The Course of Mexican Music

The Course of Mexican Music offers a full panoramic view of Mexican music, using history as a point of departure and linking Mexican music across eras, styles, and performance traditions. The aim is to understand what music Mexicans view as theirs, and how that music contributed to the creation of Mexico as a nation. In doing so, students learn both repertory and the musicians. The text brings together a full package of resources that students and instructors can use to explore the character, range, and scope of Mexican music from antiquity to the present. It includes a website that links to audio and video tracks.

Special features:

- A complete course—with important resources compiled in one place, many not found in previous works on Mexican music—access to 90 audio tracks, 17 video links, and 130 illustrations
- Comprehensive introduction to musical styles and practices within historic narrative—folkloric, popular, and classical—in Mexico from pre-colonial times to the present
- Builds upon the basic premise that understanding the relationship between historical circumstance and contemporary practice is critical to understanding the diversity, development, and contemporary potency of Mexican music

Janet L. Sturman is Professor at the Fred Fox School of Music and Associate Dean of the Graduate College at the University of Arizona.

The Course of Mexican Music

Janet L. Sturman

University of Arizona

Routledge
Taylor & Francis Group

NEW YORK AND LONDON

First published 2016
by Routledge
711 Third Avenue, New York, NY 10017

and by Routledge
2 Park Square, Milton Park, Abingdon, Oxon, OX14 4RN

Routledge is an imprint of the Taylor & Francis Group, an informa business

Library of Congress Cataloging in Publication Data
A catalog record for this book has been requested

ISBN: 978-1-138-84308-0 (hbk)
ISBN: 978-1-138-84309-7 (pbk)
ISBN: 978-1-315-73115-5 (ebk)

Typeset in Stone Serif
by Florence Production Ltd, Stoodleigh, Devon

Senior Editor: Constance Ditzel
Senior Editorial Assistant: Elysse Preposi
Production Manager: Abigail Stanley
Marketing Manager: Jessica Plummer
Copy Editor: Thérèse Wassily Saba
Proofreader: Graham Frankland
Cover Design: Jayne Varney and Mat Willis

Companion website: www.routledge.com/cw/sturman

Printed and bound in the United States of America by Sheridan Books, Inc. (a Sheridan Group Company).

Contents

Figures

BOXED INSERTS

Preface

I never expected to write a textbook on Mexican music, but circumstances demanded it. Students at the University of Arizona, where I have taught for the past 20 years, have demonstrated serious interest in the topic and have filled our courses on the topic to capacity every semester. *The Course of Mexican Music* makes it easy to hire new instructors to teach the course and add value to our curriculum.

Teaching a course on Mexican music was a charge that I inherited, and although I welcomed the opportunity, the challenge lay in collating ideal materials to address the breadth of styles and to introduce a representative set of songs as linked to social context. While excellent specialized studies exist, there was not a single comprehensive text in English. Like most instructors, I assigned various readings from different authors and I identified audio and visual materials that supported those readings. Many outstanding materials are available only in Spanish; creating English translations of important information or song texts was time-consuming and often meant excluding an ideal choice. While lectures and discussions allowed me to draw connections across these materials, I found that students wanted one text that would provide a framework for identifying returning issues and factors, and that linked Mexican music across styles and over the course of time. *The Course of Mexican Music* aims to provide that unified and historically informed perspective. The book tracks key moments in Mexican history and prompts readers to explore the attitudes and activities that shaped the development of musical expression.

GOALS

The aim of this text is to bring together a full package of resources that students and instructors can use to explore the character, range, and scope of Mexican music from antiquity to the present. While the history of Mexico provides a frame for introducing music, the discussion is not bound to a strict chronology. History also provides a point of departure for discussing contemporary reception and performance.

An important goal of the text is to introduce students to repertory and musicians. For this reason, chapters highlight individual songs, and profile composers and performers. Choosing representative examples is always a difficult task. The book introduces less celebrated music alongside well-known examples, including several favored by other authors in other texts. This is not an unusual practice; authors of music appreciation texts feel no need to apologize for including yet another treatment of Beethoven's Fifth Symphony (or any other Beethoven symphony) in their introduction to Western classical music. It can easily be argued that some selections—such as "La Maldición de Malinche" in the context of *nueva canción*—must be highlighted in any responsible discussion of a particular genre.

Even with intentions to represent scope, it is impossible to be truly comprehensive. Some important musicians and musical examples must be left for readers to explore on their own. The purposefully ample list of resources for reference and further research that close each chapter, as well as the suggested study questions, are designed promote student exploration and may also guide instructors who want to locate additional material.

INTENDED AUDIENCE

The text is designed to serve several kinds of students, principally American college students. It is meant to introduce students to music as a subject of study, and to Mexican music as an engaging example of creative expression and influence. For that reason, musical terminology is introduced early in the text, and each chapter offers readers opportunities to expand their abilities to listen with focus and analytically.

The text is written to serve English-language readers and non-Spanish speakers. Many students bring a knowledge of the Spanish language to the course, but many do not. English translations of Spanish terms and lyrics are provided throughout the text. Every effort has been made to include full translations of song texts so that students can explore the expressive intent, and the connections between the verse and the music.

Students who enroll in a course dedicated to Mexican music tend to fall into two big categories: a) those with Mexican heritage who desire to expand their knowledge of the music; and b) those with little or no knowledge of Mexican music or history. This text aims to serve them both, by providing engaging content in a historical and social context, and by guiding students to explore songs and settings from many angles. Chapter 1 sets this tone by introducing students to some larger philosophical and social issues that may be applied to their musical study.

ORGANIZATION

Apart from the opening chapters, which introduce basic concepts and terminology, the text introduces topics along a general historical chronology. Yet, there are necessary and important departures from this sequence. The first half of Chapter 3, for example, introduces musical practices of the indigenous peoples who lived on Mexican territory prior to European contact. The actual sounds of pre-conquest music have not been preserved without alteration and are thereby subject to contemporary imagination. Thus the chapter jumps to modern times when discussing reconstructed performances and recordings. The second half of the chapter offers some initial examples of living indigenous music-making, raising issues of cultural preservation as well as contemporary identity.

The desired result of this zigzag dynamic within chapters—organized in a diachronic sequence but incorporating synchronic comparisons— is to illustrate the continued value of music. The aim is to reveal examples of a basic principle of musical practice, by illustrating how people imbue musical traditions with new value in contemporary contexts. Not only does this help to explain how and why music matters, but it should also help students to understand that the process of conferring value is ongoing and often differs depending on who participates.

Chapter 1 introduces the goals of the text, the reasons for studying Mexican music, and presents a set of basic concepts to guide ways of thinking regarding the subject matter. It introduces a set of basic issues that will be examined throughout the text.

Chapter 2 introduces basic listening skills and musical vocabulary and prompts students to examine how the ways that individual listeners and communities respond to music shape the meanings that accrue to individual songs and practices.

Chapter 3 explores archaic indigenous musical practices, the historical circumstances that shaped their development, and the limits of our knowledge regarding them. Also introduced are examples of music representing living, indigenous practice. Readers are prompted to reflect on the greater value that dominant Mexican society has placed on the archaic indigenous legacy as opposed to its discriminatory treatment of living indigenous populations.

Chapter 4 examines the musical and cultural legacy of the arrival of the Spaniards on Mexican soil. Legend and song—with special attention to the poetic romance and to the *villancico*— reflecting the multicultural development of Spanish culture prior to and during the age of conquest, guides our exploration of the imposition of religious and secular philosophies, including the persisting attitudes regarding race, gender, and ethnicity.

Chapter 5 explores regional identity as expressed by the confluence of poetry, dance, and instrumental music in the signature genre known as *son*. Students will learn that, under the umbrella of one nation, there exist many Mexicos—with contrasting customs marked by colonial history, geography, culture, and economics—each producing distinct musical traditions.

Chapter 6 explores the role music played during the era of Independence when Mexico established itself as an independent republic and when residents turned to music to both create and challenge the development of a unified and centralized national identity. The chapter explores the continued importance of music associated with the struggle for independence and examines selected musical practices representing different sectors of society defined by race, class, and ethnicity.

Chapter 7 introduces popular forms of urban musical entertainment—including the middle-class favorites of the *zarzuela* and the *orquesta típica*—as it explores the development of music during the years that Porfirio Díaz held office as Mexico's president (intermittently from 1876–1911), an era of unprecedented building, modernization, and cosmopolitan exchange, but which also exacerbated the gap between the rich and the poor.

Chapter 8 introduces the genre of the *corrido* in the context of the upheaval of Mexico's revolution that began in 1910. Audio examples illustrate how historical figures such as Porfirio Díaz, Pancho Villa, Francisco Madero, Victoriano Huerta, and Venustiano Carranza were portrayed in *corridos*. Treatment of women in *corridos* and the modern uses of the genre provide additional opportunities for readers to explore how social values circulated and were questioned through music. Guidelines are presented for students to actively engage by composing their own *corridos*.

Chapter 9 addresses the impact of the media on Mexican music during the first half of the twentieth century. It explores the rise of radio stars, the establishment of an international music and entertainment industry, the cultivation of cultural icons such as the singing cowboy and the mariachi, as well as the lasting importance of signature music from the golden era of Mexican film with the *canción lírica*, *ranchera*, and *bolero*.

Chapter 10 explores two important lines of modern urban song in Mexico allowing students to contrast and compare the growth of Mexican rock 'n' roll with a parallel development of a socially conscious urban folk music. Audio examples date from 1954 to 2011 and illustrate the regular exchange across styles and with international trends as Mexican musicians increasingly made local concerns matter to international audiences.

Chapter 11 introduces a range of modern regional Mexican popular styles defined by affiliation with different strata of society from the early twentieth century to the present, presenting *norteño* and *banda* as pillar styles, and exploring the rise of the *cumbia* to its ubiquitous presence in modern dance formats. Audio examples invite reflection on how migration and routes of information exchange resulted in the new prominence of northern Mexican music in contemporary international entertainment circuits.

Chapter 12 presents five important modern classical music composers and their individual efforts to bridge divisions of place, social class, time, style, or media in order to reach new audiences. Readers are introduced to the vitality of artistic activity in Mexico City and its radiating influence extending well beyond that central orbit.

Chapter 13 closes with a reflection on stereotype, resistance, reinterpretation, and performance of the *ranchera* "Cielito lindo," prompting students to review the social and cultural significance of the many blends of musical style, influence, and practice explored throughout this text and to recognize that Mexican music—like its people—may be best understood as a constellation of expressions, not as a single entity.

FEATURES OF THIS BOOK—A SUMMARY

- A complete course—with important resources compiled in one place, many not found in previous works on Mexican music
- Comprehensive introduction to musical styles and practices— folkloric, popular and classical— in Mexico from pre-colonial times to the present
- Builds upon the basic premise that understanding the relationship between historical circumstance and contemporary practice is critical to understanding the diversity, development, and contemporary potency of Mexican music
- Offers a historical narrative of Mexican music—presents a connected historical narrative for Mexican music, with a basic historical timeline providing the organizational frame. Yet no chapter is limited to music of a single era
- Reveals the scope of musical power through specific songs and performance situations, guiding inquiry as to:

  1. Who makes music?
  2. How is music made?
  3. Why is the music composed, created, or performed?
  4. Who listens? (When and why?)
  5. How have people responded?

- Examines and provides access to 90 audio tracks, and 17 video links
- Illustrations—127 photos and diagrams
- Concluding Reflections section initiate reflection on the concepts introduced in the chapter through listening to an audio example
- A review of terms used appears at the end of each chapter
- Discussion questions follow each chapter, as well as a discography, references to other websites, and further reading suggestions.

HOW TO USE THIS BOOK

Instructors will likely want to teach one chapter per week, with most requiring three class hours of discussion. Chapters 1 and 2 are short and depending upon the academic schedule and the amount of initial exploration preferred by the instructor, might be combined into a single week. Instructors who have tested this book have typically devoted two weeks to Chapter 3, exploring the archaeological record in the first week, and introducing living indigenous traditions in a second week. Chapters 7 or 9 may require extra time, depending on what aspects the instructor wishes to emphasize.

The text lends itself to customization, and to active, student-centered learning strategies. Assigning individual students to be responsible for providing a brief commentary or introduction to any of the musical examples can be a valuable way to initiate class discussion. The discussion questions at the end of each chapter can be used in many ways. Some instructors divide them among the students when assigning the chapters to help learners focus their attention when reading and come to class prepared to contribute to an in-class discussion. Other prefer to use them as homework assignments and some of the questions are better suited as prompts for take-home essay assignments or term paper topics. All may be considered points of departure for the instructor's own assignments.

Audio and video performances are notated with icons in the margins adjacent to the narrative when first introduced, for example:

- 2.2 —The song "Sandunga" offers an example of the complexity of stylistic exchange. We will listen to two different compositions and performances based on this song.

- 7.3—the video "Danza (Romance)" from *Chin Chun Chan* performed by University of Arizona musicians with David Troiano.

The icons are numbered, keyed to the List of Audio Examples and Credits and List of Video Examples and Credits at the back of the book and on the companion website.

Students should listen to the audio examples before coming to class and be able to explain how each relates to the central themes of the chapter. Most chapters include more audio examples than can be listened to in a single class hour. I have chosen specific performances of each song or composition and provided readers with access to each; the performance matters as much as the composition. Students today enjoy using subscription services such as Spotify, or accessing YouTube to listen to music, and some of the discussions direct readers to special videos made available by that service. Students should know, however, that for the discussions in this book, the individual performance matters as much, if not more in some circumstances, than the song itself. In most cases, performances have been chosen because of the specific artist(s), setting, or rendition represented, and in several instances readers are asked to compare different performances of the same song. Even with the wide array of musical examples offered in this book, plenty of great music and many important musicians could not be represented. The foundation provided in the text can guide readers for exploring more music on their own. In many cases, the links provided will lead readers to related music and performances and invite exploration. My aim has been to balance selected opportunities for in-depth comparison with the important goal of representing the all-too-often unrecognized scope of Mexican music.

Companion website: www.routledge.com/cw/sturman

- Links to audio and video examples
- Powerpoint slides
- Interactive quizzes
- Sample tests
- Links to related websites and resources.

NOTES ON FORMAT

Unless otherwise indicated, all English text translations are by the author, who frequently benefited from collaborators' suggestions. Non-English words are italicized the first time they appear, and not thereafter unless they might be confused with English words. The signature example of the latter is *son* (musical format) and son (family relation).

Acknowledgments

The project of compiling the material for this text was not a solitary one. My work benefited from the ongoing conversations, advice, and scholarship proffered by valued colleagues to whom my gratitude is sincere. Among the most important are Richard Obregon, who initiated the course at the University of Arizona and who shared his extensive library with me, later donating many volumes to the UA Center for Latin American Music as a gift in honor of his mother. Sydney Hutchinson later shared her perspectives and materials that she compiled when she taught the course. My work also profited from conversations with experts on the music of Mexico, who generously shared recordings, publications, and ideas. I am particularly grateful to Aurelio Tello, Craig Russell, John Koegel, Luis Jaime Cortez, Luisa Vilar Paya, Brenda Romero, Raquél Paraíso, Luis E. Coronado Guel, Edgar Alejandro Calderón Álcantar, and Ingvi Kallen. Reviews of draft sections of the text by Brenda M. Romero, Sydney Hutchinson, and Raquél Paraíso, and an anonymous reviewer, were of enormous value and I thank them for their many useful suggestions. William Beezley, my friend and distinguished colleague from the University of Arizona Department of History, deserves special thanks for inspiring me to explore Mexican history in the service of this course, sending me excellent students, and for encouraging me to write this book.

Refining the ideas of any book is challenging, but I was aided in the practical demands of editing and testing each chapter by Natalia Duarte and Gabriel Venegas, two Costa Rican musicians and scholars who worked with me as graduate teaching assistants and brought important insights to the material in each unit as they assisted with conceptual and editorial matters. They devoted numerous hours to mechanical review and offered thoughtful reflections that unquestionably improved the book and for which I am most grateful. Luis Coronado Guel, historian and music lover from San Luis Potosí freely shared research, resources and insights with me that contributed greatly to the text. The Mexican historian María Concepción Márquez Sandoval lent her astute eyes to reviewing the chapters and was a tremendous help in securing permissions for illustrations and audio examples. She assisted with revisions and securing permissions, all the while engaging in valuable dialogue. Jen DiLallo, a former undergraduate student who used an early version of this text, offered thoughtful contributions to the questions sets at the end of each chapter. Guitarist and scholars, José Luis Puerta and Juan Carlos Merello assisted with final preparation of score samples, audio examples, and website content. Juan Carlos provided additional help with the teaching resources and the music permissions, and Cecilio Novillo assisted with the Index. The perseverance and encouragement of Routledge acquisition editor, Constance Ditzel, who believed in this project from the start, has been so important. Finally, I must thank my family, Art, Michael, and Andrea for their love, patience, inspiration, and encouragement. To all I've mentioned and the many more whose names cannot be listed: ¡Mil gracias!

Janet L. Sturman
Tucson, Arizona
11 January 2015

Full credit acknowledgments for the cover images are as follows:

Left image: "Yolotlapalazintzin" ("Los Colores del Alma"/The Colors of the Soul) (2007) mural in the courtyard of the Escuela de Iniciación Musical Ollin Yoliztli, Mexico City. Eduardo Juárez, Alexis Rodríguez, Ladislao Franco, Javier Botista, René Rivero. With collaboration from Mónica Sánchez, Karla Mandujo, Mariana Escamilla, Paulino Reyna, Antonio Julián, Raúl Urbina, Enrique Samudio, David Hernández, Dianey Reyes, Nancy Romero, Neom y David, Clauda Castellanos (UAM Xochimilco—Taller de Gráfica Monumental). Photo by Janet Sturman.
Center image: Son jarocho musicians with an *arpa*, a small jarana (*mosquito*), and a medium jarana (*tercera*). Photo by Janet Sturman.
Right image: Photo by Ricardo Almanza Carillo. Used with kind permission.
Bottom and back panel image: Photo by Janet Sturman.

Introduction

FIRST ENCOUNTERS

In 1995, on one of my first study trips to the interior of Mexico, I traveled to the picturesque port city of Tlacotalpan, on the left bank of the Papaloapan River near the Gulf Coast in the state of Veracruz, to observe musical activities associated with the celebration of the Fiesta de la Candelaria. From the minute I stepped off the local bus onto the main street of the town, I felt the collective anticipation of that special weekend. Every inn in town was full, and I was sent to a café to inquire if Maria, who opened her home to visitors, had a bed to rent. For that weekend, I shared a room with her *abuela* and young daughter. I met Maria's grown children who returned home for the festival and accompanied them to the signature events over a three-day whirlwind of activity. I helped her granddaughter dress for the *cabalgata* where little girls and young women wearing white lace frocks rode on horseback through the town. The dance and song competitions where local poets held forth from the gazebo in the central plaza, taking on challengers by creating song verses on the spot introduced me to the tradition of *son jarocho* and *huapangos* from this coastal region. What a contrast with the banda music playing classical marches and popular tunes that led the next evening's parade of giant puppets and costumed revelers known as the *mojiganga*, or the recordings of Grupo Limité and other pop groups blaring from the loud speakers of local *cantinas* during the afternoon *toreada*, or running of the bulls. Late at night, I danced to the DJ's mix of popular and international dance music in the local night club—surprised to find the "Macarena" by the Andalusian pop group Los del Río to be a favorite. At dawn on Sunday, I awoke to the voices of stalwart women singing *alabanzas*, simple hymns of devotion, as they processed to Mass. More music would accompany the afternoon procession with the statue of the Virgin to the banks of the Papaloapan where citizens set afloat paper boats carrying burning candles. Being part of that experience sparked my interest in building on the friendships I formed and learning more about Mexican music in all its traditions. Living and teaching in southern Arizona gave me plenty of opportunities. As an ethnomusicologist, I have always seen music as opening windows for understanding individual cultures; my experience in Tlacotalpan opened a new window, initiating my commitment to promoting recognition and understanding of the music and cultures of Mexico.

The scope of Mexican music, encountered even in that single event, is often unrecognized. In my teaching at the University of Arizona, it was not unusual for a student to tell me: "I never realized there was Mexican classical music; I only know mariachi." Knowing mariachi meant different things to different individuals, from merely recognizing the style to knowing it well. Too often, when I would ask students to name a mariachi song, they might hum a few trumpet fanfares, but were hard pressed to name a title. These were not the students who grew up hearing mariachi and other Mexican music at family affairs or performing with folkloric dance groups. Plenty of students with Mexican heritage knew many songs and had their favorites, but they often knew little about other styles, and many expressed a desire to know more about the history of Mexican music and to explore its distinct genres. Such experiences guided my efforts to create a book that would provide a more comprehensive view of Mexican music.

CHAPTER 1

Why Study Mexican Music?

MUTUALLY ENGAGED AUDIENCES

"Why Mexican music?" was a question I heard often when I told people that I was writing an introduction to Mexican music for university students in the United States. People asked: "Why not write a book about Latin American music in general? Why not broaden your scope?" Why the focus on Mexican music? My answer begins by pointing out the great influence that Mexican music has exerted on musical culture throughout the Americas, meaning all the countries of North, Central, and South America. It can be argued as well that the mutual engagement between the United States and Mexico stands as the most powerful international relationship in the hemisphere. The fortunes of Mexico and the United States are inextricably related and any study that promises deeper insight into the history, culture, and values of people, as our investigation of music certainly will, is well worth the effort. Mexico has shaped what U.S. citizens call American culture,[1] past and present, just as the United States has influenced the course of history in Mexico. The observations of historian Juan Gonzalez address this link and remind us of its complicating tensions:

> The Mexican Diaspora is at the core of our country's Latino heritage. Not only are two of every three Latinos in the United States of Mexican origin, but only Mexicans can claim to be both early settlers on U.S. soil and the largest group of new arrivals. So many Mexicans have come since 1820 that they are now the second-largest immigrant nationality in our history. No Hispanic group has contributed more to the nation's prosperity than Mexicans, yet none makes white America more uneasy about the future.
>
> (Gonzalez 2000:96)

Gonzalez's statement resonates with the contemporary politics that frame American scholarship and study of Mexico. In Arizona, to take one state at the center of current debates regarding immigration policies, the rhetoric regarding Mexico has been heated, vacillating between interest and dismissal; acceptance and rejection. Yet, despite the Arizona legislature's suspicion of ethnic studies courses and the ruling by the state board of regents to eliminate or marginalize Mexican studies courses in K-12 education in Arizona public schools,[2] the University of Arizona remains a leader in Mexican and Mexican-American studies, as well as in Latin American studies in general. Furthermore, the University of Arizona's course on the Music of Mexico, which inspired this book, is so popular that students have filled every one of the 50–70 seats available each semester since 1980, when the course was first offered.

Mexico is not simply a neighbor to the United States; the destinies of these two nations are linked. Equally important, Mexico has been described as a gateway to Latin America. Mexican music has a long history of interaction and exchange with music throughout Latin America, where we find shared legacies, formats, and contemporary concerns, despite important cultural distinctions. Profitable comparisons may be made between Mexico and virtually any nation in the Americas and the Hispanic world.

To explore the culture of Mexico is to engage with the scope and grandeur of the American experience writ large. As a specific case study, our investigation allows us to explore in depth forms and processes that reveal the power of music to enrich human experience. The study of Mexican music, like that of any music, offers a productive and positive avenue to deepen understanding of a culture while also developing an appreciation for the role of music in society and the generalizable power of human creative genius.

EXAMINING MUSIC AS AN INTEGRATIVE FRAME

The concept of integration unifies this text. There is no single activity that speaks to the genius and expressive power of Mexican music overall more than the process of integration. At every turn in history, and in different ways in different communities, Mexican musicians have adopted foreign elements, integrating some of them into existing practices, and transforming the result into expressions that serve local needs. However, the musical integration, like that of cultural and social integration, has been selective and uneven. Only in recent decades, for example, have the music and culture of Afro-Mexicans been promoted, or some cases even recognized, as with the *Mascogo capayuye*, the black gospel singers of Coahuila (Madrid 2011:171–190). Nor did the official narrative of *mestizaje* (racial mixture) give much attention to Mexicans of Chinese ancestry, despite the strong presence and contributions of this population. Chinese-Mexican presence in life and music is explored in Chapter 7. The process of merging people, perspectives, and resources is one that Mexico shares with many nations and cultures. Throughout this text, we will explore the choices of the Mexican people, to discover what makes them distinctive, as well as what we can learn from them.

The contents of this book integrate music of various musical styles, contrasting contexts, and different time periods, connecting them all to the practices and expectations of various communities of people. Individuals and groups divided by ethnicity, social class, occupation, economic status, gender, or age are often united through music—even when that same music once served as a marker of exclusion or difference. While a truly comprehensive treatment is neither possible nor desirable in a textbook, this book aims to reflect the rich scope of Mexican musical life. It is the author's hope that the material included in this text will stimulate individual investigations and invite additional examination of the social and artistic interactions that are often obscured by our custom of thinking in simple categories.

IMMIGRANT IDENTITIES AND CONTRIBUTIONS

Migration and immigration are processes that have affected Mexican culture in much broader ways than most Americans recognize. Music resulting from migration is an important subject of this book. U.S. residents tend to focus on the migration of Mexicans into the United States. There is little question that the back and forth travel that characterizes Mexican–U.S. migration has shaped culture on both sides of the Rio Grande. Less recognized however, is the scope of foreign immigration into Mexico. Spaniards may be considered the first immigrants, and we will explore the results of Iberian rule in Chapters 3–5. The musical legacy of French and German influence in later decades is explored in Chapter 6.

Cosmopolitan aspirations stimulated internal migration from the provinces to the cities, as well as Mexican travel abroad, a topic explored in Chapter 7. As historian Theresa Alfaro-Velcamp (2007) points out, trade with Asia stimulated migration from the Near East, particularly merchants from Turkey, Christians from Lebanon, and Jews from Syria. The richest man in Mexico, and currently in the world, Carlos Slim Heliú, offers a prominent example. His father immigrated to Mexico from Lebanon in 1902 and his mother's parents, also Lebanese, arrived in the nineteenth century. Social histories by Romero-Chan (2010), Truett (2006), and others, document the arrival of businessmen and laborers from the Far East, particularly China, Korea, and Japan, who began coming in large numbers in the nineteenth century to Mexico. Russian immigration swelled in the years surrounding the Revolution of 1910. In the years following the Mexican Revolution, people of various backgrounds considered Mexico as a promised land (Katz 1981). Migrants from Central Europe and the Near East acted on this belief, and those arriving in Mexico seeking fortune or relief from religious persecution during the nineteenth and twentieth centuries included Mormons, Mennonites, and Jews (Buchenau 2001).

The nation did not always welcome immigration without discrimination, and Mexican laws to limit foreign immigration initiated after 1920 are but one example of concurrent resistance to a multicultural society.

Nonetheless, integration proceeded, even if its constituents were submerged in the official narratives of *Mexicanidad* (Mexicanness). The constant effort to adjust the blend, as reflected or guided by music, pervades discussion throughout this book.

GEOGRAPHIES AND CONTEXTS

Place matters. People turn to musicians to help them mark territory, and like food and dress, music also serves as an important calling card for regional identity and pride. A comfortable knowledge of the geographical map of Mexico, including knowing the names and locations of the 32 federal entities of the modern United States of Mexico, is essential for informed reflection on Mexican music. See Figure 1.1 for a map showing the states of Mexico, which readers are encouraged to memorize. Our study of the long-standing associations of music with specific geographic regions of Mexico peaks with our examination of regional poetic dance song *(sones regionales)* in Chapter 5. Discussion throughout the text, and particularly in Chapters 7–12, invites consideration of persistent distinctions between center and periphery, with examples that show how musical practice both reflects and promotes political position, economic power, local values, and transnational experience.

EXAMINING DIFFERENCE, EVALUATING CONCEPTS OF THE ESSENTIAL

Exploring music as a social act as well as a sonic act is a complex project. Often what most interests listeners and the music student are those aspects of musical practice that differentiate one culture's music from another. Yet, as anthropologist Lila Abu-Lughod (2006) has noted, celebrating difference without examining and critiquing the philosophies and habits of mind that promote those differences, may lead to promoting social inequities. Reducing people and their cultural expressions to a limited set of essential characteristics, a process that critics refer to as "essentialization" (see Krupat 1996), leads to static or confining stereotypes. Ronald Radano (2000) offers an example of this process with his discussion of how Americans in the first decades of the twentieth century came to view the so-called "hot rhythms" of jazz as representing the essential quality of all African-American music. While white Americans considered the hot rhythms of African-American jazz as different and exciting, they also associated them with beast-like primitivism, thus reinforcing justifications for racial segregation and discrimination. At the same time, Radano observes, society's enthusiasm for hot rhythm helped create new professional opportunities for black musicians. Similar contradictions can be observed in the ways that Mexican society simultaneously and over time, stereotyped, rejected, consumed, and incorporated minority or foreign musical styles, including American jazz and Cuban music. As we will explore, the gradual creation of an official mariachi repertory that both homogenized and celebrated regional practices, or the early development of a tradition of classical art music that both reinvented ancient indigenous music, focusing on a few select characteristics, while rejecting local Indian peasants provide two other examples colored by processes of cultural essentialization. Careful readers will look for how nuances of identity, and correspondingly, recognition and value, may have been lost in the process of integration and promotion. Readers of this text should think reflexively about the processes of simplification, including those necessary for their own understanding. Consider how the promotion of various music reflects social policies, reinforces or denies power, and undergirds creative expression. As we shall see, a society's celebration of essential qualities carries social and artistic consequences.

To question cultural essentialization is not to dismiss the value of generalizations in all contexts. While there are good reasons to resist reducing complexity to a set of simple principles and forms, the purpose of any introductory text is to make the complex comprehensible. As I was writing this book, I was reading *Six Easy Pieces*, a set of introductory lectures by the late Nobel Prize-winning physicist Richard P. Feynman (2005). He begins by reminding us that even in physics, a discipline driven by the quest for a fundamental understanding of the laws of nature, learning is a dance between acquiring an understanding of simple principles—often approximates, and the more accurate but philosophically difficult corrections to those simplifications. This is a position I've tried to adopt in this text. Like Dr. Feynman, we should be equally inspired to seek relationships between branches of knowledge by seeking meaning in relating music to other realms of activity.

HISTORICAL FRAMES AND CONTEMPORARY PRACTICE

Constructing a connected historical narrative for Mexican music is a difficult enterprise, including deciding when to begin the story. A growing body of literature examines the archaeological record regarding the music of indigenous people prior to the arrival of Hernán Cortés and the period preceding Spanish rule. Much more attention has been devoted to music after the time of Independence, when Mexico came into its own as a nation. Still the greatest body of scholarship addresses musical practices after the Revolution that began in 1910, for it is during the twentieth century that Mexico as a modern nation presents itself and its music to the world. Around those guideposts is an important body of musical literature and practice awaiting more critical study. This text builds upon the basic premise that understanding the relationship between historical circum-stance and contemporary practice is critical to understanding the diversity, development, and contemporary potency of Mexican music. The narrative zigzags between the past and the present. A basic historical timeline provides the organizational frame, but no chapter is limited to music of a single era. Although musical activities and genres are introduced in a rough chronological sequence, we will regularly shift our focus to modern engagement and performance. One of our goals is to explore how our views of the past are shaped by contemporary performance.

HARMONIZING CONFLICTING REALITIES

Music is an important tool for reflection, celebration, and often, for creating and sharing idealized visions of the world. Song, dance, and musical occasions can be important settings for uniting people and ideas, or for creating an opportunity for contradicting realities to be expressed. As you read, think about the ways that music brings together people of different generations and social positions, and how each may experience that music differently.

The value of mixture: racial, social, and above all, musical, has long been celebrated in Mexico. The concept of *mestizaje*, the Spanish term for mixture used in reference to racial blending, stands as the salient example of selective integration and the core of Mexican identity. Many scholars have explored how the understanding of mestizaje has changed over time (see Alonso 2004, Miller 2004, Velázquez and Vaughan 2006) and we will too, particularly in regard to music. We will examine what elements musicians and listeners have selectively incorporated, celebrated, rejected, or ignored. We will also explore what those choices represent and what actions they have inspired. In this regard, our exploration of Mexican music illustrates a mode of analysis that may be adopted for the study of the process of selection in other music, cultures, and contexts.

PERSPECTIVES FOR STUDY

Recognizing that people use music to define their circumstances and values becomes powerful knowledge when we can point to specific strategies and examples. Each chapter in this text aims to reveal the scope of musical power through specific songs and performance situations. Several basic questions should guide our inquiry (numbered only for convenience of discussion, not necessary by priority):

1. Who makes music?
2. How is music made? (What strategies, techniques, or intentions distinguish the composition and/or performance?)
3. Why is the music composed, created, or performed?
4. Who listens? (When and why?)
5. How have people responded?

These questions prompt us to investigate both the products and the processes of music-making. Drawing upon a famous recommendation by the ethnomusicologist Alan Merriam, our study of music considers three broad and interlocking dimensions: 1) sound, 2) concept, 3) behavior (Merriam 1964:32). In Chapter 2, we will review initial guidelines and vocabulary for examining the properties of musical sound in any single performance or composition. Discussions throughout the rest of the book aim to refine your listening skills, and to prompt your examination of musical sound. We will also explore the concepts associated with that sound (the ideas and motivations that guide how people create, consume, or share music). When considering musical behavior, we may explore the techniques used to make or produce the music, as well the actions of people in response to that music, including dance.

PERFORMANCE AND RECEPTION

The study of how people respond to music must take into account performance as a social act, an important topic in the arts and in modern scholarship in general. There are many ways to discuss performance and a corresponding number of ways to understand the term. In colloquial conversation, one way that people use the term performance is to refer to an individual's ability to accomplish daily tasks or succeed at work. We all understand that this kind of performance differs qualitatively from the realization of musical, theatrical, and other performance presented on stage or for entertainment. The distinction between "performance in daily life" and the so-called "extra-daily performance" has been explored by Erving Goffman (1990), Richard Schechner (2013), Eugenio Barba (1995), Harris Berger and Giovanna Del Negro (2004), to name just a few. The focus of these scholars on technique is complemented by academic atten-tion to the performance of social engagement. Both perspectives are relevant to our study of Mexican music. Studies of how individuals and groups "perform" identity represent an important trend in contemporary music scholarship, ranging from studies of hip hop (Dimitriadis 2009) to the examination of festivals in colonial Mexico (Curcio 2004). Musicologist Alejandro Madrid reduces the difference between these two types of performance to two basic questions: 1) "How do musicians make music?"; or 2) "What happens when music happens?" (Madrid 2009). We will explore these two questions as intrinsically related.

As we consider contemporary reactions to music past and present, take time to explore your own responses as well as those of our subjects. Consider what touches your heart, makes you sing or dance, speaks to your experience, or simply connects you to the makers and listeners of Mexican music.

KNOWING MEXICO

Place matters in our study of Mexican music. It is important that the student of Mexican music learn the names and locations of the states of the Mexican nation from memory. Use Figure 1.1 to guide this study. Memorizing the states will allow you to easily match people and specific examples to specific locations, and to follow discussions throughout this book.

CONCLUDING REFLECTIONS

One Example, Many Experiences

🎧

1.1

Listening to "Las nereidas," a *danzón* by Amador Pérez Torres, composer from Oaxaca (*c*.1930) performed by the Banda Filarmónica del Centro de Capacitación y Desarrollo de la Cultura Mixe, CECAM, with guest performer saxophone player Miguel Ángel Samperio.

To initiate reflection on the concepts introduced above, listen to audio example 1.1, a performance of "Nereidas" performed by the Banda Filarmónica del CECAM (the Philharmonic Band of the Center for Learning and Development of Mixe Culture). The players for this performance are high school-age youth who live in the mountains of Oaxaca (see Figs 1.1,

Figure 1.1
Map showing the
states of Mexico.

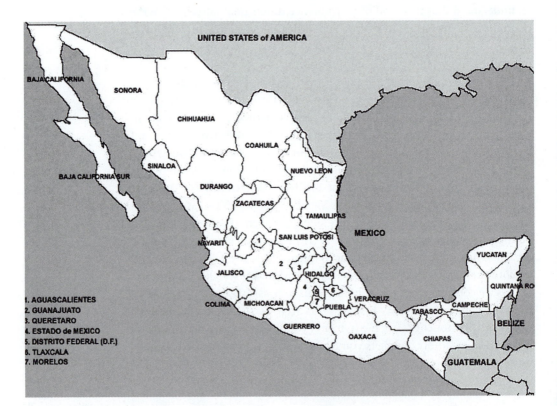

1.2). They attend CECAM, a special school that uses music as a means of teaching young people their native language and culture, something we will explore more in future chapters. Many overlapping aspects of history and experience contribute to this single performance. First, it reflects the results of a 500-year-old process of adopting European wind band traditions by a Mexican indigenous population. Second, it reflects the integration of the nineteenth-century Cuban dance form known as the *danzón* into the repertory of Mexican music forms. It also celebrates a Mexican approach to the *danzón* by the Oaxacan-born composer Amador Pérez and the importance of the *banda de viento* (wind band) in Oaxaca and in Mexico in general. The prominence of Oaxacan wind players in both isolated rural environs and national settings is a point of pride and a credit to training programs like CECAM. The participation of the professional saxophone player Miguel Ángel Samperio in this performance, further underscores the respect these young musicians have earned. Production support for the recording, came from the Xqenda Cultural Association, founded and managed by the internationally celebrated singer Susana Harp Ituribarria, who was born in Oaxaca. One of her stated goals for the foundation is to support young Mexican musicians with a solid education in their own country so they won't feel the need to leave the country for study.[3]

Notice how the illustration on the album cover (Fig. 1.2) showcases the local style of dress worn by these young players and the active

Figure 1.2
Cover photo from the CD *Sones de Tierra y Nube*. Photo by Blanca Charolet; graphic design: Grupo Charolet; producer: Asociación Cultural Xquenda, A.C. Used with permission.

participation of young female instrumentalists in the school and band. Implicit recognition of recent history is evident in the musical arrangement as well, for while this song was composed in the 1930s, the recording was released in 2009 and the performance by the *banda juvenil* (youth band) reflects modern popular and jazz-inspired aesthetics, and *not* the widely recognized, but distinct instrumental practice associated with mariachi.

In later chapters we will examine the development of the wind band tradition in Mexico and its many functions, including support of indigenous culture. As with all the chapters that follow in this book, this one closes with a set of questions to prompt deeper reflection on the topics covered and to guide your study of music as a route for understanding people and their culture.

CRITICAL THINKING AND DISCUSSION PROMPTS

1. A definition of Mexican music is not explicitly offered in this introduction. What definition(s) are implied? What makes the performance of "Las nereidas" an example of Mexican music? How would you define Mexican music?

2. Describe some of the different interpretations of the term "folk music." With which interpretation do you most agree or find most useful? Explain why.

3. List as many types of Mexican folk music as you can think of. Describe the similarities and differences among these types.

4. In what ways is Mexican music part of your life? Identify one example to share with class.

5. In your own words, define what it means to "essentialize" a style of music. What are some examples of this process in musical genres with which you are familiar?

6. Keeping in mind the social and cultural dimensions of musical performance, can you identify some ways that the music you listen to is performed to specifically appeal to you?

7. What details do you notice regarding the performance of "Las nereidas" by CECAM? Do any of these qualities surprise you? Why or why not?

8. We often think of integration solely in terms of a coming together of racial or ethnic differences. What other kinds of identities might be combined? Provide one musical example, selection, or setting that illustrates such a merger.

9. What are some of the reasons that people might resist musical or social integration?

10. In what ways does place and location matter to sound preferences and music making? Visit the Sound Map of Mexico (http://fonomaps.herokuapp.com) and find examples of distinct types of music and sound associated with different places in Mexico.

KEY TERMS, PEOPLE, AND PLACES

banda de viento	indigenous
CECAM	Mexican diaspora
cosmopolitan	Mexicanidad
culture	mestizaje
danzón	musicologist
essentialization	performance
integration (musical, cultural, social)	stereotype
immigration	

NOTES

1. There is no easy solution to the overlapping meanings of the terms America and American. U.S. citizens appropriate the hemispheric term as theirs, referring to themselves as Americans, and their nation as America. Of course, Latin Americans, whatever their country, also see themselves as Americans, particularly when comparing themselves to Europeans or Asians. In general, I will use the plural term Americas when meaning to include people residing in North America (Canada, United States, and Mexico), as well as the Central and South American nations. It is hoped that my use of the term American, particularly when appearing in quotations, will be clear from the surrounding context. If there is an implied contrast with Mexico or another Latin American nation, the term American likely refers to the United States.

2. The debate on teaching Mexican-American studies, ignited in 2012 in the Tucson Unified School District, remains heated and a dispassionate summary of the ruling is hard to find. In February 2013 a U.S. Judge ordered TUSD to reinstate culturally relevant classes, but in January 2015, Arizona Schools Chief John Huppenthal declared such courses to be in violation of state law. Both H.T. Sanchez and Diane Douglas, who respectively assumed city and state superintendent roles in January 2015, vowed to bring Arizona schools in compliance with federal law. See the *LA Times* report on earlier stages of the controversy: http://latimesblogs.latimes.com/nationnow/2012/01/tucson-ethnic-studies-program-violates-arizona-law-state-funding-to-be-withheld.html (posted January 6, 2012). Summary reports on the Arizona Senate Bill 1070 can be found at: www.azleg.gov/legtext/49leg/2r/summary/s.1070pshs.doc.htm (accessed June 5, 2015). For his television show, Jon Stewart created a review of the issue as well: www.thedailyshow.com/watch/mon-april-2-2012/tucson-s-mexican-american-studies-ban

3. Susana Harp. Wikipedia. http://es.wikipedia.org/wiki/Susana_Harp (accessed February 12, 2015).

FOR REFERENCE AND FURTHER STUDY

Abu-Lughod, Lila. 2006. "Writing Against Culture." In Richard G. Fox (Ed.), *Recapturing Anthropology: Working in the Present*. Santa Fe, NM: School of American Research Press, 137–162.

Alfaro-Velcamp, Theresa. 2007. *So Far from Allah, So Close to Mexico: Middle Eastern Immigrants in Modern Mexico*. Austin, TX: University of Texas Press.

Alonso, Ana. 2004. "Conforming Disconformity: Mestizaje, Hybridity, and the Aesthetics of Nationalism." *Cultural Anthropology* 19(4):459–490.

Barba, Eugenio. 1995. *The Paper Canoe: A Guide to Theatre Anthropology*. New York: Routledge.

Barba, Eugenio and Savarese, Nicola. 2006. *A Dictionary of Theatre Anthropology*, 2nd ed. New York and London: Routledge.

Berger, Harris and Del Negro, Giovanna P. 2004. *Identity and Everyday Life: Essays in the Study of Folklore, Music and Popular Culture*. Middletown, CT: Wesleyan University Press.

Buchenau, Jürgen. 2001. "Small Numbers, Great Impact: Mexico and its Immigrants, 1821–1973." *Journal of American Ethnic History* 20(3):23–49.

Chao Romero, Robert. 2010. *The Chinese in Mexico, 1882–1940*. Tucson, AZ: University of Arizona Press.

Curcio, Linda Ann. 2004. *The Great Festivals of Mexico City: Performing Power and Identity*. Albuquerque, NM: University of New Mexico Press.

Dimitriadis, Greg. 2009. *Performing Identity/Performing Culture: Hip Hop as Text, Pedagogy, and Lived Practice*. 2nd ed. New York: Peter Lang.

Goffman, Erving. 1974. *Frame Analysis: An Essay on the Organization of Experience*. Cambridge, MA: Harvard University Press.

Goffman, Erving. 1990. *The Presentation of Self in Everyday Life*. 15th ed. New York: Penguin Press.

Gonzalez, Juan. 2000. *Harvest of Empire: A History of Latinos in America*. New York: Penguin.

Katz, Friedrich. 1981. *The Secret War in Mexico: Europe, the United States, and the Mexican Revolution*. Chicago, IL: University of Chicago Press.

Krupat, Arnold. 1996. *The Turn to the Native: Studies in Criticism and Culture*. Lincoln, NE: University of Nebraska Press.

Madrid, Alejandro. 2009. "Why Music and Performance Studies? Why Now?: An Introduction to the Special Issue." *Trans. Revista Transcultural de Música* 13:1–8. www.redalyc.org/articulo.oa?id=82220946003 (accessed January 12, 2015).

Madrid, Alejandro, 2011. "Transnational Identity, the Singing of Spirituals, and the Performance of Blackness among Mascogos." In Alejandro Madrid (Ed.), *Transnational Encounters: Music and Performance at the U.S.–Mexico Border*. New York: Oxford University Press, 171–190.

Merriam, Alan. 1964. *The Anthropology of Music*. Evanston, IL: Northwestern University Press.

Miller, Marilyn Grace. 2004. *Rise and Fall of the Cosmic Race: The Cult of Mestizaje in Latin America*. Austin, TX: University of Texas Press.

Radano, Ronald. 2000. "Hot Fantasies: American Modernism and the Racial Imagination." In Ronald Radano and Philip Bohlman (Eds.), *Music and the Racial Imagination*. Chicago, IL: University of Chicago Press, 459–480.

Schechner, Richard. 2003. *Performance Theory*. Rev. ed. New York: Routledge.

Schechner, Richard. 2013. *An Introduction to Performance Studies*. 3rd ed. New York: Routledge.

Truett, Samuel. 2006. *Fugitive Landscapes: The Forgotten History of the U.S.–Mexico Borderlands*. New Haven, CT: Yale University Press.

Velázquez, Marco and Vaughan, Mary Kay. 2006. "Mestizaje and Musical Nationalism in Mexico." In Stephen Lewis and Mary Kay Vaughan (Eds.), *The Eagle and the Virgin: National Identity, Memory and Utopia in Mexico, 1920–1940*. Durham, NC: Duke University Press, 95–118.

DISCOGRAPHY

Banda Filarmónica del Centro de Capacitación y Desarrollo de la Cultura Mixe, CECAM. 2009. *Sones de Tierra y Nube*, Vol. II. Audio CD. México: Conaculta.

WEBSITES

CECAM. 2014. Banda Filarmónica del Centro de Capacitación y Desarrollo de la Cultura Mixe. www.cecam.org.mx/inicio.html
Mapa Sonoro de México (Sound Map of Mexico). Conaculta/Fonoteca Nacional. http://fonomaps.herokuapp.com

CHAPTER 2

Defining and Listening to Mexican Music

EVOCATION AND PERCEPTION

🎧
2.1

Listening to "La Plaza," a soundscape composed by Evaristo Aguilar and Jorge Valdez, from Evaristo Aguilar—*Ritmos de la Huasteca*, 2006. Courtesy of Evaristo Aguilar.

Picture yourself strolling through the central plaza of a Mexican town. You will hear many sounds, the cries of vendors, the tolling of church bells, perhaps street musicians, perhaps noise from cars and trucks passing by, or recorded music from restaurants and shops on the side streets. Figure 2.1 shows marketplace images to help you visualize sights associated with those sounds. Evaristo Aguilar's composition "La Plaza" [2.1] is meant to evoke that experience. It also invites reflection on the very nature of music, what defines it, and our engagement with it.

Few of us would disagree that sound is the most basic element of music. We will start our study of Mexican music with a set of principles for studying sound. To a physicist or sound engineer, sound is created by vibrations in the air, creating what we call **sound waves**. Sound waves are characterized by frequency, amplitude, shape, and duration, and we can use those fundamental structural properties as touchstones for talking about basic musical properties: **pitch**, **volume**, **timbre**, and **rhythm**. However, not all sound is music. The elements of sound structure are important, but unlike physics where essential features are defined by their intrinsic properties, music is ultimately defined by social criteria. How we use and interact with sound determines whether we consider it to be music or something else. So to study the music of Mexico, we must start with how people in Mexico have engaged sound in ways that matter to them.

"La Plaza" begins with a variety of interesting percussive sounds. At 1'20" we hear the sounds of a vendor selling *chiles*, at 5'30" we hear another sales interaction, some church bells, and other sounds of people in the plaza. We would not normally refer to these verbal interactions as music, yet many ambient recordings are included in Evaristo Aguilar's

02 *La Plaza*

Mercado huasteco semanal al aire libre / **Weekly outdoor market in the Huasteca**

Ambiente grabado en Huejutla, Hidalgo y Axtla de Terrazas, SLP - Ambience recorded at Huejutla, Hidalgo and Axtla de Terrazas, SLP

Figure 2.1 (see Plate 1)
Marketplace image. Photo by Evaristo Aguilar, 2006 Graphic Design by Michelle Cházaro. *Ritmos de la Huasteca* Universidad Autónoma de Tamaulipas, Facultad de Música. Courtesy of Evaristo Aguilar.

recording *Ritmos de la Huasteca*. To him, such sounds are more than music to his ears; they may also be considered music by listeners who take time to accept them in a musical framework. You may agree, perhaps because you too have shared some experience with the sounds in the composition. Ideas about music shape what people welcome as music. Aguilar, the composer of "La Plaza," combined ambient sounds of the weekly marketplaces in Huejutla, Hidalgo, and Axtla de Terrazas, San Luis Potosí and found inspiration in the sounds and rhythms of life for his artistic composition. (For a map with those locations, see Fig. 2.2). Like his other compositions, "La Plaza" captures Aguilar's love of place, particularly of the Huastecan region of Mexico where he grew up, and his deep appreciation for the human interactions that shape those places.

CATEGORIZING MUSIC

"La Plaza" with its evocation of a specific soundscape also invites us to reflect on categories of music. We often speak of music using broad categories such as folk, popular, or classical. Where would "La Plaza" fit? When do such categorizations matter?

The great scholar of Mexican folk music and the founder of the Folklore Society of Mexico, Vicente T. Mendoza (1894–1964) was one of the first

Huasteca Region

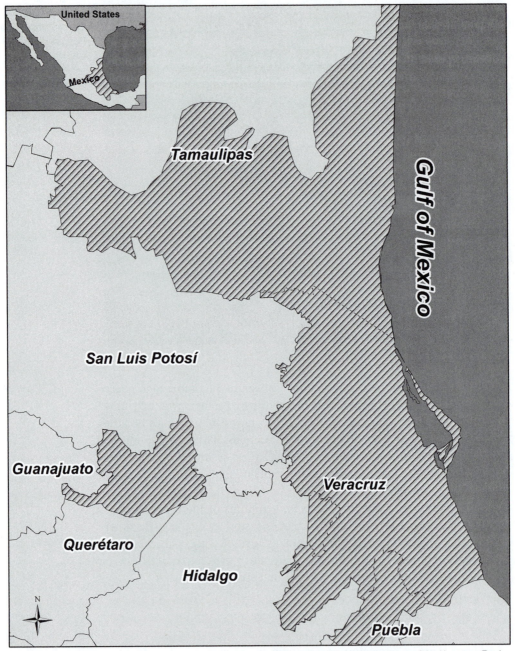

Cushman, Rachael, 2015 Geographical map of the Huasteca Region

Figure 2.2
Geographical map of the Huasteca region of Mexico. Rachel Cushman, 2015. Adapted from Canvas/World_Light_
Gray_Reference.ESRI, HERE, DeLorme, MapmyIndia, © OpenStreetMap contributors and the GIS users community.

to systematically investigate Mexican folk culture. A prolific author of dozens of books and articles, he worked with his wife Virginia Rodríguez Rivera, also a trained folklorist, to document the full scope of Mexican folk and popular music. Still, Mendoza struggled to define and classify Mexican music in non-contradictory ways.

In a signature article exploring the borders between popular and folk music in Mexico, Vicente T. Mendoza identified **popular music** as "fashionable" music and noted the historical and ongoing practice of local communities taking fashionable music and creating local variants, resulting in musical expressions that we might label folk (Mendoza 1955). Like Mendoza, we will consider folk music to be defined as much, if not more, by acts of transmission, treatment and placement, than by sound characteristics alone.

For our purposes, **folk music** may be understood as music that customarily circulates via oral tradition, transmitted by word of mouth rather than through notation. Conventionally viewed as music performed by rural or impoverished people, it may be viewed as the common property of a community, rather than the product of a single author. In many instances, folk musicians have adopted and adapted music from outside the community, including formally composed or classical works. Still, the origin or composer of a folk song is often unknown or lost in the shrouds of time, and typical versions of folk songs may have resulted from the collective contributions of many different performers over time.

Adopting a focus on transmission may guide our understanding of art music traditions as well, since the flow of influence may also move in the opposite direction, from folk to art music. The song "Sandunga" [2.2, 2.3] offers an example of the complexity of stylistic exchange. We will listen to two different compositions and performances based on this song.

STYLISTIC EXCHANGE: "SANDUNGA"

"Sandunga" is a song considered to have originated in the Isthmus of Tehuantepec in the state of Oaxaca, the narrowest part of southern Mexico, which separates the Gulf of Mexico from the Pacific Ocean. (See Fig. 2.3). Associated with a slow dance, itself known as the *sandunga*, it represents precisely the kind of transformation referenced by Mendoza. According to Henrietta Yurchenco (1976), the melody of "Sandunga" can be traced to a tune from a popular musical theater work of the type known as *tonadilla*, performed at the National Theatre in Mexico City in 1850 by the theatrical company of María Cañete. The tune captured the imagination of an Oaxacan military leader named Máximo Ramón Ortiz, who composed his own lyrics to the tune when he arrived home from battle to find his dear mother had died. The word *sandunga* (sometimes spelled *zandunga*) has many meanings. Some suggest that the word is a Náhuatl derivation of the Spanish word *fandango*, and as such refers to a dance or celebration. It has become a reference for a graceful Tehuantepec woman. It also defines

Istmo de Tehuantepec

Figure 2.3
Geographical map of
the Isthmus of
Tehuantepec. Rachel
Cushman, 2015.

Cushman, Rachael, 2015 Geographical map of the Istmo De Tehuantepec

Figure 2.4
Dancing the *Sandunga.*
Photo by Matías
Romero.

a category of *son* (dance song)—another famous *sandunga* is "La Llorona."
"Sandunga" became the unofficial anthem of the Isthmus of Tehuantepec,
and is a signature folk song performed at weddings, fiestas, and funerals,
often by wind bands or on marimba. So iconic is the *sandunga* of Oaxaca
and the Isthmus of Tehuantepec, that the celebrated film-maker Sergei
Eisenstein used it as inspiration for an entire section of his 1930 film *¡Que
Viva Mexico!*[1] "Sandunga" moved from folk to popular status in the classic
Mexican film *Águila o sol* (1937), featuring the iconic comic actor Mario
Moreno, known to the world as "Cantinflas."

   Audio Examples 2.2 and 2.3 offer two different versions of this song
that illustrate the re-integration of the folk song into cosmopolitan frames.
The first is a contemporary rendition with jazz inflections by the Oaxacan-
born singer Lila Downs (b. 1968); the other is a piano composition by the
classically trained Mexican art music composer Miguel Bernal Jiménez
(1910–1956).[2]

TERMS AND PERSPECTIVES FOR ASSESSING SOUND

Our attention to social frames does not eliminate the need to notice and
comment upon aspects of sound. Audio recordings, videos, and better yet,
live performance are our most important primary documents in any study
of music. Thus, the best way to learn about Mexican music is to listen and
notice details. Doing so may take some practice, even for people who are
music lovers. Often when we hear music we do not pay close attention to
what we are hearing. Learning to notice and acquiring the vocabulary to
document, describe, and critically examine what is noticed—in this case,
heard—is a valuable skill and a mark of an educated person. To cultivate
these skills, the next section of this chapter is dedicated to developing the

tools to sharpen your ability to listen, describe, and discuss music. There will be ongoing opportunities for you to develop skills of listening and critical perception throughout the text.

🎧

2.2

Listening to "Sandunga" a *son istmeño*, or dance song from the Isthmus of Tehuantepec, Oaxaca, performed by the popular contemporary singer Lila Downs (1999).

Lila Downs gained attention for her performances on the soundtrack for the movie *Frida* (2002). Her recording of "Sandunga" may serve as a rich example for exploring some of the basic terminology used to describe musical characteristics.

We can begin our study of musical characteristics by identifying some of the rhythmic features of the song. Can you locate the **beat** or underlying basic pulse of the song? Try tapping your foot or snapping your fingers along with the music. When you do this you are recognizing the beat. Downs's performance begins with a **prelude** that feels improvisatory. In this opening section the beat is not accented and we do not sense any regular **meter** (measure or grouping of the beat), and so we might describe it as being in **free meter.** Once the guitar enters, we feel a regular pattern of beats that fall in measures of three beats, with the first stronger than the next two. Thus, we might say that the song is in **triple meter,** familiar for most listeners who have heard or danced to a waltz. You can hear and feel that waltz-like dance rhythm throughout the rest of the performance, most clearly in the 1–2–3, oom-pah-pah strumming of the guitar.

Return to the opening of the song and notice how Downs sings. Notice the shifts in **volume** in the prelude. Downs sings some **pitches** very quietly, others more loudly, and on some she **crescendos**, beginning softly and gradually growing louder. Later in the song she will do the opposite, and **decrescendo.**

Listen closely to the pitches Downs sings. She begins on a **high** note, in the upper **register** of her voice and slides down to lower pitches, pausing twice in that descent, as a way of drawing in her listener. The three sustained pitches in that opening flourish outline a **minor chord** and introduce the **key** or **scale** of the **melody** that soon follows. Here the singer delivers each pitch in succession. When the pitches are played simultaneously, as they are by the guitarist, they create the **harmony.** It is helpful to notice the minor key and harmonies of "Sandunga," since being in a minor key (also referred to as minor **mode**), along with triple meter, is a predictable characteristic feature of the larger category of dance songs from Oaxaca known as *sandungas*.

We can hum or sing along with Downs as she sings the melody throughout the song, particularly because the sequence of pitches that comprise the melody becomes predictable through repetition. Tracking repetition, variation, and contrast in melody is one way to distinguish the overall **structure** of a song. Types of songs are often defined in part by their compositional structure. **Strophic** songs, like "Sandunga," use one basic melody, repeated for each verse, and strophic form is often called **verse-form**. Read the lyrics as you listen to the recording to see if you can hear the return of the melody with each verse. You may note one verse repeatedly returns in alternation with each new verse, serving as a refrain. In some songs the refrain is set to a different melody than the other verses; is this the case with "Sandunga"?

Fans love Lila Downs in part because of the character of her voice. Musicians use the term **timbre** to refer to the quality of sound. Not only does timbre distinguish one voice or instrument from another, but skillful performers manipulate timbre to add color and variety to their sound to be more expressive. What varieties of timbres do you hear in this recording? Can you identify all the instruments used in the recording?

Try singing "Sandunga" on your own or in class (see Figs 2.5 and 2.6 for lyrics and guitar music). Now that you have some acquaintance with musical terminology and with the melody of "Sandunga," you are ready to explore a more complex musical treatment and discussion.

Listening to *Carteles No. 5* Allegro Molto—"Sandunga" by Miguel Bernal Jiménez, composed in 1952, performed and recorded in 2010 by pianist Ahmed Fernando Anzaldúa.

2.3

Mexican pianist Ahmed Fernando Anzaldúa taught at the Conservatory of Music in Chihuahua and is currently part of the Conducting Graduate Program at Western Michigan University. In his blog, he writes: "One of my favorite Mexican composers is Miguel Bernal Jiménez. He is mainly known for his sacred music, but I think that his best writing is in his secular works. Of his keyboard compositions, the one that stands out for me is *Carteles* (pastels or posters, not a criminal organization)" (Anzaldúa 2010).

"Sandunga" is the fifth piece in *Carteles*. Miguel Bernal Jiménez sets the melody in a complex manner requiring the pianist to use some showy techniques like crossing hands, and rapidly repeating notes (**tremolo**) in one hand while playing contrasting rhythms in the other. The piece falls into sections that we may label A-B-A, followed by a brief closing or **coda** section. In the opening section, A, the pianist plays descending **chromatic** scales (a scale using all of the 12 basic pitches in the octave) with the left hand in the **bass** or low register of the piano that contrast with the melody played by the right hand in the upper (or **treble**, i.e. high) register of the instrument. The opening section builds around an A minor scale, with additional chromatic notes that give it a modern flavor. The contrasting B section of the piece shifts into the major mode (first A major and then F major), presenting a waltz-like melody harmonized in parallel sixths (where "sixth" refers to the **interval** or distance between two pitches; a very common harmony in Mexican music in general), giving this section a bright dance-like quality. The middle section is followed by a return of the music heard in the A section, and the piece closes with a contrasting closing section that features punctuating seconds (smaller more **dissonant** intervals) and a rising chromatic passage.

The shift from minor to major is customary in *sandungas* in general. Other distinctively Mexican characteristics include the use of the 6/8 time signature (**compound meter**, a metric grouping that can be divided in more than one way). Like so much Mexican music, Bernal Jiménez exploits the options for shifting the metric accent within that time signature. Often we feel an accent on the third beat (1 2 **3** 4 5 6), creating two uneven large groupings. Other times, the accent shifts to emphasize two groups of three, more like 3/4 time, and akin to a waltz. This flexibility of accentuated grouping is a feature of compound meters like 6/8. We hear the waltz-like feel in the B section of the piece. Note also how the phrases end with a downward inflection. Anzaldúa compares this pattern of inflection to the way people who live in southern and central Mexico speak (Anzaldúa 2010). Such subtle reference illustrates but one way that music is able to intrinsically express local identity.

CONCLUDING REFLECTIONS

The aim of this chapter has been to introduce basic terms and concepts useful for any serious study of music, while also introducing you to several characteristics commonly found in Mexican music of many styles. Establishing categories is difficult in music, as it can be in any field of study, but it is a necessary task to allow us to investigate and compare musical examples and activities. Learning to discern details of musical sound and structure is also an important task. Sharing our observations requires us to use shared terminology in discussion and writing. Scholars often use different terms to organize their work than do local experts, and as our examination continues we will often study native as well as academic terminology. Both will be useful in achieving our larger goals which include: 1) learning to recognize and know by name a representative set of Mexican music; 2) sharpening our ability to notice and discuss musical sound; and 3) gaining an awareness of how musical events, activities, and ideas connect and even shape the lives of individuals and communities.

If these goals sound too formal, think of them in more practical terms. When you have finished with the course you should be able to request songs from a mariachi, find a new recording, recognize music on a concert program, and find new pleasure in a wider palate of musical options. Our purposes are two-fold: to develop your understanding of music, as well as the history, concerns, and passions of the Mexican people.

CRITICAL THINKING AND DISCUSSION PROMPTS

1. Using the terms introduced in our discussion of "Sandunga" (highlighted in bold type), return to "La Plaza" [audio example 2.1] and describe what you hear.

2. Compare Lila Downs's version of "Sandunga" to the fifth piece from a set for piano solo known as *Carteles* (Posters) composed by Miguel Bernal Jiménez in 1952 and performed by Mr. Ahmed Fernando Anzaldúa. How does each integrate various aspects of Mexican identity and reflect creative adaptations?

3. Identify a classmate who plays guitar (or another musical instrument) who has the skill to accompany your class in singing a simple version of the song "Sandunga" (see Figs 2.5 and 2.6 for lyrics and guitar music). Sing the song as a group, using that experience as a way to further explore the musical elements discussed in this chapter and to enjoy the experience.

4. Compare the composition of Evaristo Aguilar to one by another composer who experiments with incorporating sounds from daily life and non-traditional instruments as part of musical composition (John Cage is a possible choice). How do the purposes and approaches of the two composers differ? How are they similar? Do you find their approaches effective? Why or why not?

Figure 2.5
Lyrics for "Sandunga."
Traditional.

Ay, Sandunga	**Ay, Sandunga**
Sandunga mamá por Dios	Sandunga mama, for God's sake
Sandunga no seas ingrata	Sandunga don't be ungrateful
Mamá de mi corazón	Mama of my heart
Ay sandunga . . . [estribillo]	Ay, sandunga . . . [refrain]
Ante noche fui a tu casa	Last night I went to your house
Tres golpes le di al candado	Three times I knocked on the door
Tu no sirves para amores	You are no good for love
Tienes el sueño pesado	You are sleeping heavily
Ay sandunga . . . [estribillo]	Ay, sandunga . . . [refrain]
[interludio]	[instrumental interlude]
Me ofreciste acompañarme	You offered to come with me
desde la iglesia a mi choza	From the church to my hut
pero como no llegabas	But because you didn't arrive
tuve que venirme sola	I had to come alone
Ay sandunga . . . [estribillo]	Ay, sandunga . . . [refrain]
A orillas del Papaloapa	On the banks of the Papaloapa
me estaba bañando ayer	I was bathing yesterday
Pasaste por las orillas	You passed by the shore
y no me quisiste ver	And you didn't want to see me
Ay sanduga . . . [estribillo]	Ay, sandunga . . . [refrain]

Sandunga

Traditional

Figure 2.6
Melody and guitar accompaniment for "Sandunga." Score prepared by José Luis Puerta.

KEY TERMS, PEOPLE, AND PLACES

ambient sound	minor chord
beat	key
composition	scale
folk music	mode
free meter	melody
prelude	harmony
meter	structure
triple meter	strophic
duple meter	pitch
compound meter	soundscape
volume	timbre
crescendos	Evaristo Aguilar
decrescendos	Vicente T. Mendoza
high note	Lila Downs
interval	Miguel Bernal Jiménez
register	Máximo Ramón Ortiz

NOTES

1 The film was never completed by Eisenstein, but a posthumous version created by Grigori Alexandrov in 1979 is available and makes for a visually compelling introduction to Mexico in the decades immediately following the revolution. The musical score attempts to honor Eisenstein's plan to connect a single musical composition to each scene.

2 For a performance of Miguel Bernal Jiménez's "Sandunga," *Carteles No. 5*, as played by Ahmed Fernando Anzaldúa, at: http://youtu.be/hqabq9_UxMw

FOR REFERENCE AND FURTHER STUDY

Anzaldúa, Ahmed Fernando. 2010. "Sandunga." Allegro Molto (posted February 24, 2010). http://ahmedfernando.wordpress.com/2010/02/24/sandunga/ (accessed January 12, 2015).

Mendoza, Vicente T. 1948. *Mexican Folksongs*. New York: Hispanic Institute in the United States.

Mendoza, Vicente T. 1955. "The Frontiers between 'Popular' and 'Folk'." *Journal of the International Folk Music Council* 7: 24–27.

Samuels, David, Meintjes, Louise, Ochoa, Ana Maria, and Porcello, Thomas. 2010. "Soundscapes: Toward a Sounded Anthropology." *Annual Review of Anthropology* 39:329–345.

Shiner, Larry E. 2001. *The Invention of Art: A Cultural History*. Chicago, IL: University of Chicago Press.

Yurchenco, Henrietta. 1976. Liner Notes and Translations. *Mexico South: Traditional Songs and Dances from the Isthmus of Tehuantepec*. New York: Folkways Records, FE 4378. http://media.smithsonianfolkways.org/liner_notes/folkways/FW04378.pdf (accessed January 12, 2015).

DISCOGRAPHY

Aguilar, Evaristo. 2006. *Ritmos de la Huasteca*. Audio CD. Mexico: Autonomous University of Tamaulipas, 2006.

Anzaldúa Ahmed Fernando. 2010. Bernal Jiménez, Miguel. *Carteles No. 5.* piano. (performer's own recording).

Downs, Lila. 1999. *Sandunga*. Audio CD. San Miguel de Allende, Mexico: Hit Records.

Various Artists. 1976. *Mexico South: Traditional Songs and Dances from the Isthmus of Tehuantepec*, recorded by Peter and Henrietta Yurchenco. Washington, DC. Smithsonian Folkways Records, FW04378_102.

CHAPTER 3

Pre-Cortesian and Indigenous Music, Past and Present

PART I
Ancient Voices

AN OPENING SONG

The first verse of a song by the princess poet-singer Macuilxochitzin opens this study of pre-Cortesian music,[1] and native practice in the era preceding the arrival of the Spanish conquistadors led by Hernán Cortés. Macuilxochitzin was born in 1435, on the fifth day of the flower month, hence her name meaning Five Flower. As the daughter of a powerful advisor to Aztec kings, she lived her life in the splendor of the court at Tenochtitlán. An historian from that era, Fernando de Alba Ixtlilxochitl of Texcoco, described Macuilxochitzin "as wise and as competent as the king" (León-Portilla 1994:195). Her adventurous poetry reflected her insider knowledge of the ruler and the politics of the kingdom. Macuilxochitzin's legacy confirms that in Aztec society women, as well as men, cultivated the art of poetic song, and both boys and girls received training in special schools in the great cities of ancient Mexico. Even beyond the court, the practice of what historian Susan Kellogg calls "gender parallelism" (Kellogg 1994) in pre-Hispanic indigenous societies offered girls and women parallel social and opportunities with boys and men, if not full equality in social status. The remainder of Macuilxochitzin's song documents the victory of her

Figure 3.1
Lyrics from "The Song of Macuilxóchitl" in Náhuatl, Spanish, and English. Miguel León Portilla, *Quince poetas del mundo náhuatl*, (Mexico City: Editorial Diana) 1994: 204–205.

Macuilxochitzin icuic	Canto de Macuilxochitzin	Song of Macuilxóchitl
A nonpehua noncuica,	Elevo mis cantos,	I raise my chants,
ni Macuilxochitl,	Yo, Macuilxóchitl,	I, Macuilxóchitl,
san noconahuiltia in ipalnemoa,	con ellos alegro al Dador de la vida,	with them, I cheer the Giver of Life,
¡yn maconnetotilo!	¡comience la danza!	let the dance begin!

people over the fierce Otomíes, who had previously settled in the central plateau. It includes a verse celebrating the women who aided in the victory. Shortly thereafter, the Aztecs, known among their indigenous contemporaries as the "Mexica" and as the "conquerors of the world," faced an even more formidable foe.

EARLY HISTORY

We might start the story of indigenous Mexico as early as 14,000 years ago, when ecological conditions in the ancient territory of Beringa made it possible for migrants from Asia and Siberia to start the move across the Bering Land Bridge and make their way into North and South America.[2] From those first inhabitants a great diversity of cultures and practices emerged, encompassing over 108 different tribes and more than 54 distinct languages.

Highly sophisticated civilizations developed in central and southern Mexico and the first permanent settlements in middle America date from 1500 BCE. These societies were agricultural, used mass labor, and organized life according to a 10-month calendar based on astronomical cycles. They built monumental architectural structures, as evidenced by archaeological ruins dating back to the golden classic era of 200–800 CE, such as Teotihuacán, Monte Albán, or Mitla, and practiced complex religions that placed priests in a special elite class and trained musicians for ritual service. Some of the oldest notations of poetic song, written in a pictographic language, appear etched in the stone structures of Monte Albán.

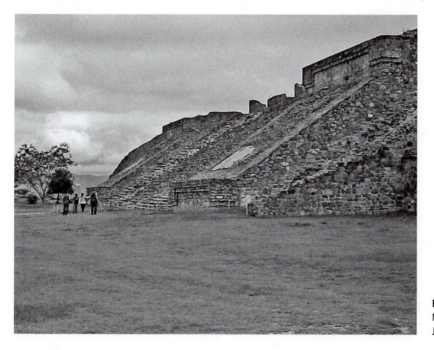

Figure 3.2
Monte Albán. Photo by
Janet Sturman, (2011).

Among the oldest layers of civilization was the monumental culture of the Olmec people who settled along the Gulf Coast (see Fig. 3.3). Olmec art, beliefs, and heroes influenced surrounding and subsequent cultures, including the Zapotec and Mixtec people who still live today in the state of Oaxaca. These groups and the Maya from the south traded with Toltecs, another group that built great temples. Many Mayan dialects are still spoken today in Chiapas and Guatemala, and elsewhere in Mexico indigenous languages are being revitalized.

Despite the wide range of indigenous people, the Aztecs stand out in history and in the modern imagination. According to their legend, the Aztecs moved south from Aztlán[3] in the twelfth century. They spoke Náhuatl, which became a common language for many Mexican groups. Their capital city, and the seat of the triple alliance of once rival city-states (after 1428), was Tenochtitlán, situated in present-day Mexico City.

Figure 3.3
Map showing Olmec settlement and influence. Rachel Cushman, 2015.

The Aztecs were empire builders. They created a strong military regime that successfully dominated fellow native groups, conquering at the peak of their empire in the mid-fifteenth century all of central Mexico. In the sixteenth century they fell to a foreign empire, at the hands of the Spanish explorer Hernán Cortés and his invading forces. Despite this fateful

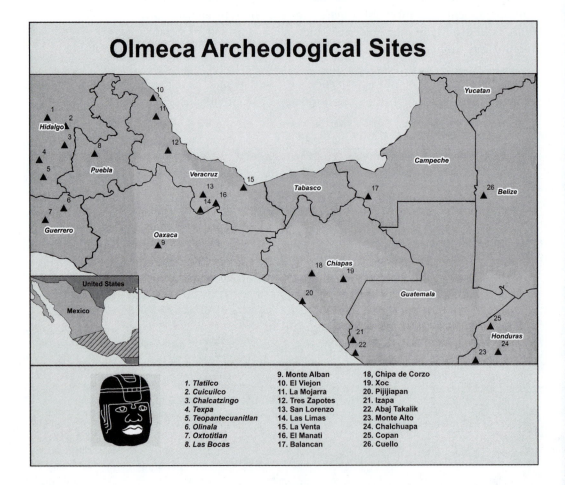

Olmeca Archeological Sites

1. Tlatilco	9. Monte Alban	18. Chipa de Corzo
2. Cuicuilco	10. El Viejon	19. Xoc
3. Chalcatzingo	11. La Mojarra	20. Pijijiapan
4. Texpa	12. Tres Zapotes	21. Izapa
5. Teopantecuanitlan	13. San Lorenzo	22. Abaj Takalik
6. Olinala	14. Las Limas	23. Monte Alto
7. Oxtotitlan	15. La Venta	24. Chalchuapa
8. Las Bocas	16. El Manati	25. Copan
	17. Balancan	26. Cuello

encounter, the legacy of the Aztecs and fellow native peoples did not vanish. The indigenous heritage lives on in the transformed ways of life of contemporary Indian and mestizo people. This legacy distinguishes Mexico, and at key moments in modern history the nation's leaders have chosen to highlight the legacy of ancient indigenous peoples like the Aztecs in their efforts to forge an independent identity and unify the nation of Mexico. We shall see this attention emerge in one way after the nation gained independence from Spanish rule, and again, a century later after the revolution.

While the archaeological record indicates that music was an important aspect of daily and ceremonial life, the ancient ancestors of native Mexicans did not notate their music in a manner that allows us to recapture the sounds of those early practices. For this reason, we must rely on an imperfect collection of materials to piece together an understanding of what music was like before the arrival of the Europeans. These materials include archaeological findings of ancient instruments, many of which are inscribed with pictographs explaining how and when they were played, as well as stone carvings with text and graphics that scholars have only recently decoded and still struggle to interpret. Among the most valuable records are the illustrated treatises written by European explorers, missionaries, and native scribes such as the ethnographic history compiled in the sixteenth century by the friar Bernardino de Sahagún.

MUSIC IN ANCIENT INDIGENOUS LIFE: ANCIENT BELIEFS AND PRACTICES

Historian Julio Estrada (1992) reminds us that the myths that ancient peoples told each other and shared with ancient scribes may serve as another resource for information regarding beliefs and attitudes towards music, even if we cannot rely upon them for details regarding actual practice. An ancient origin myth offers insight into how the Nahua people viewed the relationship between divine and natural power. The myth tells how Quetzalcóatl journeyed to the underworld to gather bones from the Lord of Death, known as Mictlantecuhtli, to create humans. Mictlantechuhtli gave Quetzalcóatl a conch shell, directing him to sound the shell and, take four turns round a circle in order to gain his help. But there were no finger holes to control the sound, so Quetzalcóatl summoned the worms to bore holes and directed the bees to fly into the sacred shell to make it sound. Upon hearing the sound, Mictlantecuhtli, recognized his visitor's power, and told Quetzalcóatl to go ahead, take the bones. Thus, the birth of a new people, the ancestors of modern Mexicans, began from the sounding of the conch, the sacred *atecocolli*, (Fig. 3.4), and sounds made possible by animals (Fig. 3.5).

The ancient Nahua believed that song embodied divine breath, a view evident in the conch myth as well as in their pictographs. The pictograph for music was the same as for poetry, there was no distinction. Song appears

Figure 3.4
Atecocolli. Conch
seashell used as
musical instrument.
Museo Nacional de
Antropología e
Historia, Mexico City
(2009).

Figure 3.5
Jaguar deity playing
the sacred conch shell.
Image painted on wall
of the Palace of the
Jaguars in
Teotihuacán. Photo by
Janet Sturman, (2009).

in manuscripts such as the Bourbon Codex[4] as flowered speech, a fitting graphic since the Nahua believed that their gods lived in the flower world (Fig. 3.6). Lines from a poem by Netzahualcóyotl (1402–1472) state "En cantos floridos yo vivo, como si fuera de oro, como fino plumaje de quetzal . . ." (In the flowered songs I live, as if out of gold, like the fine feathers of the quetzal . . .) (Netzahualcóyotl 2010:36).

As ancient society developed, humans retained contact with the authors of creation through zoomorphic instruments fashioned to resemble animals and the powers associated with those deities. The music and shape of the instruments provided links between the world of the creators and the world of the created. Instruments reflected the attributes of the gods

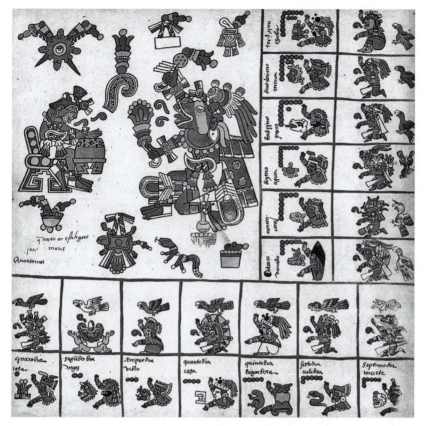

Figure 3.6
(see Plate 2)
Pictograph of Xochipilli, Prince of the flowers, deity of song, music and festival, singing to Quetzalcóatl, reproduction of page 4 from the Códice Borbónico. Bibliothèque de l'Assemblée Nationale, Paris. Used with permission.

as well as the musical resonance associated with natural beings and phenomena; thus, a shell was associated with the wind, a bell was associated with a snake, a rattle was associated with rain, seeds, or motion (see Fig. 3.7). These associations are evident in the musical personification of the gods as well as in the masks and dress worn for rituals and celebrations.

Figure 3.7
Modern recreations of zoomorphic whistles in the shape of a jaguar and turtle. Photo by Janet Sturman, (2014).

PROFESSIONAL TRAINING—PICTURE YOURSELF AS A *CUICAPIZTLE*

While the actual sounds of ancient Aztec and Mayan music are not preserved, we do have more detailed records regarding the poetic verse, as well as the training and responsibilities of native musicians. Poetry and song were inseparable, known as *cuicatl*, flowery speech. Pictographs of musicians in ancient documents and stone etchings indicate song by depicting the spiral speech glyph decorated with flowers. Professional musicians, known as *cuicapiztles*, constituted an elite segment of society. Young boys and girls received training beginning at age 12 in special schools called *cuicacallis* (song houses) (Brill 2011:65).

To appreciate the responsibilities of the cuicapiztle, imagine yourself as a musician apprentice in the Aztec court. Your songs and dance connected your people to the gods, serving the most important ritual functions of your society. You trained for many hours each day to learn everything by heart. Your performance had to be technically perfect, for any slip might enrage the gods. If you erred you expected severe punishment. You might lose a hand or foot, or be put to death.

As a cuicapiztle you were expected to compose new songs for theatrical performances and contests and simply to mark the days of the calendar. As a poet-singer you honored great warriors and noblemen with epic songs that recounted heroic feats of your ancestors and related their accomplishments and lineage to those of current leaders in flowery verse, which as always, you created on demand or delivered from memory. With these great responsibilities came great privileges. You enjoyed many of the luxuries of the elite and you were exempt from paying taxes. As a court musician, you were not expected to perform music for the daily sacrifices and ritual ceremonies at the temples; those duties belonged to the priestly musicians. You enjoyed the occasional opportunity to play outside the court when a local merchant might hire you for private celebrations (Both 2007:101).

NATIVE MUSICAL INSTRUMENTS

Musical instruments were used by native peoples in many contexts, including the founding of cities, the naming of towns and individuals, for adornment, for singing poetry, for festivals and sacrifices, for going to war, and to honor the dead. Among the most important instruments heard at Tenochtitlán and elsewhere in Mesoamerica is the *huéhuetl*, a large drum carved from a hollowed tree trunk with a stretched animal skin on top (see *membranophone*). Accounts in native manuscripts indicate that the Nahua viewed the three-legged huéhuetl as manifestations of deceased court singers or as deities speaking through the instrument to help people communicate (Both 2007:95). The huéhuetl was traditionally played during war and religious ritual ceremonies. It can produce two tones, one by playing in the center of the drum head, and the other by striking near the rim.

The *teponaztli*, is a sculpted slit-drum made from a hollowed hardwood log, beaten with rubber-tipped wooden mallets called *olmaitl*. For temple ritual ceremonies, the teponaztli was placed on a stand resembling a throne, and for dances it was set upon an x-shaped stand to boost its resonance. Like the *huéhuetl*, the teponaztli produces two pitches (Fig. 3.8). We find a parallel in the Nahua language which also uses two basic tones, one high, and one low, to distinguish meaning in words.

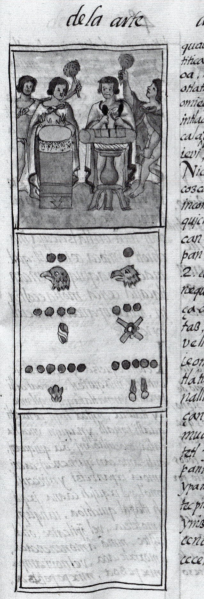

Figure 3.8
(see Plate 3)
Aztec musicians playing *huéhuetl* (footed drum), *teponaztli* (log drum), and *ayacachtli* (gourd rattles). From the Florentine Codex, Book 4. Biblioteca Medicea Laurenziana (Laurentian Library, Florence, Italy).

Figure 3.9 shows a selected inventory of instruments used by native peoples prior to European contact, many of which produce two independent or simultaneously sounding pitches. Return to this collage to test your ability to identify and categorize pre-Hispanic instruments, many of which are still used today.

Native ideas and beliefs that shaped how music was made and how these instruments sounded are just as interesting, but recreating this knowledge is an ongoing puzzle. By comparing and combining data from oral and written legend, iconographic records, and living indigenous practices, scholars have learned that native people valued nuances in the quality of musical sound, the aspect that musicians call "timbre," often viewing it as more critical than pitch. Sound was meant to be evocative rather than beautiful. Many wind instruments, such as the *huilacapitztli* or clay flutes, whistles, and ocarinas (globular flutes) were crafted in the shape of animals and spirit beings (see Figs 3.7, 3.10, 3.11), and designed to produce sounds resembling the cries and calls of those animals. These sounds provided a bridge for communicating between humans and animals. Many native people believe that songs were taught to humans by animals that also represented powerful divine spirits as well as the voices of deceased human ancestors. Such instruments could be played by trained celebrants during religious and civic ritual, as well as by commoners in practical circumstances such as hunting.

Music scholar Arnd Adje Both reminds us the very word "music" is a European imposition upon Native Americans.[5] When the Nahua spoke of the *cuicatlamatilztli*, the art of song, they included the playing of musical

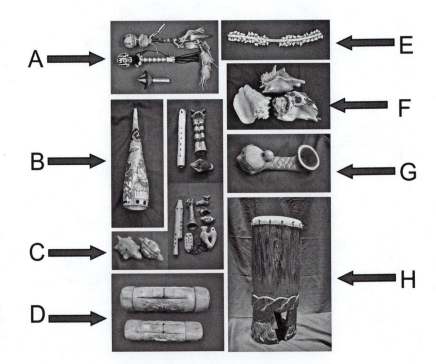

**Figure 3.9
(see Plate 4)**
Collage of indigenous instruments. Photos courtesy of Ricardo Almanza Carillo.

Figure 3.10
Zoomorphic clay whistle
from the Gulf region.
Photo courtesy of UNAM.

instruments as an extension of this art. It appears that they viewed musicians as singing through their instruments, rather than thinking of instruments simply as supplemental to or accompanying song.

NAMES AND CATEGORIES OF ANCIENT AZTEC INSTRUMENTS

To keep an open mind regarding the potential use of indigenous instruments, scholars often avoid grouping indigenous instruments by conventional European categories. Instead they may choose to classify them into one of four categories developed to compare music instruments in 1918 by scholars Curt Sachs and Erich von Hornbostel: *idiophones, membranophones, chordophones*, and *aerophones*. These categories are distinguished by the aspect of the instrument that generates the principal sound vibrations. Native musicians were more likely to categorize these instruments according to their use, their symbolic associations, as well as by who played them. Common people played the smaller hand rattles and scrapers, while the large and highly decorated instruments were played by trained musicians and reserved for religious and civic rituals in the service of the temple or court.

As you read the Náhuatl names and the subsequent descriptions for the instruments in each category, try to picture these instruments and re-order them according to how they might be used and by whom. Try to reconstruct the setting for performance in your mind. Remember that each instrument type listed here might take any of several different forms and sizes, depending on its purpose, the setting, and even the whim of the maker.

Idiophones

Idiophone means "self-sounding." This first category includes all instruments where the body of the instrument itself generates the primary sound vibration. It includes the: *ayacachtli* (gourd rattles), *ayotl* (turtle shell), *cacalachtli* (rattle of clay vessel with seeds inside), *chicahuaztli* (a long pole representing a ray from the sun, filled with seeds and played like a rattle during rituals), *chililitli* (copper disks struck with mallets), *coyolli* (metal bells, or cocoon rattles—often strapped to the legs of dances), *omichicauaztli* (a rasp made from a deer bone), *teponaztli* (log drum, some with appended gourd resonators called *tecomapiloa*), and *tetzilacatl* (metal gongs).

Membranophones

The category of instrument where a stretched membrane generates the primary sound is known as membranophones, and includes: the huéhuetl (single-headed drum with a carved wooden base) and variants thereof, such as the *panhuetl*.

Aerophones

The category of aerophones, comprising instruments where sound is generated by trapped or forced air, is well represented in pre-colonial

Figure 3.11
A set of indigenous aerophones: single and double *tlapitzalli* (flutes), *huilacapitztli* (ocarinas), *atecocolli* (seashell); membranophones: clay and ceramic drums. Photo by Ricardo Almanza Carillo (2008).

Mexico. Examples include the *chichitli* (whistle flutes), *cocolocti* (buzzing, reed flute), *huilacapitztli* (ocarinas and vessel flutes), *tlapitzalli* (clay duct flutes, may have multiple chambers or pipes), and *tepuzquiquiztli* (copper or gourd trumpets) (Fig. 3.9).

Chordophones (post-contact)

The category of chordophones, string instruments, is one for which we find no evidence of indigenous practice prior to European contact. The *mitote*, or musical bow, discussed in the second section of this chapter may represent an exception. After the fifteenth century, indigenous people learned to play European string instruments. Recognizing native talent, and because of the high cost of importing instruments, the Spaniards taught native artisans to make string instruments. One such teacher was Vasco de Quiroga, Michoacán's first bishop, known as Tata Vasco. In 1941, composer Miguel Bernal Jiménez, introduced in Chapter 2, wrote an opera titled *Tata Vasco* to celebrate the life of this bishop. The opera offers additional examples (available on YouTube) of a modern composer's recreations of indigenous musical expression in the era of Cortés (see Saavedra 2007). Tata Vasco established string instrument workshops and trained native artisans in Paracho, Michoacán. The instruments from Tata Vasco's shops gained fame for their superior sound quality and masterful construction, and the legacy persists in today's *guitarras de Paracho*. An important result of this long legacy is that local artisans created their own versions of European instruments and adopted them for use in their own distinctive music.

WHAT DID THE MUSIC OF ANCIENT AZTECS SOUND LIKE?

Listening to "Raíz Viva" (Living Root), composed by José Ávila and performed by Los Folkloristas.[6]

3.1

The instrumental piece "Raíz Viva" composed in 1977 by José Ávila, founder and director of Los Folkloristas, represents one reconstruction of ancient Aztec music. Los Folkloristas is an ensemble dedicated to performing a full range of Mexican and Latin American music and exploring links between ancient and contemporary practices (Fig. 3.12). Inspired by urban artists and musicians throughout the Americas, who recognized folkloric and indigenous culture as a means of drawing attention to the rights of ignored populations, Ávila also drew inspiration from archaeological and ethnographic findings, seizing an early opportunity to play archaic instruments housed in a museum in Veracruz, Mexico. He and his colleagues composed "Raíz Viva" to evoke the character of pre-Cortesian rituals and to introduce listeners to more than 40 different examples of instruments, including the huéhuetl, huilacapitztli, and tlapitzalli.

Figure 3.12
Members of Los
Folkloristas. Courtesy
of José Ávila and Los
Folkloristas.

As you listen to "Raíz Viva" review the inventory of archaic indigenous instruments above and check off as many as you can hear in this performance. Los Folkloristas has prepared a YouTube video that introduces this piece with samples of various instrumental sounds. You may enjoy locating it and listening to it as part of your personal investigation and also to confirm your answers.

RECONSTRUCTION AND MOTIVATIONS

The power of the ancient Aztec ancestors looms large in modern Mexican history and thought. Efforts to reconstruct ancient Aztec and other indigenous music of Mexico reflect differing philosophies, depending upon any number of conditions, including the fashion and resources of a particular era, politics, aesthetics, and positions of advocacy. The musical examples in this chapter allow us to examine three different approaches to the reconstruction of archaic indigenous music. It will become evident that different aims and philosophies result in distinct musical realizations.

Los Folkloristas became famous during the 1970s, a decade when many popular musicians used folk music to advocate for civil rights and political reform. Their efforts aligned in many ways with the folk-rock movement launched by Pete Seeger, Bob Dylan, Joan Baez, and groups like the Weavers, and Peter, Paul and Mary in the United States. In Latin America, folk-rock musicians initiated their own new folk song movement known as *Nueva Canción* (New Song), or *Nueva Trova*. They shared a goal with folk-rock musicians elsewhere in the world to celebrate traditional forms in modern contexts. For Los Folkloristas, this aim included reviving ancient Aztec music, exploring its affinities with those of other Amerindian practices, including Andean music, and working to document living indigenous and roots practices. We will examine Los Folkloristas and the New Song movement in the context of twentieth-century popular music in Chapter 10.

> Listening to "Teponazcuicatl" (Procession of the Drum), a sixteenth-century piece reconstructed in 1990 by Christopher Moroney and performed by the San Antonio Vocal Ensemble (SAVAE).[7]

3.2

"Teponazcuicatl" is the 44th song in set B from the codex *Cantares Mexicanos*, compiled between 1550 and 1580 in Mexico City. Its setting by Christopher Moroney for the San Antonio Vocal Arts Ensemble, known as SAVAE, represents another approach to the reconstruction of ancient indigenous music.

The motives guiding the musicians of SAVAE overlap in some ways with those of Los Folkloristas, but SAVAE represents a different era and other perspectives. Like Los Folkloristas, SAVAE aims to promote cultural recognition of indigenous heritage, but their rendition of "Teponazcuicatl" suggests relationships between native cultures of the United States and Mexico, reminding listeners of shared perspectives across contemporary political borders. Promotion of intercultural understanding seems to guide their work as much as the aim to reconstruct an ancient song.

The sixteenth century in Mexico was a period of transition between indigenous rule and the early period of Spanish control, conversion and education, a matter we will examine more in subsequent chapters. The song "Teponazcuicatl" was originally a native song honoring the corn goddess of that name. She represented one aspect of Tonantzín, the Mother Earth deity of war, childbirth, and sustenance.

A Christianized vision of Tonantzin was cultivated among the Aztecs in form of the Virgin of Guadalupe, an indigenous manifestation of the Virgin Mary, who appeared to Juan Diego, a Nahua convert, in the second week of December in the year 1531 (Fig. 3.13).

Diego witnessed the Virgin at the sacred site of Tepeyac where the Aztecs once worshiped Tonantzin. Spanish religious leaders made good use of this miracle to foster additional conversions and the Virgin of Guadalupe eventually became the patron saint of Roman Catholic Mexico. Náhuatl accounts report that on December 26, 1531, devotees sang "Teponazcuicatl" in celebration as the faithful converts processed from the Metropolitan Cathedral in the center of Mexico City to the far northern district of Tepeyac, carrying as a banner Guadalupe's image on Juan Diego's cloak. Her image (see Fig. 3.13) has become an icon of Mexican identity; you have probably seen it many times.

The rhythms you hear in this performance of "Teponazcuicatl" are adapted from syllabic drumming patterns found in the codex *Cantares Mexicanos*, a collection of song lyrics compiled in the sixteenth century by Aztec musicians and historians. Christopher Moroney of SAVAE explains

Figure 3.13
Illustration of
Apparition of the
Virgin of Guadalupe.
Courtesy of the
Biblioteca Teológica
"Lorenzo Boturini,"
Basílica de Santa María
de Guadalupe.

how he and the chorus drew upon this manuscript to reconstruct the music
heard on the recording:

> No written music exists for this or any other song in the *Cantares*, and no
> rhythmic structure or rhyming scheme is evident in the Náhuatl verses.
> However, a drum pattern in the form of onomatopoeic Nahua syllables
> (tico toco toco tiquitiquiti quiti quito) starts the song followed by the
> instruction: "Just thus it will come back in." By assigning pitches from the
> pentatonic scale of the Aztec huilacapitztli (clay flute) to these syllables as
> well as adapting the syllabic pattern to the drums, a driving melodic and
> rhythmic figure emerged. Not only did the words fit the melody beautifully,
> but each Náhuatl verse formed a set of four melodic repetitions with the
> words actually rhyming at the end of each repetition! It felt as if we had

"decoded" part of a musical system that had been recorded for posterity by the Aztecs over 400 years ago.[8]

The syncretism of Christian and pre-Christian belief is evident from the translation that Mooney offers of the song's lyrics (Fig. 3.14). SAVAE does not set all the original verses found in the manuscript of the *Cantares Mexicanos*, instead the group performs a combination of selected verses.

"Teponazcuicatl"—Náhuatl text, from the *Cantares Mexicanos*.	"Song of the Drum (Teponaztli)"— English translation.
Tico Toco Toco tiquitiquiti quiti quito Can ic mocueptiuh	*Tico Toco Toco tiquitiquiti quiti quito* Just thus it will come back in
[I] Ÿ tlapapalxochicentli niyol aya nepapā tonacáxochitl moyahuaya oncuepontimoquetzacoyan aya aya yeteoya ixpan tona a Santa María ayyo.	[I] "Painted by the flowering ear of corn my heart comes to life." Now the various flowers of our sustenance are scattered about, bursting into bloom in front of the divine presence of our mother, Holy Mary.
[III] Çan ca tlacuilolpā _nemia moyollo amoxpetlatl ypan toncuicaya tiquimonyai'totia teteuctin aya in obispoya çan ca totatzin aya oncā_titlatoa atl itempā _ayyo.	[III] Your heart is alive in your painting. And we, the lords of this land sing all together from the book of songs. In perfect harmony we dance before you. Oh Bishop, Our Father, you preach over there by the water.
[IV] Yehuan Dios mitzyocox aya xochitla ya mitztlacatili yan cuicatl mitzicuiloa Santa María in obispoya [III] çan ca totatzin aya oncā_ titlatoa atl itempā ayyo.	[IV] In the beauty of the flowers did God create you. He paints you as a song, oh Holy Mary. Oh Bishop, Our Father, you preach over there by the water.
[V] Tolteca ihcuilihuia ahaa yaha ontlantoc amoxtliya moyolloya onaya moch onahciticac oo toltecayootl a ycaya ninemiz ye nicā _ayyo.	[V] The Toltecs are painted, yes, completed are their books. Your whole heart came to be perfect. "Here, with the Toltec art, I'll live."
[X] Tel cacahuaxochitl ahuiac xeliuhtihuitz a ihpotocaya in ahuiyac poyomahtlin pixahuia oncan nine'ne'nemi nicuicanitl yye ayao ohui yonca quiya itzmolini ye nocuic celia	[X] The flowers of the fragrant cocoa come scattering down spreading perfume. Fragrant poymatli drizzles down. And there, I, the singer, will walk. Listen, oh listen to my song of joy!
[XI] notlatollaquillo ohua in toxochiuh ycac y quiapani ayao.	[XI] Our flowers are arisen in this place of rain.

Figure 3.14
Lyrics from "Teponazcuicatl." Translation by Christopher Moroney, from the program notes of the album *El Milagro de Guadalupe*. Used with permission.

BUILDING A NEW NATION UPON ANCIENT SOUNDS

Aztec musical practices also attracted the attention of Mexican political and intellectual leaders in the first decades of the twentieth century, in the wake of the Mexican Revolution from 1910 to 1921. This period was known as *el Renacimiento azteca*, the Aztec Renaissance. The most famous Mexican composer at that time was Carlos Chávez (Fig. 3.15). He saw the arts as a critical tool for building a new nation. In addition to his work as a journalist and composer, Chávez served as the director of Mexico's National Symphony and the National Conservatory of Music. Like so many of his post-revolutionary contemporaries, he saw the ancient Aztecs as the fountain of a unique Mexican identity. Chávez carefully studied indigenous instruments and descriptions of ancient music in the accounts of early Spanish historians. He first used indigenous instruments in his two Aztec ballets composed in the 1920s, *El fuego nuevo* (New fire) and *Los cuatro soles* (The four suns).

3.3   Listening to "Xochipilli, An Imaginary Aztec Music: Allegro Animato," from *Complete Chamber Works, Vol. 3* by Carlos Chávez, Southwest Chamber Music with the Tambuco Percussion Ensemble, Cambria Master Recordings CD8852 (2005).

Chávez wrote *"Xochipilli"* (An Imagined Aztec Music) in 1940 for four wind players (two flutes, one doubling on piccolo, and one E-flat clarinet) and six percussionists, each of whom plays several different instruments over the course of the performance. The composition represents Chávez's systematic effort to evoke pre-conquest music for modern listeners. In addition to requiring European concert instruments to simulate ancient ones, such as the trombone conveying the sound of the conch shell, Chávez included parts for ancient Aztec instruments, the teponaxtli and the huéhuetl.

In his own program notes for *Xochipilli*, Chávez acknowledges the impossibility of directly quoting ancient music. He then explains that the sources of his inspiration grew from ancient sculptures, buildings and art, as well as living indigenous practice.

> *Xochipilli* is the result of my thoughts on topics of Mexican antiquity and of my unlimited admiration for pre-Cortesian sculpture and painting. Although referring to different arts, there is a common denominator in the various expressions of a given culture so that it is not impossible to derive from plastic arts a sensitivity that can be transcribed to music. Also, many times during my childhood I heard in the country Indian ensembles deeply rooted in the old traditions, something that is now lost, which made it possible for me to delve into the aesthetics of those cultures: sobriety, conciseness, purity and vigor.

(Chávez 1940)

Figure 3.15
Mexican composer,
Carlos Chávez as a
young man. Source:
Library of Congress.

Xochipilli means "flower prince" in Náhuatl and was the name of the Aztec god of art, games, beauty, dance, flowers, and song (Fig. 3.6). He was also the patron of the monkey calendar sign, homosexuality, and male prostitutes, perhaps stemming from Toltec association (Greenberg 1990:195). In the preface to his score, Chávez also recounts the specific practices of Aztec music that inspired him to compose *Xochipilli*. He was forced to imagine aspects that could not be certified, but we can sense his pride in the grandeur and intensity of music produced by Mexico's ancestors and his view of the continuity of certain fundamental practices and values.

There is no certainty of the style or aesthetic nature of the music of pre-Columbian civilizations. We deal with hypotheses, though these can be based on somewhat sensible considerations. At least two main genres can be distinguished: music for sacred festivities and that which accompanied poetical expressions of a deep lyrical or religious character. The latter were sung and must have corresponded to the same poetic expression of the lyrics, which fortunately have been transmitted to us, and which we admire

Figure 3.16
Uncovering a temple at Teotihuacán. The protruding stone heads include the image of Quetzalcoatl on the left wall. Photo by Janet Sturman, 2008.

for their deep poetic content. Being vocal music, we must surmise that it corresponded to a continuous melodic line more or less varied, although undoubtedly based on the repetition of simple musical phrases. In contrast to this lyrical expression, the music of the great sacred festivities was preponderantly rhythmical and active, meant to accompany enormous ensembles of dancers. It must have been rather tremendous music, implacable in its rhythm, strong and obstinate.

(Chávez 1940)

Chávez's concert masterpiece falls into three sections or movements. He tells us that in the first and third sections flutes and percussion depict the grand but fearful festivals at the *teocalli*, the pyramid-shaped temples, an example of which appears in Figure 3.16. The gentler, middle section of *Xochipilli* features melodies of "deep concentration" designed to evoke the powerful lyrical poetry of the cuicapiztle discussed earlier.

RECLAIMING INDIGENOUS AUTONOMY

In the plazas of Mexico City and in cities in the United States, such as Los Angeles, Tucson, Chicago, or Austin, you may encounter dance groups who identify themselves as concheros or as performers of Danza Azteca or Danza Mexica. Performers in these ensembles typically wear replicas of the feather headdresses and body ornaments treasured by the ancient Aztecs while they dance and play indigenous instruments (Fig. 3.17).

These groups trace their legacy back to the pre-Cortesian times, a claim that outsiders charge as remote at best and fabricated at worst. Several types

**Figure 3.17
(see Plate 5)**
Danza Azteca in front
of the Metropolitan
Cathedral in Mexico
City beneath the
decorations for the
2011 celebration
honoring the nation's
Independence on
September 16.
Photo by Janet
Sturman, 2011.

of conchero groups complicate practitioners' claims of ancestral affiliation. One line of practice is distinguished by the aims of participants to engage in *danzas de promesa*—dances to manifest religious vows and devotion. A second line of practice is maintained by dancers who emphasize the political implications of re-enacting ancient ritual as a rejection of European imperialism initiated by the imposition of Hispanic culture. Susanna Rostas (1991) explains that these groups, who often prefer to self-identify as Mexica, may include participants of non-native and non-Mexican ancestry who support the political aims of the group and its desire to promote ascendancy of indigenous culture and authority. Still a third line of performance is that of theatrical performance groups, including the national folkloric ballet, that adapt the conchero traditions for staged presentation and the entertainment of tourists.

The name conchero, comes from one of the instruments used in the devotional groups. It is a small, guitar-like instrument, a native adaptation of the Spanish guitar called the *guitarra conchera* since it was originally made from an armadillo shell (Fig. 3.18). The concha has five double-course strings, tuned as paired octaves to B-flat, E-flat, A-flat, C, and F. We find similar instruments in the Andes regions of South America where descendent of the Incas in Bolivia and Peru created the *charango*, also using the armadillo shell. The concha was an essential instrument used by religious brotherhoods, known as *cofradías* or *mesas*, who supported an early merger of native and Catholic customs maintained by the concheros. The newer urban and more radical Danza Mexica groups eschew the concha as representing unwanted Hispanic influence (remember, the inventory of archaic indigenous musical instruments showed no evidence of string instruments prior to European contact).

Figure 3.18
Concha and concheros. Photo by Ricardo Almanza Carillo (2008).

The older line of conchero practice is only one example of religious ritual that merged native beliefs within a Christian framework. Building upon the foundations of the conversion dramas, known collectively as *moros y cristianos* (Moors and Christians), native people re-enacted tales of good versus evil. They retold stories of conquest and invading forces in new formats that accommodated Catholic worship, while also honoring native custom. Over time, they blended and syncretized multiple tribal and Catholic customs. Concheros may perform in private ceremonies or in public outdoor settings, such as the plazas in front of the very churches built upon the ruins of indigenous temples, as are so many in Mexico. The dances may go on for several days, and often all night in ceremonies called *velaciones*, as the concheros support vigils of religious devotion. Community residents may participate by singing *alabanzas*, hymns of devotion, before and after the devotional conchero dances.

In former, stricter times, conchero dancers were prohibited from sleeping or stopping their performance, which may last several days. Vigilance and endurance were viewed as evidence of devotion and strength of will, qualities valued in the quest to uphold tradition or combat domination. Some songs in the conchero repertory date back to 1537 and tell the story of the battle of Cortés with the Chichimecas, a native population that fiercely resisted conversion. According to legend, the Spaniards called upon Santiago—Saint James the Apostle, the patron saint of Spain—to aid them during the battle. There was an eclipse and in the sky appeared the image of Santiago carrying a banner with a cross surrounded by light. The apparition was interpreted by the Spaniards as a victory for Spain and Christ, while the Chichimecas recognized in it their symbol for life and cosmic unity. Thus ceased the fighting at Sangremal hill where the city of Querétaro, the land of the concheros, was founded and this moment in history, according to one leader, initiated the tradition of the concheros (see Proveda 1981:285).

Seeing themselves as warriors for "the good," concheros use a vocabulary rich in military references. The dancers, known as soldiers, march in strict formations outlining a cross—whose four corners also correspond with indigenous reverence for the four cardinal corners of the universe. Later, they form a circle for their dances. They follow the orders of a captain and his lieutenant and other officers, including two concha-players of the right and two more concheros of the left, which according to Proveda (1981), represents a merger of Spanish and native posts. Some concheros carry banners, usually bearing Christian emblems such as the cross, the image of Jesus, or a specific saint being honored. Once in position, dancers perform a sequence of dances. The choreography uses rapid foot movements and relatively little movement from the upper body. Although contemporary dancers speak of the choreography as an unchanged continuation of ancient practices, if we compare the detailed accounts offer by dance scholar Gertrude Kurath (1946) with that of Susanna Rostas (1991), we find that conchero choreography has changed considerably even in the past 50 years. The specific dances may vary from group to group but typically include a dance to the sun, a dance for Malinche, as well as eagle, frog, and deer dances.

The Mexica or Aztec dancers are less bound by affiliation with a closed religious community than the conchero brotherhoods just described, and most participants are modern Mexicans (or Mexican-Americans) of mixed race (*mestizos*). Although few claim direct indigenous ancestry, they are dramatic in their promotion of a purely indigenous perspective. Dancers wear large and elaborate feathers and dance barefoot. They use native drums and percussion instead of conchas and do not carry the Christian banners. These organizations often function as educational units, promoting the learning of indigenous languages, particularly Náhuatl, and seek recognition of the strengths and values of native Mexican culture.

Listening to "Danza de los concheros," performed by Los Folkloristas.[9]

3.4   The audio example provided here is another recording by Los Folkloristas, this time representing the *danzas de los concheros*. You can hear from the audio that it was performed for a concert, so in some ways it represents a third line of conchero practice, that which is staged or prepared for viewers outside the circle of practitioners. Beyond that frame, we might consider which of the other two lines of practice is being represented here: the older line of syncretic religious ritual, or the newer re-imaged Aztec identity in the service of political advocacy. Try to identify the instruments you hear and their role in the music texture and performance scenario.

Audio-visual exploration and documentation of the concheros practice exist in Bruce Lane's film *The Eagle's Children* (1985) and Jaime Bofill's *Danzas de Conquista: Continuities and Change of a Millenary Tradition* (2011). Keep in mind that many of the ritual observances of the concheros are private, and fittingly, there are few films or videos that capture the full depth of the practice beyond its public face. The film *The Eagle's Children* indicates the spread of the conchero practice in the United States and stresses the formation of communities that share sympathies across physical and temporal borders.

The fact that many modern performers do not self-identify as indigenous in their daily lives outside of the dance gatherings has led some scholars and critics to deny the tradition as inauthentic, while Gerard Behague (2000) is among those who argue that historical accuracy and authenticity are less important than the value of serving authentic contemporary needs. Modern performers draw spiritual and political inspiration from the proud concheros of history who insisted on dancing their old dances, even if it meant modifying them with choreography that also recognized the military and religious power of the Spaniards conquerors.

REFLECTING ON ARCHAIC INDIGENOUS PRACTICE

The aim of the first part of this chapter has been to illustrate the bond between archaic indigenous traditions and modern contemporary imagination. We have seen how archaic music, viewed as the true, original, or autochthonous Mexican music, is reinterpreted, often most dramatically by people who do not identify themselves as indigenous. We have seen how various individuals and communities turn to the ancient cultures of Mexico for inspiration, studying, borrowing, and recreating indigenous ways. The examples in this chapter illustrate how archaeological excavations, long legacies of adaptive practice, re-imaginings and re-constructions all gave rise to new musical practices promoted as representing ancient Mexico.

Modern fascination with the high cultures of ancient Mexico has, however, too often left living, indigenous people ignored. Some of the best preserved archaic indigenous practices are not those of the urban Aztecs and Mayans but rather those of the nomadic and rural tribes, like the Seris, Yaquis, and Huicholes. In Part II of this chapter we will look at the practices of living people who persist, often in the face of considerable strain and discrimination, to identify themselves as indigenous. Before moving on, review Questions 1–9 at the end of this chapter, and take time to reflect on how the musical examples discussed so far differ in their portrayal of indigenous tradition. Try to summarize the ways each addresses contemporary needs, as much as, if not more than, historic reality.

PART II
Living Indigenous Music, Traditions Apart

WHO ARE THE LIVING INDIGENOUS PEOPLE OF MEXICO?

While many Mexicans consider themselves to be the descendants of indigenous people, far fewer self-identify as indigenous and assert tribal affiliation in regular daily interaction. While ancient native culture has been idealized, romanticized, and appropriated for artistic and political use, in mainstream practical contexts indigenous culture is stigmatized as impoverished, backward, and isolated. That reality reminds us that people recognize ethnic identity in Mexico by culture—that total complex of ways of life, beliefs, and behavior—as well as economic and social status, and above all by language.

There are 62 indigenous languages in Mexico, with 288 language dialects,[10] and between 70 and 100 indigenous *pueblos* (tribal communities or societies).[11] The Mexican states with the largest indigenous populations are: Oaxaca, Chiapas, Veracruz, Yucatán, Puebla, Quintana Roo, and Hidalgo. The map in Figure 3.19 shows the concentration of indigenous languages in Mexico and the relative strength of languages within regional populations. We can see that except for pockets in the northern and western region, the dominant concentrations lie in Mexico's southern states.

It can be argued that Mexico has the largest indigenous population in Spanish America, and while only 10 percent of Mexicans identify as indigenous, 10 percent of a populous nation of 106 million people exceeds the total in other nations, such as the 40 percent indigenous in Guatemala, or the 25 percent in Ecuador.[12] Despite the numbers, indigenous Mexicans remain largely isolated from the privileges and opportunities associated with full participation in Mexico's civic life. Despite national efforts to develop native communities, such as the CDI, the National Commission for the Development of Indigenous Peoples, and their advances in education and social equity, at least two million indigenous Mexican children still receive no schooling. Indigenous Mexicans experience higher levels of poverty than others, as a result of long-term marginalization.

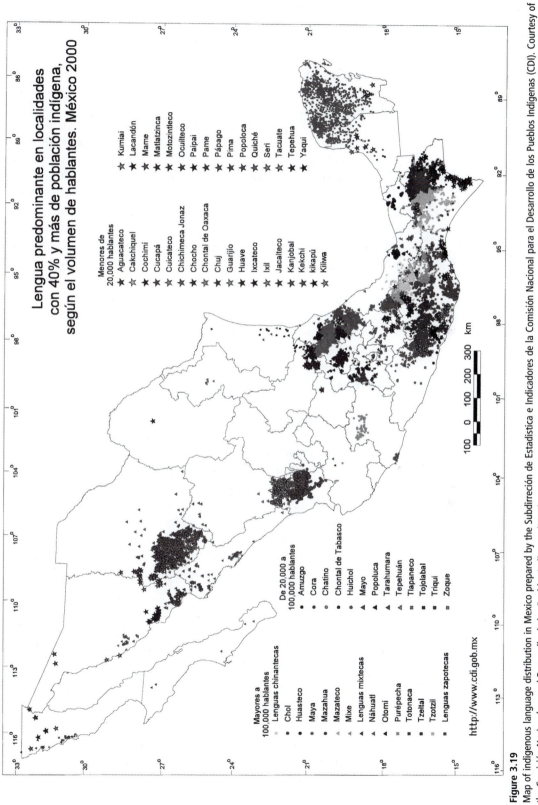

Figure 3.19

Map of indigenous language distribution in Mexico prepared by the Subdirreción de Estadística e Indicadores de la Comisión Nacional para el Desarrollo de los Pueblos Indígenas (CDI). Courtesy of the Comisión Nacional para el Desarrollo de los Pueblos Indígenas (2010).

Poverty leads to migration, both internal and external. Thus, we find as many as 30,000 migrants of Mixtec ancestry now living in California alone (also many Triquis, Purépechas, Mayas, and other groups), as just one example (Kresge 2007).[13] Migration influences the maintenance of culture as well as group identity and native languages. Music is an important tool for sustaining culture, but cultural change often brings musical adaptation as well, as evidenced in the YouTube clips of a Gueleguetza, Oaxaca's celebrated annual traditional dance festival—itself an adaptation of a much more ancient ceremony, recreated in San Marcos, California.[14]

The condition of standing apart, whether by choice or as a result of being ignored or rejected by mainstream mestizo society, characterizes and distinguishes the more than 70 indigenous pueblos not only from mestizo society, but also from each other. Each tribal population differs from another in language and system of belief, manner of ceremonial life, and social organization, as well as economic and ecological resources. Each indigenous group also has its own musical life; there is no one kind of native music, but instead, in the words of Fernando Nava, we should recognize that there are "many musics of numerous indigenous societies" (Nava 2010:29).

Mestizo Mexican culture is not homogeneous either, a topic we will tackle later, but the institutional efforts of the middle and upper classes in Mexico, as well as commercial and popular media, have created a shared mainstream culture that frequently contrasts mestizo culture with indigenous cultures, beginning with sacred sites of musical cultivation. Instead of serving great temples, cathedrals, or concert halls, the traditional music of living indigenous peoples is heard in local churches around modest altars, in homes, outdoor ramadas, caves, sea banks, or on sidewalks and mountaintops. Native musicians are part-time specialists, also laboring as farmers, ranchers, or craftsmen.

Official state or national boundaries do not easily define indigenous music. For example, the music practiced by the Tzotzil and Ch'ol speakers in Chiapas is similar to that practiced by their Quiche neighbors in Guatemala. There people consider the *tunkul* (the Maya term for teponaztli) as related to the marimba, an important instrument in both regions. Dance steps and music associated with the *Danza de Conquista*, performed by the Tzotzil and Ch'ol can be found in the Guatemalan *cakchiquel* dance called *Baile de los mejicanos*. Similarly, music and dance of the *yuto-nahua* people (O'odham and Yaqui) from the region adjoining Sonora-Arizona share features with that of the Yuma of California and the Kikapu of Coahuila and the Great Lakes. It often makes little sense to view the indigenous music of Mexico as being bound by modern geopolitical borders. As Alejandro Madrid and his co-authors illustrate (Madrid 2011), it is often more revealing to focus on how people and communities find meaning in customs of performance, despite such restrictions.

Indigenous musicians typically pass along musical knowledge by word of mouth, often in the form of mental coding. Writing music is rare, although the Zapotec and Mixe wind band leaders, discussed later, take great pride in their musical literacy and the scores they maintain for their groups. Children usually learn from elder family members and by performing alongside adults while participating in rituals and ceremonies. In the past, many indigenous communities restricted musical training by gender and age, permitting only boys and men to perform on musical instruments. However, these rules are changing as young men migrate to find jobs, leaving too few males to carry on traditions without allowing females to assume new roles. Today young women play important roles in sustaining native musical practices.

ADAPTIVE MUSICAL PRACTICE

As we will explore in the next unit, the native people of Mexico fell subject to the political rule of the Spaniards in the sixteenth century and were systematically, sometimes brutally, converted to the Catholic faith. The Spaniards also trained the native people to play European instruments, originally to serve the church. From 1500 to 1800 the most important string instruments in Iberian musical practice were the guitar, violin, and harp; all were adroitly adopted by indigenous peoples in Mexico as elsewhere in the New World.

You have already explored a few musical examples that illustrate the convergence of indigenous and European perspectives resulting from colonial encounters. Because the native peoples in Mesoamerica were so numerous and diverse, many cultures persisted. Indians intermarried with Europeans and adopted foreign customs, but they also found ways to retain aspects of their own traditions and native culture. It should be noted that once in Mexico, the Spaniards adapted their diet and adopted selected native customs, reminding us that change took place on both sides, albeit unevenly. The ensuing discussion and audio examples in the remainder of this chapter will explore examples of how the Seri, Yaqui, and Cora have held fast to native principles while adopting new influences.

CORA AND HUICHOL MUSIC

The Cora and Huichol people consider the mountain highlands of the state of Nayarit to be their homeland. These two groups are related linguistically, and both farm and raise cattle. In recent years many Cora have migrated from the Central Mexican highlands to northern Colorado, settling in the Gunnison Valley (Shoemaker 2011).[15]

Listening to "Harvest Chant," performed by a Cora shaman with *mitote*, recorded by Henrietta Yurchenco in 1952.

3.5

This chant represents a repertory of song performed for harvest ceremonies and is sung during the preparations for the feast day as well as during the festive dancing that follows the feast and continues throughout the night. The singer in this example is a shaman, a native priest or spiritual leader who accompanies himself on the *mitote*, a musical instrument shaped like a hunting bow. The bow is set on a gourd resonator to amplify the sound, produced by striking the string with two wooden sticks. Other tribal peoples, including the Seri and Apache adapted the musical bow, developing ingenious one-string fiddles with a body made from agave stems. The "Paths of Life" exhibit in the Arizona State Museum on the campus of the University of Arizona includes several examples of these musical bows.

3.6

Listening to "Wiricuta"—Huichol fiddle music (also known as Wirarica). Mariano, Pablo, Rosenda, and Augustin singing and playing the *raweri* (fiddle), the *kanari* (guitar), and rattles. Recorded in 1996 by Professor Ernesto Cani Lomelli from University of Guadalajara in Jalisco.[16]

The Huichol people farm and raise cattle and are known for their beautifully embroidered clothing and their colorful yarn paintings. They retain a life rich in ceremonies, some of which employ the use of the peyote cactus. This song is one of a set of songs belonging to what is commonly called the peyote cycle. Wiricuta is a holy site in the north-eastern desert of San Luis Potosí, viewed by the Huichol as the center of creation where all the gods were born and where humans are said to have come into existence. It is also where the Huichol travel to harvest peyote for their ceremonies. The Huichol believe the world was created in five days and the number five carries deep significance to them. Wiricuta has five entrances; Christ and the Huichol gods do things five times; and Huichol songs describe the five acts performed by the deities in the course of

Figure 3.20
Huichol *raweri* and *kanari* players performing in Mexico City. Photo by Janet Sturman (2009).

creation. The Huichol instrument known as the *raweri* resembles the Renaissance fiddle known as the *rebec*, although it is sometimes referred to as a folk violin. It has four strings: two made of horsehair and two made of metal. The *kanari* guitar, also heard in 3.6, has only five strings.

YOEME (YAQUI) RITUAL AND MUSICAL PRACTICE

Listening to "Tlaxcala, Tlaxcala"—Yaqui deer dance song. Source: *Indian Music of Mexico*, recorded by Laura Boulton, 1957.[17]

3.7

Viewing *Seyewailo: The Flower World* [3.1].[18]

3.1

The Yoeme or Yaqui people live along the Yaqui river in the Mexican state of Sonora. Their traditions illustrate how music and dance may connect a pueblo to their deities and to supernatural power. The Yaqui recall how during their early contact with European missionaries and settlers their ancestors called upon a team of angels to "sing the borders" of their land to help them preserve their territory (Arizona State Museum).

Living in the harsh Sonora desert helped the Yaqui earn a reputation for being among the fiercest of native peoples. Until the 1930s they resisted Mexican rule and it was only after their mass conscription into the Mexican army during World War II that the government was able to successfully move them off their land. Today, many Yaqui live in southern Arizona. The Pima and O'odham people are related tribes.

Despite their long history of resistance against Spanish, the Yaqui accepted Christianity early. In the seventeenth and eighteenth centuries the Jesuit priests recognized the tenacity of the Yaqui and permitted them to keep their traditional dances and pantomime dramas by fusing them with Christian practice. In the process the Yaqui merged pre-Hispanic and European music customs to create rituals that they identify as purely their own. The *pascola* ceremonies and the deer dance, described below, are two of the most important Yaqui rituals of this kind.

Yaqui adaptation to cultural change did not stop during the colonial era. As the Yaqui relocated and interacted with other communities, they adopted musical practices at each stage. Contemporary Yaqui musicians also play mariachi, norteño, and sing corridos in Spanish and in the Yaqui language. In ceremonial contexts, Yaqui *matachines* (contradance musicians) devoted to the Virgin, play violins and guitars in ways that also sustain the old traditions of New Spain.

The most distinctive of the Yaqui ritual dances persists in the *pascola* (*pahko'ola*) ceremony. Two types of music, distinguished by different instruments, define the Spanish versus the Native aspects of the ceremony. Music played on violin and harp thus alternates with the music played on flute and drum that accompanies the *danza del venado* or deer dance. The dance belongs to a complex of activity observed during Holy Week and the Lenten period leading to it. Men wearing masks and dressed as

Chapayecas or Pharisees rule the community during Lent, collecting alms to support the fiesta that begins on Holy Saturday.

On Holy Saturday the pascola deer and coyotes dance in a special arbor (*ramada*). The main dancer is the deer. His chest is bare and he wears a *rebozo* (shawl) as a wrap around the waist. Deer antler rattles hang from his waist and rattles made from butterfly cocoons filled with seeds encircle his ankles. He runs from the other dancers, known as pascolas, who eventually hunt him down and kill him.

In the film *Seyewailo: The Flower World* you will witness how the pascolas, the "old men of the fiesta," serve as ritual hosts who make speeches, act as historians, and perform as clowns to keep participants

Figure 3.21
Figurine of Yaqui deer dancer. Arizona State Museum Collection, The University of Arizona. Photo by Janet Sturman, (2014).

awake during the all-night ceremony. They also dance and sing ceremonial songs. First, they dance to the *apaleo* (European) music, sones played on harp and violin. Their dance contributes to the musical rhythm with the sounds of the *tenevoim* (cocoon rattles) on their legs and the bells on their belts. The rattles celebrate the singing of the insect world. When the pascolas put on the sacred masks over their faces, they dance to *tampaleo* (Yaqui) music with flute and drum, while playing complex rhythms on a hand-held sistrum, a shaken idiophone with metal jingles. Then the deer dancer enters the ramada. His dance is accompanied by three deer singers who describe events in both the flower world and the present world, using an ancient form of the Yoeme language. Two of the singers play rasping

Figure 3.22
Figurine of Yaqui pascola dancer. Arizona State Museum Collection, The University of Arizona. Photo by Janet Sturman, (2014).

Figure 3.23
Yaqui water drum.
Pascua Village, Tucson,
Fiesta of San Ignacio,
1955, photographer,
George Iacono.
Photograph courtesy of
the Arizona State
Museum, The
University of Arizona.

sticks or *hirukiam*, which rest on *bweheim*, half-gourd resonators. The third singer plays the *vaa'a kuvahe*, the water drum (Fig. 3.23). The drum is made from a half gourd that floats in a basin of water. It is beaten with the *hiponia*, a drumstick wrapped with corn husks. The water drum represents the heartbeat of the deer, whom the Yaqui view as their "Little Brother," and the rasping sticks represent his breathing.

CONCLUDING REFLECTIONS

The twentieth century brought great changes to indigenous people and communities in Mexico. The post-revolution indigenismo movement, exemplified here by the work of Carlos Chávez, launched new intellectual interest in indigenous traditions, particularly archaic practices, which might be romanticized and imagined in formats that suited a national narrative of independent identity but required no direct contact with the complicated lives of living indigenous people. Within Mexico's mestizo society during the twentieth century, indigenous music surged with new energy. Among mestizo populations, already integrated Indians continued to practice select traditions, and some maintained their native language.

Academic study of folklore led by pioneer Vicente T. Mendoza, prompted scholarly documentation of the living indigenous traditions. The development of radio spurred the recording of indigenous music to further supplement folkloric scholarship. The American scholar Henrietta Yurchenco was one of the first to record on-site the music of native pueblos in Mexico, including some of the examples used in this chapter. The founding of government agencies to support indigenous rights and development, known by their acronyms INI (Instituto Nacional Indigenista) and CDI (Comisión Nacional para el Desarrollo de los Pueblos Indígenas), brought new attention to the persisting discrimination against indigenous people. Indigenous public schools emerged in the 1970s and even in the national public school curriculum, songs in indigenous languages were taught to children in public schools.

Ethnomusicology became a career option at Mexico's National University (UNAM) in 1985, and a number of graduates have focused on expanding the study of native musical cultures. Schools of dance and music, in public and private settings, have fostered new interest concerning indigenous cultures. While this work has helped focus attention on the value of living indigenous musical and cultural practices, many people living in indigenous communities continue to lack economic and educational opportunity.

The general public still tend to view indigenous music and culture as exotic ethnic nationalism, and native people have turned to marketing select cultural traditions for tourist consumption, both local and foreign. Folk dance and musical gatherings (*encuentros*), fairs, radio and television programs, and certainly festivals like the Guelagüetza in Oaxaca, and the Huey Atlixcáyotl in Puebla, promote the maintenance of indigenous custom in showy formats that transform and commercialize the very traditions they promote and seek to sustain. At the same time, exchange facilitated via migration and improved access to entertainment media have influenced native musical tastes and practices. Native musicians listen to commercially popular music and some also perform rock, metal, cumbia, hip hop, and the latest techno styles.

Mexico established an Indigenous Agency for Education (Dirección General de Educación Indígena, or DGEI) in the 1980s to create bilingual schools that would promote Spanish literacy, while also retaining indigenous languages.[19] The success of these new formal schools in promoting the retention of indigenous language and customs has been uneven. Indigenous schools are often poorly funded. Training teachers has been difficult and so also has been matching the standardized Mexican education curriculum with indigenous curricular designs. Such efforts however do seem to represent a positive step forward from the intentions of President Lázaro Cárdenas to absorb the indigenous into the mestizo identity. At the first Interamerican Indigenous Congress in Pátzcuaro, in 1940 he stated, "Our indigenous problem is not in conserving 'the Indian' in the Indian, nor to indigenize Mexico, but to Mexicanize the Indian."[20] That kind of integration threatened to obliterate indigenous culture, relegating it to the status of a museum artifact.

Efforts to Mexicanize the indigenous people began with the imparting of Hispanic culture. This chapter has introduced several contrasting examples of how indigenous tradition has resisted complete integration and continued to flourish. We have also explored how native practices inspired music which is created to represent Mexico as a nation, advocate for civil rights, and promote spiritual strength. In subsequent chapters we will encounter additional examples of living indigenous music in other contexts. Chapter 4 moves forward in the historical narrative to consider the musical legacy of life when Mexico was the most glorious vice-royal state of New Spain.

CRITICAL THINKING AND DISCUSSION PROMPTS

1. Would you want to be a cuicapiztle? Why or why not? What modern and ancient resources might you use to learn more about them?

2. In what ways does "Raíz Viva" draw listeners into a world of ancient sounds?

3. What aspects of "Raíz Viva" might prompt us to argue against its representation of the actual sounds of ancient Aztec music?

4. How does "Teponazcuicatl" compare to "Raíz Viva"? Remembering our discussions of performativity, discuss differences in sound and in the conceptual motivation that supports both the original song for historic listeners and its rendition for contemporary listeners.

5. How does Carlos Chávez link the ancient and modern worlds in *Xochipilli*? Discuss aspects of the composition and performance including melody, rhythm, instrumentation, and formal structure. What impressions are you left with after listening? To further develop your analysis, read more about the life of Carlos Chávez and offer an analysis of how he and his contemporaries viewed indigenous arts and what those positions may have meant to the development of Mexican music and nationhood.

6. Find recorded examples of Miguel Bernal Jiménez's *Tata Vasco* on YouTube and compare the way he represented indigenous music to that of Carlos Chávez in *Xochipilli*. Expand your analysis by reading Leonora Saavedra's examination of music nationalism in the 1940s (Saavedra 2007).

7. Susanna Rostas (1991) states that "for the concheros, the reconquest of Mexico did not end in 1910." Describe how her use of the term "reconquest" differs and compares to the way that term is used by Chicano activists in the United States.

8. Using the sources listed at the end of this chapter or others from your library or the internet, learn more about the conchero tradition. How is the *danza de los concheros* used today to battle for indigenous autonomy? Mention specific choreographic, musical, and conceptual details in your answer. Do you think the danza is an effective political tool? Why or why not?

9. Watch Bruce Lane's film *The Eagle's Children* and compare what you learn in that film about the conchero tradition to what you've read here. Note how the practice spread to the United States. How has widespread adoption and new purposes affected the maintenance of indigenous tradition?

10. Watch Jaime Bofill's film *Danzas de Conquista: Continuities and Change of a Millenary Tradition*, available at: www.jaimebofill.com/Jaime_Bofill/Documentales_y_videos.html What insights does this film offer regarding the authenticity and meaning of the tradition to contemporary participants?

11. Have modern developments made it easier or more difficult for native peoples in Mexico to retain their own music and culture?

12. Discuss the pros and cons of assimilation for indigenous cultures in Mexico.

13. Which living native tradition of Mexico most interests you and which would you like to learn more about? Beginning with the bibliography at the end of this chapter, identify several resources that you might use in your investigation.

14. Watch the film *Tree of Life* by Bruce "Pacho" Lane about the *voladores* tradition practiced by the Totonac people. Describe in your own words the legend upon which this tradition is based and evidence of religious syncetism in current ritual. What musical instruments are featured in the video and what role do they play in Totonac culture?

15. Listen and watch a contemporary treatment of indigenous culture and Tarahumara soundscapes (2011) by the composer Luis Jaime Cortez from his opera *Luna* (https:// www.youtube.com/watch?v=e7OKhw_n4qk). How does his treatment compare to the other compositions in this chapter?

16. Explore the CDI website. View some of the videos posted on the music and culture of individual tribes and language groups. How do the examples on the site compare to the ones in this chapter? Describe some important ways that music figures into the lives of the native peoples profiled by the CDI?

KEY TERMS, PEOPLE, AND PLACES

Tenochtitlán	Macuilxochitzin
atecocolli	Quetzalcóatl
cuicatl	Hernán Cortés
cuicapiztles	Carlos Chávez
cuicatlamatilztli	SAVAE
huéhuetl	Los Folkloristas
teponatzli	Bernardino de Sahagún
huilacapitztli	CDI
idiophones	"Raíz Viva"
membranophones	*Xochipilli*
chordophones	"Teponazcuicatl"
aerophones	Yaqui deer dance
concheros	Cora "Harvest Chant"
concha	"Wiricuta"
Danza Azteca	Huichol fiddle music
Danza Mexica	

NOTES

1. Pre-Columbian (in Spanish, *precolombiano*) is a more familiar designation for this era, but for Mexico the explorer and conqueror whose arrival impacted history most definitively was Cortez (Cortés, in Spanish), thus this text favors pre-Cortesian.

2. Scholars contest the details regarding this migration, the dates of the earliest settlements in the Americas, and mode of travel. Some argue that the migrants traveled by sea, not by land. Archaeological findings confirm human occupation in the Americas during the Clovis era dating from 11,500 years ago, but some archaeologists, led by Tom Dillehay (2001), argue that settlement occurred even earlier and spread rapidly southward, citing as evidence the remains at Monte Verde in Chile, a pre-Clovis settlement in the Americas dating 12,500 years ago. The essential point in this chapter is that the history of the Mexican people, and therefore Mexican music, really begins thousands of years ago.

3. The location and boundaries of Aztlán have never been incontrovertibly determined. Conflicting locations range from Lake Chapala in the modern state of Jalisco, to Puget Sound, near Seattle, Washington. There is some consensus that the ancient territory was on the island of Mezcaltitlán in Nayarit, Mexico. The name Aztlán surfaces in ancient documents such the *Crónica Mexicayotl* written *c.*1499 by Tezozómoc. It is depicted as the ancestral homeland of all the Nahua people. The cartographer Alexander von Humboldt (1769–1859) associates it with the ruins of Chaco Canyon in modern New Mexico, while Lewis Henry Morgan believed it to be the site of Cibola, the spot referenced by Coronado in his exploring journal. Contemporary Chicano activists use Aztlán as a symbol of ancestry associating it with the lands of Greater Mexico lost to the United States. See: *Enciclopedia de México*. Director, José Rogelio Álvarez, (Mexico City: Impresora y Editora Mexicana, 1978) pp. 1078–82; Michael Pina, "The Archaic, Historical and Mythicized Dimensions of Aztlán," in Rudolfo A. Anaya and Francisco Lomelí (Eds.), *Aztlán: Essays on the Chicano Homeland* (Albuquerque, NM: University of New Mexico Press, 1991), pp. 14–48.

4. The Bourbon Codex gets its name from where is housed today, the Library of the Bourbon Palace in Paris. Digital copies of each page can be found on the internet, at: www.famsi.org/spanish/research/loubat/Borbonicus/thumbs0.html

5. Carolina Robertson explores the imposition of the European concept of music on native peoples of the Americas in "Latin America. Indigenous Music," Grove Music Online, (Ed.) L. Macy (2002), at: www.grovemusic.com/shared/views/article.html?section=music.16072.1 For a detailed, comparative examination, see Laura Cervantes, "Sounds like Music: Ritual Speech Events among the Bribri Indians of Costa Rica" (PhD diss., The University of Texas, Austin, TX, 2003), 92–93.

6. José Ávila. *Raíz Viva. Los Folkloristas.* Disco Mexico Horizonte Musical, 1988.

7. From the album *Milagro de Guadalupe* (1999) by SAVAE, the San Antonio Vocal Arts Ensemble. The performers are: Covita Moroney—alto, guitar, teponaztli, huilacapitztli, atecocolli, and Náhuatl readings; Lee P'Pool—tenor, huéhuetl, small hand drum, and tambourine; Christopher Moroney—baritone, teponaztli, huilacapitztli, lajas, atecocolli, ayacaxtli, omichahuaztli, and Náhuatl readings; Tanya Moczygemba—alto, teponaztli, deer antlers, Native American drum, and ayacaxtli; Kathy Mayer—soprano, recorder, teponaztli, tambourine, and chayahuatzli; Jody

Noblett—tenor, Native American flute, huilacapitztli, deer antlers, and huéhuetl; Paula Olsen—soprano, recorder, and ayacaxtli.

8. Program notes for the CD *El Milagro de Guadalupe*, by Christopher Moroney, http://savae.org/milagro.html. See also: Christopher Moroney, "The Unabridged Interview: Early Music America Magazine," www.savae.org/emmaginterview.html, and Tina Chancey, "Voices from the Cutting Edge: Medieval and Renaissance Groups Challenge Listeners and Themselves with Innovative Performance Practices," *Early Music America*, 7.2 (Summer 2001): 28–29.

9. Los Folkloristas. *México: Horizonte Musical*. Fonarte Latino, 1988.

10. Comisión Nacional para el Desarrollo de los Pueblos Indígenas, 2000, at: www.cdi.gob.mx/images/mapa_nacional_lenguas_indigenas_cdi.jpg

11. E. Fernando Nava L., "Las (muchas) músicas de los pueblos y las (numerosas) sociedades indígenas," in Aurelio Tello (Ed.), *La Música en Mexico, Panorama del siglo XX* (Mexico City: CONCULTA, 2010), p. 29.

12. Sylvia Schmelkes, Lecture on Indigenous Education in Mexico, University of Arizona (March 24, 2010); Warman 2003 in CDI 2006.

13. Lisa Kresge. 2007. "Indigenous Oaxacan Communities in California: An Overview." California Institute for Rural Studies.

14. "Danza de la Pluma Zaachila en San Marcos CA 2011." http://youtu.be/EPNU04vRm8c.

15. Will Shoemaker, "The Cora Connection: The Life of Indigenous Mexicans in Colorado's Mountains," *Colorado Central Magazine* (June, 2011). http://cozine.com/2011-june/the-cora-connection-the-life-of-indigenous-mexicans-in-colorado's-mountains/

16. *Wood that Sings. Indian Fiddle Music of the Americas*. Washington: Smithsonian Folkways (SWF40472, 1997). See also YouTube, at: http://youtu.be/cgzf9-uPHwI

17. *Indian Music of Mexico*. Recorded by Laura Bouton (Washington, DC: Smithsonian Folkways, 1952).

18. http://parentseyes.arizona.edu/wordsandplace/seyewailo.mov

19. The government's efforts to promote bilingual education combining native and Spanish languages began with José Vasconcelos and his creation of the Secretariat of Public Education in 1921. He promoted the translation of the classics like the *Iliad* into native languages and created education brigades to teach natives in their territories.

20. "Nuestro problema indígena no está en conservar 'indio' al indio, ni en indigenizar a México, sino en mexicanizar al indio." Lázaro Cárdenas del Río, Discurso del Presidente de la República en el Primer Congreso Indigenista Interamericano (Discourse by the President of the Republic at the First Interamerican Indigenous Congress). Memoria Política de Mexico (Political Memories of Mexico) Mexico City: El Instituto Nacional de Estudios Políticos, A.C. (INEP). www.memoriapoliticademexico.org/Textos/6Revolucion/1940PCM.html

FOR REFERENCE AND FURTHER STUDY

Barnes, William. 2005. "Secularizing for Survival: Changing Depictions of Aztec Rulers in Early Colonial Texts." In Elizabeth H. Boone (Ed.), *Painted Books and Indigenous Knowledge in Mesoamerica: Manuscript Studies in Honor of Betsy Smith*, MARI Publication 69. New Orleans, LA: Middle American Research Institute, 319–340.

Behague, Gerard. 2000. "Boundaries and Borders in the Study of Music in Latin America: A Conceptual Re-Mapping." *Revista Música Latinoamericana/Latin American Music Review* 21(1):16–30.

Bierhorst, John (trans.). 1985. *Cantares Mexicanos: Songs of the Aztecs*. Stanford, CA: Stanford University Press.

Both, Arnd Adje. 2007. Aztec Music Culture. *The World of Music* 49(2):91–104.

Brill, Mark. 2011. "Mexico." In *Music of Latin America and the Caribbean*. New York: Prentice-Hall (Pearson).

Chávez, Carlos. 1940. *Xochilipili (An Imagined Aztec Music)*. New York: EMI Publishers.

CDI [no author listed]. 2006. *Lenguas indígenas en riesgo: Pápagos, México* [Indigenous languages at Risk: Pápagos, Mexico] CDI Comisión para el desarollo de los pueblos indigenas [Commission for the Development of Indigenous Peoples].

CDI Website. Commission for the Development of Indigenous Peoples. www.cdi.gob.mx. www.cdi.gob.mx/images/mapa_nacional_lenguas_indigenas_cdi.jpg (accessed January 12, 2015).

Delgado-Gomez, Angel, exhibition author. 2010. *Spanish Historical Writing about the New World*. The John Carter Brown Library at Brown University. www.brown.edu/Facilities/John_Carter_Brown_Library/spanishhistorical/pages/indians.html (accessed July 22, 2011).

Dillehay, Thomas. 2001. *Settlement of the Americas: A New Prehistory*. New York: Basic Books.

Dultzin Dubín, Susana and Nava Gómez Tagle, José Antonio. 1984. "La Música en el Panorama Histórico de Mesoamérica: El mundo musical prehispánico." In Julio Estrada (Ed.), *La Música de Mexico, I. Historia*. Mexico City: Instituto de Investigaciones Estéticas. Universidad Nacional Autónoma de México, 17–34.

Estrada, Julio. 1992. "The Emergence of Myth as an Explanation." In Carolina Robertson (Ed.), *Musical Repercussions of 1492: Encounters in Text and Performance*. Washington, DC and London: Smithsonian Institution Press, 337–350.

FAMSI—Foundation for the Advancement of MesoAmerican Studies, Inc. www.famsi.org

Gómez G., Luis Antonio. 2008. "Los instrumentos musicales prehispánicos: Clasificación general y significado." *Arqueología mexicana* 16(94):38–46.

Greenberg, David. 1990. *The Construction of Homosexuality*. Chicago, IL: University of Chicago Press.

Harrison, Frank Llewellyn. 1973. *Time, Place and Music: An Anthology of Ethnomusicological Observation c.1550 to c.1800*. Ann Arbor, MI: University of Michigan.

Hornbostel, Erich von and Curt Sachs. 1961. "Classification of Musical Instruments," translated from the original German by Anthony Baines and Klaus Wachsmann. *The Galpin Society Journal* 14:3–29.

Kellogg, Susan. 1994. "The Woman's Room. Some Aspects of Gender Relations in Tenochtitlan in the late Pre-Hispanic Period." *Ethnohistory* 42(4): 563–576.

Kurath, Gertrude Prokosch. 1946. "Los Concheros," *The Journal of American Folklore* 59(234):387–399.

León-Portilla, Miguel. 1994. *Quince poetas del mundo náhuatl*. Mexico: Editorial Diana.

Jennings, Gary. 1980. *Aztec*. New York: Forge (Tom Dohery Associates).

Madrid, Alejandro (Ed.). 2011. *Transnational Encounters: Music and Performance at the U.S.–Mexico Border*. New York: Oxford University Press.

Maroney, Christopher. 1999. Program notes for the CD *El Milagro de Guadalupe* http://savae.org/milagro.html (accessed January 12, 2015).

Martens, Frederick H. 1928. "Music in the Life of the Aztecs." *The Musical Quarterly* 14(3):413–437.

Martí, Samuel. 1954. Precortesian music, *Ethnos: Journal of Anthropology* 19:1–4, 69–79.

Martí, Samuel. 1968. *Instrumentos musicales precortesianos*. 2nd ed. Mexico City: Instituto Nacional de Anthropología e Historia.

Mendoza, Vicente T. 1962. *La canción Mexicana* [Mexican Song]. Mexico City: Fondo de Cultura Económica.

Nava L., E. Fernando. 2010. "Las (muchas) músicas de los pueblos y las (numerosas) sociedades indígenas." In Aurelio Tello (Ed.), *La Música en México, Panorama del siglo XX*. Mexico City: Consejo Nacional para la Cultura y las Artes, 29–105.

Nezahualcóyotl. 2010. *Poemas*. Barcelona: Lingua Digital.

Proveda, Pablo. 1981. "Danza de concheros en Austin, Texas: Entrevista con Andrés Segura Granados" [The Dance of the Concheros in Austin, Texas: Interview with Andres Segura Granados]. *Latin American Music Review* 2(2):280–299.

Rostas, Susanna. 1991. "The Concheros of Mexico," *Dance Research: The Journal of the Society for Dance Research*, 9(2):3–17.

Saavedra, Leonora. 2007. "Staging the Nation: Race, Religion, and History in Mexican Opera of the 1940s." *Opera Quarterly* 23:1–21.

Sahagún, Bernardino de (1950–82) [*c*.1540–85]. *Florentine Codex: General History of the Things of New Spain*, 13 vols. in 12 vols. I–XII. Charles E. Dibble and Arthur J.O. Anderson (Eds., trans., notes and illus.) (translation of *Historia General de las Cosas de la Nueva España*). Santa Fe, NM and Salt Lake City, UT: School of American Research and the University of Utah Press.

Shoemaker, Will. 2011. "The Cora Connection: The Life of Indigenous Mexicans in Colorado's Mountains." *Colorado Central Magazine* (June). http://cozine.com/2011-june/the-cora-connection-the-life-of-indigenous-mexicans-in-colorado's-mountains/ (accessed January 12, 2015).

Stevenson, Robert Murrell. 1952. *Music in Mexico: A Historical Survey*. New York: Crowell.

Stevenson, Robert Murrell. 1968. *Music in Aztec and Incan Territory*. Berkeley, CA: University of California Press.

Stone, Martha. 1975. *At the Sign of Midnight. The Concheros Dance Cult of Mexico*. Tucson, AZ: University of Arizona Press.

Tello, Aurelio. 2010. *La Música en Mexico: Panorama del Siglo XX*. Mexico City: Consejo Nacional para la Cultura y las Artes.

Torquemada, Juan de. 1969. [1615] *Los veinte y un libros rituales y Monarchia Indiana, Biblioteca Porrua*, vols. 41–43. Mexico City: Editorial Porrua.

DISCOGRAPHY

Chávez, Carlos. *Complete Chamber Music,* Vol. 3. Southwest Chamber Ensemble, Jeff von der Schmidt, cond., Cambria Records, 2005.

Indian Music of Mexico, recorded by Henrietta Yurchenco, Washington: Smithsonian Folkways, (FW04413), 1957.

Indian Music of Mexico—Zapotec, Otomi, Yaqui, Maya, recorded by Laura Boulton, Washington: Smithsonian Folkways Recordings, (FW08851/FW 8851), 1957.

Los Folkloristas. Audio CD. México: Horizonte Musical. Fonarte Latino, 1988.

San Antonio Vocal Ensemble, SAVAE. *Milagro de Guadalupe,* Iago Records/ Talking Taco, 1999.

Wood that Sings. Indian Fiddle Music of the Americas. Washington, DC: Smithsonian Folkways (SWF40472, 1997).

FILMS AND VIDEOS

Bofill, Jaime. 2011. *Danzas de Conquista: Continuities and Change of a Millenary Tradition*. Video. www.jaimebofill.com/Jaime_Bofill/Home.html

Cortez, Luis Jaime. 2012. *Luna* (A short film based on the opera *Luna* (Moon) about the Tarahumara by Luis Jaime Cortez. https://www.youtube.com/watch?v=e7OKhw_n4qk

Lane, Bruce. 2005. *Tree of Life: Totonac Indians of Mexico*. DVD. Rochester, New York: Ethnoscope.

Lane, Bruce. 2005. *The Eagle's Children*. DVD. Rochester, New York: Ethnoscope.

López, Hilario. 2010. Wirikuta de hilario lópez, Música huichola. YouTube. http://youtu.be/cgzf9-uPHwI

Seyewailo. University of Arizona. http://parentseyes.arizona.edu/wordsandplace/seyewailo.html

Majesty, Machismo, Mestizaje, and Other Legacies of the Vice-Kingdom of New Spain

ROMANCES AND RELATIONS: SEX AND GENDER IN SONG AND DEED

The rustic quality of Crescencio M. García's performance of the ballad of "Delgadina" [4.1] makes it easy to picture the tired soldiers who accompanied the conquistador Hernán Cortés at camp for the night, hearing the dark tale of a selfish king who lusted after his own daughter. When the princess refuses to comply with her father's unprincipled demands, he locks her up and coldly allows her to die of thirst and hunger. Clearly women in this king's court, and elsewhere in Spain, were viewed as property and mistrusted. The story of "Delgadina" told in the lyrics depicts a court where women were expected to serve and please men, no matter what the cost. Although incest was not a condoned behavior, the Iberian custom of *machismo* which venerated the strong man who asserted his superiority over others, particularly women, is evident in this song, as it was in the behavior of the conquistadors.

According to Bernal Díaz de Castillo (1492–1581), the *romance*, the ballad song and ancestor to the modern *corrido*, was one of the most popular songs types enjoyed by Cortés and his men (Sonnichsen 1994). The romance "Delgadina" is one of the oldest and most widely circulated of these venerable poetic songs. Spanish explorers carried this and other romances with them on their journeys. Juan de Oñate, Hernán Cortés's son-in-law, is an example of such an explorer. In 1598 he forged a path north, establishing New Spanish settlements in what is now the U.S. state of New Mexico, from where Mr. García, the singer of our opening example, hails. Like other romances, "Delgadina," tackles the subject of love, power and treachery in aristocratic quarters. Spaniards of all backgrounds enjoyed hearing these spicy moralistic tales sung in strict poetic and musical form of 32-syllable stanzas.

Listening to "Delgadina," a romance performed by Crescencio M. García in 1970.[1]

4.1

Figure 4.1
Lyrics to "Delgadina."
Source: Jack Loeffler,
et al. (Eds.), *La Música
de los Viejitos* (1999),
p. 3. Used with
permission.

Delgadina se paseaba en su sala muy cuadrada, con su manto de hilo de oro que en su pecho iluminaba.	Delgadina was strolling in her well-squared hall, with her mantle of golden threads that illuminated her breast.
"Levántate, Delgadina, ponte tu falda de seda, porque nos vamos a misa a la ciudad de Morelia."	"Arise Delgadina, put your silken dress because we are going to Mass in the city of Morelia."
Cuando salieron de misa su papá le platicaba, "Delgadina, hija mía, yo te quiero para dama."	When they left Mass, her father said, "Delgadina, my daughter, I want you as my mistress."
"No lo quiera Dios, papá ni la Virgen Soberana Es ofensa para Dios y traición para mi mamá."	"God would not wish that, father, nor the Sovereign Virgin It is an offense against God and treachery against my mother."
"Luego que lleguemos a casa yo te pondré en castigo por hija desobediente no a vedar lo que te digo." "Júntense los once criados," dice el padre de Delgadina. "Enciérrenla en un cuarto oscuro donde la voz sea ladina.	"After we get home I will start your punishment for being a disobedient daughter who should not deny what I ask." "Bring forth my eleven servants," says Delgadina's father. "Confine her in a dark room where her voice will sound foreign.
Si le dieren que comer la comida muy salada si le dieren que tomar la del agua sorrostrada."	If you feed her give her very salty food, and if you give her drink, throw water in her face."
"Madrecita de mi vida, tu castigo estoy sufriendo. Regálame un vaso de agua que de sed me estoy muriendo."	"My dearest mother, I am suffering your punishment. Give me a glass of water for I am dying of thirst."
"Júntese los once criados," dice la madre de Delgadina. Llévele agua a Delgadina en esos vasitos de oro, sobre bordados de China."	"Bring forth my eleven servants," says Delgadina's mother. "Take water to Delgadina in these golden glasses, on Chinese embroidery."
Cuando le llevaron el agua, Delgadina estaba muerta, como gallo, boca arriba, tenía su boquita abierta.	When they took her the water, Delgadina was dead, like a rooster, face up, with her little mouth open.
La cama de Delgadina de ángeles está coronada, y la de su papá el rey de demonios apretada.	Delgadina's bed with angels was crowned, while that of her gather the king, was crowded with demons.
Ya con ésta me despido por los azahares de lima, aquí se acaba cantando la obediente Delgadina.	With this I take my leave by the blossoms of a lime tree, here I cease singing of the obedient Delgadina.

Figure 4.2
Spanish Baroque guitar.
Photo courtesy of:
www.toddgreen.com/

In his performance of "Delgadina" [4.1], Crescencio M. García of Mimbres, New Mexico, accompanies himself on a modern acoustic guitar. More likely the men in Cortés's retinue would have played a much smaller Spanish guitar, popular during the Baroque era (fifteenth–seventeenth centuries)[2] featuring five courses (sets) of strings. This instrument represented a bridge between the Andalusian lute and the Spanish *vihuela* (which had six courses of double strings). In Mr. García's rendition of "Delgadina," the slightly askew alignment of the sung melody with the harmony produces a discordant tension that seems appropriate to the sentiment of the lyrics.

The rhythmic qualities of García's performance are also striking. As you listen to the guitar accompaniment, note how each verse begins clearly in duple meter, but as the verse progresses, the strumming pattern changes, shifting the accent across that original pulse, so that we feel the pulse in a slow three. Some musicians refer to this shift as a hypermeter; no matter what we call it, the technique commands the listener's attention by breaking the pattern of expectation.

MESTIZAJE AND THE LEGENDS OF LA MALINCHE

Another iconic and complex female image, La Malinche, stands at the heart of the Spanish invasion and persists in the performances that keep alive memories of that time. As races and cultures mixed in the process called mestizaje, so did musical traditions. The process of blending may be traced to the arrival in the Yucatán of the intrepid Spanish explorer Hernán Cortés in 1519. While in Yucatán, Cortés secured the first of two important translators, Jerónimo Aguilar, a Franciscan priest and victim of a shipwreck in 1511, who had learned the Mayan language while in captivity. Later that year in the battle of Centla in Tabasco, Cortés received a second translator, the one who was to change history: Malintzin, a Nahua woman and one of 20 slaves given to him by the vanquished Tabascan natives. Malintzin became the mistress of Cortés and was rewarded with land property by Cortés for her services. She became the mother of his son Martín, considered the first mestizo Mexican. She is known by various names including Doña Marina,[3] La Malinche, and Malinalli. Since she was raised on the Gulf Coast, Malintzin knew the workings of the Aztec state and customs and could speak both Náhuatl[4] and Maya. Although she died in her 20s of smallpox, like thousands of natives during the encounter, she became an invaluable aid to the conqueror. Modern Mexicans remember her in conflicting ways, honoring her as the mother of a new race but also scorning her as a traitor to her people. Her image and legacy surface in many examples of song, dance, and artistic expression, as evidenced in her appearance in the recently examined concheros dances, and in our future explorations of *matachines* dances and protest songs, where for example she has become an important symbol for the Chicano movement.

Historians highlight the shrewd strategies Cortés employed in his battles along the Yucatán (see Burkholder and Johnson 2003). Mounted on the horses brought from Spain, Cortés's men quickly overtook the flanks of Indians armed only with bows and arrows. After conquering a tribal state, Cortés would integrate the surviving native men among his troops. By this means, the number of native auxiliaries came to exceed the Spaniards as the invaders headed into the Aztec capital of Tenochtitlán. While it might seem ironic that native tribes assisted the foreign conquerors, the tribes who joined the Spaniards such as the Tlaxcaltecas had been

Figure 4.3
La Malinche interpreting for Cortés and Tlaxaltecan leaders in "Negociaciones con los españoles," a mural by Desiderio Hernández Xochitiotzin in the Palacio de Gobierno (Governmental Palace) in Tlaxcala city. Photograph by Wolfgang Sauber. Creative Commons License, Wikimedia.

exploited and abused by the Aztec, whose military empire forced them to provide high taxes and also provide men for their sacrificial rites. The subdued tribes joined the Spaniards hoping to get rid of the Aztec yoke.

Spanish reports claim that Moctezuma, the reigning Aztec monarch of the time, perceived Cortés as the embodiment of the Toltec deity Quetzalcóatl, the feather-serpent god destined to usher in a new era. Cortés, knowing of this legend, perhaps from Malintzin, did nothing to dissuade Moctezuma. The myth did not persist throughout the war; the Aztecs soon realized that Cortés and the rest of the Spaniards were not emissaries of Quetzalcóatl and Moctezuma tried to fight back, but the damage was done. Cortés had gained the upper hand. He also took advantage of existing tensions among native populations and realms subject to Aztec rule. He enlisted the aid of men living in Cempoala, and conquered the city states of Tlaxcala and Cholula before attempting to enter Tenochtitlán as an emissary. Moctezuma, impressed by Cortés's military successes, greeted him with gifts, and housed him in Axayacatl, his father's palace. Spurred by the gold and splendor he saw around him, Cortés responded by luring Moctezuma to Axayacatl and holding him hostage. From this vantage point, the conquistador immediately began to convert the natives to Christianity and secure their pledges of loyalty to King Charles I.

Full victory over the Aztec capital was neither immediate nor painless for either side. In the historic battle of *La noche triste* (the Sad Night) in 1520, Moctezuma was killed, but the Aztecs succeeded in pushing the Spanish garrison out of Tenochtitlán. After the loss of half his troops from persistent attempts to regain advantage, Cortés and his men returned to Tenochtitlán in 1521. They crossed the canals leading into the island city and finally bridged the walls surrounding the central palace. From there they conquered the fierce but starving inhabitants who had been further weakened by smallpox, a disease introduced by the Spaniards and for which natives had no antibodies. In 1524, Cortés executed Cuauhtémoc, the last of the Aztec rulers, confirming Spanish dominion over Tenochtitlán, the Aztec or Mexican capital. Establishing Spanish influence in other territories of what was to become Mexico took longer, but this step defined the trajectory.

Mexico's Palacio Nacional (National Palace) sits on the ruins of the royal residence of Moctezuma. Once the site of vice-royal power and authority, today the National Palace houses federal government offices, the national archives and also serves as a museum. Among its treasures is a stunning mural depicting the arrival of Cortés, just one of the historic encounters dramatically depicted by the painter Diego Rivera that adorn the walls of the interior of the palace (accessible in a virtual webtour).[5]

IMPERIAL CATHOLIC RULE AND MUSIC

With the defeat of Cuauhtémoc, Spain established Mexico City as a principal seat of the vice-royal kingdom in North America. Americans often refer to the period before Independence as the colonial period but the distinction between a colony and a vice-kingdom is important and affects our understanding of music during this period. The ruling Spaniards saw themselves as an extension of the Spanish court in Madrid, and Cortés and his men sought to recreate its splendors in the New World. The Spaniards did not wait until they had established New Spain to enjoy music. Even during the days of battle, Spanish soldiers entertained themselves with the story songs of their home country.

As Spain extended its empire by conquest overseas, it linked imperial rule to religious order. The Spaniards claimed their military conquest of Mexico was to save souls and to convert natives to the service of the Catholic monarch, thus justifying economic and political avarice as well. As soon as a native state was conquered, the Spanish converted the residents, razed native religious structures, planted the cross and built churches on the most sacred of indigenous sites. With the church in place, religious instruction could take place and that included musical training and employment for musicians. As a principal seat of power in the extensive realm of New Spain, Mexico City was also the seat of cosmopolitan learning and artistic activity. European composers taught Mexicans the continental fashions with which they themselves were expected to compete and adopt as their own. Much of the most sophisticated musical composition was that associated with Catholic worship services.

Juan Gutiérrez de Padilla (1590–1664) was one of the early composer–teachers in Mexico. Born in Málaga, Spain, Gutiérrez moved to Puebla, Mexico in 1622, site of the second largest cathedral in New Spain, and a city with vast resources for the patronage of artistic endeavors. After several years as assistant and apprentice to music master Gaspar Fernandes at the Puebla Cathedral, Gutiérrez rose to become *maestro de capilla*, the post he held until his death. His duties included composing and directing music for all worship, including daily Masses, sacred festivals and holidays. Over 700 of his compositions survive in manuscript form and his *Missa Ego Flos Campi* is among his most celebrated works.[6] The contrast between the formal style heard in the *Kyrie* of that Mass and his music for the lively dance known as a *jácara* (also spelled *xácara*, pronounced HA-ka-ra) illustrate the versatility of this master.

🎧

4.2

Listening to *Kyrie* from *Missa Ego Flos Campi* ("I am the Flower of the Field" Mass) by Juan Gutiérrez de Padilla, performed by the Schola Cantorum Mexico, under the direction of Benjamín Juárez Echenique in 2000.[7]

The Kyrie is the first section of the Mass set for voices and orchestra. The title of the Mass comes from the biblical Song of Solomon, with reference to the lines "I am the flower of the field," often translated as I am the Rose of Sharon and the Lily of the Valley. The Kyrie is just one of the five sections of the Mass ordinary (regular Mass), and the only one with lyrics in Greek. The other sections are in Latin, the language of the Roman

Kyrie eleison	Lord have mercy upon us
Christi eleison	Christ have mercy upon us
Kyrie eleison	Lord have mercy upon us

Figure 4.4
Text from the *Kyrie*.

Catholic Church and the language used by composers like Gutiérrez de Padilla for much sacred music.

Listen closely to the recording. What instruments do you hear? How does the setting evoke grandeur appropriate to both the religious sentiment and the original performance setting? The form of the music closely aligns with the text.

Listening to "A la xácara xacarilla" (A la jácara jacarilla) by Juan Gutiérrez de Padilla as sung by Maria Cristina Kiehr, Adriana Fernández, and the Ensemble Elyma, in 2011.[8]

4.3

The *jácara* was a type of burlesque song and dance used for festivities adopted from the elite Madrid theater tradition (Davies 2007). The lyrics often depict street folk of vulgar background, who nonetheless exhibit a high moral character in the context of the song setting. The boasting of the opening "character" and the chorus of onlookers shouting "¡vaya!," the lengthy narrative of the many *coplas* (poetic verse with paired rhyming lines)[9] are typical of jácaras on both sides of the Atlantic. Other musical features, such as the two-against-three rhythms known as *hemiola*, distinctive melodic patterns in the supporting bass parts (descending motives in the Phrygian mode), are typical of Gutiérrez de Padilla in Puebla. Cathedral composers in early seventeenth-century Spain found the Christmas story an ideal theme for the jácara, and the lyrics in Figure 4.5 demonstrate a celebration of the nativity. Though the music invites dance, jácaras were not intended for dance in church, but rather to highlight the festive nature of special celebrations. A similar effort to engage popular dialect and music can be found in other early church music such as the *villancico* (discussed below).

RELIGIOUS DANCE DRAMAS

Among the tools Spaniards used to convert native Mexicans to Christianity were the religious dance dramas that had gained popularity in late fifteenth-century Iberia known generically as *moros y cristianos* (Moors and Christians), and lively dance music helped this task. The example of the *concheros* musicians and dancers introduced in Chapter 3 is but one legacy of the conversion practice; another is the *matachines* practice discussed in this chapter. Native converts held on to many of their own traditions, often integrating them with European customs. As we shall see, new

Figure 4.5
Lyrics for "A la xácara xacarilla" (*To the Dance and Song Fest!)* with poetic English translation by Juan Pedro Gaffney Rivera, Director, Coro Hispano San Francisco. Used with permission.

"A la xácara xacarilla"
[Original text]

A la xácara xacarilla
de buen garbo y lindo porte
traygo por plato de corte
siendo pasto de la villa.

A la xácara xacarilla
de novedad de novedades
Aunque a más de mil novedades
que alegra la navidad.

Vaya vaya de xacarilla
que el altísimo se humilla
vaya vaya de xácara vaya
que el amor pasa de rraya

1. [contralto]
Agora que con la noche
se suspenden nuestras penas
y a pagar culpas agenas
nace un bello Benjamín
si el Rey me escuchara a mí
o que bien cantara yo
como ninguno canto
del niño más prodigioso!

2. [tenor] (Con licençia de lo hermoso)
Rayos desembayna ardientes
¡escúchenme los valientes!
esta verdadera historia
que al fin se canta la gloria
y a el la cantan al naçer
general se vio el plaçer
quel velo a la tierra embia.

3. [tiple]
Que en los ojos de María
madrugaba un claro sol
Con celestial arrebol
mostro la aurora más pura
muchos siglos de hermosura
en pocos años de edad
sino sol era deidad
y el sol es quien la a vestido.

A la xácara xacarilla . . .

"To this dance-feast and song-fest"
[Poetic English translation]

To this dance-feast and song-fest,
though it be but village fare
I bring my song with style and flair
as if a platter of the best.

To the dance that tells a tale,
what's happening, the latest hit:
against a thousand songs to praise
the Birth, this is the best of all.

Tell the tale, tell it, then:
that the Most High became most low!
tell this story in dance and song,
that Love exceeded nature's bounds.

1. [alto]
For now and always, on this night
all that's wrong is held at bay;
and to set right others' wrongs
a child of grace is born this day.
If my voice could reach this king,
O! how well this song I'd sing
like no song ever sung before
in praise of this wondrous child!

2. [tenor] (With permission of the muses)
Like burning rays this one'll hit you;
listen up, homeboys—I mean you!
check it out, hear the corrido
of a real hero—a tale that's true!
The glory-song sung at the end
began the moment he was born.
Yeah, everybody danced for joy
to see what heav'n sent us that morn!

3. [soprano]
Reflected in María's eyes
a brilliant sun begins to rise,
sending fire throughout the heavens
to reveal a dawn beyond all dawns
with the beauty of the ages
in her but few years of age.
For this sun that so adorns her
is the Godhead Sun itself.

To this dance-feast and song-fest . . .

4. [contralto]
¿Quien como ella le ha tenido?
¿quien como ella le tendrá?
Virgen y madre será
del ques sin principio y fin
Serrana y más serafin
que serrana y que muger
porque Dios quiere nasçer
Apercive su jornada.

4. [alto]
Who like her ever had such beauty?
who like her could ever have it?
Maid, yet mother she will be
of Him without beginning or end.
Village-girl, yet more an angel
than maiden, or any woman,
for God now chooses to be born,
and sees in her his handiwork.

5. [tenor]
La bella bien maridada
de las mas lindas que vi
bien es que se diga aquí
de su esposo lo galante
El más verdadero Amante
y el mas venturoso joben
Sin que los yelos la estorven
dentro de un ave María.

5. [tenor]
That beautiful girl—and I've seen beauties!
she married well, I'll tell you that.
The one she married, what a guy!
A gentleman, a real lover,
He does whatever it takes, and then some,
to take good care of her. Ice and snow
won't slow him down longer than
it takes to say a Hail Mary.

6. [tiple]
Muerta de amores venía
la diosa de los amores
saludánla rruiseñores
y por madre de la vida
la daban la bienvenida
perla a perla y flor a flor,
A un portal los llevo amor,
y en la noche más helada.

6. [soprano]
Dying now of love she comes,
goddess of love, and lover of God;
the nightingales sing her welcome
and greet her, as is right they should
to the mother of Life itself—
pearl to Pearl, and flower to Flower.
To a lowly stable love guides them,
and on this coldest night of nights.

A la xácara xacarilla . . .

To this dance-feast and song-fest . . .

7. [contralto: al portal]
Miran de çierra nevada,
Altos y encumbrados rriscos
En los grandes obeliscos
ya no ay piedra sobre piedra
escollo armado de yedra
Yo te conocí edificio
Ya se miran por resquisio
las glories a manos llenas

7. [alto: addressing the stable]
Jagged rocks and lofty crags
look down from the snow-capped Sierra;
on those obelisks of nature
there's not a stone upon a stone.
Shelf of rough rock, framed in ivy—
yet I see in you a temple!
For on these early-morning visits
glory shines on us in plenty.

8. [tenor: siguiendo el tema]
En un rretrete que apenas
se divisan las paredes
esta para hacer mercedes
que en su primer arrebol
dividido se vio el sol
en breve espaçio de çielo

8. [tenor: embroidering on the theme]
In an alcove-space, where hardly
can you see a wall, He lies there,
gently working mercies. In his
first-dawn, not-yet-morning glow,
the Sun begins to shine upon
this tiny piece of heaven here;

Figure 4.5
continued

Su gloria puso en suelo Con la voluntad mas viva.	brings his brightness down to earth with a heart aflame with love
9. [tiple] Quien liverta descautiva Quien rroba la voluntad La noche de navidad la tierra vio su alegria Al pie de una peña fria ques madre de perlas ya tierno sol mostrando esta opuesto al yelo y al ayre	**9. [soprano]** That freely frees from evil's thrall, and takes away our will for ill. Tonight, the night on which He's born, all earth rejoices in his joy! At the foot of a frost-chilled stable— changed by his breath to mother-of-pearl— this gentle Sun already shines his warmth against our winter air.
A la xácara xacarilla . . .	To this dance-feast and song-fest . . .
10. [contralto] Valentia en el donayre y donayre en el mirar para empesar a pagar de un criado obligasiones Bañando esta las prisiones con lagrimas que derrama Tiene de campo la cama de yelo puesto al rigor.	**10. [alto]** Valiantly He shares his grace, graciously He shines his face on us, and thus begins to pay the debts our sins incur, though we but servants be. Our prison-cells He bathes with tears! His battlefield? The crib that's set against the chill and rigor of sin's winter-cold.
11. [tenor] Ay verdad es que en amor siempre fuistis desgraçiadas las promesas confirmadas El mas Tosco mas se afila Y a la gayta baylo Gila que tocaba Anton Pascual dejemosle en el portal con principios de Romançes.	**11. [tenor]** Hey, check it out: when it comes to love, you guys have always dragged behind! Never mind who talks the line: it's the rough-shod one dances the finest. Look at Jill! dancin' up a storm to Tony, jammin' on his horn! Well, leave 'em there, then, by the crib, singin' hero-songs to our Hero-Kid.
12. [tiple] Y pues no a de ver mas lançes y mi xacarilla buela Acabose y acabela que era de vidrio y quebrela Acabela y acabose que estava al yelo y quebrose Acabose y acabela que estava al yelo y quebrela.	**12. [soprano]** And now I've done with all my verses, my jacarilla goes its way. It comes to its end, so let it end! It was but glass, so let it break! End it now, and it is ended, For it's no more than ice that shatters. It's at an end, so wrap it up! it was of ice, so break it up!
A la xácara xacarilla . . .	To this dance-feast and song-fest . . .

traditions combining Continental and native practice developed in all social circles of New Spain and thus appear as well in many musical styles from folk to classical. The institution of the Catholic Church stood at the core of religious, economic, and artistic life, and provided the framework for education. As a result, virtually all Mexican music can claim some distant lineage to the installation of the Catholic faith in colonial times.

RACIAL, ETHNIC, AND SOCIAL DIVISIONS, AND RESULTING MUSICAL PRACTICE

New lines of social and ethnic stratification slowly emerged during the vice-royal period. By the end of the seventeenth century social interactions involved four main classes, defined first by ancestry and then by the related combination of governing authority, political power, and economic status. Spaniards, known as *peninsulares* (those born on the Iberian Peninsula) held the most authority. Native-born descendants of Spaniards, known as *criollos* (creoles),[10] were next in social status, followed by various stations of mestizo descendants of Spanish–Indian intermarriage, many known simply as *castas* (caste).[11] People of indigenous ancestry were rarely given positions of authority over *peninsulares*, and the residents of mixed race, including descendants of African slaves, found themselves living and laboring on the outskirts of social power.

In addition to the separate social domains, there existed at least three general but distinct musical domains across which influences were often exchanged. European-style church music, cultivated by the social elite and exemplified by formal compositions for multi-voice choirs and instrumental orchestras was one domain. Music in this category developed in the chapel schools of the cathedrals and parish churches. Musicians who had been born or educated in Europe taught composition and performance to Mexican natives and later mestizos, many of whom quickly acquired the expertise and experience to rise as masters themselves. A diverse and important second category includes non-religious music for dancing, theater, or other entertainment such as song contests. Entertainment music was created as often by amateurs as by specialists and occurred, as it does today, in private homes and public settings. Finally, Indian music persisted in semi-isolated communities, where performers selectively assimilated European practices from both secular and sacred realms. We shall explore examples from each category.

FROM THE CHAPEL SCHOOLS TO THE PEOPLE— THE *VILLANCICO*

One of the most important genres of music that developed in vice-regal Mexico was the *villancico*. Initially imported from Europe, the villancico resulted from an ongoing exchange of musical styles and customs across social strata, a process important to Mexican music in general. Villancicos are art music with popular appeal. While the Mass and other formal sacred music were sung in Latin, villancicos were typically sung in Spanish or other native languages, and the music supporting that vernacular verse often incorporated popular melodies and dance rhythms.

Literally translated "villancico" means "rustic song," from *villano* meaning villager or commoner. In fifteenth-century Spain, the genre emerged as a poetic secular song form. The villancico gained prominence in religious contexts as it became a Hispanic custom to insert songs in popular style into the formal liturgy. The distinctions between the villancico in Spain and the genre as it developed during the sixteenth and seventeenth centuries in Mexico involve the texts, which came to resemble dialogue or short plays know as *juegos*. These mini-dramas, not meant to be staged, featured local characters, often combining folk and popular elements such as gypsy dance songs and rhythmic refrains in Negro dialect. The most renowned poet of all Mexican villancicos was the nun Sor Juana Inés de la Cruz (1648?–1695).[12] Her verses were set by several prominent Mexican composers, including Manuel Sumaya (*c.*1658–1755), the first native-born composer to hold the prestigious position of chapel master at Mexico City's Cathedral, discussed below. Figure 4.6A–B shows samples of a handwritten manuscript of a musical score by Sumaya. The state of this manuscript offers some indication of the detective work that music scholars must undertake on a piece to reconstruct the history and the compositions from the colonial era.

By the eighteenth century composers had developed the villancico into an elaborate form of sacred music featuring a linked set of songs set in multiple sections for choir and orchestra, with stylistic features reminiscent of opera. During that century grand and glorious religious compositions marked the waning power of a church facing growing competition with new civic, artistic, and political institutions. By the end of the 1700s, few composers created new villancicos, and most of those that have survived and now circulate in popular custom are extracts and simplified versions, often sung at Christmas time. Indeed the common understanding of the term villancico across the Spanish-speaking world is as a type of Christmas carol.

In Mexico today, as well as elsewhere in the Spanish-speaking world, classical concert musicians are showing new interest in reviving the historical masterpieces of New Spain. Leaders emerging after Mexico declared independence from Spain in 1810 viewed music with such direct Spanish and European ancestry as not authentically Mexican and as too elite. The manuscripts with notation for these sacred compositions have languished in archives and the backrooms of churches. Today, views have changed. Villancicos and other genres from the colonial era are regularly performed in concert settings and released on new recordings by early music ensembles, such as the Capilla Virreinal de la Nueva España (the Vice-regal Chorale of New Spain) directed by the distinguished musicologist and composer Aurelio Tello, featured on the next audio example [4.4].

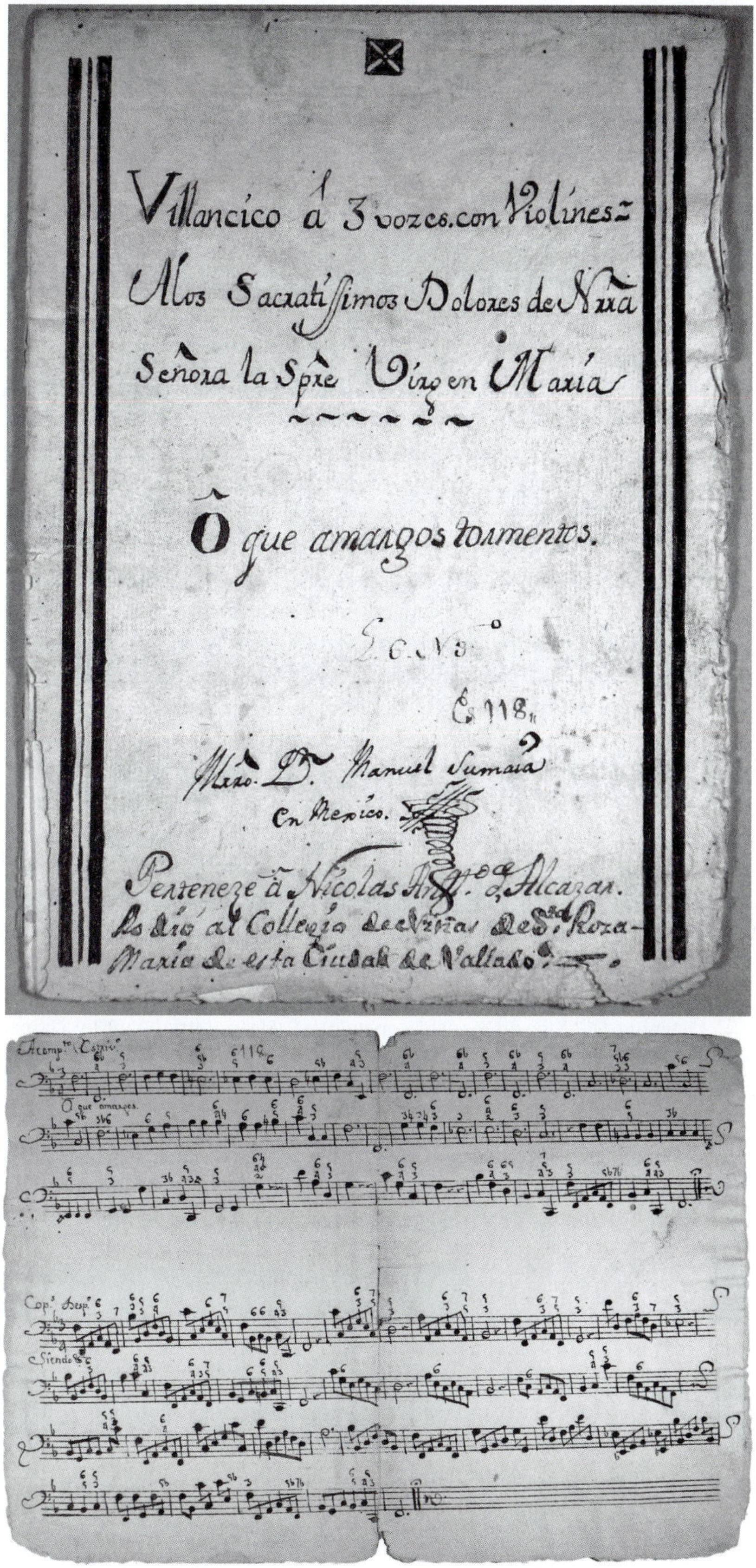

Figure 4.6A–B
The cover and a fragment of the accompaniment part of the handwritten score for a *villancico* by Manuel Sumaya. Courtesy of the Archives of the Conservatorio de las Rosas in Morelia, Michoacán, Mexico.

Overall, there exists a growing recognition that vice-regal Mexican art music emerged from a combination of native genius and cosmopolitan interaction. The result is sophisticated and delightful music which is important not only in Mexico but also in the modern international concert repertory.

TWO *VILLANCICOS* BY GASPAR FERNANDES

Gaspar Fernandes (1566–1629), was a Portuguese-born composer who served as chapel master (*maestro de capilla*) in the cathedrals of Guatemala (1599–1609) and in Puebla, Mexico (1609–1659). While in Guatemala, Fernandes compiled a collection of important music of the era, including his own compositions, known as *El cancionero de Gaspar Fernandes* (the Songbook of Gaspar Fernandes) collated between 1609 and 1616. The villancicos we will be examining come from this collection. In Puebla, Fernandes taught and conducted singers of African and American-Indian ancestry in his choir and he concentrated on creating music, primarily villancicos for the matins services (the night Mass that ends at dawn), that integrated African and indigenous languages and traditions with European models. Much of this music is notated in the Codex Fernández Leal compiled in Oaxaca and now housed in the Bancroft Library in Berkeley, California. The career of Fernandes illustrates several important points. First, the value of contributions made by peninsulares to Mexican musical culture; second, the sympathy that various missionaries and composers held for the native and African residents of New Spain; and third, the regular exchange that existed not only between Europe and America but also between the centers of power in the Americas (Mexico and Guatemala, for example).

Listening to "Xicochi xicochi conetzintle" (Sleep, Little One) by Gaspar Fernandes *c.*1609, as performed by the Capilla Virreinal de la Nueva España in 2005.[13]

4.4

As you listen to the villancico "Xicochi xicochi conetzintle" notice the patterns of musical stress on the repetition of words. Examine the song text and notice how the verse integrates ideas and lyrics in the Tlaxcalan dialect of Náhuatl with Spanish words. What is the meter of this selection? Most Indian music employs duple meter; do you hear that in this recording? Does the rhythm and melodic flow suggest a rocking motion to you?

Linguist David Shaul has observed that the short–long rhythmic pattern in the melody provides not only a rocking lilt appropriate for a lullaby but also preserves the main stress on the customary antepenultimate syllable of the Náhuatl spoken prosody, suggesting that Fernandes was sensitive to native language and music characteristics (2007).

"Xicochi" is a simple villancico without the customary verse and refrain exchange found in longer, more complex examples. It may represent

Xicochi, xicochi conetzintlé [:]	Go to sleep, go to sleep revered baby, the
ca ōmitzhuihuixocoh in angelosmeh. Alleluia	angels already rocked you. Alleluia.

Figure 4.7
Lyrics for "Xicochi xicochi conetzintle." English translation by David Shaul (2007).

a verse once used in combination with other music, but in its present form it retains considerable popularity with modern singers as a Christmas lullaby. Choral groups in Mexico, the United States, and across Europe perform it and popular singers, such as Linda Ronstadt, have recorded it as well.

Listening to "A negrito de Cucurumbé" (The Black Boy from Gurumbe) by Gaspar Fernandes *c.*1609, as performed by Harry Christophers, Kaori Muraji and The Sixteen in 2007.

4.5

"A negrito de Cucurumbé" is another villancico composed by Gaspar Fernandes *c.*1619 and it illustrates the breadth of the composer's style and interests. The direct reference to a young black boy reminds us that the population of Mexico in the seventeenth century included people of African descent who came to New Spain first as slaves and formed a distinctive, if marginalized, segment of the population. Villancicos incorporating African elements were themselves known as *negritos*, and like our example, the lyrics reflect a blend of languages making them difficult to translate. Fernandes indicated in his composition that this piece was to be accompanied by percussion, presumably integrating rhythms and instruments from Africa.

The term "cucurumbé" has a long and curious legacy in Mexico and the Caribbean revealing the attraction and resistance to African importations in Mexico. Related to the word "Gurumbe," it refers to a kind of African dance attributed to Guinea practiced by Africans living in New Spain. Some claim that it is a derivation of the term *cumbe*, an African word for the belly button or navel, while others note common usage of the term to mean "irregular." The sixteenth-century Spanish poet, Eugenio Salazar mentioned the *cumbe* and *guineo* dances in his letters, and the modern musicologist José Antonio Cahero-Robles has documented the dance in the eighteenth century (Masera 2000). Craig Russell writes that the dance was a popular component in eighteenth-century Mexican theatre, noting that it may also be the progenitor of the popular *maracumbe* dance still practiced today in Michoacán (1995:72).

The performance in our example is a complex one. A solo singer delivers the opening *coplas*, beginning the story. She is answered by another singer who helps her complete the verse. Then the full chorus comes in the *estribillo*, or refrain, highlighting the word "Gurumbe." The choir breaks into a polyphonic repetition of the opening coplas, overlapping words in an exciting blend. After another repeat of the estribillo, the soloist moves on to the next set of coplas, a lesson of the transformative power of

Figure 4.8
Lyrics to "A negrito de Cucurumbé" (The Little Black Boy from Cucurumbé). Source: *Into the Light.* The Sixteen and Harry Christophers, featuring Kaori Muraji.[14]

A negrito de Cucurumbé	**The black boy from Gurumbe**
A negrito de Cucurumbé	The black boy from Gurumbe
Bisicaino lo sá mia fé;	Vizcayno knows my faith
qui vai buscán a mé,	He went looking for me
¿Y si cansarte?	Does it make you tired?
Ma si qui cánsame.	Yes, that tires me.
Que preso hártame	How that prisoner annoys me
de si pan que dame	and of the bread they give me
qui tasi pañoli	if of the clothes
de Santo Tomé,	of Saint Thomas
Cucurumbé	Gurumbe
Coplas:	*Verses:*
Si día piensas	If you think daily
Si día bebes,	If you drink daily
mientes sangre de Dios es,	As long as it is the blood of God,
que por eso tanto puedes,	For that, as much as you can.
que vuelves hombre al revés	So that you should again become a man
cuando comas como debes.	When you eat as you should.

devotion. From a modern perspective it may be hard to reconcile the joyful setting with the not-so-subtle implication that marginalized populations especially needed the saving grace of the church.

The leading character in this villancico, led to a racial stereotype later transformed to "La negrita Cucurumbé," the little black girl of the children's song composed by Francisco Gabilondo Soler (1907–1990), known as Cri-Crí.[15] Cri-Crí was the beloved singing cricket created and voiced by Gabilondo who appeared on radio XEW from 1934 to 1954. Like Walt Disney, his legacy continues to entertain Mexican children today. The lyrics for this popular children's song tell the tale of a young girl who steps into the ocean, hoping that the white foam of the waves will whiten her black skin; when a talking fish wearing a bowler hat swims by and tells her that she is beautiful just as she is. Like the villancico, the song illustrates a mainstream complicity with racial marginalization, even as it documents racial difference and rebukes those who refuse to recognize beauty in blackness. New Spain may have been a multiracial society, but as elsewhere in the Americas, it was also a racist society. Traces of that legacy persist in the modern era, resulting in general denial of the significance of black heritage, what Alejandro Madrid has referred to as "the erasure" of African presence in Mexican mestizaje (Madrid 2011:186).

Listening to Manuel Sumaya's "Villancico a 6 al príncipe de la iglesia, el señor San Pedro" (Villancico for 6 voice parts to the prince of the church, the lord Saint Peter), as performed by members of the Capilla Virreinal de la Nueva España, directed by maestro Aurelio Tello. Josué Efraín Piedra is the tenor soloist.[16]

4.6

This villancico for Saint Peter represents the work of one of Mexico's most distinguished early composers, Manuel Sumaya (c.1658–1755). As noted earlier, Sumaya held the post of chapel master at Mexico City's Cathedral from 1715 to 1738, the first mestizo to earn such status. In 1738 Sumaya moved to follow his dear friend, the Bishop Tomás Montaño to Oaxaca, where he assumed the post of chapel master at the cathedral in that city, a job he held until his death. Sumaya is renowned for composing the first New World opera, *Parténope*, the tale of one of the sirens who tempted Odysseus. It premiered in Mexico City in 1711, but unfortunately, the music to this opera has since been lost.

In "Del vago eminente," as the song begins, is a villancico for six voices with instrumental accompaniment; the coplas, or verses, are sung by a solo tenor who is accompanied by either a harpsichord or an organ paired with a violoncello. In one section we hear the violoncello playing a rising musical scale to indicate St. Peter's ascension to heaven. This rhetorical technique of making music that literally depicts the text is called "word painting." Sumaya's elegant villancico is beautifully balanced and clearly designed for a formal setting and occasion.

As you listen to Sumaya's villancico to St. Peter, explore the composer's artistry. See if you can discern how the coplas contrast with the estribillo. Do you detect any musical or textual overlap? Do you hear sections where one voice repeats a phrase sung by another (imitative polyphony)? How does the estribillo differ from the coplas? Does the estribillo share any musical characteristic with the coplas? How do these techniques contribute to the overall character of the music?

INSTRUMENTAL MUSIC LEGACIES

Listening to "Juan Charrasqueado" featuring the *chirimía*—an ancient double-reed instrument, in a recording by Charles M. Bogert and Martha R. Bogert in the Tarascan Pueblo [Michoacán] in the mid-twentieth century.[17]

4.7

We have already discussed how the Spaniards introduced bowed and plucked string instruments to Mexican natives. One of the oldest wind instruments introduced by the Spaniards to native Mexicans was the *chirimía* [listening 4.7]. This instrument is still used in some indigenous communities, while in European-inspired bands and orchestras it has been replaced by the oboe. Early music enthusiasts, such as Los Ministriles de Marsias in Europe, resurrected their extinct chirimías in part by studying

Figure 4.9
Lyrics for the
"Villancico a 6 al
príncipe de la iglesia,
el señor San Pedro"
("Del vago eminente
imperio que dora") by
Manuel Sumaya, as
they appear in the
booklet for the CD,
*La Música de la
Catedral de Oaxaca,
Vol. II, México, Manuel
de Sumaya: Capilla
Virreinal de la Nueva
España*, Aurelio Tello,
director (Quindecim,
2005).[18]

*Villancico a 6 al príncipe de la iglesia,
el señor San Pedro,* **"Del vago
eminente imperio que dora"**

Del vago eminente imperio que dora
De Pedro los rayos,
huyendo las sombras,
Por el aire que arguye derechos,
El águila regia salió caudalosa.

Coplas:
[1]
Si águila es Pedro que al alto
Sacro imperios se remonta,
Por que el clemente vago
No ha de decir que le toca.

[2]
Que es águila bien lo dice
En las plumas que enarbola,
Pues a Dios, de hito en hito,
Cual sol de justicia goza

[3]
Corona sacra se ciñe
cuando el pastoral le adorna,
Y asi se lleva la palma
Cuando águila se corona.

[4]
Con sus hijos de la iglesia
Surca rumbos amorosa
Anunciándole depeá os
Al que al sol Cristo no adora.

[5]
Sus vuelos al aire encumbra
A la más ardiente zona,
Donde el padre de las cumbres
Por hijo suyo le adopta.

[6]
Luego el aire de sus timbres
Es la vocinglera trompa
Con que desterrando penas
De Pedro canta las glorias.
Del vago eminente imperio que dora
De Pedro los rayos,
huyendo las sombras,
Por el aire que arguye derechos,
El águila regia salió caudalosa.

*Villancico for 6 voice parts to the
prince of the church, the lord Saint
Peter* **"From the empire of
ungraspable heights that gilds"**

From the empire of ungraspable height,
That gilds Peter with its rays,
Fleeing the shadows,
The majestic eagle departs in plenty
Through righteous air.

Verses:
[1]
If the eagle,
Arising form the high sacred empire, Is
Peter, why the ungraspable and merciful
Does not say that he is of him.

[2]
That he is an eagle,
Is well expressed by the feathers he raises
So to God, from sign to sign
What sun of justice he enjoys

[3]
A sacred crown encircles him
When the pastoral adorns him,
As thus he bears the palm
When as eagle he is crowned.

[4]
With his sons of the church
He heads through amorously,
Announcing ruin to those
Who do not adore Christ's sun

[5]
His airy flights raise him
To the most fervent zone
Where the father of the heights
Adopts him as his son.

[6]
Later, the air of his timbre
Forms the roaring horn
Which, banishing sorrows,
Sings of Peter's glories
From the empire of ungraspable height,
that gilds
The rays of Peter
Fleeing the shadows
Through the righteous air,
The majestic eagle departs mightily.

Figure 4.10
Chirimía played by by Joaquim Guerra Codina, a member of Los Ministriles de Marsias, an ensemble from Spain specializing in early music. Photo by Janet Sturman, (2012).

Mexican folk preservation. The tune played in our recorded example dates from a 1947 movie theme song by Victor Cordero, and is thus far more modern than the instrument performing it. The legacy of chirimía, rooted in the early vice-regal church and state, directs our attention to the era's contribution to modern wind instrumental music in Mexico.

TRANSFORMATIVE FRAMES: FROM THE CHAPEL SCHOOL TO WIND BAND

The power of the vice-regal cathedral music did not perish when Mexico gained independence from Spain in the nineteenth century. Even if the recent renaissance of choral music in modern concert settings never took place, much of the music once cultivated and sung in the chapel choir schools (also known as *capillas*) was adopted by musicians working outside of religious settings and performed in new ways. We have explored one such example with the trajectory of "Cucurumbé." The transformation also affected purely instrumental music. A remarkable example of the transformation of the legacy of the capilla, both in educational practices and repertory, can be found in the development of the wind bands in Oaxaca. The chapel schools also trained instrumentalists to support music for religious service; over time the training of wind musicians became even more important than the training of singers. You heard a modern example of the Oaxacan wind band with the performance of "Las nereidas" in Chapter 1 [1.1]. Below we briefly explore how the modern wind bands in Mexico owe their origin to the training of instrumental musicians in the cathedrals.

The impact of the musical training provided by the church during the vice-regal period has been long lasting. Writing about the history of *bandas populares* in Oaxaca, anthropologist Sergio Navarrete (2001, 2008) explains that over time the music education once provided by the chapel schools in each town's cathedral or parish church, eventually became the responsibility of the town band. He connects this transfer of responsibility first to secularization inspired by national independence, and later to the period of agricultural reforms under President Lázaro Cárdenas (1934–40). Beginning in the nineteenth century, the repertory of masses, vespers, matins, nocturnes, and responses, tones, and other sacred compositions, was expanded to include performances of overtures, fantasies, variations, marches, and dances such as waltzes, mazurkas, two-steps, polkas, schottisches, quadrilles, and other traditional dances such as *fandangos*, *sones, jarabes*, and *chilenas*. We will discuss those styles in more detail in later chapters, for now the point is to recognize the enduring impact of historic capillas. Expanding the instrumental training to include wind band music eventually transformed the capillas themselves. The long-favored string orchestras with organ that supported vocal choruses were overshadowed by the popularity and flexibility of the wind band. The band schools honored the chapel tradition of educating the local populace and in many communities, particularly in the state of Oaxaca; the civic band became, and still is, the central institution for indigenous advancement, employment, and municipal leadership.

OAXACA'S FAMOUS WIND BAND SCHOOLS

In the mountains of twenty-first-century Oaxaca, home to the Zapotec, Mixtec and Mixe Indians, as well as to mestizo residents, music is integral to life. Training to play in the wind band initiates formal education for many native children. Reading music is their first step to learning to read and write in Spanish as well as their native language. Musical training puts young people on track for a serious education, enabling them to serve as leaders in their communities. Following a tradition of music instruction established by the Catholic priests and choirmasters dating from the sixteenth century, four-year-old children are given two years of *solfege* instruction where they learn to sing and hear pitches and match them to musical notation. After learning to sing, primary school children are given the chance to play wind or percussion instruments in a band. There are 1,000 municipalities in Oaxaca and every town in each municipality needs a band to play for civic and religious celebrations, as well as for family events such as baptisms, weddings, and funerals. Many towns have standing adult bands, but there are so many events requiring music that youth bands quickly assume the responsibility of leading the community. One famous school for advanced instruction in music and indigenous culture sits high among the cloud-tipped mountains of Oaxaca and is known by the acronym CECAM. Some of the finest conductors and wind players performing today in Mexico, in bands and orchestras of all types, acquired their foundational training in the Oaxacan youth band programs.

> Listening to two examples of Mixe wind band music with sacred roots. "Himno de los Mixes" [4.8], arranged by Antonio Romero and Chuy Rasgado and performed by the Bandas de Santa María Tepantlali, Tenetze de Zaragoza, and San Pablo de Ayutla[19] and "Son de la Danza de los Mixes" [4.9], performed by Zapotec musicians in Oaxaca recorded in 1993.[20]

🎧 4.8

🎧 4.9

The indigenous Oaxacan wind band can be heard in "Himno de los Mixes." The Mixes (pronounced "Mee-hays") are another indigenous language group with a presence in the Oaxacan highlands (*Mix* is a Náhuatl word for cloud, so Mixes, like their neighbors the Mixtec are both cloud people (see Fig. 4.11). The simple title of this piece reveals the overlap and exchange of native traditions as well as the integration of European instrumental practices. Like the hymn, the "Son de la Danza de los Mixes" is music

Figure 4.11
Location of Mixe and Mixtec populations.
Source: Summer Institute of Linguistics in Mexico.

Figure 4.12
Youth Band in San
Bartolomé de
Quialana, in Oaxaca.
Photo by Janet
Sturman, 2011.

originally conceived for sacred purposes and spiritual devotion. In the Mexican state of Oaxaca, the Zapotec people include selected music of their Mixe neighbors in their repertory of songs for sacred festivals. This second example of Mixe band music represents a genre known as *sones divinos*, or sacred dance songs, that also blend indigenous performance practices and sensibilities with European musical techniques evident in part by the insistent and repetitive melodic structure of the examples. The intonation or tuning of the ensemble reflects native preferences rather than European standards. These *sones* represent a contrast of purpose with the constellation of regional dance songs generically called *sones* that we will examine in Chapter 5. The Mixe band selections offer a mere sample of the innumerable variants of inseparable blendings or syncretisms that have shaped folkloric music in Mexico and which reflect both selective and imposed integration of competing indigenous and foreign practice.

FUSING HERITAGE AND PURPOSE—THE EXAMPLE OF THE *MATACHINES*

One way that Mexico's indigenous people held on to their heritage was to integrate adopted Christian religious beliefs with their native religious practices. Ritual dance dramas involving masks and pantomime were already part of indigenous practice when the Spanish arrived in Mexico bringing with them their own pantomimes in the form of *autos sacramentales* (religious plays concerning the subjugation of the Turkish or Arab infidels). Those dramas were also influenced by the characters and costumes of the Italian comic theater known as *commedia dell'arte*. The drama of the matachines ceremony (or *matachina*, as it is known in New Mexico) involves the pantomimed enactment of a king's victory and features four main characters: *el monarca* (the king who struggles to vanquish evil, often a symbol for Moctezuma), *La Malinche* (Malintzin, Cortés's interpreter, the first female convert, and mother of a new people), the *abuelo* (the grandfather or the old one, *el viejo* representing the wisdom of the elders, often a burlesque character), and the *toro* (the unruly bull who distracts the king and his followers from their mission). During the stages of the pantomime, the four characters dance around rows of matachines, the soldiers of Christ, in some instances viewed as representing the twelve apostles, in other instances the soldiers of the Holy Virgin of Guadalupe. Each part of the play is accompanied by violin and guitar.

> Listening to "Matachines Dance Tunes," performed by Charles Aguilar, violin; Jerry Hopkins-Velarde, guitar; Eddie Guitiérrez, *guaje* (shakers) in 1992.[21]
>
> 4.10

The "Matachines Dance Tune" is a purely instrumental selection recorded in New Mexico, land that belonged to New Spain. After Independence, it belonged to the nation of Mexico until 1848 when it was ceded to the United States. The persistence of the matachines tradition, not just in Mexico, but also in the south-western United States well into the 1990s when this recording was made, reminds us of the Mexican presence in the United States. It also illustrates the success of the syncretic blend of European and indigenous customs underlying the tenacious survival of this tradition. Matachines dances accompany many festivals in Mexico, particularly those honoring saints' days and holy festivals such as the fiesta of the Holy Cross and the Celebration of the Virgin of Guadalupe. Researchers in Tamaulipas have documented its role in the annual Fiesta de la Santa Cruz in the mountain village of Palmillas as just one example (Vargas Mendoza 2008). In 2008, New Mexico Arts sponsored a conference to examine the wide variety of matachines traditions and published a collection of essays resulting from that gathering that illustrate the convergence and divergence of practice (Stephenson 2008).

Matachines dancers with their colorful garments and pantomine-like choreography often attract more attention than the musicians who supply the music for their dancing. The tunes played on the violin and guitar take their names from the stock characters and dramas in the stories of religious conversion that date back to the autos sacramentales: *son de La Malinche, son del toro* (bull). The matachine tradition is not limited to Mexico and the United States. We find matachines in Colombia, Chile, and elsewhere in Spanish America. Not surprisingly, while some basic practices are shared, such as dances illustrating the triumph of good over evil, each community has distinctive elements of performance, as Brenda Romero documents in her examination of Native American and New Mexican matachine performance techniques and customs (Romero 1997).

Figure 4.13 (see Plate 6)
Photo of Pueblo of Jemez Matachina, August 28, 2010, in Ponderosa, NM, a tribute to Adelaido Martínez, who played the violin for the Matachina for 30 years. From left to right: Monarcha (facing left), Abuelo (facing back), Malinche; the rest are *Matachina danzantes*. The Toro is not visible in this photo. Courtesy of Brenda M. Romero.

The inclusion of social dance and non-sacred music in celebrations that are ostensibly religious is common in Mexico. Religious holidays provide the general public with a chance to rest and socialize, and to enjoy music and dance purely for entertainment. We will continue to explore the overlap of context in the next chapter dedicated to an investigation of regional practices.

CONCLUDING REFLECTIONS

The mark of Iberian *machismo* on gender and race relations in the history of the founding of New Spain is recorded in song as well as in deed, particularly in the popular music of the romances that entertained the imaginations of Hispanic listeners of all social classes. The form of the *romance* was quickly adopted in New Spain and was later developed into the *corrido*, a form we will examine later.

This chapter stresses the role of the Catholic Church in establishing Spanish rule in Mexico and in shaping its musical traditions, including paving the way for blending styles across racial and class divides.

Sophisticated music for formal worship was created first by composers born and trained in Europe; Gaspar Fernandes, and Juan Gutiérrez de Padilla are but two examples. Later, native-born, criollo music masters, notably Manuel Sumaya, created new compositions that not only served local needs, but in turn influenced composers in Europe. These composers worked to create music at the highest artistic standards, but they also explored popular and native styles, integrating them into forms like the villancico that merge elite and common elements.

Simultaneous with the practice of high art music, new traditions among native peoples developed. Rituals that began with conversion activities were adopted and transformed by native people. In previous chapters we explored the concheros dance, and the Yaqui pascola ceremony. In this chapter we added the matachines as another widespread adaptation of the moros y cristianos dramas of music and dance that fused narratives of good vanquishing evil, with Christian victory over heathen practice. It may seem ironic that native people appropriated the victory of conversion, but claiming that victory as theirs and adapting Christian and European formats to retain select native religious beliefs and cultural practices provided a measure of control over their customs and space to create their own interpretations.

In addition to training composers, the Catholic cathedral music schools also trained many anonymous performers to supply the choirs and orchestras needed to perform music in support of worship in the church. The feast days of the church calendar provided ample occasion for outdoor music-making, and wind and percussion instruments were especially well suited for parades and processions associated with those celebrations. The legacy of the chapel schools for wind bands in the state of Oaxaca contributed to the rise of numerous youth band schools that exist throughout Mexico, and which now provide Zapotec, Mixtec, and Mixe children with foundational education and native-language instruction as well as music training.

The audio examples supporting this chapter were chosen to reflect the diversity of practice across social classes but they also provide you with the opportunity to explore details of musical form and structure associated with each style of music. In addition to learning about the genre of the villancico, you also learned about the estribillo and copla as structural elements that later generated their own forms. Our brief consideration of the matachines drama introduced the concept of native religious dance tunes called sones. Another example of sones with religious legacies, are the hymns and religious dance tunes played by the Mixe bandas. In both instances we see how indigenous people adopted European musical instruments, customs, and musical forms to keep alive their own practices even as they accepted the frames of Catholic worship.

We will continue to explore the interplay of form and structure with social custom as we move to the next chapter on regional legacies and learn about non-religious forms of *sones*.

CRITICAL THINKING AND DISCUSSION PROMPTS

1. Compare the music and delivery of "A la xácara xacarilla" to that of the Kyrie. How does Gutiérrez de Padilla confirm his intentions to reach non-elite listeners with this song? Do you find that it shares any feature with the romance "Delgadina"?

2. Locate additional performances of "Xicochi" on YouTube and the internet. Compare two or more performances, noting how different performers have chosen to realize the score. Describe those differences using terms and criteria discussed in this chapter and in the listening guide from Chapter 2.

3. As you listen to "A negrito de Cucurumbé," see if you can hear the distinction between the estribillo and the coplas. What musical features help distinguish the song form and highlight the narrative? What do these lyrics reveal about racial politics and religious policy in Mexico during the time of Gaspar Fernandes?

4. Compare the villancico "A negrito de Cucurumbé," to other Mexican songs about Afro-Mexicans, beginning with Cri-Crí's songs "La negrita de Cucurumbé." "Negrito sandía" (Little Black Watermelon Boy) is another Cri-Crí song in this category. Can you compare it with other music, art, or literature from the United States or elsewhere in the Americas?

5. Compare various recordings of Mexican indigenous wind bands to the examples offered in this text. The "Son de la danza de los Mixes" that appears on the Smithsonian/Folkways recording *Creation's Journey* (see discography), offers a nice point of departure.

6. As you listen to the "Matachines Dance Tunes" [4.10], answer these questions: How does the combination of instruments represent the blend of indigenous and European practice? What other elements of the music reflect European practice? What elements reflect indigenous practice? How can you tell that this is dance music? Consult one of the references in the bibliography to learn more about this tradition. Identify at least one practice that you find significant and explain why.

KEY TERMS, PEOPLE, AND PLACES

Vice-royalty of New Spain	Maestro de capilla
peninsulares	Oaxacan bandas juveniles
criollos	jácara (xácara)
villancico	matachines
romance	chirimía
coplas	sones
estribillos	moros y cristianos

Crescencio M. García	"Kyrie Eleison"
Juan Gutiérrez de Padilla	*Missa Ego Flos Campi*
Gaspar Fernandes	*"Xicochi xicochi conetzintle"*
Manuel Sumaya	"A negrito de Cucurumbé"
Malinche	"Del vago eminente"
Moctezuma	"Juan Charrasqueado"
Cuauhtémoc	"Danza de los Mixes"
Mixes	Matachines Dance Tune
vice-regal	word painting
"Delgadina"	

NOTES

1. *La Música de los Viejitos. Hispano Folk Music of the Rio Grande del Norte.* Jack and Katherine Loeffler and Enrique R. Lamadrid. Albuquerque, NM: University of New Mexico Press (1999), 3CDs. Recording used by permission.

2. Some historians, among them, David Brading (1993), have observed that Baroque influence in Mexico extended into the eighteenth century.

3. For more details on Doña Marina with links to primary sources consult, *Dona Marina, Cortés's Translator* by Dana Liebsohn and Harriet Lillich, a module in the online publication *Women in World History* (Roy Rosenzweig Center for History and New Media at George Mason University, 2006). http://chnm.gmu.edu/wwh/modules/lesson6/lesson6.php?s=0

4. For a brief introduction to Náhuatl, see *Common Questions about Náhuatl.* www.sil.org/Mexico/nahuatl/10i-NahuatlQuestions.htm. See also the Náhuatl Pronuciation Guide, at: www.native-languages.org/nahuatl_guide.htm

5. Virtual Museum of the National Palace of Mexico. The video tour of the interior of the National Palace is available with narration in Spanish and English. The section on murals gives a brief introduction to Diego Rivera's famous depictions of Mexican history. www.hacienda.gob.mx/cultura/museo_virtual_pal_nac/shcp_mv.htm

6. *Classical Archives LLC*, at: www.classicalarchives.com/work/525217.html

7. *Baroque Music*—Cabezon, A.—Padilla, J.G. de—Clemens Non Papa, J.—Laba, A. (Baroque Mexico, Vol. 2). Mexico City: Urtext Recording, 2009.

8. *Hanacpachap: Latin-American Music at the Time of the Conquistadores.* Gabriel Garrido, Ensemble Elyma. CD recording. Pan Classics, 2011.

9. Coplas are poetic song composed in lines of four 8-syllable lines of verse united by a specific rhyme scheme. In the coplas of romances, verse lines 2 and 4 typically end with a rhyme (a b c b), while in coplas of the redondilla verse form, lines 2 and 3 rhyme (a b b a, or a b b c), as heard in the xácara in 4.3.

10. The subject of racial and ethnic intermarriage and interaction merits more study than this text can support. Social interpretation of intermarriage often

obscured biological reality, depending on the partners involved. While in the American South the designation Creole was commonly used to refer to light-skinned descendants of African and European ancestry, in pre-Independence Mexico the term *criollo* was typically reserved for those of European ancestry, while the designations *mulatto* or *pardo* referred to residents with African ancestry. A brief but useful discussion of mestizaje appears at: www.smith.edu/vistas/vistas_web/units/surv_mestizaje.htm Héctor Fernández L'Hoeste and Juan Poblete, *Redrawing the Nation: National Identity in Latin/o American Comics* (New York: Macmillan, 2009) compare racial politics and artistic representation in Mexico with practices in other nations.

11. Whereas the term *mestizaje* refers to the act of intermarriage and mixture, the related term *mestizo* is typically used to refer descendants resulting from Hispanic and Indian parentage. This topic is addressed more thoroughly in Ana Alonso, "Conforming Disconformity: Mestizaje, Hybridity, and the Aesthetics of Nationalism." *Cultural Anthropology* 19(4) (2004):459–490.

12. Scholars disagree on her date of birth; some maintain that she was born in 1651.

13. *El Cancionero Musical de Gaspar Fernandes.* Aurelio Tello, director, Capilla Virreinal de la Nueva España. Música de la Catedral de Oaxaca, México, vol. 1.; Esplendor de la música Virreinal. 1-CD audio recording. Mexico City: Quindecim, 2005.

14. Lyrics shown here incorporate the transcriptions created by Gabriel Garrido and Drew Davies. Garrido has also recorded this villancico with his ensemble Elyma. www.festivalubedaybaeza.org/seccion/conciertos//edicion-2007/ficha/el-siglo-de-oro-del-nuevo-nundo-villancicos-de-gaspar-fernandes-oaxaca-mexico-y-juan-de-araujo-sucre-bolivia.html

15. Cri Crí's version of "La negrita cucurumbé," also known simply as "Cucurumbé" appears at: www.youtube.com/watch?v=4Ng9iSkMl3s. Note the strong influences of Cuban music in the musical setting.

16. Manuel de Sumaya. *Música de la Catedral de Oaxaca, México, vol. 2: Esplendor de la Música Virreinal.* Audio CD. Quindecim, 2005.

17. Charles M. Bogert and Martha R. Bogert, *Chirimía Music of the Tarascan Pueblo.* Folkways Records & Center for Folklife and Cultural Heritage, Smithsonian Institution. Mexico, 1958.

18. Manuel de Sumaya. *Música de la Catedral de Oaxaca, México, vol. 2: Esplendor de la Música Virreinal.* Audio CD. Quindecim, 2005.

19. *Testimonial Musical de México, number 50, 1964–2009. En el lugar de la música.* Mexico City: Instituto Nacional de Antropología e Historia, 2008.

20. Various Artists, *Creation's Journey: Native American Music*, Charlotte Heth, Terence Winch Producer, Smithsonian Folkways Recordings, 1995.

21. *Music of New Mexico. Hispanic Traditions.* Smithsonian Folkways. Audio CD, Smithsonian Folkways, 1992.

FOR REFERENCE AND FURTHER STUDY

Barwick, Steven. 1994. "Mexico." In Curtis Price (Ed.), *The Early Baroque Era: From the Late 16th Century to the 1660s.* Englewood Cliffs, NJ: Prentice Hall, 349–360.

Brading, David. 1993. *The First America: The Spanish Monarchy, Creole Patriots and the Liberal State 1492–1866.* Cambridge: Cambridge University Press.

Burkholder, Mark and Johnson, Lyman L. 2003. *Colonial Latin America.* London and New York: Oxford University Press.

Catalyne, Alice Ray. 1966. "Music of the Sixteenth to Eighteenth Centuries in the Cathedral of Puebla, Mexico," *Anuario* 2:75–90.

Davies, Drew Edward. 2007. "Nationalism, Exoticism, and Colonialist Appropriation: The Historiographic Decontextualization of Music from New Spain." In Janet Sturman (Ed.), *Latin American Choral Music: Contemporary Performance and the Colonial Legacy.* http://web.cfa.arizona.edu/sturman/CLAM/Pub1/Davies1.html (accessed January 12, 2015).

Estrada, Jesús. 1973. *Música y músicos de la epoca virreinal.* Mexico City: Secretaría de Educación Pública (Biblioteca SEP).

Knighton, Tess and Alvaro Torrente. 2007. *Devotional Music in the Iberian World, 1450–1800: The Villancico and Related Genres.* London: Ashgate.

Laird, Paul. 1993. "The Dissemination of the Spanish Baroque Villancico." *Revista de Musicología* 16(5):2857–2864.

Laird, Paul. 1997. *Towards A History of the Spanish Villancico.* Warren, Michigan: Harmonie Park Press.

Liebsohn, Dana and Harriet Lillich. 2006. "Dona Marina, Cortés' Translator." In *Women in World History.* Fairfax, VA: Roy Rosenzweig Center for History and New Media at George Mason University. http://chnm.gmu.edu/wwh/modules/lesson6/lesson6.php?s=0 (accessed January 12, 2015).

Liebsohn, Dana and Barbara Mundy. 2010. *Colonial Latin American Visual Culture, 1520–1820.* Austin, TX: University of Texas Press. www.smith.edu/vistas (accessed January 12, 2015).

Lamadrid, Enrique R. 1994. *Tesoros del Espíritu.* Embudo, NM: El Norte/Academia Publications.

Loeffler, Jack, Loeffer, Katherine, and Lamadrid, Enrique R., (Eds.). 1999. *La Música de los Viejitos: Hispano Folk Music of the Rio Grande del Norte.* Albuquerque, NM: University of New Mexico Press.

Madrid, Alejandro (Ed.). 2011. *Transnational Encounters: Music and Performance at the U.S.–Mexico Border.* New York: Oxford University.

Masera, Mariana. 2000. "El nuevo mundo y el viejo mundo en la canción tradicional mexicana: del villancico a la copla." *Acta Poetica* 21:255–277.

Navarrete Pellicer, Sergio. 2001. "Las capillas de música de viento en Oaxaca durante el siglo XIX." *Heterofonía* 124:9–27.

Navarrete Pellicer, Sergio. 2008. "Entre la trompeta y el barítono hay un refifi que solo la tuba puede acompañar." Program Notes for the CD Recording Set *"En el lugar de la música." Testimonial Musical de México* 50, 1964–2009, 97–111.

Ramírez Cárdenas, Sergio and Claudia Walls. 2007. *Antología coral infantil Cri-Cri. Cantemos todos, vol. 3.* Mexico City: Sistema Nacional de Fomento Musical.

Robertson, Carolina. 1992. "Dance of Conquest." In Carolina Robertson (Ed.), *Musical Repercussions of 1492: Encounters in Text and Performance.* Washington, DC and London: Smithsonian Institution Press, 9–33.

Romero, Brenda M. 1997. "Cultural Interaction in New Mexico as Illustrated in the Matachines Dance." In Kip Lornell and Anne K. Rasmussen (Eds.), *Musics of Multicultural America.* New York: Schirmer Books, 155–185.

Russell, Craig. 1964. "Mexico City Cathedral Music: 1600–1750." *The Americas* 21:111–35.

Russell, Craig. 1992. "Musical Life in Baroque Mexico: Rowdy Musicians, Confraternities and The Holy Office." *Inter-American Music Review* 13(1):11–21.

Russell, Craig. 1995. *Santiago de Murcia's Códice Saldívar No. 4: Commentary.* Chicago, IL: University of Illinois Press.

Shaul, David Leedom. 2007. "An Appraisal of Spanish Colonial Era Music with Náhuatl Texts." In Janet Sturman (Ed.), *Latin American Choral Music.* Tucson, AZ: University of Arizona—Center for Latin American Music. http://web.cfa.arizona.edu/sturman/CLAM/Pub1/Shaul.html (accessed January 12, 2015).

Sonnichsen, Philip. 1994. Liner notes for *Corridos y tragedias de la frontera*. 2 CDs. Arhoolie/Folkloric 7019–7020.

Stephenson, Claude (Ed.). 2008. *Matachines! Essays for the 2008 Gathering*. Albuquerque, NM: New Mexico Arts. www.nmarts.org/matachines/Matachines_Essays.pdf

Stevenson, Robert. 1968. *Music in the Aztec and Inca Territory*. Berkeley, CA: University of California Press.

Stevenson, Robert. 1970a. "The First New World Composers: Fresh Data from Peninsular Archives." *Journal of the American Musicological Society* 23(1): 95–106.

Stevenson, Robert. 1970b. *Renaissance and Baroque Musical Sources in the Americas*. Washington, DC: General Secretariat, Organization of the American States.

Stevenson, Robert. 1994. "Ethnic Impulses in the Baroque Villancico." *Inter-American Music Review* 14(1):67–106.

Tello, Aurelio. 1990. *El Archivo Musical de la Catedral de Oaxaca*. México, D.F.: CENIDIM.

Truitt, Jonathan. 2012. "Adopted Pedagogies: Nahua Incorporation of European Music and Theater in Colonial Mexico City." *The Americas* 66(3):311–330.

Vargas Mendoza, Mariana de Jesús and Vergara de los Ríos, María del Carmen. 2008. *Rescate y preservación de la música y danza vivas en Tamaulipas. Fiesta de la Santa Cruz en Palmillas*. A documentary video. Universidad Autónoma de Tamaulipas.

DISCOGRAPHY

Creation's Journey: Native American Music. Various Artists. Charlotte Heth, Terence Winch, Producer, Audio CD. Smithsonian Folkways, 1995.

El Nuevo Mundo. Folías Criollas. Hesperion XXI. Jordi Savall, director. Audio CD. Alia Vox, 2010.

Hanacpachap: Latin-American Music at the Time of the Conquistadores. Ensemble Elyma, Gabriel Garrido, director. Audio CD. Pan Classics, 2011.

Into the Light. Harry Christophers, Director. Kaori Muraji, guitar and The Sixteen, choir. Decca Music Group, Ltd., 2006.

La Música de la Catedral de Oaxaca, Vol. II. Manuel de Sumaya. Capilla Virreinal de la Nueva España, Aurelio Tello, Director. Mexico City: Quindecim, 2005.

México Barroco, Puebla II. Various Ensembles. Audio CD. Urtext Records, 2000.

Music of New Mexico. Hispanic Traditions. Various Artists. Audio CD, Smithsonian Folkways Recordings, 1992.

Tarascan and Other Music of Mexico: Songs and Dances of the Mexican Plateau. Recorded by Charles M. Bogert and Martha R. Bogert. Folkways Records & Center for Folklife and Cultural Heritage, Smithsonian Institution, 1958.

Testimonial Musical de México, number 50, 1964–2009. En el lugar de la música. Mexico: Instituto Nacional de Antropología e Historia, 2008

CHAPTER 5

Colonial Legacies and Regional Responses: Sones Regionales

A MODERN *TRÍO* REFLECTS

The year is 2007; three musicians in their early twenties sit in a small apartment in Tampico, huddled around a CD player as they listen to old recordings. As a trio they often perform Huastecan traditional music, but tonight they are relaxing after returning from their regular day jobs. Lorena works as a physician's assistant; she plays *jarana huasteca* (small five-string lute) and sings with the trio. Her sister, graphic designer Orlanda, plays supporting bass on the *quinta huapanguera* (large lute with eight to ten strings in five courses). Both learned to play and sing from their father. Recently they have been performing with their former classmate and friend Osiris, now a violinist of such renown that he makes a living teaching and playing from performing for festivals, weddings, and workshops. Lorena explains, that in the past, girls were not encouraged to play *sones* and *huapangos*, (two types of poetic song with instrumental interludes and music for dance), certainly not in public; that work was left to men. Both women are proud that they are breaking stereotypes and have earned respect as outstanding performers in a tradition that was not only a male preserve, but until recently was also neglected by young adults.

One recorded selection catches their attention: "La petenera" (the title references an alluring woman).[1] Each knows it with a different set of verses and melodies. They identify it as one of the oldest *sones*, music with deep roots extending back into the colonial era. "Have you heard the French recording of 'La petenera'?" Orlanda asks her friends [5.1]. "It uses ancient instruments." Osiris makes a face, "yes, but ironically, the rhythms and vocals seem too modern to me." He prefers a version like one he recorded with the Trío los Guardianes de la Huasteca (Guardians of the Huasteca Trio).[2]

Despite these criticisms, the performers are pleased that new audiences from around the world are drawn to music from their region of Mexico and that professional musicians working in the international field of early music include the song type in their repertory.

They turn to a set of recordings compiled by Mexican researchers working the 1970s. Here they find two other versions of "La petenera" and they begin discussing regional approaches to the song and different playing styles. "The instrumentation is different; there is no violin, and the tempo is much slower," observes Osiris, in reference to the performance by the group Los Azohuaztles from Tixtla [5.2].

Observing the trio's fascination with regional approaches to the *son* offers us a window from which to view the historical trajectory of one of the most important categories of Mexican music, a practice that remains vital today. Their comments also remind us that for much of the nation's history there were many Mexicos, with regions separated by topography and cultural traditions, sporadically bridged by trade, politics, or the demands of battle.

HISTORICAL PERSPECTIVES: MANY MEXICOS

Residents and foreigners alike could identify many Mexicos during the vice-regal period from 1500 to 1821. The Spanish imposition of religion, culture, and language (an incomplete imposition in the case of many natives who held on to their own language and traditions) was not enough to unify Mexico as a nation. Environmental and geographic conditions varied across the land, separating communities and shaping regional experience. In previous chapters we have explored the results of some of the racial, ethnic, and social distinctions promoted by the conquistadors and the Spanish crown. In this chapter we look at the musical relationships among regions within Mexico. We will see how local responses to imported musical traditions produced related, yet distinct, musical practices as we focus on the development of the regional varieties of the category of poetic song, music and dance that Mexicans call *son* (pronounced SEW-N; the word literally means "sound"; its plural is *sones*). So varied is this category, that some scholars prefer to speak of Mexican *son* as a "complex" of practice and form linking sung poetry, instrumental music, and dance, as we will discuss presently.

Local specialization was important to the economy of New Spain. Exports from Mexico were strictly regulated, licensed, and taxed by the Spanish Crown, resulting in little local profit and thus for the majority of residents, internal commerce was more profitable. Local exchange was also the more practical option, given the challenges posed by Mexico's complex landscape to transportation and communication before the arrival of the railroad in the late nineteenth century. As a result, the 1700s saw a rise in regional specialization of local products, crafts, manufacturing, fishing, and agriculture. Regional distinctions in local goods and services were mirrored in identifiable differences in musical styles and practices. By the end of the eighteenth century, the various regions of Mexico were rather sharply distinguished not only by geographic features and resulting agricultural traditions, patterns of labor, and local religious and civic customs, but also by the ethnic make-up of the population, which reflected a mix of indigenous and imported populations specific to each region. Musical practices were among the distinctive local customs developed in each province, and the wide variety of regional sones reflects this process. Regional customs of production and cultural expression continued to represent Mexico's many distinct geographic and cultural regions long after improved transportation, migration, intermarriage, and cultural exchange blurred provincial boundaries.

The term *son* is widely used in other Hispanic countries to describe musical styles, songs, and instrumental compositions, particularly in the Caribbean and Central America, but it should be noted that the varieties of rural Mexican *son* differ substantially from *son* in Cuba—particularly the urban *son* that led to *salsa*—or in other regions of Latin America.

Mexican *son* is typically joyful music, but can be used to express melancholy and sorrow as well. Lyrics may convey irony, offer political critique, often relying on *doble sentidos*— words with double meaning, or puns known as *albur* where one of the meanings carries sexual overtones (recall the lyrics of "Las naguas blancas" for example). *Albur* is a key component in popular Mexican culture and humor and its prevalence in sones made them a target of censure from the church and particularly during the colonial era when "El Santo Oficio" prohibited the performance of sones and jarabes as sinful and prone to forbidden sexual connotations. Musicians today continue to perform sones to accompany the full range of lived experience, happy and sad. As the vignette at the start of this chapter illustrates, people still perform sones to mark special moments in their lives and in settings where they entertain themselves, as well as their friends, families, communities, and guests. While some performers are paid for playing, singing and dancing, many more perform out of a sense of

Oral History and Invented Tradition

Another source of information regarding popular and folkloric music practiced during the vice-regal era is the body of stories passed along from generation to generation, the lore of continued practice, often accessed via oral histories. Deciphering cultural memory is a challenging process. Contemporary performers may hold dear facts that have undergone considerable re-interpretation, yet those perspectives may still reveal a great deal about the persisting value of a tradition and the meanings that various generations invest in it. The British historian Eric Hobsbawm (1980) studied how people, and particularly governments, shape cultural memory by processes of selective reinterpretation that he labeled "inventing tradition." Communities may do the same and while the notion of inventing tradition might initially carry negative connotations, Hobsbawm and his co-authors show that the process is universal. Nonetheless, each instance is distinct and those differences reveal the concerns and values of any particular community. We can use the concept of invented tradition as a useful framework for exploring the historical and ongoing development of regional popular music in Mexico.

responsibility—for honor, love, and respect. As musicians perform sones, they also reinforce their connections to complex historic legacies, linking modern concerns and contexts to valued past traditions.

POPULAR MUSIC DURING THE COLONIAL ERA

By the 1770s, theater was the most popular form of shared entertainment in the cities of New Spain, with opera holding the attention of the elite. Meanwhile, new forms of popular theater, including musical dramas, such as the *zarzuela* and the more compact *tonadilla escénica*, captured the hearts of the bourgeoisie. As we shall see, the music associated with these dramas acquired a life of its own in Mexican New Spain. In particular, song forms rooted in literate practice crossed social divides and were adopted by urban workers and rural folk who transformed them to appeal to local audiences.

Studies of music during the colonial era have focused on music cultivated in the royal chapels and cathedrals, in part because much of this music was notated and there exist archival collections of written scores, or parts of them, to examine. Less attention has been given to popular music prior to Independence. Most of this music was not notated and instead was circulated by word of mouth. Public records, commentaries, diaries, and narrative accounts of musical activity, written by people who lived during the colonial era, provide some information regarding musical practice. Given that few popular musicians were literate, such accounts were often provided by upper-class observers or foreign visitors (Koegel 2002:365–367).

Son and its Theatrical Roots

Although music historians typically discuss the development of the *son* in Mexico during the nineteenth century, the form and its customs originated much earlier. Music scholar Thomas Stanford (1972) dates the common use of the term in Spain to 1671, but he traces the practice of *son* in Spanish theater back to the 1500s. The first documented use of the term *son* in Mexico surfaces in 1766 in a set of verses from Veracruz, however, once again, scholars believe that practice pre-dates the label. Thus, we may surmise that Mexicans did not wait until the nineteenth or even the eighteenth century to cultivate their own approaches to the instrumental music and sang verse that Spaniards imported to accompany dance and enliven drama.

We may trace the roots of *son* in Mexico to the glorious period of Spanish literature known as the *Siglo de oro* (Golden Century, but it would be more accurate to speak of the plural *Siglos de oro*, since the period extended from the end of the fifteenth century to the late seventeenth century). In this era the poetry and dramas of Lope de Vega, Miguel de Cervantes, Calderón de la Barca, and other master authors were enjoyed not just in Spain but were also imported to New Spain. To cater to a variety of tastes and to keep audiences alert, theatrical impresarios often inserted short compositions for popular entertainment between the acts of longer formally staged dramas. Such *intermedios* or *entremeses* included songs and dances reflecting local custom, provincial dances for example, such as the *seguidillas* of Castile, as well as the *matachines* and *mojigangas* that persist today in the Americas.[3]

Later, during the 1700s, songs involving dialogue, called *tonadillas*, once performed between the acts of larger theatrical works, eventually expanded to become short music dramas on their own accord, known as *tonadillas escénicas*. Hundreds of tonadillas were composed, so many that they were considered disposable, and few notated examples of this early music survive. Vicente T. Mendoza (1984) believed that the best record of the tonadilla lives on in the popular songs of the Mexican nation.

The tonadilla also gave rise to more complex types of musical theater, including the *zarzuela*, a play with spoken and sung verse, somewhat like American musical theater with more operatic music. These lyric plays featured music based on a wide array of dance music from the many regions of Spain, including *seguidillas*, *boleros*, and *jotas*, as well as flamenco styles, particularly *malagueñas* and *peteneras*, the genre we will explore in more detail. Popular theater songs quickly entered the repertory of ordinary city residents and were sung and whistled by street vendors. Indians and *campesinos* (peasant farmers) who came to the city to sell their wares took songs back with them to their towns and villages, and *mestizo* Mexicans created their own versions of these musical genres. This is the music that influenced the development of regional sones, but the process was not unidirectional. As people moved around, sometimes by choice, and other times by force, so did their music. Certainly, the ethnic make-up of each city influenced musical practices. As slave traders imported Africans via the port of Veracruz, black musicians added their traditions and sensibilities to the music made in Mexico. Similarly, the runaway slaves on the other coast, in the Costa Chica of Guerrero, and the freed slaves in Mexico City, contributed musical practices that helped define the sones of those regions. Acapulco and Guerrero became important enclaves of black settlement and Guerrero remains one of the states with the highest population of African descent in the country, with several mostly black communities.

CHARACTERISTICS OF *SON*

Stanford calls *son* a mega-genre because it includes a variety of constituent types. Three dimensions of performance help define and distinguish the different types: 1) music, 2) verse, and 3) choreography. Music for sones is typically realized by a combination of string instruments, such as one or two violins accompanied by a strummed counterpart—either a guitar or similar instrument, a harp, or sometimes both. Such instrumentation reflects the basic combination of instruments favored in Spanish theatrical productions, and even in seventeenth-century churches and chapels, although by and large the *son* developed as secular music.

The musical form of *son* is strophic song (repeating melody with each verse) most typically with a *compás* (meter) of 6/8 or 3/4, characterized by shifts in rhythmic accentuation from a two-beat stress to a three-beat stress (**1**–2-3 **4**–5-6 =**1** + a **2** + a) (**1**–2 **3**–4 **5**–6 =**1**+ **2**+ **3**+). This kind of mixed meter is called *sesquiáltera* (six that alters). The poetic verse of the *son* may feature classic lines of text, but singers often improvise verse while performing. They must adhere to the classic rules of rhyme and syllabic structure while spinning short poetic rhyming stanzas called *coplas*.[4] (You are already familiar with coplas from our earlier discussion of that structure in the villancicos, another source of influence for the sones.) The poetic subject matter of sones commonly concerns women and matters of love, often in a suggestive and clever manner, rich with double meaning and sexual innuendo. The lyrics of some sones were so salacious that religious authorities in New Spain attempted to ban all performances of the genre (Sheehy 1979:27).

The choreography of sones features a foot-stomping dance called *zapateado*. The dancers' movements often simulate courtship rituals and are customarily performed on a raised wooden platform known by various names depending on the region: *tarima* (Huasteca), *artesa* (Costa Chica), or *tabla* (Tierra Caliente, Guerrero). The sound of the dancers' stomping feet contributes to the overarching quality of the music and the steps highlight the shifting rhythmic accents in the music. Each type of *son* has its own dance steps. Similarly, the garments worn by the dancers, especially in staged performance, represent traditional regional dress and distinguish one regional style of *son* from another.

One of the goals of this chapter is for readers to recognize some of the major styles of *son* and be able to distinguish among them. Pay attention to the differences in instrumentation, the manner of playing or singing (including vocal timbre and register), favored song repertories, as well as the dance steps and customs of dress that differentiate one style from another.

VARIETIES OF *SON*

There are at least ten different kinds of *son* associated with a particular region of Mexico: 1) *son jarocho* from Veracruz, from the southern regions of that Gulf Coast state, and the northern region of the state of Tabasco; 2) *son calenteño* from the hot lands, or Tierra Caliente in the state of Michoacán—in the Tepalcatepec region along the river's southern shores—and in the state of Guerrero—region of the Río Balsa—also called *son guerrerense*; 3) *son abajeño* associated with the lowlands and the Purépecha Indians of Michoacán and into Jalisco; 4) the *son jalisciense* from the state of Jalisco; 5) *son huasteco* and *huapango* originating in those regions populated by Huastec people in the states of Hildago, Veracruz, Tamaulipas, San Luis Potosí, Puebla, and Querétaro (see Fig. 2.2); 6) *son guerrerense* from the state of Guerrero and sometimes called *son calentaño* which features different instrumentation from the earlier mentioned *son calenteño*; also from the region known as the Tierra Caliente along the Balsas river; 7) *son istmeño* or *son Oaxaqueño* from the southern coast of Oaxaca and parts of nearby Chiapas; 8) *son de Tixtla*, also from Guerrero; 9) *son arribeño*, from the Río Verde region; and 10) *sones de Tabasco* (see Fig. 5.1—map of *sones*).[5] As we will see in our exploration of the first eight styles, each regional tradition reflects a different blending of Hispanic and Indian practices, with additional contributions from African, Arabic, and other Latin American practices distinguishing several of the styles.

In addition to regional varieties, there exists a distinction between indigenous sones and mestizo sones. Indigenous sones are often defined by association with particular ethnicities, for example the Yaqui in the northern borderlands, or the Zapotec in the south. Many indigenous sones are used in ritual and ceremonial circumstances. There are also secular indigenous sones performed outside of religious settings, such as for social occasions. A popular category of indigenous *son* found in the U.S. state of New Mexico is the *indita*.[6] The more widespread category of the so-called *mestizo sones* has roots in the regional forms mentioned above. Modern mariachis have adopted mestizo sones into their repertory, creating arrangements that suit the mariachi instrumentation and style, rather than the instrumentation and approaches associated with the regions' traditions discussed in this chapter. The historical link between the modern mariachi tradition and the performance of regional sones appears at the end of this chapter.

Figure 5.1
Map of the principal regions of *sones*. Courtesy of Raquél Paraíso (2010).

Map of regional *sones*

"LA PETENERA": REGIONAL INTERPRETATIONS OF HISPANIC LEGEND

Whether you are in Guerrero or listening to *trovadores* (poet singers) in the Huasteca, you may encounter the *son* "La petenera," the subject of the conversation that opened this chapter. It is one of several old song types that illustrate the long history of the *son* and its debt to Spanish poetic masters, as well as the connections to flamenco dance rhythms and theatrical inspired song.

Those who love flamenco may recognize the name *petenera* as a flamenco *palo* (a basic style defined by its patterns of harmony, tonality, poetry, singing, and above all, by rhythm). The *petenera* is a 12-beat pattern with the following accentuation: **1** 2 3 **4** 5 6 **7** 8 9 **10** 11 12, or 1–2–3, 1–2–3, 1–2, 1–2, 1–2. This beat pattern matches that of the sixteenth-century Spanish dance the *zarabanda*[7] and the *jácara*. The flamenco petenera is accompanied by a guitar, and performed with a slow and solemn character. There are local variants of peteneras in various Spanish regions such as Castilla y León, Valencia, and Extremadura. They are sung and accompanied with musical instruments from these regions such as guitars, *bandurrias* (short-necked lute with 12 strings), *dulzainas* (double reed aerophone), and *tamboriles* (barrel shaped folk drum).

Folklorists trace the title and the subject of the petenera to a legend about a woman from Paterna in Cádiz whose seductive power drew men to ruin. The specific lyrics of "La petenera" sung in Mexico vary depending on the style, and when and where it is performed. We have been discussing the *son* petenera as an import from Spain into Mexico, but scholars classify the genre as "son de ida y vuelta," (a round trip song type) which means that the genre could have been born in the Americas and brought to Spain through the port of Cádiz.

With the coming and going of practices, peteneras developed differently in Mexico and Spain. Nonetheless, certain themes seem to persist: "La petenera" remains a beautiful woman, she may be a mermaid or siren, her status is alternatively cast as divine or dangerously seductive, and the singer's rhetoric often unfolds as if he knows her. One verse may seem to have little to do with the next, but the singer may also connect the *femme fatale* to the surrounding environment, as he weaves in advice to listeners. "La petenera" is popular in the Huasteca, along the Costa Chica of Guerrero, and in the Isthmus of Tehuantepec, and each locale supports a different approach. Using audio examples 5.1–5.3 and audio video example 5.1 we can, like the trio of friends at the start of this chapter, compare several contrasting versions of "La petenera" to better understand historic and regional treatments of this song.

🎧

5.1

Listening to "La petenera," performed by the modern ensemble L'Arpeggiata with Christina Pluhar (theorbo—bass lute), Patricio Hidalgo (guitar and voice) and Béatrice Mayo-Félip (soprano).[8]

This example recreates a version of "La petenera" using instruments, rhythms, and customs that date directly from the vice-regal era, but are performed for listeners with modern sensibilities. Notice in particular the use of the *salterio* (psaltery—a kind of hammered dulcimer) accompanying the singer in the first strophe, and the *theorbo* (a long-necked lute with extended bass strings) in strophe two. The *cornetto* (a Baroque trumpet) and Spanish castanets are heard in the instrumental interludes between verses. These instruments enjoyed popularity in the eighteenth century in New Spain as well as Spain. The performers in L'Arpeggiata merge Spanish, specifically Andalusian, historical practices with Mexican folkloric ones, expanding the appeal of this music to international devotees of early music.

> Listening to "La petenera," a *son* from the Costa Chica as performed by Los Azohuaztles from Tixtla.[9]

5.2

Audio example 5.2 begins with a *jarabe* as an introduction. Banned as a lascivious dance in the 1700s, the jarabe surged in popularity after independence, to earn recognition as in the early 1900s as the "national dance of Mexico." Performances of sones from Tixtla in the state of Guerrero Mexico prompt energetic stomping dancing on a wooden platform, leading local residents to refer to this style as "*sones de tarima*" (see Fig. 5.3).

The sones of Tixtla reflect, in the instrumental practice and song delivery, the influence of African traditions alongside Hispanic and indigenous contributions, sharing this legacy, although realized differently, with sones from the Costa Chica, the 200-mile stretch along the Pacific coast (see Fig. 5.2) to the south. This region of the country has a sizeable Afro-Mexican population and African musical customs have influenced

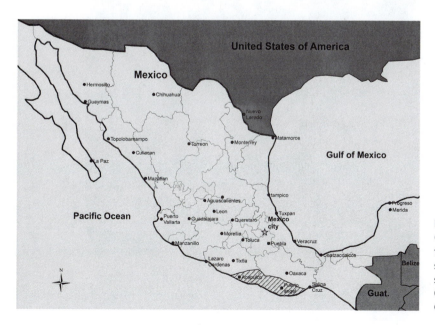

Figure 5.2
Geographical map of the Costa Chica region, shaded portion, of the states of Guerrero and Oaxaca. Rachel Cushman, 2015.

music practiced here dating back to the era of the slave trade. Evidence of the African influence can be heard in the use of percussion that accompanies the singing and playing of guitars, vihuela, harp, and sometimes a five-string bass guitar known as the *bajo sexto*. Los Azohuaztles, the performers heard in 5.2 play vihuela, guitarra de golpe, and *cajón* (wooden box). The percussionist uses his hands or a small block to strike the sides of the cajón. The dance platform, called a *tarima* in Tixtla, is known as *artesa* in Costa Chica, also serves as a percussion instrument, and in rural settings it is sometimes made from a hollowed trunk of the *ceiba* tree.

Notice how the singers share in the delivery of the verse. This dialogic, call-and-response style of delivery, is typical of African singing. Consider how this give-and-take affects the way you listen to the narrative of the song.

5.1 You can view and listen to yet another version of "La petenera" [5.1] performed by another trío from Tixtla.[10] The photo near the end of the sequence in the video shows both the artesa and dancers on the tarima. This example makes for an interesting comparison to the version heard in 5.2.

Audio example 5.3 is a version of "La petenera" sung by soneros from the Huasteca region of Mexico (see Fig. 2.2). The instrumentation features the instrumental trio encountered in our opening scenario: violin, quinta huapanguera (often just called "huapanguera")—a large flat-backed guitar, with five courses of strings and a deeper sound than a conventional acoustic guitar; and a *jarana*—a smaller five-string mate of the huapanguera (not

Figure 5.3
The musicians Los Azohuaztles playing cajón, vihuela, and guitarra de golpe. Source: Música Tradicional Mexicana. Courtesy of Guerrero Cultural Siglo XXI, A.C.

to be confused with the double-strung jarana used in the *son* jarocho style discussed later in this chapter). The singers employ a technique of high singing called falsetto distinctive of Huastecan style.

Juan Jesús Aguilar León (2000) reports that a popular Spanish expression "salirse por peteneras" means the equivalent of "going off on a tangent," both referring to leaving the topic at hand for a discussion on a new point. While Gypsies in Spain used the term "petenera" to refer to a beautiful woman who bewitches men, in the Huasteca, singers deliver poetic references to sailors, fisherman, and coastal life troubled by enchanting sirens of the sea. Although the singer may develop a principal theme or topic throughout the verses, the lyric content from one stanza to another may not be related. Singers choose from an extensive lyric repertory of stanzas associated with a particular *son*, or compose their own (Sánchez 2010).

As you listen to each version of "La petenera," compare the lyrics of sung verse (see Figs. 5.4–5.6) as well as the sounds in the supporting music. Consider how the verses illustrate the themes mentioned above.[12] Look for elements that are shared as well as what is different among the versions. Consider how the musicians perform and sing. How does the musical delivery affect the character of the song and how do you respond to it? Can we really say that each of the renditions is the same song? Which do you prefer and why? Contemporary musicians are devoting new attention to regional sones, as evidenced by the 2012 release of the recording *El gusto: 40 años de son huasteco*.[13] In your view, what factors account for such new interest?

Listening to "La petenera," in a performance by the Trío Cantores de la Huasteca.[11]

5.3

"La petenera" [5.1] as performed by the ensemble L'Arpeggiata	"La petenera" [5.1] as performed by the ensemble L'Arpeggiata
Una doncella se fue a vivir al mar profundo, [2x] pero ante noche soñé que en alguna parte del mundo [2x] cantando la encontraré.	A maid went away to live in the deep sea But last night I dreamed That in some part of the world Singing, I will find her.
Ay soledad, soledad, soledad que yo quisiera. [2x]	Ah solitude, solitude Solitude, that I wish for
Que usted se volviera anona pa' que yo me la comiera, ay madurita, ay madurona que del palo se cayera.	That you became a soursop So that I could eat it Ay, little ripe one, That fell from the branch.

Figure 5.4
Lyrics for "La petenera." Traditional. As sung by the ensemble L'Arpeggiata. Transcribed by Gabriel Venegas.

[instrumental interlude]

Quien le puso Petenera
no la supo bautizar, [2x]
le hubiera puesto siquiera
la musa de mi cantar [2x]
y en mi corazón viviera.

[instrumental interlude]

Ay soledad, soledad,
soledad que yo quisiera. [2x]

Que se formara un columpio
solito ya lo ves.
Que se formara un columpio
para que yo me meciera.

[instrumental interlude]

Whoever named her Petenera
Did not know how to baptize her [2x]
He could have at least called her
The muse of my song [2x]
That would live in my heart

[instrumental interlude]

Ah solitude, solitude
Solitude, that I wish for

That a swing would be formed
By itself you see
That a swing would be formed
So that I could rock in it.

Figure 5.5
Lyrics for "La petenera," Version from Tixtla performed by the Conjunto Los Azohuastles. Lyrics from *Antología del son de México*, courtesy of Discos Corasón SA. The three-volume set of original recordings is available on itunes and www.corason.com[14]

"La petenera," [5.2] Version from Tixtla performed by Conjunto Los Azohuastles

Ten cuidado cuando vueles
del palo a la guacamaya
para que de mi te acuerdes
por donde quiera que vayas.

Dicen que la petenera
es una mujer bonita
que se va a bañar de tarde
y viene a la mañanita.

Ay, soledad,
soledad de aquél que fue
a darle agua a su caballo
que se le moría de sed.

Dicen que la petenera
es una mujer honrada
que se va a lavar de tarde
y que viene a la madrugada.

Ay, soledad,
soledad de cerro en cerro,
todos tienen sus amores
y a mí que me muerda un perro.

Dicen que la petenera
es una santa mujer
que se va a lavar de tarde
y viene al amanecer.

"La petenera" [5.2] Version from Tixtla performed by Conjunto Los Azohuastles

Be careful when you fly
From the perch to the macaw
So that you remember me
Whenever you may go

They say that the petenera
Is a pretty maid.
Who goes to bathe in the afternoon
And returns in the early morning

Oh, solitude,
Solitude of the one that went
to water his horse
That was dying of thirst

They say that the petenera
Is an honest maid,
Who goes to wash in the afternoon
And returns at the break of day.

Oh, solitude,
Solitude from hill to hill,
Everyone has a sweetheart
And here am I, all alone.

They say that the petenera
Is a saintly maid.
Who goes to wash in the afternoon
But returns at the break of day.

Ay, soledad, soledad que así decía, regálame un vaso de agua que me muero de sequía.	Oh, solitude, Solitude that said like this; Give me a glass of water, For my throat is parched.
Dicen que la petenera en una mujer bonita que se va a lavar de tarde y viene a la mañanita.	They say that the petenera Is a pretty maid. Who goes to wash in the afternoon And returns at the break of day.
Ay, soledad, soledad de aquel que fue a darle agua a su caballo que se le moría de sed.	Oh, solitude, Solitude of the one who went To water his horse That was dying of thirst
A orillas de un camposanto yo vide una calavera con su cigarro en la boca cantando la petenera.	In the corner of a graveyard A skull I did behold. With cigarette in mouth singing the petenera.
Ay, soledad, soledad del otro lado, vale más torear un toro y no un viejo alborotado.	Oh, solitude, Solitude of the world beyond, It's better to fight a bull Than a lusty old man.

"La petenera" [5.3] as performed by Trío Cantores de la Huasteca	**"La petenera" [5.3] as performed by Trío Cantores de la Huasteca**
Dicen que el agua salada tiene varias seducciones, [2x] la cosa está comprobada ay la lai, la la la la que mantiene a tiburones y a la sirenas encantadas.	They say that salty water has various seductions One thing is certain Ay la lay, la la la la That it maintains sharks And enchanted mermaids too
La sirena de la mar me dicen que es muy bonita, [2x] yo la quisiera encontrar ay, la lai, la la la la y besarle su boquita pero como es animal no se puede naditita.	The mermaid of the ocean Is very beautiful, so they say I would love to find her Ay la lay, la la la la And kiss her little mouth But because she is an animal Nothing, nothing can I do.
Pescador y marinero ha sido mi profesión, [2x] conozco al pescado mero ay la lay, la la la la también conozco al salmón ese no cae con anzuelo solamente con arpón.	Fisherman and sailor Has been my profession I know the sea-bass fish Ay la lay, la la la la I know the salmon too That one does not bite the bait It can only be harpooned

Figure 5.6
Lyrics for "La petenera" [5.3] as performed by Trío Cantores de la Huasteca. Lyrics from *Antología del Son de México*, courtesy of Discos Corasón SA. The three-volume set of original recordings is available on itunes and www.corason.com[15]

Seis años y un mes anduve	Six years and a month I roamed
de marinero en el mar, [2x]	As a sailor on the sea
por una razón que tuve	For one reason that I had
ay, la lay, la la la la	Ay, la lay, la la la la
que tú te ibas a embarcar	That you were going to embark
en una preciosa nube	On one of those lovely clouds
de las que bajan al mar.	That descend upon the sea

ADDITIONAL REGIONAL TYPES OF *SON*

Now that you have an initial appreciation for the variety of historical and regional approaches through an exploration of the petenera as song and type, we will move to a review of several other regional traditions of *son* with the aim of deepening your perception of the variety of practice. These regional and literary practices may be traced to legacies of the vice-regal era before Independence, but the bulk of the regional repertories and practices still cultivated today took shape in the nineteenth century. Thus the emphasis in this section lies more on learning to recognize and appreciate distinct regional customs than on maintaining a strict chronological sequence.

Son istmeño

You may recall our earlier of *son* in previous units. "La Sandunga" [2.2] represents one of the most celebrated of songs from the tradition of *son istmeño*. We have also discussed the important role that wind band music instruments play in civic and community celebrations in Oaxaca and neighboring Chiapas. These bands often play sones. The marimba is another important instrument for the performance of son istmeño, also known as sones de marimba. Almost as famous as the marimba as symbol of the region are the fantasy wood carvings, known as *alebrijes*, created by artisans in Oaxaca for export and trade. Figure 5.7 shows a wood carving of animals playing a marimba. In real life multiple musicians do indeed play on a single marimba in a similar manner.

🎧
5.4
Listening to "La petrona" performed by Milo Cortés's Marimba Dance Band, recorded in Juchitán, in the state of Oaxaca in 1972 by Henrietta Yurchenco and her son Peter Yurchenco.[16]

"La petrona" offers another example of son istmeño and illustrates a preference for incorporating the marimba into instrumental ensembles in this region of Mexico. This purely instrumental rendition falls into several sections. We may use the example as an opportunity to examine the treatment of musical form, which here alternates *zapateado* (stomping

dance) sections for the full ensemble with sections featuring solo instruments rather than singers. Yurchenco (1976) describes the already archaic choreography in detail, noting that Section 1 highlights the fancy footwork of the male dancers, with music played by the entire band. Section 2 is a trumpet solo to which a single couple might dance. The man dances around the woman, approaching and retreating, while she dances slowly, holding one end of her voluminous skirt to her chest, alternating sides and hands. The meter alternates between 3/4 and 6/8. Section 3 is another zapateado, and as in the first, attention goes to the footwork of the men. Section 4 is a saxophone solo. In the choreography the female dancers feign indifference but then display growing interest in the male dancers. In Section 5, the zapateado, again featuring the fancy footwork of the men, returns. Section 6, is a marimba solo where couples dance, with some improvisation. Section 7 is a final zapateado for all participants that closes with a characteristic series of descending scales passages.

The regions in the states of Oaxaca and Chiapas where son istmeño is cultivated are those with the greatest concentration of indigenous people who still speak native languages, predominantly Náhuatl, Mixtec, and Zapotec. Resistance to the Spanish language manifests itself in the sones that omit Castillian verse and instead favor instruments alone, although important exceptions exist, such as the sones abajeños and pirekuas, genres from the state of Michoacán where indigenous musicians combine verses in Spanish and Purépecha. Nonetheless, the early adaptation of European instrumental practices by indigenous communities, provided native musicians the option for letting musical sound speak for them in place of words. We have already noted the importance of the wind band tradition in Oaxaca, but the marimba is also viewed as both regional and indigenous. Oaxaca's close proximity to Guatemala and Central America, where the Mayan people have long viewed the marimba as a native instrument,[17] has also influenced this preference.

Figure 5.8
Istmeño marimba group with singer María Luisa Leyto Matanche (b. 1943), c.1960(?). Creative Commons License.

Although 5.4 is purely instrumental, the lyrics associated with "La petrona" indicate that it is yet another variant of "La petenera."[18]

We will discuss film music in a future chapter, but it is worth noting here that composers favored the son istmeño in early Mexican film, such as *Águila o sol* (1937) or *La Zandunga* (1938). We might say that these composers were engaged in what Hobsbawm (1980) would label "inventing tradition," or at least they were reinventing it, to underscore the political agenda of post-revolutionary social reformers. According to historian Zahra Moss (2012), Oaxaca and its indigenous people became important emblems of post-revolutionary conceptions of national identity. Displays of the archaeological treasures of Monte Albán between 1922 and 1933 helped "prime the public" for an interest in the indigenous people of Oaxaca and aided national initiatives to draw upon regional and indigenous identities to establish the post-revolutionary Mexican identity.

Son jarocho

Son jarocho, one of the most celebrated styles of *son*, comes from the southern Gulf Coast region of Mexico. The term *jarocho* was once a derogatory slang term for a peasant from the Veracruz region. The term no longer carries that stigma but its etymology reminds us that rural people and their customs were often snubbed by city folk. Like the other forms of *son*, the roots of son jarocho date back to the colonial period, but the establishment of a centralized recording industry in Mexico in the twentieth century brought new attention to regional music forms as profitable commodities. Today a growing number of modern urban musicians enjoy performing son jarocho, giving it a niche status all its own (Sheehy 1999:65). In the United States, son jarocho performance and instruction serve as a catalyst for artistic and political activism, particularly in California and in Midwest cities like Chicago (see Balcomb 2012; González 2011; Loza 1992). In addition to experimenting with modern approaches, revivalists have promoted a return to older techniques and as a result have led to a professionalization of folkloric practice (Kohl 2010).

In recent years, musicians have been promoting the legacy of African contributions to the development of son jarocho, using the genre to speak out against an official practice of obscuring the African roots of Mexican identity (González 2010). From the 1500s to 1900s, the port of Veracruz was one of Mexico's most important trade sites, providing important links to trade with the Caribbean islands and passage to Spain and the rest of the world. Veracruz was also a principal center during the colonial era for the importation of slaves from Africa. Many Africans passed first through Cuba or other Caribbean sites before arriving in Mexico. As a result, music from Veracruz reflects influences from both Caribbean and African practices. The blend is particularly evident in the complex rhythms that distinguish the son jarocho from other types of *son*.

One of the most famous examples of the son jarocho is the song "La bamba," made world famous in 1958 in an early rock version performed by Ritchie Valens, and later by the Los Angeles based group Los Lobos whose version reached number one on recording industry charts in the United States, and the UK in 1987.

Listening to "La bamba" as performed by José Gutiérrez and Los Hermanos Ochoa in 2003.[19]

5.5

Since the jarocho tradition prizes improvisation, the lyrics for "La bamba" vary from performance to performance.[20] However, all performances include some of the traditional verses that open by stating the need for grace in dancing the bamba, and exhortations for the rising intensity of the stomping dance (*arriba* literally means "up"). In the second verse, the singer insists he is not a sailor ("yo no soy marinero") but is instead a captain, an important distinction of status anywhere, but particularly so in a seaport city.

Listening to jarocho showman Andrés Huesca's rendition of "La bamba."
Source: *Bicentenarario, 200 Años de la Historia de la Música en México*[21]

5.6

Daniel Sheehy, an expert on the history of the son jarocho, writes that in the 1940s harpist Andrés Huesca adapted the jarocho style of performance to attract new listeners on radio, film, and recording. Instead of sitting at a smaller *arpa jarocha*, he used a larger harp and stood while playing. He liked to play very fast to dazzle his listeners with his technique. Huesca inspired other musicians, such as Lino Chávez, who moved from Veracruz to Mexico City to play with a group of musicians who called themselves Los Costeños, to create an urban style of jarocho that enjoyed considerable commercial popularity (Sheehy 1999).

How might a listener distinguish son jarocho from other types of *son*? We've already noted the fast-paced, complex rhythms associated with this style. Another distinctive characteristic of the folkloric son jarocho lies in the instrumentation. Sheehy (1999) describes the classic ensemble as having one or two harps, accompanied by two guitar-like instruments: the *jarana jarocha* (a thin-bodied instrument with ten strings, eight as double courses, and two as single strings) and the *requinto* (four–five stringed bass version of the jarana, commonly tuned ADGc, or EADGc). Although in the past musicians in Veracruz included several sizes of jaranas, including a very small jarana with five strings called the *mosquito*, and used the violin as well, the iconic jarocho trio does *not* include the violin. Since the 1990s, many performers have worked to revitalize older practices of son jarocho, connecting the renewal to contemporary issues such as racial politics and civic justice, discussed later. The result is that in the first decades of the twenty-first century, the instrumentation for son jarocho now varies widely. Raquel Paraíso (2014) notes that the violin is used in the Tuxtlas area of Veracruz and many groups use several sizes of jaranas and one (or two) requintos. There and in the United States, jarocho musicians often use a *marimbol* (plucked resonator box), *quijadas* (donkey jawbones), and a *cajón* as a new statement of Africanness. The harp, is being reintroduced, but the older smaller harp and musicians play it sitting down.

🎧
5.7

Listening to a demonstration of *jarana maniqueos*, recorded by Daniel Sheehy (1991).

The jarana plays important strumming patterns known as *maniqueos* or *mánicos* that accentuate either rhythmic units of two beats or three beats, shifting the metric feel between compound duple and triple meter (recall Chapter 2). Listen to 5.7 for examples of the part played by the jarana.

The harmonies of son jarocho follow a very predictable and repetitive sequence marking both a change of harmony and rhythmic measure or *compás*. This pattern repeats cyclically, creating a kind of groove that is characteristic of African music, but which is also prominent in the harmonic schema for a wide variety of regional sones. Figure 5.9 offers a schematic representation of the chord changes, indicated with Roman numerals, against the fundamental pulse marked by the strumming of jarana player. The asterisk indicates a strong accent. The compás may be felt as four sets of 6 beats. (Compare Figs 5.9 and 5.15 for a deeper understanding of the rhythmic feel and organization.)

Figure 5.9
Schema of standard harmonic pattern for son jarocho. Adapted from Daniel Sheehy, "Music of Mariachi and Música Jarocha."

I		IV		V7			
* ··	* ··	* ··	* ··	* ··	* ··	* ··	* ··

Jarocho singing typically includes an exchange between singers: a leader, called the *pregonero* (the caller) and one or more singers who respond as a *coro*, or chorus. While the coro repeats the line of the pregonero, he has time to think of the next clever line. As we observed with sones from the Costa Chica, this give-and-take is common in traditions influenced by African music.

The lyrics follow customary formats that we have also seen in earlier examples, including a welcoming statement, a sequence of verses alternating with instrumental interludes, and a closing farewell statement in which the singer may include a reference to himself or the ensemble, called a *despedida*. We will see a similar structure when we explore the *corrido* in Chapter 8.

> Listening to "El siquisirí," performed by José Gutiérrez and Los Hermanos Ochoa in 2003.[22]

🎧 5.8

"El siquisirí" [5.8] offers another example of son jarocho. Compare it to "La bamba." What features do they share? How do they differ? The lyrics appear below. Listen to the jarana part. As you listen, try to perceive the changes in harmony that support the melody and mark the standard compás.

Sones de arpa grande de la Tierra Caliente, the Hot Lands of Michoacán

> Listening to "Son de las naguas blancas" [5.9] performed by Don Tomás André Huato and Don Antioco G., and a demonstration of *arpa cacheteada* [5.10] performed by Timoteo Mireles and Don Tomás André.[24]

🎧 5.9

🎧 5.10

Figure 5.10 (see Plate 7) Son jarocho musicians with an *arpa*, a small jarana (*mosquito*), and a medium jarana (*tercera*). Photo by Janet Sturman (2011).

Figure 5.11
Lyrics to "Siquisirí."
Traditional.[23]
Source: *La Bamba: Sones Jarochos from Veracruz.* Courtesy of Smithsonian Folkways.

"El siquisirí"	"Siquisirí"
Buenas noches señoritas,	Good night young ladies,
muy buenas noches señores.	A very good night sirs
muy buenas noches señores,	A very good night sirs
buenas noches señoritas.	Good night young ladies
A todas las florecitas	To all the little flowers
de rostros cautivadores,	With captivating faces
van las trovas más bonitas	Go the prettiest verses
de este trío de cantadores.	From this trio of singers
¡Ay! que sí, que si, que no,	Ah! yes, ah yes, oh no
qué bella y joven Dulcinea	How beautiful and young is Dulcinea
(¡Ay! que sí, que si, que no)	(Ah! yes, ah yes, oh no)
Por pobre no merecí	Being poor, I don't deserve her
(Ahora sí, mañana no)	(Today yes, tomorrow no)
Como sufre el que desea.	How suffers he who desires
(A la grande tu,	(You with the oldest girl,
y con la chica yo)	I with the youngest one)
Y a la que yo prentendí,	Someone else gets to see
otro es el que la chiquea,	The girl I courted
no necesita de mí.	She doesn't care for me.
Qué bonito es el fandango	How beautiful is the fandango
cuando el arpa lo acompaña	When the harp accompanies it
bajo la sombra de un mango	Under the shade of a mango tree
y al olor que llega a caña,	And the smell of sugarcane
hay que ponerse muy chango	One must be very agile
para zapatear con maña.	To dance with flair.
Que ni la luna en su apogeo	Neither the moon at its apogee
ni el sol tan capacitado	Nor the sun so powerful
satisfacen los deseos	Satisfies one's desires
como el que llega a Alvarado,	Like he who arrives in Alvarado
del arpa se oye el trineo	From the harp one hears the melody
del "Siquisirí" afamado.	of the famed "Siquisiri."
Desde Alvarado portamos	From Alvarado we bring
un saludo muy decente,	A very kind greeting
lo hacemos galantemente	We do it gallantly
porque muy pronto nos vamos,	Because we are leaving soon
a todos los concurrentes	To all who are present
las buenas noches les damos.	We wish a very good night.
Que no hay muchacha que se fea	No woman is ugly
cuando viste de jarocha	When she is dressed like a jarocha
y más cuando zapatea.	And even more so when dancing
Con tu gracia de morocha	With your Moorish [dark] grace
la tarima se cimbra,	The dance stage makes you shine
y esta es mi tierra jarocha.	And this is my jarocho land.

The harp is important to more than one region in Mexico. The north-west region of Guerrero and its borders with the states of Michoacán and Mexico is the home of *son calenteño*, meaning "warm" *son*. It is also called *son de arpa grande* because many of the performing ensembles use a big harp. The *calenteño* harp has a larger sound chamber than the traditional arpa jarocha. Calenteño harpists provide a foundation to the ensemble and do not take the same kind of solo melodic role enjoyed by jarocho harpists. Other instruments used by calenteño musicians are the *guitarra de golpe* (literally, "percussive guitar," which supplies a rhythmic or percussive strumming part to the music), the vihuela, and one or two violins. The drum-like sounds that you hear in the ensemble in 5.9 results from one of the musicians rapping with his hands on the soundboard of the harp while the harpist plays the strings. This technique is known as *tamborear*, the result of that technique is called tamboreada, also referred to as *arpa cacheteada*, and this practice is illustrated solo in 5.10. With the complete ensemble the tamboreada produces an exciting, jubilant sound, well-suited for celebratory events. Raquel Paraíso documents this dynamic at a gathering of musicians and dancers in a park in Zicuirán (Huracán, Michoacán), entertaining people as they wait for a concert to honor two veteran folk violinists, Leandro Corona (99 years old) and José Jiménez (87 years old) in her blog *Ecos del sonar* (see Fig. 5.12).[25]

The vocal lines in son calenteño are customarily delivered by two male singers who favor the high registers of their voice and they often elaborate song lyrics with improvised nonsense syllables in a practice known as *jaranear*, meaning "to make merry" (Sheehy 1999). The lyrics in Figure 5.13 illustrate the integration of nonsense syllables ("tira la la") in the sung verse. Calenteño musicians, like those in the Balsas region, also play other genres of dance music including *jarabes*, *minuetes*, and *valonas*.

**Figure 5.12
(see Plate 8)**
Photo of arpa
cacheteada ensemble.
Photo courtesy of
Raquel Paraíso.

Figure 5.13
Lyrics for "Las naguas blancas" as performed by Los Marineros de Apatzingán. Lyrics from *Antología del son de México*, courtesy of Discos Corasón SA. The three-volume set of original recordings is available on itunes and www.corason.com[26]

"Las naguas blancas"	"The White Petticoats"
En la torre de un convento me jalé unas naguas blancas con unas piernas adentro. ¿Para qué quiero las naguas? Con las piernas me contento	In the tower of a convent I found a white petticoat With a pair of legs within What do I care for petticoats? The legs will do me fine.
Tira la, la, la Tira la, la, la	Tira la, la, la Tira la, la, la
Arriba de una enramada me jalé unas naguas blancas con unas tiras bordadas	Way up in a bower I found a white petticoat Laced with ribbons
Tira, la, la, la Tira la, la, la	Tira, la, la, la Tira la, la, la

Son guerrerense, from the *Tierra caliente* of Guerrero

Like son calenteño, the root practice of *son guerrerense* is from the state of Guerrero and the Río Balsas region of adjoining Michoacán, also from the Tierra Caliente. The hot lands produced several distinct styles of sones, distinguished in part by customs of instrumentation. An attentive listener will hear that the *guerrerense* ensemble includes violin (one or two), guitars (one or two six-stringed guitars, although in the past a locally made "big-bellied" guitar called the *panzona* was employed), and a *tamborita*, a small double-headed side drum (membranophone). Traditionally, only sones from Guerrero and Tabasco use a separate drum. The traditional repertory in Guerrero includes *gustos*, which are played and sung at a slower tempo.

5.11

Listening to "El gusto federal" performed by violinist Juan Reynoso. Source: *Juan Reynoso: The Paganini of the Hot Lands*.[27]

"El gusto federal," is a traditional song that extols the bravery of the forces who fought in the battle to end the French intervention in 1866 (see Chapter 8) and thus differs from the many gustos that celebrate the virtues of love and praise the beauty of the region. It is a composed song and the verses are not improvised with the kind of freedom we observed in the son jarocho or son huasteco, however variations exist. Folklorists debate who composed the first set of verses for this song. Some attribute the lyrics to one of the leaders of the republican resistance, the military general Vicente Riva Palacio (1832–1896), others to Juan Bartolo Tavira (1847–1929), a harpist who as a young man fought as a soldier in the same war. Both men were heroes from the Hot Lands. "El gusto federal" acquired anthem-like status in the state of Guerrero, and later across the country, becoming so popular that virtually all folkloric dance troupes and musicians learn to perform it.[28] Nonetheless, there are as many versions of the song as there are groups who perform it.

The flexibility of *son* performance can be illustrated in a report shared on an internet blog in 2010. A musician from Guerrero relates how once an administrative aide from the ministry of culture, who was helping to bring together musicians from the Tierra Caliente for a festival to honor the legendary violinist Juan Reynoso (1912–2006), contacted him. The aide asked him if he could arrange for all the visiting groups to unite at the end of the festival and play "El gusto federal" together. The musician answered that this would not be possible. How, he wondered could he explain to the aide that the musicians from the Hot Lands are not contemporary mariachis? There is no standard style. Each traditional group learns from family members, not in a school or academy. Each family has their own verses, their own intonations, their own improvisations—known as *adornos*, and own interpretations, some so individual that they seem to be different songs. This is the case with many sones and songs that live in the domain of popular memory. We will return to the issue of standardized song versions in the final section of this chapter.

As you listen to "El gusto federal," notice the instrumental musical interludes between the verses.[29] What instrument dominates those interludes? Can you hear the tamborita? What do you suppose is providing the other source of percussive sound in this recording? What are the roles of the instruments: who dominates; can you detect a give-and-take between instruments, instruments and singers, or dancers and instruments?

The best musicians garner great respect for their expertise and dedication to their tradition of *son*. The violinist heard on the recording of "El gusto federal" is Juan Reynoso, known as the "Paganini of the Mexican Hot Lands" because of his great virtuosity. Reynoso was also a revered teacher who in the old manner taught his sons, and many others who came to learn from him, the techniques of playing the old tunes and supporting them with disciplined improvisation.

A RETURN TO *SON HUASTECO—HUAPANGO HUASTECO*

In our review of sample versions of "La petenera" you have already encountered an example of *son huasteco*, but we have not yet discussed the *huapango* dance that animates this music. In son huasteco the choice of melodies is fixed and the emphasis lies on the delivery of elaborate poetry. With the huapango, performance emphasizes dance, and apart from the introduction, both the music and verse are improvised. The most common ensemble is a trio of musicians who sing and play the huapanguera, the *jarana huasteca*, and violin. The word huapango is a term related to fandango meaning dance party. It also refers to the wooden platform used by the dancers (*huapanco* from the Náhuatl *cuahpanco*).

Figure 5.14
Lyrics for "El gusto federal." Source: *Juan Reynoso, The Paganini of the Mexican Hotlands.* Courtesy of Discos Corasón SA.

"El gusto federal"	"The Federal Taste"
Viva Dios que es lo primero	Long live God who is the first
dijo la oficialidad,	it is officially said
viva Dios que es lo primero	Long live God who is the first
dijo la oficialidad.	it is officially said
muera el príncipe extranjero	May the foreign prince die
¡que viva la libertad!,	Long live freedom!
muera el príncipe extranjero	May the foreign prince die
¡que viva la libertad!	Long live freedom!
Bonito San Juan Huetamo	[How] Handsome [was] Saint John Huetamo
cuando la luna salió,	when the moon came out
bonito San Juan Huetamo,	[How] Handsome [was] Saint John Huetamo
cuando la luna salió	when the moon came out
se oyeron los cañonazos,	They heard the cannons
cuando Arteaga lo alistó	When Arteaga enlisted it
se oyeron los cañonazos,	They heard the cannons
que hasta la tierra tembló	until the earth trembled
En el estado de Guerrero	In the state of Guerrero
es muy libre y soberano,	Is very free and sovereign
en el estado de Guerrero	In the state of Guerrero
es muy libre y soberano,	Is very free and sovereign
con el corazón entero	With all my heart
yo digo a mi hermano	I say to my brother
dile adiós en las alturas	Tell him goodbye in the heights
del pueblo de Huetamo.	of the town of Huetamo
Santa Anna dijo en el puerto	Santa Anna said in the port
cuando ya se iba embarcar,	when he was going to embark
Santa Anna dijo en el puerto	Santa Anna said in the port
cuando ya se iba embarcar	when he was going to embark
ha dicho lo que no es cierto:	He said what is not true:
ahora acabarán de hablar,	Now they will stop talking,
ahí les dejo el gallo muerto,	Here I leave you the dead rooster
acábenlo de pelar.	so that you can finish plucking it

5.2

Viewing the Huapango huasteco "El miramar" [5.2].[30]

Observe the video example of a performance of "El miramar" from a huapango contest in held in the state of Tamualipas and focus on the dancers. Notice that there are two types of dance steps, the quiet steps performed while the singers deliver their verses, and the loud stomping steps performed during the vigorous instrumental interludes. Start with the zapateado for the interlude: feel the six beats per measure (set sets of triplets), and step your foot on each beat, alternate steps and stomping

Figure 5.15
Rhythms and dance
steps for Huapango.

Stomping steps, during instrumental interludes

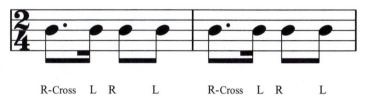

More gentle toe-cross step, during sung verses

your heel on the first of each triplet (see Fig. 5.15). During the verse, cross your right in front of the left, then alternate your feet, in a slow, quick, slow, slow, pattern (see Fig. 5.15).

Each region in the Huasteca has its own repertory of dance songs. "El miramar" is one of the classic huapangos associated with Tamaulipas. The dancers are from Veracruz and wear the traditional white garments associated with that state, but the competition is being held in Tamaulipas. The poetic verses of many huapangos refer to the city of Tampico in the state of Tamaulipas. Juan J. Aguilar León claims that is because "Tampico is to huapango what New Orleans is to jazz"; people and styles came from all over to mix together in those cities and produce a distinct new sound (Aguilar León 2000:134). Musicians from other cities in the Huasteca might make similar claims, pointing to the huapangos that refer to Tepetzintla, Veracruz, Huejutla, and Chicontepec, reminding us of how the tradition fostered pride not only in regional, but also in specific local, identities.

REGIONAL *SON* AND THE RISE OF THE MARIACHI

While this chapter opens with a reflection on colonial legacies, linking them to various moments in history and to the present, the historical development of the *son* as Mexican music gained momentum in the nineteenth century, during the era of Independence that began in 1821. We will address that era directly in Chapter 6. Although many of the audio examples we have examined in our study of regional *son* represent efforts to preserve or resurrect historic practice, they nonetheless also represent the practice of *son* in the twentieth century. In this section we will again cross time frames as we look at one of the more popular trajectories of the *son*, its incorporation into the modern mariachi tradition.

SON JALISCIENSE AND *SON ABAJEÑO*

Historians contend that the sones from Jalisco and the western region of Mexico led most directly to the modern mariachi tradition. Musicians in the northern highlands of Jalisco called themselves mariachis and represented a mestizo and criollo tradition, whereas mariachis in the lowlands (*abajeños*, from *abajo*, meaning below) performed in a distinctive manner separate from those living in the south or along the coast.

There were also indigenous musicians who called themselves mariachis among the Huichol or Wixárika, and Cora tribes. These communities exchanged practices with the Purépecha and Afro-mestizos of Nayarit, Colima, and Michoacán. *Son jalisciense*, as the *son* from Jalisco is known, also bears some similarities with sones from the neighboring states of Zacatecas and Aguascalientes. The repertories of *jalisciense* musicians included a variety of dance genres in addition to sones such as *minuetes, jarabes, jotas, chotis, valses*, and polkas. Distinctions were also cultivated within the jalisciense son repertoire, and there exist many designations for these various types of sones: highland (*alteños, arribeños,* or *serranos*) coastal (*costeños*), plains (*planecos*), lowlands (*abajeño*), with tarima, and with harp (Chamorro 2006).

🎧

5.12

Listening to the *son abajeño* "El tren," performed by the Mariachi Vargas de Tecalitlán in a historic recording made in 1938. Source: *Mariachi Vargas de Tecalitlán. Their First Recordings: 1937–1947.*[31]

The modern invention of the train, portrayed in this *son* was celebrated in a wide range of music composed, beginning in the early nineteenth century and continuing to the present.[32] Audio Example 5.12 features the celebrated Mariachi Vargas de Tecalitlán. Tecalitlán is a village in the southern part of the state of Jalisco, recognized as farming and ranching territory. The original members of Mariachi Vargas formed in 1898 and represented the rural, all-string instrument mariachi format common in that region, dating back at least to the early 1800s. The original group included Gaspar Vargas on *guitarra de golpe* (five-string rhythm guitar), Manuel Mendoza on harp, and Refugio Hernández and Lino Quintero on violin and lead vocals. By 1921, the group replaced one violinist with Don Gaspar's son Silvestre, and added an additional violinist, Nicolás Torres, bringing the group to five members (Clark 1992).

Like other early mariachis from the region, Mariachi Vargas originally wore simple country clothing. For their first performance tour to the United States in 1931, Mariachi Vargas wore a uniform inspired by typical Indian dress of loose fitting pants and shirt made of white cotton, a belt of red sash at the waist, straw sombreros and a red bandanna tied at the neck. Shortly after Mariachi Vargas won a competition in Guadalajara, they were invited to travel to Mexico City to perform for the inauguration of President Lázaro Cárdenas in 1934. The president gave the group a position as the official musicians for the Mexico City police department, a post that they held for 20 years, making it possible for Mariachi Vargas to stay in Mexico City and establish themselves as the nation's premier mariachi. You can read more about the history of the mariachi in Daniel Sheehy's book *Mariachi Music in America* (2006).

The *son abajeño* is a genre cultivated by the Purépecha Indians of Michoacán and the Tierra Caliente of west central Mexico (Morales Rivera 1990:14).[33] The name is a reference to the sones played in that lowland region. Like the previous examples, this is music we might hear performed for festivities, family celebrations and dancing, although in the abajeño tradition only men dance the lively stomping steps of the *zapateo*, while women dance more subtle contrasting steps. Abajeño style favors a rapid tempo and lively character.

Early mariachis in this area were mostly string ensembles. The trumpet was added in the 1930s when mariachis began performing for radio and making recordings to represent the nation, and while Mariachi Vargas occasionally played with a guest trumpet player before then, it was not until the 1940s that Don Silvestre Vargas hired trumpeter Miguel Martínez as a regular member of the group.

We can tell from the lyrics that "El tren" is a nineteenth-century *son* composed after 1837 when the first railroad line was established in Mexico, linking Veracruz to Mexico City (Fig. 5.16). In this recording the musicians combine forces to simulate train sounds, particularly evident in the closing instrumental section where we also hear clear shifts in metric accent.

Listening to the *son jaliciense* "La negra," performed by the Mariachi Tapatío. Source: *Mariachi Tapatío de José Marmolejo "El Auténtico."*[34]

5.13

Another historic performance of a song that has come to represent son jaliciense, elements of abajeño style, and early modern mariachi can be heard in Audio Example 5.13 with Mariachi Tapatío's performance of the iconic *son* "La negra."[35] The word *tapatío* refers to Guadalajara, the capital of Jalisco and the home of the group's founder Francisco Marmolejo. In 1922 Francisco moved to Mexico City and began playing vihuela with the mariachi of his uncle Cirilo Marmolejo, a founder of Mariachi Coculense, the first mariachi to perform in Mexico City. While in Mexico City, Francisco Marmolejo formed his own group, Mariachi Tapatío, which enjoyed the patronage of the wealthy Eusebio Acosta Velazco, owner of the Autobuses de Occidente bus line. Mr. Acosta would host magnificent fiestas in his home and for the city, paying Mariachi Tapatío to provide the music.

Tapatío was one of the first mariachis to include trumpet, and we can hear trumpeter Jesús Salazar in this 1925 recorded performance. The other

Figure 5.16
Lyrics for "El tren."
Traditional, Public
Domain.

"El tren"	"The Train"
Oigan señores el tren, oigan el tren caminar que lejos me va llevando.	Listen Gentlemen to the train Listen to the train moving That is taking me far away
Oigan los silbidos que echa cuando ya va caminando.	Listen to the whistle it makes When it is running
Oigan y oigan señores, oigan el tren caminar	Listen and listen gentlemen Listen to the train moving
el que se lleva a los hombres al otro lado del mar	It carries men To the other side of the sea
Al pasar por Zapotiltic me dijo una bonita: qué dice señor, ¿me lleva? ya traigo mi maletita.	While passing through Zapotiltic A pretty girl said to me: Sir, will you take me with you? I'm already carrying my suitcase
Señora no me la llevo porque tengo a quien llevar.	No, miss, I can't take you Because I already have someone to bring
Hasta lloraba la ingrata Porque se quería enganchar	The ingrate even cried Because she wanted to hook up

instruments in the ensemble are two violins, two vihuelas, and one *guitarrón* (bass guitar). Notice that there are no guitars in this early mariachi and that the singers repeat and recombine the verses in the song as they alternate with long instrumental passages designed to encourage dance.

La negra	The Black Girl
Cuándo me traes a mi negra que la quiero ver aquí, con su rebozo de seda que le traje de Tepic.	When will you bring me to my black girl For I want to see her here With her silk shawl That I brought her from Tepic
Negrita de mis pesares ojos de papel volando, a todos diles que sí pero no les digas cuándo, así me dijiste a mí, por eso vivo penando	Little black girl of my grief Eyes like flying paper You tell everyone yes But you don't tell them when That's what you told me For that I am suffering

Figure 5.17
Lyrics for "La negra."
Traditional, Public
Domain.

MARIACHI INSTRUMENTS

The guitarrón heard in "La negra" [5.13] is essentially an acoustic bass guitar, and can be considered to be the first horizontal string bass. The modern guitarrón has six nylon strings, instead of ones made from animal gut as in the past. It is tuned A'-D-G-c-e-A.[36] Historians have located instruments called *guitarrones* in seventeenth-century Spain (Contreras Arias 1988:101). It shares the rounded back of the vihuela, its partner harmony and rhythm instrument. The vihuela (aka Mexican vihuela, as opposed to the historic Spanish vihuela) is a small guitar with five strings that produces a high-pitched sound. The strings are tuned A-d-g-B-e. The vihuela is normally smaller than the requinto guitar, but like a guitarrón, the vihuela also has a vaulted back. This deep, convex-curved body of the vihuela helps to amplify its tone. The rounded back links this instrument to its ancestor, the Arabic *ud* (lute). The vihuela, like the classical acoustic guitar, has nylon strings. However, three of the strings are tuned up one octave in order to produce a higher-pitched sound.

The use of the requinto guitar in classic mariachi reflects the synthesis of regional styles that took place in the first half of the twentieth century as performers from various regions of the country moved to Mexico City and began performing in mariachis promoted to represent the entire nation. The requinto is a small acoustic guitar with six nylon strings tuned at A-D-G-c-e-a. It is generally about 15–20 percent smaller than a standard acoustic guitar and has a deeper body. Requinto players use a pick to strum the strings when performing.

JÁUREGUI'S HISTORY OF MARIACHI THROUGH "LA NEGRA"

Jesús Jáuregui, author of *El Mariachi, Símbolo de México* (1990), has traced the origins of the *son* "La negra" in a manner that allows us to gain a feeling for the complex ways that musicians adapted the rural mariachi tradition for urban practice, a transformation that led to mariachi's iconic status representing Mexico to the world (Jáuregui 2010). Some of his questions concern the lyrics of "La negra" and their structure; others concern matters of origin and representation. Like him, we might ask: What is the importance of the reference in the opening *cuarteta* (four-line verse) to *rebozos de seda* (silk shawls) from Tepic? Was "La negra" originally a *son* from Jalisco, or is its history more complicated? If not, why has it become recognized as a quintessential example of son jaliciense, and if so, why don't we find it in some of the oldest song collections from that region? Why are there so many recorded variants of the lyrics prior to 1940? How did "La negra" come to represent the very tradition of mariachi, and even Mexico as a nation?

To answer such questions, Jáuregui examined printed, recorded, and archival sources, and interviewed musicians who performed with various mariachis in the first decades of the twentieth century. Their recollections challenge some of the cherished myths about the development of the mariachi and illustrate the process of give-and-take practiced by working mariachis as they adapted their rural experience to the demands of working in Mexico City.

We cannot know for certain when "La negra" first arose as a *son* performed by mariachis. In trying to trace the song's origins, Jáuregui finds that the version documented by Higinio Vázquez Santa Ana in his distinguished 1925 collection of sones from Michoacán, Guerrero, and Guanajuato does not come from Jalisco nor does not it match the version recorded by Mariachi Vargas. It does not correspond to the one recorded in 1925 by Mariachi Coculense, nor the one performed by the once famous Mariachi Concho Andrade, the first group to perform as a resident mariachi in the, now legendary (and still operating), cantina El Tenampa in Mexico City's Plaza Garibaldi during the 1920s. In short, before the 1930s there were many versions and they reflect the custom of acquiring, exchanging, and adapting songs across regions.

5.14

Listening to *Sones de Mariachi* by Blas Galindo (1940) performed by the Orquesta Sinfonica de Xalapa, Herrera de Fuentes, conductor.[37]

The Mexican composer Blas Galindo (1910–1993) is one of the musicians interviewed by Jáuregui. Galindo's 1940 composition *Sones de Mariachi*[38] incorporated "La negra" as one of three folk songs representing the nation. The others were "El zopilote" (The Vulture) and "Los cuatro reales" (The Four Coins).[39] Galindo was a practicing mariachi well before the tradition took root in the nation's capital.

Galindo grew up in San Gabriel, Jalisco, a city later renamed for former president Venustiano Carranza and one of the cities viewed as the cradle of the modern mariachi tradition. As a child Galindo sang in the church choir, studied organ and *solfege* (sight singing), played guitar, and performed with mariachis. He remembers that

> in my town everyone was a musician and since there was no television or radio in those days, in the evenings we would gather to make music . . . I remember people calling to me from the streets to "grab my guitar and come play."
>
> (Jáuregui 2010:272)

Of course not all players were equally skilled at remembering lyrics or realizing a melody, and despite their best efforts this also led to variants. Galindo's memories help us understand that spontaneous music-making was part of rural music life and formed the heart of regional practice. Music played a central role in the lives of people around the nation. Maintaining that place represents a signature achievement for Mexicans wherever they live, past and present.

Galindo recalls how the mariachi tradition stemmed from exchange across regions and was rooted in performance of sones.

> Mariachi can be traced to the central region of Mexico defined by the states Michoacán, Nayarit, Jalisco, Colima. For many years people have claimed the origin of mariachi in Cocula, Guadalajara because this is where the two groups who traveled from there to Mexico City were from, but now we know that the music corresponded to the entire region.
>
> The music performed by these [regional] ensembles was called *son*. Typically, musicians sung while playing, other times they alternated singing and playing. There could exist different versions of the same song in different sites of the same region. Good mariachis distinguished a song according to the region. Thus the song "El toro," as it is known in Jalisco, is known as "La vaquilla" in Nayarit. The song that people in Michoacán know as "La Morena" is known as "La negra" in Jalisco. . . . The basic melodies are the same, but there may be differences that we can attribute to the restlessness of the musicians and to their inability to exactly duplicate each other's songs.
>
> (Jáuregui 2010:285)

Equating "La negra" with "La morena" reminds us that the lyric may address as easily a dark-haired, dark-eyed beauty, as a dark-skinned girl.

Another venerable mariachi, Blas Martínez Panduro (b. 1913), who performed with Mariachi Vargas before their move to Mexico City, recalls "La negra" as a piece he and his bandmates learned from musicians while performing in the state of Colima (Járegui 2010:288). He also recalls melodic and rhythmic varieties before the version most commonly heard today became an imposed standard.

The existence of a set of "La negra" variants and musical exchange should not surprise us. In this chapter we have already discussed the wide range of performance traditions associated with the *son*. Before radio, film, and recording facilitated the spread of music freely across geographic boundaries, local musicians took special pride in acquiring songs they learned while traveling, or from visitors, and in adapting those pieces to the tastes and conventions of listeners in their home regions. Many hands and voices contributed to these distinct lines of practice in both lyrics and music realization.

By challenging the assumption that "La negra" originated in Jalisco, Jáuregui also challenges the common claim that Jalisco was the single geographical birthplace of mariachi. His research confirms that the roots of modern mariachi lie in a blend of several traditions from central and west central Mexico. The modern mariachi also reflects the process of transforming regional practices to suit the cosmopolitan needs of performance in Mexico City and distribution via recordings, radio, and film. Instrumentation that once identified rural practices changed in urban practice. Blas Galindo explains that the mariachis of his youth did not use trumpet nor did many include other instruments that we now consider essential to the modern mariachi.

> The mariachi that I knew was all strings: one or two violins, generally one, vihuela, the "panzona" (big belly) guitar, today forgotten, and the harp. There was no guitarrón. In the harp, one hand played against the beat and the other provided the bass line. In Apatzingán, in the Hot Lands, they played on the harp box.
>
> (Jáuregui 2010:272)

The standardization of lyrics was another result of modern urban perspectives on the mariachi. Jáuregui suggests that the two canonic stanzas of "La negra" likely arose from different traditions, each one representing a longer set of verses and poetic practice. The *cuarteta* (the four-line verse) that opens the song likely represents one line of influence and contrasts in structure, tone and, inference with the *sextilla* (six-line stanza) that closes the song. Over time, mariachis combined and condensed the stanzas to make a shorter song in order to respond to the economic realities of the developing mariachi tradition in urban venues.

Don Blas Martínez Panduro (b. 1913), harpist and multi-instrumentalist famed for his long association with Mariachi Vargas, confirms this view, observing that the lyrics associated with the *son* "La negra" today are the same as what he learned in the 1930s. He explains: "We discarded a section and made it shorter to more quickly earn money" (Jáuregui 2012:289). The lengthy recitations appropriate for rural gatherings prior did not work well for musicians who were paid by the song in urban restaurants and other settings where patrons were far more mobile.

The meanings associated with the reference in the cuarteta to *rebozos de seda* (silk shawls) from Tepic, a port city in Nayarit, are equally significant. Tepic was an important site of international maritime commerce as well as home to two major textile factories during the nineteenth century. Silk shawls, once imported from China via the Philippines, were later manufactured locally. The prominent reference to the rebozo, links the song to the era of Independence after 1821, when silk shawls were no longer worn exclusively by elite women but had become a fashion standard for women of all ages and social classes, worn even while dancing, during which they might be skillfully employed in the choreography. Retaining this reference not only links the song to the history of the nation, but it also evokes the visual image of the garment that now stands as a symbol of Mexican femininity and national pride.

A final step in establishing the standard version of "La negra," occurred when Mariachi Vargas recorded it on a 1958 album devoted to sones jaliscienses and again in 1963, copyrighting the song in the names of Rubén Fuentes and Silvestre Vargas. By that time Mariachi Vargas was already billing itself as the "best mariachi in the world" and Rubén Fuentes served as the master arranger of songs for the group. His arrangements formalized the integration of repertory, instrumentation, and performance techniques that made Mariachi Vargas stand out among modern mariachis.

The story of the first resident trumpeter with Mariachi Vargas, Miguel Martínez Domínguez (b. 1921), further illustrates how the demands of the emerging market for mariachi music influenced the formation of standard practices. When Martínez first came to Mexico City to make his way as a musician, he played with musicians outdoors in the Plaza Garibaldi. He recalls that:

> in the 1930s being able to play mariachi inside the restaurant/bar El Tenampa in the Plaza Garibaldi was ... like performing at Bellas Artes [Mexico City's most elegant concert hall]. ... No more than five groups played in the plaza and only mariachi Concho Andrade played in Tenampa.
> (Jáuregui 2010:289–290)

He remembered how one day, Andrade's trumpeter, "El Pitayo," stayed drunk for a month and Andrade had enough. Don Concho called out to Martínez to come in and help him out. His recollections confirm the versatility required of mariachis, as well as the importance of sones to their repertory.

> We had to learn many sones, all in a day. We played sones as well as popular songs from the cinema, but if someone requested two songs, it was because they had already heard eight sones. A musician who couldn't play sones was not a mariachi.
> (Jáuregui 2010:293)

Competition existed between the mariachis performing during that era, and each had its own style. Initially, Mariachi Tapatío was the most celebrated mariachi on the radio. Martínez recalls that Tapatío had three shows per week on radio XEW while initially Vargas had one only every five days.

Mariachi Pulido was favored by President Lázaro Cárdenas, who gave the members appointments in the Secretariat of Education. They played for school children and for government ceremonies. The appeared on the radio and had many *chambas* (hired performing gigs). One day Martínez was asked to join them. At first he was afraid, because this was a group he had heard on the radio. Then he realized that this was the group he wanted to perform with. They worked during the day and he could continue to perform with other mariachis at night. Once he realized the potential, he grew excited: "I called my mother and told her she could quit ironing" (Jáuregui 2010:294). His experience highlights the real distinctions in mariachi performance conventions.

> With Don Concho in Garibaldi we played the style from Cocula. With El Pulido, what a difference! They were two different worlds. Pulido brought in the Negrete brothers and they knew more sones than Don Concho;

what musicians they were! They were from Jalisco and played violin. Some of these sones we later played in Mariachi Vargas. The style was different from how I had learned with Don Concho. Eventually that seemed too dry to me and that style was forgotten.

(Jáuregui 2010:294)

Martínez's experiences and the history of the song "La negra" neatly illustrate the complex set of factors that influenced the early development of the urban mariachi tradition and its deep connections to the history of the regional *son* in Mexico. All along the way, musicians, audiences, and promoters responded to the changing circumstances of their lives, and to the demands of the marketplace, by selecting from a range of musical resources, and integrating them into a new and vibrant practice.

CONCLUDING REFLECTIONS

The *son* stands at the heart of Mexican identity, embracing history and regional diversity. Modern realizations of sones form a central part of the repertory of contemporary mariachis and the transformation of those sones propelled the mariachi on its rise to iconic status. Despite that important legacy, the *son* retains its value to Mexican musical practice apart from its association with mariachi.

This chapter began with reflections on variant versions of a single *son*, "La petenera," and ended by reflecting on variants of another, "La negra." The first comparison allowed us to explore the roots of the genre, dating from the years prior to Independence to the present, and introduced the concept of individual regional traditions. Jáuregui's research on "La negra" connects musical practice in the era following Independence, when the inventive practice of regional *son* flourished, with the post-revolutionary era. In those first decades of the twentieth century, the practice of regional *son* gave rise to cosmopolitan standards created to unify diverse factions and tastes. In a very real sense, the urban mariachis aimed to unify the many Mexicos into one, even if the integration was uneven, favoring some *son* styles over others.

Radio, recording, and film played an important role in further unifying regional customs into new forms and fortifying standard practices. The influence of these media on Mexican music in general will be addressed in a subsequent chapter, but we cannot overlook how despite the changes prompted by such media, they have also validated older practices. The crystallization of regional practices took place in the 1800s, yet our knowledge of early *son* and rural practice is heavily dependent upon oral history, and local memory. With the exception of the closing examples of historic mariachi sound recordings made in the 1930s, most of the audio examples in this chapter were recorded in the past 50 years. The examples were chosen because they capture the persistence of difference rooted in regional customs, despite inevitable change.

Our closing discussion of the son jalisciense and the early mariachi traditions underscores an overarching point: while each region developed its own customs, techniques, and repertory, in every case the resulting musical practices resulted from an integration of forms and practices exchanged over time and across communities and cultures. It is impossible to speak of a pure *son* style and no region is without influence from another.

While official Mexican policy today recognizes the diversity of regional cultures with pride, this was not always the case. Many urban residents and government officials viewed rural customs as backward and potentially seditious. Separatist sentiments threatened the formation of a strong national union in the years preceding and following Independence. It was not until after the Mexican Revolution that mariachis received government posts and were expected to combine regional music to represent the unity and diversity of Mexico. These efforts transformed the sones of the countryside, attracting new audiences. While the rise of the urban mariachi ostensibly promoted regional music, it did little to promote the careers of local musicians like Juan Reynoso, who directed their artistry towards preserving traditional sones apart from the new mariachi format. Despite new opportunities, the struggle of mariachis to gain respect was a long one. Well-to-do Mexicans often associated mariachis with alcohol and unstable lifestyles and looked down on those musicians. In later chapters we will explore how mariachi performance helped strengthen immigrant communities in the United States and inspired musicians around the world. Linda Ronstadt's 1987 recording *Canciones de mi Padre*, for which she collaborated with Rubén Fuentes of Mariachi Vargas, reached a large crossover audience bringing new enthusiasts to the music.

This chapter links the historical emergence of the contemporary mariachi tradition to the history of the *son*, a vibrant tradition in its own right. The performance traditions of early sones were once influenced by melodies performed by Spanish theatrical orchestras that included violins, guitars, and harp. Musical groups performing *son* were small and generally not known outside of the region from which they came. That reality changed somewhat with the rise of the mariachi and with the rise of the recording industry and radio in the 1930s that provided new, if limited, opportunities for regional musicians to share *son* with larger audiences (Paraíso 2014). We might even say that the practice of sones arranged for orchestra came full circle as the folkloric practice was re-integrated into the formal orchestra with compositions for symphonic orchestra such as Blas Galindo's *Sones de Mariachi*.

The importance of Mexican *son* should not be measured by its connections to historic and contemporary mariachi but by its importance to local communities. There is a tendency to think of folkloric forms as static, but current engagement with *son*, such as the vibrant, transnational, modern son jarocho movements in Los Angeles, Chicago, and Veracruz, or the metal rock band Noesis from Oaxaca that mixes son istmeño with a range of styles, exemplifies the constant transformation—sometimes subtle, other times dramatic—that contemporary performers and participants exact from tradition.[40] We may conclude that living folk traditions, like the *son*, remain dynamic to serve contemporary needs.

CRITICAL THINKING AND DISCUSSION PROMPTS

1. In what ways can we use the *sones regionales* to illustrate cultural, musical, and historical integration? In your answer, contrast sones from two different regions offering details regarding at least sound, concept, and behavior associated with at least two specific musical selections to support your answer.

2. Discuss how the sones regionales influenced the development of the modern mariachi tradition. Offer at least three specific examples to support your points.

3. So iconic is the *son* "La negra" that it was the song chosen to represent the Americas in the 2008 Olympic Ceremony held in Beijing, China. For that performance an all-female mariachi performed and they altered the verse citing the rebozo to credit its source from Peking, not Tepic. Find another recording of "La negra" and compare it with 5.15. Pay careful attention to the dates, circumstances, and any adjustments made in the recordings you select. Identify some aspects of mariachi practice and history reflected in your chosen example.

4. Compare mariachi renditions of the *son* "El tren" to one or more of the classical compositions featured in the 2013 concert at the National Train Museum in Puebla (see Note 32).

5. Listen to a local mariachi performance. How do the musicians interact with those who come to hear them? What does that interaction reveal about the status of these musicians and their music? Where do sones fit in their repertory?

6. Review Note 40 and the list of references that close this chapter to identify resources regarding new and contemporary uses of the *son*. Write a summary of one new practice that you find interesting and explain why.

KEY TERMS, PEOPLE, AND PLACES

sesquiáltera	son calenteño
trovador	tamboreado
son istmeño	son guerrerense
son jarocho	Tierra Caliente
son abajeño	gusto
son calentano	huapango

son huasteco	fandango
son jalisciense	corrido
mariachi	despedida
tarima	guitarra de golpe
zapateo/zapateado	vihuela
polka	guitarrón
bolero	huapanguera
arpa cacheteada	jarana
mánico	cuarteta
tapatío	

NOTES

1. There is no simple translation for this song title. Some say that petenera refers to a woman from Paterna (a place in Cádiz, Spain), but this is debated. "The woman from Petén" might seem logical, referring to the ancient Mayan city of Petén, in Guatemala, but this is not a common understanding.
2. www.youtube.com/watch?v=l4nK2ngfsLw
3. Brenda Romero, personal communication, June 13, 2014.
4. Sones are structured around coplas or short poetic rhyming stanzas of four, five, six, or ten lines that are generally octosyllabic, or 8 syllables per line.
5. *Revista de Literaturas Populares*, x/1–2 (2010): 151–182. This particular issue of the Revista is devoted entirely to new research on the *son* and is highly recommended reading. A pdf version is available on the internet at: http://ru.ffyl.unam.mx:8080/jspui/bitstream/10391/2833/1/RLP_X_1-2_2010.pdf
6. Brenda Romero (2002) notes that if one considers the *son* "Una indita en su chinampa" an indita, we can trace the genre back to the theater in Teatro Coliseo in Mexico. Vicente Mendoza traces that song to Puebla in 1880 and confirms its popularity in theatre repertory (Mendoza 1991: 164). Romero points out that inditas as a genre developed in New Mexico as feminine versions of the corrido.
7. Scholars believe that the dance known as the sarabande in Europe originated in New Spain as the zarabanda and was later imported to Europe during the sixteenth century where it inspired variants in Spain, Italy, and France. The earliest printed references to the zarabanda come from Panama in a 1539 poem by Fernando Guzmán Mexia. Diego Durán refers to the zarabanda in Mexico in his *Historia de las Indias de Nueva Espana* (1579). King Philip II banned performance of the zarabanda in Spain in 1583 because the dance was considered too overtly sensual. *Oxford Music Online. Grove Music Online* (accessed September 12, 2012).
8. *Los impossibles*. L'Arpeggiata, Christina Pluhar, conductor, with the Kings Singers. Audio CD, Naïve Records, 2007. The ensemble Arpeggiata, founded

by Christina Pluhar in 1992, experiments with old and new music and is based in Paris.

9. *Antología del son de México. Anthology of Mexican Sones.* Baruj Lieberman, Eduardo Llerenas, and Enrique Ramírez de Arellano. Corasón. Distributed by Rounder Records, Cambridge, MA, 1985. CD2—Tixtla, Costa Chica, Istmo y Veracruz.

10. http://youtu.be/iF3otLcmkkQ

11. *Antología del Son de México. Anthology of Mexican Sones.* CD 3—Huasteca. Mexico City: Corasón. Cambridge, MA: Rounder Records, 1985.

12. See sacred songs with similar text, at: www.scribd.com/doc/19328563/Cancionero-Cristiano.

13. *El Gusto: 40 años de son Huasteco,* introduced by Beto Arcos for The World, PRI. www.theworld.org/2012/02/el-gusto-mexico/

14. *Antología del Son de México. Anthology of Mexican Sones.* CD 3—Huasteca. Mexico City: Corasón. Cambridge, MA: Rounder Records, 1985.

15. *Antología del Son de México. Anthology of Mexican Sones.* CD 3 Huasteca (track 15). Mexico City: Corasón. Cambridge, MA: Rounder Records, 1985.

16. From the album *Mexico South: Traditional Songs and Dances from the Isthmus of Tehuantepec.* Smithsonian-Folkways, 1972.

17. While indigenous residents claim the marimba as original to Southern Mexico and Central America, scholars have concluded that it arrived in the Americas from African slaves brought to the region by the earliest European colonizers. Indigenous people already had a tradition of playing tuned wooden idiophones in the form of slit drums such as the Mayan *tunkul, tun tun* akin to the Náhuatl *teponaztli,* introduced in Chapter 2, and this practice likely facilitated Central American adoption of the African marimba. An excellent and succinct overview of the academic scholarship regarding the passionate debate that still takes place about the provenance of the Central American marimba can be found in Sergio Navarette-Pellicer, *Maya Achi Marimba Music in Guatemala* (Philadelphia, PA: Temple Press, 2005), pp. 70–74.

18. Lyrics for "La petrona" can be found at Aqui Oaxaca—www.aquioaxaca.com/index.php?option=com_content&view=article&id=145&Itemid=72 (accessed August 17, 2014).

19. *La Bamba: Sones Jarochos from Veracruz.* Smithsonian Folkways Recordings, 2003. A video of Los Hermanos Ochoa, along with additional information about the musicians and son jarocho, appears on the Smithsonian Folkways website, at: www.folkways.si.edu/explore_folkways/jose.aspx

20. The lyrics as sung by José Gutiérrez and Los Hermanos Gutiérrez in 5.5 (with English translations) can be found at: www.folkways.si.edu/resources/pdf/40505lyrics.pdf. They illustrate the custom and artistry of the performers in adapting this song for a specific setting.

21. Jésus Escalante and Pablo Dueñas. *Bicentenario, 200 Años de la Historia de la Música en México.* [Bicentennial, 200 Years of Music History in Mexico], includes 4 CDs. Mexico City: Sony Music, 2010.

22. *La Bamba: Sones Jarochos from Veracruz.* Smithsonian Folkways Recordings, 2003 [track 2].

23. Another, more modern treatment of this song and other son jarocho numbers can be found on the album, *Son de Madera,* Smithsonian Folkways (SFW40550), 2009.

24. Various Artists. *Cantos y Música de Michoacán: Testimonios musicales de México.* Instituto Politécnico Nacional. Recording by René Campos. Ediciones Pentagrama, 1998.

25. More pictures and additional discussion appear at: http://raquelparaiso.blogspot.com/2006/12/msica-y-baile-en-zicuirn.html

26. Music, text, and translation from *Antología del Son de Mexico*, 5th ed., Corasón Records MTCD 101/3 (1993).

27. *Juan Reynoso: The Paganini of the Hot Lands*. Historic Recordings 1972–1993. Mexico: Corasón, 2010.

28. Agencias. Las Polémicas de El Gusto Federal. Posted October 7, 2010. http://guerrerocultural87.blogspot.com/2010/10/las-polemicas-de-el-gusto-federal.html (accessed August 17, 2014)

29. Zecerro and Soto Correa (2006:103–104) provide us with an illustration of the variation associated with this *son*. The verses match those in the recorded example except lines four, five, and six which are: Carlota y Maximiliano /vinieron a estos lugares (x2); formaron bastantes tropas/de belgas y australes/pero cual fue su derrota/El Indio Benito Juárez/Cuando el gran Benito Juárez/sentenció el Maximiliano/El cielo cubrió de gloria/a este suelo Mexicano/donde se rendía tributo/al poder republicano. The author's English translation of these verses is: Carlota and Maximilian/came to these places (x2)/Enough troops formed/of Belgians and Austrians/but they were routed by/the Indian, Benito Juárez /When the great Benito Juárez/sentenced Maximilian/The sky covered in glory/ this Mexican ground/where tribute is now [being] paid/to the republican power.

30. Video of Huapango danced Hidalgo style in YouTube collection. http://youtu.be/zTBiDW6vJ6E (accessed August 17, 2014).

31. *Mariachi Vargas de Tecalitlán. Their First Recordings: 1937–1947*. Mexico's Pioneer Mariachis, Vol. 3. Arhoolie, CD, 2004.

32. In 2013 the National Train Museum in Puebla, Mexico presented a concert of this music. It included *Sinfonía Vapor* written in 1869 by Melesio Morales for symphonic orchestra, band and trains; *Música para charlar*, a film score composed in 1938 by Silvestre Revueltas; and *Las cuatro estaciones*, published by Arturo Márquez in 2004, which refers to the important train stations in Aquascalientes, San Luis Potosí, Veracruz, and Puebla. In 2005, the National Train Museum in Puebla commissioned the composition *Máquina férrea (Toccata ferrocarrilera)* (Iron machine; The Ironrail Toccata) from Leonardo Coral (b. 1962), a composer currently living in Mexico City. See www.conaculta.gob.mx/detalle-nota/?id=31109#.U5q4thaCYjU (accessed June 2014).

33. Examples of folkloric *son abajeno* played by Tarascan musicians (the San Lorezo String Ensemble) can be heard on *Music of the Tarascan Indians of Mexico: Music of Michoaca and Mestizo Country*, Smithsonian Folkways, FW04217/AHM 4217 (1970).

34. *Mariachi Tapatío de José Marmolejo "El Auténtico."* Mexico's Pioneer Mariachis, Vol. 2. Arhoolie Folklyric, CD 7012 (1994).

35. While literally this translates to the black girl, in Mexico the terms *negro* and *negra* are often used as terms of endearment, somewhat the equivalent of darling or my dear one.

36. A shorthand for indicating pitch and register uses "c" to denote middle C on the piano. A capital "C" indicates the octave below middle c, while a superscript comma, c' indicates the octave above.

37. *Huapango. Orquesta Sinfonica de Xalapa*, Herrera de Fuentes, conductor. Guild Records (2001).

38. There are several easily accessible recordings of Blas Galindo's *Sones de Mariachi*. Another example can be found at: https://itunes.apple.com/us/podcast/sones-de-mariachi/id547455233?i=118480857&mt=2

39. Blas's original arrangement featured symphonic chamber orchestra and a mariachi. That score did not include trumpet. He later created the more familiar arrangement for full orchestra, with trumpets, heard in 5.14.

40. An examination of new trends in the performance of regional *son* are beyond the scope of this chapter. Interested readers are directed to the scholarship of Hannah Balcomb (2012), Norma González (2009), Randall Kohl (2007, 2010), Raquel Paraíso [González-a] (2014a, 2014b), and Robin Sacolick (forthcoming) for an evaluation of contemporary attitudes towards twenty-first-century performance practices.

FOR REFERENCE AND FURTHER STUDY

Aguilar León, Juan Jesús. 2000. *Los trovadores huastecos en Tamualipas*. Mexico City: Color Box.

Balcomb, Hannah Eliza Alexia. 2012. "Jaraneros and Jarochas: The Meanings of Fandangos and Son Jarocho in Immigrant and Diasporic Performance." Master's thesis, University of California, Riverside, CA. http://escholarship. org/uc/item/81t598fs (accessed January 12, 2015).

Chamorro, J. Arturo. 2006. *Mariachi antiguo, jarabe y son: símbolos compartidos y tradición musical en la identidades jaliscienses*. Guadalajara: Secretaria de Cultura, Gobierno del Estado de Jalisco.

Clark, Jonathan. 1992. Liner Notes. *Mexico's Pioneer Mariachis, Vol. 3: Mariachi Vargas de Tecalitlán (1937–1947)*. Arhoolie Folklyric CD 7015.

Clark, Jonathan. 1993. Liner Notes. *Mexico's Pioneer Mariachis, Vol. 1: Mariachi Coculense "Rodríguez" de Cirilo Mammolejo (1926–1936)*. Arhoolie Folklyric CD 7011.

Clark, Jonathan. 1994. Liner Notes. *Mexico's Pioneer Mariachis, Vol. 2: Mariachi Tapatío de José Marmolejo*. Arhoolie Folklyric CD 7012.

Clark, Jonathan. 1998. Liner Notes. *Mexico's Pioneer Mariachis, Vol.4: Cuarteto Coculense (1908–1909)*. Arhoolie Folklyric CD 7036.

Contreras Arias, Juan Guillermo. 1988. *Atlas of Musical Instruments*. Mexico City: SEP.

Escalante, Jésus and Pablo Dueñas. 2010. *Bicentenarario, 200 Años de la Historia de la Música en México*. [Bicentennial, 200 Years of Music History in Mexico], includes 4 CDs. Mexico City: Sony Music.

González, Anita. 2010. *Afro-Mexico: Dancing between Myth and Reality*. Austin, TX: University of Texas Press.

González, Martha. 2009. "Zapateado Afro-Chicana Fandango Style." In Olga Nájera-Ramírez, et al. (Eds.), *Dancing across Borders*. Chicago, IL: University of Illinois Press, 359–78.

González, Martha. 2011. "Sonic (Trans) Migration of Son Jarocho 'Zapateado': Rhythmic Intention, Metamorphosis, and Manifestation in Fandango and Performance." In Wilfried Raussert and Michelle Habell-Pallán (Eds.), *Cornbread and Cuchifritos*. Tempe, AZ: Bilingual Press, 59–72.

González-Paraíso, Raquel. 2014. "Re-contextualizing Traditions: The Performance of Identity in Festival of Huasteco, Jarocho and Terracalenteño Sones in Mexico." PhD diss., University of Wisconsin.

Hobsbawm, Eric and Ranger, Terence. 1980. *The Invention of Tradition*. Cambridge: Cambridge University Press.

Jáuregui, Jésus. 1990. *El Mariachi, símbolo de México*. Mexico City: Banpais/ INAH.

Jáuregui, Jésus. 2010. "El son mariachero La Negra: de gusto regional independista al aire nacional contemporáneo." *Revista de Literaturas Populares* 10(1–2):270–318.

Koegel, John. 2002. "Music in Ibero-America to 1850: A Historical Survey." *Notes* 59(2):365–367.

Kohl, Randall. 2007. *Ecos de "La Bamba." Una historia etnomusicológica sobre el son jarocho de Veracruz, 1946–1956*. Xalapa: Instituto Veracruzano de la Cultura.

Kohl, Randall. 2010. *Escritos de un náufrago habitual: Ensayos sobre el son jarocho*. Veracruz: Universidad Veracruzana.

Loza, Steven. 1984. "The Origins of the Son." *Aztlán: International Journal of Chicano Studies Research* 15(1):105–121.

Loza, Steven. 1992. "From Veracruz to Los Angeles: The Reinterpretation of Son Jarocho." *Latin American Music Review* 13(2):179–194.

Mendoza, Vicente T. 1984. *Panorama de la Música Tradicional de México*. Mexico: Universidad Nacional Autónoma de México.

Mendoza, Vicente and de Mendoza, Virginia R.R.. 1991. *Folklore de la Región Central de Puebla*. Mexico City: CENIDM.

Morales, Juan. 1996. *The Mariachi Harp*. www.ifccsa.org/mariharp.html (accessed April 2, 2003).

Morales Rivera, Ubaldo. 1990. *Cuaderno de Musicología 6: Sones y abajeños p'urhepecha de San Ángel Surumucapio, Michoacán*. Morelia: University of Michoacán, San Nicolás de Hidalgo (Centro de Investigación de la Cultura P'urhépecha).

Moss, Zahra. 2012. "The Golden Treasures of Monte Alban: Mexican Representation and Exhibition Controversy, 1933–1936." PhD diss., University of Arizona.

Ochoa Serrano, Alvaro (Ed.) 2001. *De occidente es el Mariache y de México . . .* Zamora, Mexico: El Colegio de Michoacán.

Paraíso, Raquel. 2010. "Las redes de globalización y sus efectos en las músicas folklóricas: el caso de los sones mexicanos." *Revista de Literaturas Populares* 10(1–2):151–182.

Paraíso, Raquel. 2014a. "Recontextualizando tradiciones alrededor de la tarima: un fandango en Huetamo." In *El Fandango*. Serie Testimonios de México. Mexico City: INAH. Article and ethnographic recordings.

Paraíso, Raquel. 2014b. "Re-contextualizing Traditions and the Performance of Identity in Festivals of Mexican Huasteco, Jarocho, and Terracalenteño Sones." PhD diss., Ethnomusicology, University of Wisconsin at Madison.

Romero, Brenda. 2002. "La Indita of New Mexico: Gender and Cultural Identification." In Olga Nájera-Ramírez and Norma Cantú (Eds.), *Chicana Traditions: Continuity and Change*. Chicago, IL: Chicago University Press, 56–80.

Sánchez, Rosa Virginia. 2010. "Lírica nueva en sones viejos de la Huasteca poblana." *Revista de Literaturas Populares* 10(1–2):11–37.

Sánchez García. 2009. *XXIII—Antología poética del son huasteco tradicional*. Mexico City: CENIDIM.

Sheehy, Daniel. 1979. "The *Son Jarocho*: The History, Style and Repertory of a Changing Mexican Musical Tradition." PhD diss., University of California, Los Angeles.

Sheehy, Daniel. 1999. "Popular Mexican Musical Traditions: The Mariachi of West Mexico and the Conjunto Jarocho of Veracruz," In Daniel Schechter (Ed.), *Music in Latin American Culture*. New York: Schirmer Books, 44–79.

Sheehy, Daniel. 2006. *Mariachi Music in America: Experiencing Music, Expressing Culture*. New York: Oxford University Press.

Stanford, E. Thomas. 1972. "The Mexican Son." *Yearbook of the International Folk Music Council* 4:66–86.

Villacis, Antonio and Francillard, Francisco. 1995. *De Cocula es el Mariachi: 1545–1995, 450 años de Música Coculense*. Mexico City: Secretaría de Cultura.

Zerecero, Anastasio and Soto Correa, José Carmén. 2006. *Biografía de C. Benito Juárez*. Madero, México: Instituto Politécnico Nacional.

DISCOGRAPHY

Juan Reynoso: The Paganini of the Hot Lands. Historic Recordings 1972–1993. Mexico: Corasón, 2010.

Los impossibles. L'Arpeggiata, Christina Pluhar, conductor. Audio CD, Naïve Records, 2007.

Mariachi Vargas de Tecalitlán. Their First Recordings: 1937–1947. Mexico's Pioneer Mariachis, Vol. 3. Arhoolie, 2004.

Various Artists. *Antología del son de México. Anthology of Mexican Sones*. 3 CDs. Baruj Lieberman, Eduardo Llerenas, Enrique Ramírez de Arellano. Corason Records. Distributed by Rounder Records, 1985.

Various Artists. *Cantos y Música de Michoacán: Testimonios musicales de México*. Instituto Politécnico Nacional. Recording by René Campos. Ediciones Pentagrama, 1998.

Various Artists. *La Bamba: Sones Jarochos from Veracruz*. Smithsonian Folkways Recordings, 2003.

Various Artists. *Mexico South: Traditional Songs and Dances from the Isthmus of Tehuantepec*. Smithsonian-Folkways, 1972.

FILMS AND VIDEOS

Germano, Roy. *A Mexican Sound/Un Son Mexicano*. Roy Germano Films, 2013.

Lane, Brue, Reynoso Portillo, Juan, and Anastasio, Paul. *Viva mi tierra caliente: The Music of Juan Reynoso*. Rochester, NY: Ethnoscope, 2000.

Plate 1 (see Figure 2.1)

Marketplace image.

Photo by Evaristo Aguilar, 2006. Graphic design by
Michelle Cházaro. *Ritmos de la Huasteca.* Universidad
Autónoma de Tamaulipas, Facultad de Música. Courtesy
of Evaristo Aguilar.

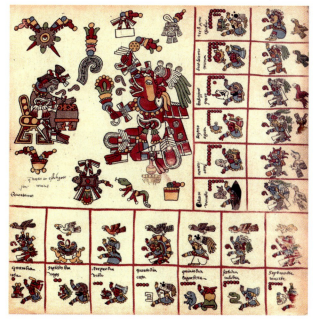

Plate 2 (see Figure 3.6)

Pictograph of Xochipilli, Prince of the flowers, deity of
song, music and festival, singing to Quetzalcóatl,
reproduction of page 4 from the Códice
Borbónico.

Bibliothèque de l'Assemblée Nationale, Paris. Used with
permission.

Plate 3 (see Figure 3.8)
Aztec musicians playing huéhuetl (footed drum), teponaztli (log drum), and ayacachtli (gourd rattles).

From the Florentine Codex, Book 4. Biblioteca Medicea Laurenziana (Laurentian Library, Florence, Italy).

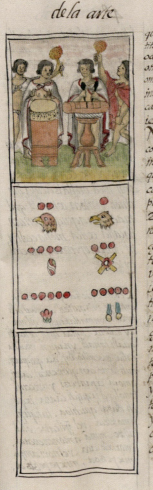

Plate 4 (see Figure 3.9)
Collage of indigenous instruments. See Chapter 3 for a discussion of this figure.

Photos courtesy of Ricardo Almanza Carillo.

Plate 5 (see Figure 3.17)
Danza Azteca in front of the Metropolitan Cathedral in Mexico City beneath the decorations for the 2011 celebration honoring the nation's Independence on September 16.

Photo by Janet Sturman, 2011.

Plate 6 (see Figure 4.13)
Photo of Pueblo of Jemez Matachina, August 28, 2010, in Ponderosa, NM, a tribute to Adelaido Martínez, who played the violin for the Matachina for 30 years. From left to right: Monarcha (facing left), Abuelo (facing back), Malinche; the rest are Matachina danzantes. The Toro is not visible in this photo.

Courtesy of Brenda M. Romero.

Plate 7 (see Figure 5.10)

Son jarocho musicians with an *arpa*, a small jarana (*mosquito*), and a medium jarana (*tercera*).

Photo by Janet Sturman, 2011.

Plate 8 (see Figure 5.12)

Photo of arpa cacheteada ensemble.

Photo courtesy of Raquel Paraíso.

Plate 9 (see Figure 7.5B)
Cover of sheet music for "Sobre las Olas."

Courtesy Collection of Carlos Monsiváis.

Plate 10 (see Figure 8.9)
Image of Lydia Mendoza on U.S. postage stamp.

Used with permission from USPS.

Plate 11 (see Figure 10.3)
Alex Lora, lead singer of the legendary Mexican band El Tri, poses for a photo on Sunset Blvd., in Los Angeles.

(AP Photo/Nick Ut, file). Used with permission.

Plate 12 (see Figure 11.5)
Mexican performers Banda El Recodo sing during the Billboard Latin Music Awards at the Bank United Center in Miami Thursday April 28, 2011.

(AP Photo/Carlo Allegri)

Diego Rivera. (1886-1957)
El Hombre en el Cruce de Caminos
"El hombre controlador del universo"
1934. Fresco sobre bastidor metálico móvil
4.80 m x 11. 45 m

Instituto
Nacional de
Bellas Artes

CONACULTA
Consejo Nacional para la Cultura y las Artes

u·tour

Plate 13 (see Figure 12.2)
Fresco by Diego Rivera, "El hombre en el cruce de caminos." Copyright MPBA—Museo del Palacio de Bellas Artes.
Photo by Tomás Casademunt. ARS Artists Rights Society. Used with permission.

Plate 14 (see Figure 12.3)
The glass curtain and concert hall interior of the Palacio de las Bellas Artes.
Photo by Brenda Blanco Perea.

Plate 15
"Yolotlapalazintzin" ("Los Colores del Alma"/The Colors of the Soul) (2007) mural in the courtyard of the Escuela de Iniciación Musical Ollin Yoliztli, Mexico City. Eduardo Juárez, Alexis Rodríguez, Ladislao Franco, Javier Botista, René Rivero. With collaboration from Mónica Sánchez, Karla Mandujo, Mariana Escamilla, Paulino Reyna, Antonio Julián, Raúl Urbina, Enrique Samudio, David Hernández, Dianey Reyes, Nancy Romero, Neom y David, Clauda Castellanos (UAM Xochimilco—Taller de Gráfica Monumental). Photo by Janet Sturman.

Plate 16
Choir performing with orchestra in the Cathedral, Morelia, Michoacán. Photo by Janet Sturman, 2011.

CHAPTER 6

Sound Foundations for Independence

FROM BATTLE CRY TO THE NATIONAL ANTHEM

Every school child in Mexico knows the story of the events that led to Mexican Independence, for they are recounted in the lyrics of the national anthem and celebrated annually with colorful festivities and formal re-enactments on the national holiday of 16 September *(dieciséis de septiembre)*. On that morning in 1810 the priest Father Miguel Hidalgo y Costilla (1753–1811) rang the bells of his parish church to summon his parishioners—*mestizos* and Indians alike, in the little town of Dolores, Guanajuato. There he delivered the famous "Grito de Dolores," the call for independence, ending with the cry "death to the *gachupines*," rallying residents to take up arms and take back their land from the peninsular Spaniards. His group of rebels marched towards the wealthy city of Guanajuato, carrying before them the banner of the Virgin of Guadalupe. Their successes launched the eleven-year struggle to win full independence from Spain. While Hildalgo's call for death to the Spaniards spurred initial revolt, it was the more conservative proposals outlined by the military officer Agustín de Iturbide (1783–1824) in his *Plan de Iguala* that secured support from both liberals who favored complete independence, and conservatives who hoped for a constitutional monarchy, that would ultimately secure independence on September 27,1821.

> Viewing the video clips: "Independencia—(03) Hidalgo" [6.1][1] and "Independencia—(05) El Grito de Dolores" [6.2]. Source: Historia de Alto Vuelo, Mexico 2010.[2]

6.1, 6.2

> Listening to the *Himno Nacional*, a remastered historic recording from 1908 performance by Manuel Romero Malpica and the Banda Artilleria (Artillery Band). Source: *Bicentenario, 200 Años de la Historia de la Música en México.*

6.1

Mexico's National Anthem is heard in the background of patriotic films such as the series created for the *Bicentenario*, the celebration of 200 years

Figure 6.1
Image of Father Hidalgo. Lithograph by Luis Garces. Source: Manuel Rivera Cambas. *Los gobernantes de México: Galería de biografías y retratos de los vireyes, emperadores, presidentes y otros gobernantes que ha tenido México, desde Don Hernando Cortés hasta el C. Benito Juárez*, vol. 2. Mexico City: Imp. de J.M. Aguilar Ortiz, 1873, p. 2. (Public Domain).

of Independence held in 2010 and is of course performed during the annual celebrations for *el dieciséis de septiembre*. It originated in 1853 as a result of a contest initiated by Antonio López de Santa Anna, who was president of the nation at that time.

The music for this anthem was composed by a Spanish-born (Catalán) band director, Jaime Nunó Roca. The lyrics to the anthem were composed by Francisco González Bocanegra, a talented poet of the era whose fiancée, according to popular legend, forced him to reflect on patriotic themes in a locked room until he arrived at the verses that won Santa Anna's

National Anthem of Mexico

CHORUS:
Mexicans, at the cry of battle
lend your swords and bridle;
and let the earth tremble at its center
upon the roar of the cannon.

I
Oh motherland! Your temples shall be
girdled with olive garlands
by the divine archangel of peace,
For in heaven your eternal destiny
was written by the finger of God.

But should a foreign enemy
Profane your land with his sole,
Think, beloved motherland, that heaven
gave you a soldier in each son.

CHORUS
II
War, war! without intent of truce
of the motherland to stain the blazons!
War, war! the banners of the nation
are soaked by waves of blood.
War, war! in the mountain, in the valley
the dreadful sounding cannons roar
and sonorous echoes resonate
with the voices of Union!, Liberty!

CHORUS
III
Before, Mother Country, the necks of your
defenseless children bent beneath the yoke,
your countryside is watered with blood,
and on blood they set their feet.
And your temples, palaces and towers
collapse with a horrid roar,
and their ruins remain, saying:
a thousand heroes of the mother country
were here.

CHORUS
IV
Motherland, motherland, your children
promise their breath in your cause,
If the bugle in its belligerent tone
calls upon them to struggle with bravery.
For you the olive garlands!
For them a memory of glory!
For you a laurel of victory!
For them a tomb of honor!
CHORUS

Figure 6.2
Lyrics of National
Anthem of Mexico.
Source: Ley sobre el
Escudo, la Bandera y el
Himno Nacionales.[4]

competition.[3] The official version of the national anthem was not legally recognized until 1943, and further refinements were recorded in the legal record in 1984 which stipulates that only verses 1, 5, 6, and 10 of the original poem, plus the chorus, would constitute the official anthem. Shorter versions of the anthem are performed at soccer games and other public events. This historic recording features the operatic baritone singer Manuel Romero Malpica, also known as M.R. Manolito (1874–1935). Born in Puebla in 1874, he traveled to New York City to train with opera stars at the Metropolitan Opera, later performing throughout Europe and the Americas. He was one of the first Mexican singers to make recordings in the early twentieth century.

MUSIC IN IMPERIAL MEXICO

The period that followed Independence remained turbulent. Fighting between central Mexico and other regions in the nation persisted as local *caudillos* (political leaders) fought to avoid the concentration of resources and power in the central zone. Agustín de Iturbide directed the special military force that he had formed to help wrest Mexico from Spain towards shoring up his position, thus initiating what was to become an ongoing custom of self-serving military alliance with governance. Iturbide adopted the title Emperor of Mexico in 1822 and focused more on creating a splendid independent court than on solving domestic problems. After only ten months of rule, he was forced to abdicate the throne on March 19, 1823.

Polite and polished music, following the fashions of Europe, formed an important part of imperial life during Iturbide's rule. His wife took keyboard lessons from the most celebrated composer in Mexico of that time, José Mariano Elízaga (1786–1842), whom the Emperor honored with the appointment and title of Maestro de Capilla Imperial Mexicano (Master of the Imperial Mexican Chapel). Elízaga later went on to found the short-lived Philharmonic Society in 1825, a music publishing company in 1826, and an Academy of Music in his hometown of Valladolid (today, Morelia) in 1840. The city had already earned a reputation for fine musical instruction with its Conservatory of the Roses (El Conservatorio de las Rosas) established in 1743 as a girls' school and which gave rise to today's distinguished modern music conservatory, with programs ranging from preparatory through university levels.

Mexican composers like Elízaga who operated in the elite circles needed to compete with imported concert music from Europe. Italian operas, particularly works by Gioachino Rossini (1792–1868), were all the rage. Thus, composers earned the most attention and status by composing opera and works for piano. Following elite fashion in Europe, well-bred women in the Mexican capital and provincial cities became adept keyboard players and hosted musical entertainments for intellectuals and upper-class patrons in the salons of their homes.

Listening to *Últimas variaciones*, composed in 1826 by José Mariano Elízaga (1786–1842). Recorded performance by pianist Silvia Navarette in 2009.[5]

6.2

An example of Elízaga's compositions are his "ultimate" variations for keyboard in a style inspired by the Viennese composer Franz Joseph Haydn (1732–1809), an early master of the classical style. The variations were composed around 1826, after the fall of Iturbide's empire, when Maestro Elízaga was then professor at the Conservatory in Morelia. His clear intention to please noble female patrons remains evident (although it appears that he strove to hide the identity of the dedicatee). The printed cover to the musical score, discovered by Professor Ricardo Miranda, carries this inscription:

> *Últimas variaciones/del profesor michoacano/D. Mariano Elízaga/Que compuso y consagró/a la tierna memoria de la señorita / Dª. G.G. de G. / tocadas a primera vista por la joven señorita / Dª. Dorotea Losada* (Ultimate variations/by the Michoacán professor/ Sir Mariano Elízaga/Who composed and dedicated/to the tender memory of the young lady/ Miss G.G. de G./first played by the young lady/Miss Dorotea Losada)

Elízaga also founded the first music publishing press to operate in Mexico, and he advertised in a periodical dedicated to the arts, known as *El águila mexicana*. Such magazines often included sample compositions for readers to play on their home pianos. In addition to promoting his "Ultimate Variations," Elízaga posted an advertisement for a set of waltzes, the most popular dance of the era, six of them composed for guitar, and one dedicated to the Italian opera composer Gioachino Rossini.

The structure of the variations is distinctive and rather complex. There are three double variations that follow the statement of an opening theme in C major followed by a contrasting section, called the "trio" also in C major. Hence the form can be outlined as: A(theme) B(trio), A1 B1, A2 B2, A3 B3. This is a structural order that the European master Franz Joseph Haydn used in some of his piano sonatas. Drawing inspiration from Haydn was surely no accident. The Viennese composer was greatly admired in Mexico as elsewhere in the Americas for his breadth of expression, for his sonic encapsulation of logical order, and for his sensitivity to nature. Like the solid and industrious Haydn, Elízaga was a musician who believed in the power of the musical arts to elevate the human spirit and promote social cohesion (Miranda 1998). We know few details of Elízaga's life and many of his compositions are lost, but we do know that Elízaga was a composer, teacher, and founder of orchestras, conservatories, and publishing enterprises. As Miranda reminds us, Elízaga dedicated his life to establishing the musical foundations of his new country during its most fragile moments of independence.

SANTA ANNA'S REBELLIOUS REPUBLIC

Imperial order gave way to the formation of a republic in 1824, led by a team of three leaders, again with military backgrounds. The country's first president was Guadalupe Victoria (1755–1843). While enjoying some success with international diplomacy, Victoria did little to solve growing domestic chaos and stimulate the flagging economy. His successor, President Vicente Guerrero abolished slavery in 1829, a pronouncement first made by Hidalgo and followed by Iturbide, and with the help of General Antonio López de Santa Anna (1794–1876) repelled Spain's attempt to regain Mexico, an event that prompted the exile of Spaniards still living in the nation; those who chose to stay were discouraged by a law that expelled all peninsular Spaniards and expropriated their businesses and haciendas. These actions set the stage for Santa Anna to assume the presidency in 1833, a position he held, intermittently, until 1855.

Santa Anna initially gave his Vice-President, Valentín Gómez Farías, extraordinary power to deal with domestic issues, resulting in reforms that reduced the power of the military and church. However, the President later revoked most of those liberal moves, abolished the federal republic and established a centralized state, giving himself dictatorial power. Discontent regarding the reduction of the rights of states and territories prompted a series of revolts that defined the presidency of Santa Anna and Mexican life for the first half of the century. We will look at music connected to two such revolts during Santa Anna's dictatorship: the first, the Caste War of Yucatan in 1847, was not officially resolved until 1901.

CONFLICTING IDENTITIES: MAYAPAX FIDDLE MUSIC AND THE CASTE WAR OF THE YUCATAN

In the early years of the new republic, one-third of Mexico's population was Indian and most of them lived in small communities known as *pueblos*. Except for the parish priest who headed the church in the larger Indian towns, whites and mestizos rarely lived in the pueblos, but they still exerted control over the economic well-being of those communities. There were few schools in the pueblos and most Indians spoke little or no Spanish. They lived in small homes constructed of sticks with thatched roofs or adobe with dirt floors and slept on straw mats or hammocks. Most sold crafts or operated small farms, and relied upon a system of internal barter with limited cash exchange to sustain themselves.

After the wars of independence, the national government was faced with the challenge of creating a nation out of disparate people of unequal status, a task which was made exceedingly difficult given the continuing distrust among political factions and the ongoing revolts and counter-revolts in various regions of the country. The Caste War of Yucatan illustrates the clash between separatism and unity that troubled the era, and the complicated cultural syncretism that native people used to resist persisting discrimination. The Caste War began in 1847 when the native Maya people rebelled against those of European descent, known as the *Yucatecos*, who exerted exclusive control over politics and the economic activity in the Yucatan peninsula and who had a history of conscripting the Mayans and turning them against each other. As the aggression mounted, the Mayans moved into even more remote areas of the peninsula. Mayan leaders solicited support from neighboring Belize and Honduras and united their people by drawing upon indigenous rituals and practices, including music.

The Mayans have always been a prophetic people. Scholars like Ana Juárez (2002) attribute their acceptance of Christianity in part to this world view, noting that Mayan sacred texts had predicted a conquest. Other factors aided the Spaniards in the conquest, including famine and disease that decimated the native population, and the creation of little towns called "reducciones de indios," where Spaniards controlled the land, local production, and oversaw conversion to Christianity. Throughout the colonial era individual Mayans willingly allied with various Hispanic factions, accepted appointments as landowning *hidalgos*, and served in military commands. Discrimination and economic depravation eventually provoked the Mayans to rebel, but they did not abandon their acceptance of Christian and Hispanic customs. Their leaders cultivated the belief that the rebellion was sanctioned by God, as manifested by a Talking Cross, and a group named themselves followers of the cross or *Cruzoob* (Spanish for cross, with the Mayan plural suffix). The Cruzoob rebels established a stronghold in the territory that is now the modern state of Quintana Roo, claiming it as an independent state until 1901 when the Mexican army took it back. Tension and fighting persisted well into the 1920s in remote villages where some still refused to acknowledge Mexican control.

Listening to Mayapax music: "Aires Fandango," performed by Marcelino Poot Ek, violin; Pedro Ek Cituk, *tarola* (snare drum); Esteban Caamal Dzul, *bombo* (bass drum). Recorded in the state of Quintana Roo in 1993 by researchers at the National Indigenous Institute in Mexico City. Source: *Wood that Sings*.[6]

6.3

Ironically, the music known as Mayapax that helped rally Mayas to rebellion was not purely Mayan, nor was it overtly political. In "Aires Fandango" [6.3] we see an illustration of how the Mayas adopted the European violin and the dance music of the Andalusian fandango, making both their own. Fandangos were performed on festive occasions such as *fiestas* and bullfights as well fairs (*ferias*) and patron saint celebrations, the very occasions that would bring together communities across social and racial divides, making them important sites for the musical displays of identity. In this modern recording of a nineteenth-century fandango air (melody), we hear a bass drum called the *bombo*, and a snare drum, known as *tarola*, accompanying the violin. The "sounding" of complex identity can be very subtle; the way the violin is played, and the intentionally raspy tone produced, differs considerably from the timbres cultivated by European musicians. Other instruments associated with Mayapax music, not heard in this recording, include the iron bell, turtle-shell percussion, and harmonica, integrating European, Afro-Caribbean, and indigenous customs.

GERMAN AND IRISH IMMIGRATION TO MEXICO

Settlers from Europe migrated to northern Mexico to take advantage of the vast stretches of open land available for ranching, farming, and dairy production. Graham Davis (2002) argues that the Irish were among the first European immigrants to take the land grants they received and use them as entrepreneurs to build profitable enterprises in ranching and other development, attracting other immigrants to join them in Texan–Mexican territory.

Scholars often explain migration in terms of "push" and "pull" factors, and in addition to the pull factors of opportunity for agriculture and business, Europeans responded to push factors as well. Swedes and Norwegians came as early as the 1820s to evade hardship and famine in Scandinavia. The most famous early settlement of Germans in Mexico was at the site of what is today Austin, Texas in the 1830s, but the largest and most diverse wave of immigration to Mexico began in the 1840s and continued until the early twentieth century. In addition to the Spanish, migrants from Britain, the Austro-Hungarian Empire, Holland, Ireland, France, and Italy came to settle in Mexico. Migration from the Middle East, particularly from Syria and Lebanon, also began in the first half of the nineteenth century.

Not only did these new arrivals transform industry and commerce in Mexico, but they also influenced politics and took sides in battles. While some of the Irish settlers in Texas territory sided with the United States in battles with Mexico, a large group of the Irish Catholic immigrants living in the northern territory chose to side with Catholic Mexico in the Mexican–American war from 1846–1848.

THE MEXICAN–AMERICAN WAR

The most destructive of the revolts during Santa Anna's presidency began in the territory of Texas and led to the devastating war with the United States. We will not explore the details here, except to introduce a few of the many songs that reference this decisive event and the hostilities surrounding it. The war ended with the signing of the treaty of Guadalupe in 1848 and resulted in the loss of Texas and the huge California and New Mexico territories to the United States. The war left Mexico insolvent, stalled improvements to infrastructure, industry, and foreign trade, and established attitudes of cultural mistrust that shaped not only the remainder of the century but which persist to this day.

Figure 6.3
Monument to the Irish soldiers who fought for Mexico during the Mexican–American War at the Museo Nacional de las Intervenciones (formerly the Monastery of Churubusco) in Coyoacán, Mexico, D.F. Photo courtesy of Leigh Thelmadatter (2009). Wikimedia cc by SA 3.0.

Listening to "March to Battle across the Rio Grande," performed by the Chieftains with Banda de Gaita de Batallón de San Patricio, Liam Neeson, Los Cenzontles, L.A. Juvenil.[7]

6.4

Paddy Maloney, leader of the famous Irish music group the Chieftains states that he created the "March to Battle across the Rio Grande" to sing the story of the Irish who fought for Mexico, known as the San Patricios (Saint Patrick's Battalion).[8] In reality the battalion, founded and led by Patrick Riley, was only about 60 percent Irish, with runaway American slaves, Canadians, and other ethnic minorities completing the ranks. A number of them had defected from the U.S. army where they had once been conscripted or served as mercenaries, but very few were actual U.S. citizens. The San Patricios espoused strong religious sympathies with the Catholic Mexicans and they fought five decisive battles against U.S. forces.

Understandably, there are differing views regarding the valor of these fighters. The United States considered the San Patricios to be traitors, but Mexico honored the battalion for its fierce support (Miller 1997). After the war, United States forces court martialed 45 of the captured soldiers from the battalion and hanged them for treason in a public display of the ultimate punishment for desertion.

THE FRENCH INVASION AND THE LINGERING FAREWELL

The United States and Spain weren't the only foreign powers with whom Mexicans engaged contentiously in the nineteenth century; there was also, and most significantly, France. Tensions began with the so-called Pastry

War of 1828, when France levied a charge of damages after Mexican soldiers commandeered and ate the wares of a French pastry chef. This led to the battle of Veracruz in 1838, where Santa Anna lost his left leg driving back the first French invasion.

The most influential leader of the middle of the nineteenth century, Benito Juárez (1806–1872), won the presidency in 1861 and he too faced the French. As the nation's first indigenous president, Juárez initiated far-reaching reforms that limited the hold of the church on civic life, forced it to sell its non-ecclesiastic property, and began efforts to equalize rights of citizens, but his efforts were compromised by ongoing civil wars and foreign interventions, with the French proving most intrusive.

In 1861 the French landed in Veracruz, following Spanish and British forces who had come to collect long outstanding debts. The Spanish and British went home, but Napoleon's French army did not. Rallying after several defeats, the French succeeded in taking the city of Puebla and then moving into Mexico City in 1863. Shortly thereafter, Napoleon III installed the Austrian archduke, Maximilian of Hapsburg as the emperor of Mexico, a post he retained until Benito Juárez's counter-insurgent troops forced him to surrender in 1866.[9]

The influence of the French occupation of Mexico shaped fashion and culture in the cities and extended to racial blending in the villages. Turmoil in the nation and slow birth rates encouraged the administration to invite additional immigration from Europe, but it was not enough to stem the steady flow of migrants from Mexico to the United States. In 1876 only about 25,000 people in Mexico were foreign-born and they almost all resided in the larger cities (Meyer 2007:365). As we will see, it was not until the early twentieth century that the government moved to more fully integrate immigrants and their contributions into the national identity.

Mexican musicians contributed to the political debates during the French occupation with volleys of patriotic and satiric songs, illustrated here by the still popular *canción*, "Adiós, Mamá Carlota."

6.5   Listening to "Adiós, Mamá Carlota" composed in 1866 by Vicente Riva Palacio and Sebastian Iradier. Recorded performance in 1970 by Amparo Ochoa, Mili Bermejo, Arturo Alegro, Raúl Díaz, el "Mago del salterio."[10]

When the empress Carlota of Belgium, wife of the Emperor Maximilian, departed in 1865 on a voyage from the Yucatan to Europe, she told those who gathered to see her off that they should "consider her the mother of all Mexicans." That phrase prompted one of the leaders of the republican resistance, the intellectual general Vicente Riva Palacio (1832–1896), to compose verses parodying the patriotic poem "Adios, oh patria mía" by the Spanish-born poet Rodríguez Galván. That poetic parody gained fame as the popular song "Adiós, Mamá Carlota." In 1866 the Empress made one last trip to Europe to solicit aid from Napoleon and the pope for her husband's flailing imperial government. Her trip prompted Riva Palacio to circulate his verses in his satirical self-published journal, *El Pito Real* (lit.

"Adiós, Mamá Carlota"	"Goodbye, Mama Carlota"
Alegre el marinero con voz pausada canta, y el ancla ya levanta con extraño rumor.	Happy is the Sailor singing with slow voice and the anchor already rising with a strange noise.
La nave va en los mares, botando cual pelota. adiós, Mamá Carlota, adiós, mi tierno amor.	The ship travels the sea hurling like a ball Goodbye, Mama Carlota Goodbye, my tender love.
De la remota playa te mira con tristeza la estúpida nobleza del mocho y el traidor. En lo hondo de su pecho ya sienten su derrota: adiós, Mamá Carlota, adiós, mi tierno amor.	From the remote beach she watches you with sadness the stupid nobility of the fanatic Catholic and traitor Deep in their breast they already feel their defeat: Goodbye, Mama Carlota Goodbye, my tender love.
Acábanse en Palacio tertulias, juegos, bailes; agítanse los frailes en fuerza de dolor.	Finished in the Palace are the parties, games and dances agitating the friars with a painful force.
La chusma de Las Cruces gritando se alborota; adiós, Mamá Carlota, adiós, mi tierno amor. Murmuran sordamente los triste chambelanes, lloran los capellanes y las damas de honor	The crowd in Las Cruces has become excited shouting. Goodbye, Mama Carlota Goodbye, my tender love. The sad escort silently whispers the chaplains and bridesmaids cry.
El triste Chucho Hermosa canta con lira rota: adiós, Mamá Carlota, adiós, mi tierno amor.	The sad Chucho Hermosa sings with a broken lyre: Goodbye, Mama Carlota Goodbye, my tender love.
Y en tanto los chinacos ya cantan la victoria guardando tu memoria sin miedo ni rencor.	And meanwhile, the liberal soldiers already sing the victory keeping your memory without fear and resentment.
Dicen mientras el viento tu embarcación azota: Adiós, Mamá Carlota, adiós, mi tierno amor.	They say as the wind hits your boat: Goodbye, Mama Carlota Goodbye, my tender love.

Figure 6.4
Lyrics for "Adiós, Mamá Carlota" by Vicente Riva Palacios. Traditional.
Source: *Cancionero de la Intervención Francesa.* Edited by Irene Vásquez Valle and María del Carmen Ruiz Castañeda. Mexico City: INAH-SEP, 1980.

"The Royal Whistle," also the name of a local bird and a popular jarocho dance) to help muster support for Mexicans liberals to take back the government (Ortiz 1993:124). The verses circulated quickly among supporters in *cantinas* where they were originally sung to the well-known operatic melody "La Paloma" by the Spanish composer Sebastian Iradier.[11] When the general arrived in Michoacán to rally a republican army, entire communities greeted him with the song, and the title became a battle cry during the war that ensued. Eduardo Ruiz includes the song in his celebrated *History of the War of the Intervention in Michoacán*, published in 1896. In subsequent years, "Adiós, Mamá Carlota" continued to serve as an anthem to inspire liberal action and it remains a popular favorite in many forms, including satire.

So popular was the song "Adiós, Mamá Carlota" that it even makes an appearance in classical Mexican opera. Mexican composer Melesio Morales references the song in *Anita* (1910) his opera composed to honor Porfírio Díaz. *Anita* is modeled on the operatic style of the Italian composers Giuseppe Verdi (1813–1901) and Vicenzo Bellini (1801–1835), thus the original version uses Italian not Spanish lyrics (a modern restoration by musicologist Karl Bellinghausen converts the libretto to Spanish). Morales's reference to the piquant song "Adiós, Mamá Carlota" let him honor Porfirio Díaz's heroic fight against the French intervention, index Mexican popular culture, and provide a chance for the opera cast to sing in Spanish. Apart from confirming the celebrity of song, the quote also illustrates the fluid exchange between strata of musical activity in Mexico.

6.3 Viewing "La Golondrina"—a federal hymn and *despedida*,[12] composed in 1862 by the medical student and musician Narciso Serradell Sevilla (1843–1910) in a performance by the Croatian mariachi group Los Caballeros.[13]

"La Golondrina" is another *canción mexicana* that stems from the period of French intervention. The composer, Narcisco Serradell Sevilla, put himself through medical school by providing music for parties and dances. At a gathering of musical friends, a *tertulia*, he was challenged to create music for Francisco Martínez de la Rosa's elegant translation of a French poem. Embedded in Martínez's verses is a coded message, reading from top to bottom the first letter of each line reveals the sentiment: "to the object of my love" (*Al objeto de mi amor*), proffering love of country, now Mexico rather than France, in words equally suited for courtship. Serradell won the competition for the best musical setting of this clever poem. He was also a patriot who fought to restore the republic to Mexican rule and who was sentenced to exile by the French for his opposition. On his departure, he offered "La Golondrina" as his sentimental *despedida* (farewell), a role the song has retained to the present day.

The rendition in 6.3 is performed by a Croatian mariachi, a testimony to the spread of Mexican music, particularly mariachi music, around the world. We will discuss the export of Mexican music during our

La Golondrina	The Swallow
A dónde irá veloz y fatigada la golondrina que de aquí se va ¡Oh!, si en el viento se hallará extraviada buscando abrigo y no lo encontrará.	Now that the swallow departs, fast and exhausted, where will she go Oh, if she were lost in the wind, seeking shelter and not to find it?
Junto a mi pecho le pondré su nido en donde pueda la estación pasar también yo estoy en la región perdido ¡Oh, cielo santo! y sin poder volar.	Next to my bed I'll put her nest where she can spend the season. Oh God, I am also lost in the region and unable to fly.
Dejé también mi patria idolatrada, esa nación que me miró nacer, mi vida es hoy errante y angustiada y ya no puedo a mi mansión volver.	I also leave my adored country, that mansion that saw my birth. My life is now errant and stressful and I cannot go back to my house.
Ave querida, amada peregrina, mi corazón al tuyo estrecharé, oiré tus cantos, tierna golondrina, recordaré mi patria y lloraré.	Dear swallow, beloved pilgrim, I will draw together my heart to yours. I will hear your singing, tender swallow, then I will cry remembering my country.
[Al objeto de mi amor]	[The object of my love]

Figure 6.5
Lyrics from "La Golondrina" by Narcisco Serradell Sevilla. Written by Rosamond Johnson, Narciso Serradell, Armando Bergo, F. Gonzales, and C. Compagne, Harold. Used by permission of Edward B. Marks Music Company.

investigation of music during the Porfiriato, but for now let's examine the enduring appeal of this song. "La Golondrina" is often sung in Mexico and in Mexican communities in the United States as a closing number in a concert or at graduation ceremonies. Try to identify the qualities of this song, musical, textual, conceptual, that make it attractive to international audiences. How might the song's appeal to international listeners differ from how contemporary Mexicans view it? You might interview family, friends, or acquaintances to explore this topic.

MUSIC IN THE RESTORED REPUBLIC

After the successful ouster and execution of Maximilian, Benito Juárez returned to the Presidency in 1867 and the decade that followed was remarkably stable. Many historians note that the foundations of modern Mexico were laid during this era, an assessment that holds for musical activity as well. Juárez worked to build educational and economic foundations for the restored nation. Among his most notable achievements was the completion of the railroad between Mexico City and Veracruz and the establishment of the national railway system, the *Ferrocarril Mexicano*. He also pushed for the completion of a new central boulevard in Mexico

City, begun by Maximilian, but finished during the restored republic. Juárez named the grand route, *Paseo de la Reforma*, in honor of the reformers.[14] Education was a priority for Juárez, and he initiated the policy that primary school education should be mandatory, provided by the state, apart from religious institutions (in accordance with his liberal ideals and the Reform laws), and made available free of cost across the nation.

THE RISE OF THE JARABE AND OFFICIAL FOLKLORIC REPRESENTATION

The jarabe dance, which first circulated in the seventeenth century (recall the jarabe in the *son* sung by Los Azohuastles in Chapter 5), was always a dance of celebration. As people in rural towns danced jarabes at festivals and to celebrate Independence, the genre acquired official status as representing *Mexicanidad* (Mexican identity), a process explored in detail by Ricardo Pérez Montfort (2007). He notes that the jarabe became a pretext for referring to range of distinctive Mexican cultural expressions, places, and products, including food. For example, there is a "Jarabe de Chamistlán" referring to a kind of a kind of bread, and there is also the "Jarabe de Atole" referring to a typical drink made from corn meal. The names of animals, flowers, and everyday articles are frequently used to describe a jarabe: "El Durazno" (the peach), "La Perica" (the parrot), "La Pasadita" (little passageway), "La Reata" (the lariat). The word jarabe became part of daily expression, although interpretations varied depending on region, and the way jarocho musicians in Veracruz used the term varies from how mariachis from Jalisco have historically used it.

By the end of the nineteenth century, the musician José Antonio Gómez (1805–1876), inspired by Viennese concert dance sets, created a chain of Mexican popular songs and dances bound to the jarabe, calling it *jarabe encadenado*, a format that persists to this day. A popular example is *"el son de perro encadenado con jarabe"* (the chained dog song with jarabe). The jarabe encadenado became an ideal format for official music with its frame for linking songs from different regions into a single unit. This procedure gave rise to the set called "Aires Nacionales" (National Songs)

🎧
6.6

Listening to *Aires Nacionales* by Ricardo Castro, performed by pianist Silvia Navarette. Source: *Mósaico: Música de America Latina* (2011).

Audio Example 6.6 offers an example of *Aires nacionales* arranged for piano by the composer Ricardo Castro (1864–1907), who became the favorite composer of President Porfírio Díaz, discussed in Chapter 7. While politicians were struggling to define the best form of government in the new nation, musicians were "cooking up" new musical alliances to help the process (Pérez Montfort 2007). The emergence of *orquestas típicas*— orchestras formed, often with political patronage, to present music typical and representative of Mexico in civic, diplomatic, and touristic contexts—

exemplify such alliances of personnel, customs, and repertory. During the Republican period the Mexican people grew to know the customs of other regions of the country through musical sounds reproduced by instrumentalists who, as they traveled or took up residence in the cities, reinvented regional customs in a manner that helped define both Mexican music and the Mexican people. As we shall see, this is a process that continues in later eras.

ADVANCING FORMAL MUSIC EDUCATION

The spirit of educational reform and infrastructural building during the Republican era led to the first efforts to establish a conservatory for advanced music education. We have already noted José Mariano Elízaga's early efforts to formalize educational training for professional musicians. Renewed support for a national conservatory of music emerged from a group of prominent citizens, intellectuals, physicians, and lawyers—all lovers of music, who met at the home the pianist Tomás León. This group initially called themselves the Club Filarmónico. They later disbanded and reformed as the Sociedad Filarmónica de México and collected funds to support the creation of a conservatory of music that would sustain a symphony orchestra and a professional choir, and a conservatory for professional music instruction. In 1866, José Antonio Gómez (the creator of the *jarabe encadenado*) founded that conservatory of music. In 1877 it become the National Conservatory of Music, offering free professional instruction to music students.

CONCLUDING REFLECTIONS

Musical activity in Mexico during the first century of independence was diverse, depending on the community in which it originated. Still, the political demands of the era promoted and even forced, interaction between these communities and their music. Efforts to formalize musical education and performance opportunities apart from the control of the church influenced the nature of classical music composition, and also promoted new attitudes towards music in the provinces. Similarly, new options for publishing enhanced the circulation of song lyrics and printed sheet music, helping to create a shared national repertory.

It is common to hear people say that music transcends politics, but in this unit we have examples of several different ways that music and politics are overtly linked. We have explored examples of songs created in response to specific political goals of the moment: reinforcing elite order, supporting rebellion, or promoting unity or integration against internal wars and foreign invasions. Much of this music however also remains viable today, holding new meanings for new listeners in new contexts, long after the era that sparked its creation. Political relevance is not limited to songs with lyrics; Elízaga's *Últimas variaciones* illustrates that purely instrumental music may also carry political intention, however subtle, and even more importantly may inspire actions, such as the formation of arts institutions that shape the social and cultural climate far into the future.

CRITICAL THINKING AND DISCUSSION PROMPTS

1. In this unit we listened to several examples that might not seem like Mexican music to the man on the street. Is the song about the San Patricios a Mexican song or a song about Mexicans? Does it represent the Mexican-Irish who are often unrecognized in common reflections on Mexican ethnicity? Why might some listeners not consider the cosmopolitan music of Elízaga to be Mexican? What would he answer in return?

   Earlier in our exploration we asked the question: what makes music Mexican? As Mexico established itself as an independent nation, this question once again seems important. In a short essay attempt to answer those questions, justifying your responses with examples.

2. Several of the audio examples, while representing songs rooted in Mexican history, are performed by non-Mexican musicians. Does a song become less Mexican if performed by non-Mexicans? Explain your answer and offer comparable examples.

3. Choose one of the musical examples in this chapter to examine more closely. What qualities of music, such as elements of sound, text, or concept, might make this music attractive to international audiences? How might that attraction differ from the way that Mexicans, past or present, may view the song? Considering interviewing family, friends, or acquaintances to explore this topic.

KEY TERMS, PEOPLE, AND PLACES

fandango	Santa Anna
Mayapax	Narciso Serandell
corrido	"Himno Nacional"
despedida	"Últimas Variaciones"
16 de septiembre	"Aires Fandango"
Miguel Hidalgo y Costilla	"March to Battle across the Rio Grande"
Agustín Iturbide	"Adiós, Mamá Carlota"
Vicente Riva Palacio	"La Golondrina"
Maximilian	Ricardo Castro
José Mariano Elízaga	

NOTES

1. In English at www.youtube.com/watch?v=5o7Ap6eq11Q. Bicentenario Mexicano on YouTube. www.youtube.com/watch?v=VigJ0iBY5IQ&index=19&list=PL677EC9C2CE03001D Also, www.mayahii.com/#!/salon/11568/759

2. In English at www.youtube.com/watch?v=GQC85TyYM2o&list=PLFC86EF6E400D9FDB. www.youtube.com/watch?v=LRmHUe44GBc&list=PL677EC9C2CE03001D&index=21 Also, www.mayahii.com/#!/salon/11570/759

3. Himno Nacional de México. www.ieepo.gob.mx/17.htm

4. The Law concerning the Shield, the Flag, and the National Anthem http://ceremoniascivicas.segob.gob.mx/work/models/Desarrollo_Politico/Template/7/1/docs/Ley-EBHN.pdf

5. Source: Silvia Navarette. *La campana de la Independencia*. Mexico: Mosaic Editions, 2010.

6. Source: *Wood that Sings. Indian Fiddle Music of the Americas*. Smithsonian Folkways Recordings, 1993.

7. www.songfacts.com/detail.php?id=19084

8. Ibid.

9. Historian María Concepción Márquez Sandoval notes that when Juárez went to exile in New Orleans, support for his leadership persisted and Mexico literally had two rulers, a federal president and an emperor. Juárez never ceased to be Mexico's president. He never resigned, and in the view of his followers, and according to Mexican law, he remained president during the whole of the French occupation.

10. *Cancionero de la Intervención Francesa*. Recorded by Rodolfo Sánchez Alvarado. Edited by Irene Vásquez Valle and María del Carmen Ruiz Castañeda. Mexico City: INAH-SEP, 1980.

11. Juan Jesús Aguilar León, *Los trovadores huastecos en Tamaulipas* (Ciudad Victoria, Mexico: Instituto Tamaulipeco para la Cultura y las Artes), 106–107. "La Paloma" had arrived from Cuba in the early nineteenth century, likely with traveling opera companies.

12. Sheet music for "La Golondrina," dating from 1880, can be viewed at: https://jscholarship.library.jhu.edu/handle/1774.2/7659. A list of versions, performances and recordings appears at: http://instro.pmouse.nl/lagolondrina.htm

13. www.youtube.com/watch?feature=player_embedded&v=fqUeAwMXAFA

14. This project was started by Maximilian as he wanted a direct route from his palace in Chapultepec to the National Palace and Cathedral. His plan was to emulate the Champs-Élysées in Paris and name the boulevard for his wife, the Empress Carlota. He did not live to see it finished. Much of the construction is credited to president Sebastian Lerdo de Tejada. The project was completed under the presidency of Benito Juárez, who inaugurated it with sculptures of the nation's heroes and liberal reformers, and who gave it the name Paseo de la Reforma.

FOR REFERENCE AND FURTHER STUDY

Bellinghausen, Karl. 2000. *Melesio Morales, Catalogo de música*. Mexico City: CENIDIM—CENART.

Davis, Graham. 2002. *Land!: Irish Pioneers in Mexican and Revolutionary Texas*. Texas A&M University Press.

Escalante, Jesús and Pablo Dueñas. 2010. *Bicentenarario, 200 Años de la historia de la música en México* [Bicentennial, 200 Years of Music History in Mexico], includes 4 CDs. Mexico City: Sony Music.

Estrada, Jesús. 1973. *Música y músicos de la época colonial*. Revised and annotated by Andrés Lira. México: Secretaría de Educación Pública.

Herrera y Ogazón, Alba. 1917. *El arte musical en México*. Mexico City: Editorial Bellas Artes.

Juárez, Ana. 2002. "Ongoing Struggles: Mayas and Immigrants in Tourist Era Tulum." *Journal of Latin American Anthropology* 7(1):34–67.

Malmström, Dan. 1991. *Introducción a la música mexicana del siglo XX*. Mexico City: Fondo de Cultura Económica.

Mayer-Serra, Otto. 1941. *Panorama de la música mexicana; desde la independencia hasta la actualidad*. México City: El Colegio de México.

Meyer, Michael C., et al. 2007. *The Course of Mexican History*. 8th ed. New York: Oxford University Press.

Miller, Nicola. 2006. "The Historiography of Nationalism and National Identity in Latin America." *Nations and Nationalism* 12(2):201–221.

Miller, Robert R. 1997. *The Sword and the Shamrock: The Saint Patrick's Battalion in the U.S.–Mexican War*. Norman, OK: University of Oklahoma Press.

Miranda, Ricardo. 1993. "Una obra desconocida de Mariano Elízaga." *Heterofonía* 26(108):114.

Miranda, Ricardo. 1998. "Haydn en Morelia: José Mariano Elízaga." In *Revista Música Chilena*, 52(190). www.scielo.cl/scielo.php?script=sci_arttext&pid=S0716–27901998019000006#3 (accessed January 12, 2015).

Murray, Stephen. 2011 "A Hiberno-Mexican Story: The Presence of the Irish in Mexico." Paper delivered to the Academia Nacional de Historia y Geografía—National Academy of History and Geography, Mexico City, March 3, 2011.

Olavarría y Ferrari, Enrique. 1961. *Reseña histórica del teatro en México 1538–1911*. México City: Porrúa.

Ortiz Monasterio, José. 1993. *Historia y ficción. Los dramas y novelas de Vicente Riva Palacio*. Mexico City: Universidad Iberoamérica.

Pedelty, Mark. 2004. *Musical Ritual in Mexico City: From the Aztec to NAFTA*. Austin, TX: University of Texas Press.

Pérez Montfort, Ricardo. 2007. "De jarabes, dulces, y aguardientes. El azúcar y algunos de sus derivados en la expresión popular fandanguera mexicana," In *Expresiones populares y estereotipos culturales en México. Siglos XIX y XX: diez ensayos*. Mexico City: Centro de Investigación y Estudios Superiores en Antropología Social, 17–37.

Rugeley, Terry. 1996. *Yucatan's Maya Peasantry and the Origins of the Caste War*. Austin, TX: University of Texas Press.

Ruiz, Eduardo. 1975 [1886]. *Historia de la guerra de intervención en Michoacán*. Morelia: Balsal Editores.

Soto Correa, José Carmen. 2006. *Juárez. La canción durante la intervención francesa*. Mexico City: Instituto Politécnico Nacional.

Stevenson, Robert. 1971. *Music in Mexico: A Historical Survey*. 2nd ed. New York: Thomas Y. Crowell.

Stevenson, Robert. 1982. "Haydn's Iberian World Connections," *Inter-American Music Review* 4(2):3–30.

DISCOGRAPHY

Cancionero de la Intervención Francesa. Recorded by Rodolfo Sánchez Alvarado. Edited by Irene Vásquez Valle and María del Carmen Ruiz Castañeda. Mexico City: INAH-SEP, 1980.

Silvia Navarette. *La campana de la Independencia*. Mexico: Mosaic Editions, 2010.

Silvia Navarette. *Mosáico: Música de América Latina*. Mexico: Silvia Navarrete (7503007392022), 2011.

Wood that Sings. Indian Fiddle Music of the Americas. Washington, DC: Smithsonian Folkways Recordings (SFW40472), 1997.

FILMS AND VIDEOS

Eduardo Flores Torres (TATO), director and photography. 2010. *Historia de Alto Vuelo: Independencia*. In English as *High Flying History: Independence*.

Vimeo (posted 2011), at: http://vimeo.com/channels/historiadealtovuelo/1980 5387; YouTube (posted September 14, 2010). www.youtube.com/watch? v=5o7Ap6eq11Q

WEBSITES

500 años de México en documentos (500 Years of Mexico in Documents). www.biblioteca.tv/artman2/publish/miguel_hidalgo/Miguel_Hidalgo_y_C ostilla_Documentos_de_1810_y_1811.shtml (accessed October 5, 2014).

Art Music of Mexico and Guatemala. (University of Massachusetts) July 8, 2011. Excellent biographies of representative musicians, including Melesio Morales, Manuel Ponce, and Juan Carillo. Includes links to NAXOS recordings of representative music. http://artmusicmexicoguatemala. wordpress.com/category/the-art-music-of-mexico/

Mayo, C.M. On Maximilian and Mama Carlota. www.cmmayo.com/ maximilian-adios-mama-carlota.html (accessed October 5, 2014).

Melesio Morales. A collection of videos and links to sound recordings, supporting biographical and contextual information. Video clips from *Anita* (uploaded July 15, 2014). http://wn.com/Melesio_Morales

Mexico 2010. Bicentenario Independencia. Centenario Revolución, at: www.bicentenario.gob.mx/english/index.php [site has ceased operation]

Mozaic Editions. A source for scores and bibliographies for Mexican and Spanish music. Much of it suitable for performance by skilled amateurs as well as trained artists. www.mozaic.cat/store/partitures-scores-partituras

Northern Belize.com—Caste War. www.northernbelize.com/hist_caste.html (accessed October 5, 2014).

CHAPTER 7

Immigration and Cosmopolitan Identity during the Porfiriato

SETTING THE SCENE: AN EPISODE FROM *CHIN CHUN CHAN*

The date is 1904, the set, an opulent and elegant hotel in Porfirio Díaz's Mexico City. On stage, two Chinese gentlemen face each other, surrounded by solicitous staff and hotel guests. The gentlemen bow and after an uneven exchange of greetings in which each has clearly offended the other, they sit in stony silence and amazement while the hotel manager invites a group of French cabaret singers to entertain them with a saucy number about the modern wireless telephone, and its seductive uses. The chorus girls sing:

> *To communicate with a young lady you put the device close to you and just RING RING. That sound arrives in front of the mouth with sweet tingle that repeats. RING RING. Come closer Lady, come closer Gentleman, now gently push the button. Yes, I am excited. I feel electrified. I feel those tingles; now you can speak; there is communication. There is a special feeling. Leave the button, don't push it again. Now stop; quit playing, otherwise the current will end.*[1]

Viewing "El teléfono sin hilos" (The Wireless Telephone) [7.1] from *Chin Chun Chan*, University of Arizona production, January 2007.

7.1

Columbo, disguised as one of the Chinamen, applauds: "Bravo Bravo. I should like to bring one of these devices to China so I could spend the whole day 'communicating'!" His enthusiasm is interrupted by a woman pushing her way into the group: "Where is he?" she shouts. "Let me pass or else . . . I hear him. I'll strangle him. I'll make a tortilla out of you! Let me pass." Alarmed, Columbo slips out. The woman enters and begins pummeling the other Chinese man, (the real Chin Chun Chan) with her handbag. "I can see through that stupid disguise. Stop thinking you'll deceive me and get back to Chamacuero. I should kill you . . . why won't you speak Spanish?!!"

This loosely translated scene from the zarzuela *Chin Chun Chan* takes us to the heart of the drama and introduces a few of the many topics addressed in the musical comedy. In the drama, the philandering Don Columbo, from the town of Chamacuero, attempts to escape from his overpowering wife by disguising himself as a Chinaman and by traveling to the big city. The proprietors of the hotel where he registers are expecting the son of the Chinese Emperor as their guest, and thus Columbo the impostor receives an unexpectedly warm welcome. As the scene above illustrates, the plot thickens when the real Chinaman arrives.

In this comedy no one and nothing escapes parody. Provincial vacationers are ridiculed for their pretensions, migrant workers and Chinese businessmen for their inscrutable customs, naïve honeymooners for their excessive ardor, street vendors for their pandering to American tourists, Yankees for displaying their wealth and for expecting Mexicans to know how to speak English, and the elite and aspiring middle class are mocked for their obsession with foreign fashion, especially French and American entertainment. Also mimicked are the conventions of drama and musical theater, including the Italian *commedia dell'arte*, the British comic puppet theatrical tradition of Punch and Judy, and of course, opera, a fascination of the Mexican President Porfirio Díaz. All the while, the hilarious story of *Chin Chun Chan* prompts audiences to recognize the racial and social diversity of modern cosmopolitan experience. The drama and its music provide insights into the manners and concerns of Mexico as it entered the twentieth century. It also represents Mexican zarzuela at its most delightful peak—and we will return to discuss the work in detail presently, but zarzuela is just one of the genres fancied by Porfirio Díaz that left a mark on future musical practice.

The range of themes embodied in *Chin Chun Chan* characterize the years of Porfirio Díaz's presidency known as the *Porfiriato*. It was an era of modernization, new modes of travel and technology, increased immigration, and new fashions in music. President Díaz promoted pride in Mexico City and dedicated resources to impress visitors and the world at large. *Chin Chun Chan* provides a point of departure for exploring those historical issues and other competing musical activity.

DEFINING THE *PORFIRIATO*

When Porfirio Díaz assumed the presidency of Mexico in 1876, he vowed to bring order, stability, and modernity to the nation, and music was one of the tools he used to accomplish those aims. In the preceding 55 years since Independence, the presidency had changed 75 times, but Díaz would lead the country for more than three decades, linking the nineteenth and twentieth centuries in a period that came to be known as "the Porfiriato." The period ended in 1911, with Díaz exiting as a dictator. He had indeed transformed the country as promised, but not without social costs and discontent leading to revolution. During his presidency, Díaz strategically promoted music and he cultivated those musical styles that he felt would position Mexico as equal to any of the world's powerful nations.

TECHNOLOGY AND CONNECTION

Sound recording came of age during the Porfiriato. President Díaz signaled his recognition of the importance of this new sound technology by permitting his greetings to Thomas Edison to be recorded in 1901. Technological development spurred economic development, particularly during Díaz's second term of office. He oversaw the installation of hydroelectric power, the expansion of the railroads and tramways, and the installation of wireless telephones (one of the technologies celebrated in *Chin Chun Chan*), telegraphs, and submarine cables. President Díaz allowed himself to be among the first to record a verbal message on the new phonogram [7.2].

7.2

Listening to Porfirio Díaz's greetings to Thomas Edison. Source: Project Gutenburg.[2]

TRANSPORTATION, INDUSTRY, AND IMMIGRATION

Improved transportation connected central Mexico City to its suburbs, and to isolated regions of the country, thus increasing options for economic production as well as cultural interaction. As we've seen, authors Rafael Medina and José Elizondo, the playwrights of *Chin Chun Chan*, used humor to tackle the topic of migration and immigration in their collaborations with composer Luis G. Jordá.

President Díaz revived the mining industry, removing tariffs, and encouraging foreign investors who would help modernize production and boost profits. New industry developed as well, including oil drilling and refining, and beer production in breweries founded by German immigrants. Such improvements and new employment opportunities helped make the Porfiriato an era of increased immigration. In 1876 only about 25,000 people in Mexico were foreign-born and almost all of them resided in large cities. Porfirio Díaz's interest in exporting Mexican culture as cosmopolitan, and worldly rather than provincial, fostered his efforts to integrate new cultures, foreign and local, into an umbrella of Mexican national identity.

THE CHINESE IN MEXICO: SOME HISTORICAL BACKGROUND

It is easy to forget that the cosmopolitan city, defined by its diverse population and economy, owed a debt to surrounding regional and rural development. The popular Mexican music drama, *Chin Chun Chan*, invited audiences in 1904 to explore acceptance and resistance to migration from China to Mexico as well as rural laborers into the urban milieu. Even today, the non-traditional narrative of *Chin Chun Chan* offers still relevant lessons for contemporary struggles with movement across geographic, ethnic, occupational, and conceptual borders. In the nineteenth and early twentieth centuries, Mexicans and Americans joined together to transform the borderlands between the United States and Mexico into a territory of economic development. This region, geographically distant from Mexico City, helped to propel the ambitious dreams of the central government. At the same time, central leaders found it difficult to govern those living in the northern borderlands. The sparsely inhabitant region where political dissidents and bandits took refuge among the scattered and stolid indigenous communities became known as "fugitive terrain" (Truett 2006), and the efforts of miners and ranchers to tame this territory did not diminish the harsh and barren landscapes framing the region's dusty towns.

The most important wave of Chinese immigration to Mexico began with the opening of steamship lines between Mexico and China in 1890 and continued until 1930 when Mexicans imposed exclusion laws to expel Chinese residents. Roberto Chao Romero (2010) reports that during that 40-year span, more than 60,0000 Chinese immigrants came to Mexico seeking work, principally in mining and railroad construction, but also in mercantile enterprise, some of them after first living in Cuba, the United States, or other places en route.

For Mexican businessmen, the Chinese were not new partners. Beginning in the sixteenth century, interest in acquiring silver made China an important trading partner with New Spain. So important was the silver trade from 1565–1800 that the Mexican *peso* acquired the status of international currency (Chanda 1999). The Spanish Manila Galleon trade sustained interaction between Mexico, Spain, the Philippines, and China. Spaniards used Mexican silver to buy fine Asian porcelain, textiles, ivory, spices, and lacquerware from Chinese merchants stationed in Manila (Philippines) and imported them to the Americas through Acapulco and other Mexican ports.

While the Chinese silver trade was propelled by maritime trade, Chinese immigration in the nineteenth century was propelled by land activity. Chinese migrants came to Mexico for two main reasons: as a means of entering the United States, or to find employment in Mexico. The most popular destination for the wave of Chinese immigration beginning in the nineteenth century was the northern state of Sonora where there was access to the U.S. border and to the existing Chinese labor force working in the United States in mining, railroad, and commerce. The region was sparsely populated and viewed as remote from the hub of activity in central Mexico. Magdalena, a Sonoran border crossing point, exemplified such destinations (Truett 2006:121). Employment came from ranching, mining, and the railroad. Residents of the town included a community of indigenous people, the Papago Indians (known today as the Tohono

O'odham and whose music we'll explore in Chapter 11). The independent lifestyles cultivated by these residents opened space for assimilation of new migrants like the Chinese, many of whom found themselves living as indentured laborers enduring abysmal treatment by Mexican residents (Hu-DeHart 2006; 1984).

U.S. legislation further spurred migration to Mexico. The nation became an alternative destination for the Chinese after they were barred from entering the United States as a result of the Chinese Exclusion Act of 1882. The passage of this law coincided with efforts by the government of Porfirio Díaz to recruit and attract Chinese laborers to support Mexico's economic modernization. Widespread immigration was further facilitated by the Mexican Treaty of Amity in 1899, which permitted free exchange and travel of Chinese from one port to another. Chinese merchants residing in San Francisco, California might arrange for contracts and passages of Chinese coming to Mexico from numerous international points. As a result, from 1890 until 1931, when Sonora passed its own anti-Chinese labor laws, Chinese arrivals created the largest minority population in the region (Truett 2006:121). In sum, by 1924 more than 24,000 Chinese lived in Mexico overall and they constituted the second-largest immigrant group in the entire country (Chao Romero 2010:1).

The Zarzuela: From Spain to Mexico

Chin Chun Chan is classified as a zarzuela, and while it is definitely Mexican in character, it represents the continuity of a musical dramatic genre rooted in the golden age literary practice of Spain. Inspired by the *comedia*, a dramatic form combining poetry and prose with musical interludes to provide public entertainment made famous by authors such as Lope de Rueda, Lope de Vega, and Miguel de Cervantes, the zarzuela served as Spain's distinctive answer to Italian opera and the nation's signature form of lyric theater. The first work to bear the name "zarzuela" was *El Golfo de las Sirenas*, penned by Calderón de la Barca (1600–1681). At that time, the zarzuela was courtly entertainment, and Calderón drew upon classical texts for plots to please his royal patrons. He and his musical collaborators also established the combination of spoken and sung verse incorporating local references that would set the continuing standard for genre. Authors and composers of zarzuelas continued to respond to Continental trends and fashion in opera and theater, particularly those of Italy and France, and over the centuries zarzuelas became increasingly populist, addressing historic and regional themes in formats aimed to entertain the general public.

The zarzuela traveled to the Americas along with the conquistadors and was an important part of entertainment in New Spain. As in Europe, the genre made its way into the realm of public and popular entertainment. New fashions in zarzuela composition and performance were cultivated by foreign touring companies as well as local performers. A creole (native-born) tradition of zarzuela developed throughout New Spain, and Mexico was no exception. Still, despite local interest, until 1890 most Mexican zarzuelas were created by foreign-born composers.

The story of Chinese in Mexico engages us not only with immigration practices but also with the equally important and oft-ignored history of the "*cuarta raíz*," what Chao Romero calls the "fourth root of Mexican identity" (2006:25). Like most of Latin America, Mexico ascribes its identity to the merger of three racial streams: European, Native American, and African. Those with Asian ancestry, including migrants from Japan and other Asian countries, constitute a fourth stream and this presence forces us to view the process of mestizaje with fresh eyes and greater appreciation for the nuances of blended identities in Mexico and the Americas.[3]

THE CREATION OF *CHIN CHUN CHAN*

It is in the context of urban modernization and immigration that the zarzuela *Chin Chun Chan* was created for audiences to encounter musical and satiric treatment of these issues. When authors Rafael Medina and José Elizondo first published the comic drama *Chin Chun Chan* in 1904, the drama was so popular that the playscript was reprinted at least four times in that same year (see Fig. 7.1).

The work was conceived as a picaresque zarzuela, an operetta-like show with a combination of spoken and sung lines, and it soon became the most celebrated of all Mexican examples of this popular Spanish genre (Reyes de la Maza 1910). The composer, Luis Gonzaga Jordá (1869–1951), was a Catalan musician, raised in Barcelona who moved to Mexico in 1890 and lived there until 1915 when he returned to Barcelona. He collaborated with the prolific Mexican librettist Rafael Medina on several other dramatic works, including *Palabra de Honor* (1899), *Los de Abajo* (1899), *La Veta Grande* (1903), *¡Que Descansada Vida!* (1904), and *El Champion* (1905) (Leal 2002:66). Notice how quickly these works were generated. Like today's television sitcoms, zarzuelas provided timely entertainment directed towards educated audiences and the growing middle class. These light dramas led the way for the flowering of an insular literature that focused on the Mexican experience.

The historic popularity of this work results first from the genius of the drama, second from the music, and third from the comic actors who provided depth to the light-hearted commentary and story. Librettists Medina and Elizondo crafted a libretto with puns, local dialect, and colorful regional characters familiar to theater patrons of the day. The cosmopolitan bustle and glamour of Mexico City serves as the backdrop for appropriating dramatic conventions and stock characters from contemporary and international historic stage forms in vernacular guise. The clown-like *Pulchinela* from the historic *comedia del arte*[4] appears as a street entertainer, while the overbearing wife (named for the Amazon queen Hyppolyta who greeted Heracles)[5] pummels her philandering husband with her handbag in a manner reminiscent of Punch and Judy. Operatic parodies abound as well. French *can-can* girls entertain guests at the hotel, as does a mysterious

Figure 7.1
Cover page to fourth edition of *Chin Chun Chan*. Medina y Comp, 1904. Source: Google Books.

CHIN
CHUN=CHAN

CONFLICTO CHINO

en un acto y tres cuadros

original de

Rafael Medina y José F. Elizondo

música del maestro

Luis G. Jordá

(DE LA SOCIEDAD MEXICANA DE AUTORES DRAMATICOS

Y LIRICOS)

CUARTA EDICION

1904

MEDINA Y COMP., IMPRESORES
1er. Callejón de López. 8
MEXICO

operatic tenor who offers an unsolicited, but irresistible, solo aria. Most important, however, are the characters that represent the conflicting diversity of the new republic. For it is in the capital city where ranchers rub shoulders with sophisticated businessmen, immigrant Chinese laborers, clownish fellows known as *payasos*, as well as indigenous vendors trying to make a living selling wares on the street. All are introduced to audiences, but are broadly drawn as un-nuanced stereotypes.

Figure 7.2
Handbill with lyrics for the "Coplas de Charamusquero."
Source: Popular Graphics Collection of the Library of Congress.

THEATER AT THE DAWN OF THE TWENTIETH CENTURY

The dawn of the twentieth century in Mexico was a period of artistic and social transformation, but theater did not lead the way. Zarzuela and opera continued the popularity they enjoyed from the mid-nineteenth century and drew on conventional forms to tell their stories. Despite this conservative approach to form, the zarzuela and the more colorful and more loosely structured musical revue reflected local custom and concerns far more effectively than did straight theater in this era (Monterde 1970:61).

The development of modern cosmopolitan cities was an important goal of the reform policies of President Porfirio Díaz. During the Porfiriato, the wooden sidewalks of Mexico City streets were replaced with cement pavement and electric railways were built to replace mule-drawn carts. Porfirio Díaz aimed to make the federal capital resemble the great cities of Europe by constructing broad, tree-lined avenues, later realized in the construction of the Avenida Paseo de la Reforma. Theater was also an important index of modernity and Mexico City boasted several important buildings for its patrons. When *Chin Chun Chan* premiered in 1904, the Teatro Nacional (National Theater) had been torn down in preparation for a newer theater, but the Teatro Renacimiento (Renaissance Theater) had opened in 1900 and renovations on the Teatro Principal (Main Theater) were complete. Conspicuous construction and support for the arts was not limited to the capital; Porfirio Díaz had theaters built in cities around Mexico (Hardison Londré and Watermeier 2000:325).

PRODUCTION HISTORY

Chin Chun Chan debuted at Mexico City's Teatro Principal on April 9, 1904, and was subsequently performed thousands of times in theaters all over the Republic. Historian Luis Reyes de la Maza dubbed the *conflicto chino*, as the drama was subtitled, "the best-known Mexican theatrical work" (1984:340). He and other commentators credit *Chin Chun Chan* with establishing conventions that later distinguished the more overtly political musical theater of the Revolution by replacing imported Spanish formulas with broadly drawn Mexican national types and customs (Morales 1984:18).

The nation's most celebrated actors contributed a glamorous energy to the original production. Film star Manuel "Manolo" Noriega (1880–1961) played the lead character Columbo,[6] and Esperanza Iris (1888–1962), the gifted actress for whom the National Theater is now named, performed as one of the sexy telephone girls, and also as a man, portraying Ponciano in a celebrated "pants" role.

The individual songs of the zarzuela were first published separately, and then later in 1912 as a set. Likely another of the reasons the work enjoyed such renown was that its authors were clever businessmen, able to exploit publication opportunities. Jordá, Medina, and Elizondo were co-founders of the Mexican Society of Authors of Music Theater (Sociedad Mexicana de Autores Dramáticos y Líricos) (1981). The accessibility of the original drama immediately spawned adaptations. Song sheets, known as broadsides, sometimes with new lyrics (see Fig. 7.2), were printed and circulated alone as well as in popular song books known as *cancioneros*. By 1933, there were at least seven different editions of the complete work (Monterde 1970:216).

When *Chin Chun Chan* premiered, technology for sound recording was in its infancy, but the Señoritas Pérez and baritone José Torres Ovando recorded the Charamusquero trio for Victor Records in 1905.[7] A 1998

Experimental Revivals of *Chin Chun Chan*

In 1993, the National University in Mexico City (UNAM—Universidad Nacional Autónoma de México) presented a lavish revival production of *Chin Chun Chan* in the Julio Castillo Theater in a version emphasizing its links with contemporary politics, directed by Enrique (Chachirulo) Alonso (1923–2004). In another production of that same year, director Vicente Leñero emphasized the nation-building ethos inherent in the drama by setting the zarzuela inside the revolutionary drama *Las Musas del País*, another historic operetta. In 2007 a production at the University of Arizona of *Chin Chun Chan* used an original English translation of the spoken lines. For this complete staging the actors delivered the drama in English but sang the songs in the original Spanish.

---

recording, *Obras de Luis G. Jordá*, featuring the Mexican pianist Silvia Navarette with tenor Fernando de la Mora, includes the *romanza* from *Chin Chun Chan*. The tendency to record only isolated songs severed the music from the complete drama, a point to which we will return, and which continues into the present.

Ironically for a plot centered on proper Mexican identity, English speech, or attempts at it, appears with frequency in *Chin Chun Chan*, often in the context of the encroaching influence of the United States in Mexico. In Scene V of Part II, Columbo, disguised as a Chinese man, experiences trouble maintaining the appearance of speaking Chinese and tries to convince Borbolla, a hotel employee, that spending time in Mexico is confusing him. Borbolla replies that this confusion is nothing compared to that of the poor indigenous peasants who struggle to speak English because the country is so full of "gringos" who do not know Spanish. This exchange is followed by the appearance of the Charamusquero or the candy vendor and two street characters, who ridicule the mixing of Spanish and English in street commerce and daily life, and share tales of rich Americans who try to buy at bargain prices and woo pretty Mexican salesgirls. Here the display of English hovers between realized and attempted cultural sophistication and treachery (for additional discussion of such ambiguity, see Haney 2003:163–188).

CONFRONTING CHARGES OF RACISM

In recent years, *Chin Chun Chan* is rarely performed. Occasionally isolated musical numbers are performed in concert, without the original play, which includes dialogue and references to ethnic and regional prejudices that by today's standards might be deemed culturally insensitive. The drama captures and now documents a prevailing suspicion with which Mexicans once viewed foreign immigrants, particularly the Chinese, as well as the general tendency among Mexican city dwellers to view migrants from the provinces as hopeless country bumpkins. No character is given a free pass in this drama; all of their morals are subject to humorous scrutiny, satire, and caricature. Understood in its context—as a parody tackling the contradictions of an emerging cosmopolitan identity in a tongue-and-cheek manner not unlike a contemporary *Saturday Night Live* skit—the complete production offers a dramatically hilarious and musically captivating reflection on social manners of early twentieth-century Mexico. These approaches invite reflection as well as laughter, but offer little depth upon which to build agendas for social reforms that might raise the status of immigrants and provincial laborers. Hijinks and romantic intrigue overpower social satire in the drama and in the most enduring and celebrated music number, romance carries the day.

7.1

Listening to "Danza (Romance)" from *Chin Chun Chan* [recording 7.1, with Fernando de la Mora and pianist Silvia Navarette, recorded 1998; or 7.3 with tenor David Troiano, recorded 2009].[8]

7.3

The romantic "Danza," (song no. 5), the most popular of the musical numbers in *Chin Chun Chan*, is sung by Ricardo, a dashing tenor who makes a single appearance in the drama, emerging to dispel tension and entertain hotel guests with a rhapsodic serenade.

The verses continue to express amorous sentiments: "dreaming of your embrace ... those sweet lips and languid eyes ... kiss me my darling, be the sun in my sky."

Danza, like so many musical terms, has multiple meanings. Generally, when Mexicans speak of danzas they are referring to ceremonial dance such as *danza azteca* (Aztec dance), or *danza del venado* (deer dance). These more formal or ritual dances contrast with *bailes*, the term used for social dances, such as *el baile de la quebradita*. There is also however a social dance known as danza. The danza in *Chin Chun Chan* is an example of that popular dance genre named for its rhythm drawn from the *habanera* and from a complex of rhythms associated with the *contradanza* (contradance), a creolized dance genre that swept the Caribbean and which was cultivated most prominently and influentially in nineteenth-century Cuba and Puerto Rico. In his extensive study of the contradance and its history dating back to the 1700s, Peter Manuel discusses how the rhythms associated with its creole forms outlived ephemeral dance fashions. The choreography shifted from lines of dancers or partners in group formations to the ballroom style of independent couple dances (Manuel 2011:1, 26).

Figure 7.3
Opening lyrics to "Danza (Romance)" from *Chin Chun Chan*.

Cuando la luna resplandeciente	When the moon's resplendent rays
quiebra su rayos en tu balcón,	illuminate your balcony,
entre las sombras tímidamente,	In the shadows, I timidly
te espera con ansias mi corazón.	await you with anxiety in my heart.

The rhythm of the habanera (Fig. 7.4A) results from a dance rhythm designed to reproduce an African drumming pattern that sounds two beats against three, resulting in a pattern that Spanish speakers identified as *tresillo* (Fig. 7.4B). An elaboration of this pattern, known as the *cinquillo* rhythm (eighth-sixteenth-eighth-sixteenth-eighth in one bar of 2/4 time, repeated over and over as an ostinato) provides the underpinnings of the danza (Fig. 7.4D).[9] One might also start the ostinato on the sixteenth instead of the eighth, resulting in the amphibrach form (Fig. 7.4E). We hear this rhythm in the melody line of the danza from *Chin Chun Chan*, and in "La borinqueña," the national anthem of Puerto Rico, also a danza. By 1920, Mexicans viewed danzas as old-fashioned and the genre was no longer popular in dance halls, but its rhythms lived on in boleros and other popular songs and in concert music throughout Mexico and Latin America.

A) Basic habanera rhythm   B) Tresillo in 2/4 time

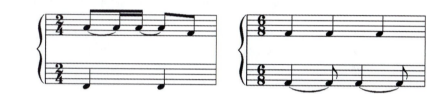

C) Tresillo in 6/8 time

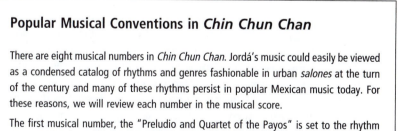

D) Cinquillo rhythm

E) Amphibrach rhythm

Figure 7.4[A–E]
Habanera rhythms and related Afro-Caribbean rhythmic patterns of *tresillo*, *cinquillo*, and *amphibrach*.
Figure prepared by the author.

Popular Musical Conventions in *Chin Chun Chan*

There are eight musical numbers in *Chin Chun Chan*. Jordá's music could easily be viewed as a condensed catalog of rhythms and genres fashionable in urban *salones* at the turn of the century and many of these rhythms persist in popular Mexican music today. For these reasons, we will review each number in the musical score.

The first musical number, the "Preludio and Quartet of the Payos" is set to the rhythm of a popular duple-meter dance known in Europe as the *schottische* and in Mexico as the *chotis* or *chote*.[10] Like other such dances popularized in the nineteenth-century ballroom, this genre became popular in music for the stage, concert hall, and salon, and later found its way into the repertory of rustic rural musicians playing in cantinas and local festivities. The Prelude begins before the curtain rises, and in true theatrical tradition foreshadows the music to come with excerpts of the numbers ahead, including a two-step and a waltz. The tempo and rhythm shift to a *chotis* as the curtain opens and the number becomes a vocal quartet sung by guests at an elegant hotel. We meet a vacationing couple from ranching territory as they dine and plan their activities in the big city and two rustic newly-weds who struggle to control their ardor in public, while other hotel guests and personnel become the chorus and offer comments on country manners, concluding that while the food in the big city is good, romance and kisses are still better.

In the nineteenth century, the *chotis* also circulated throughout Spanish-speaking regions of Latin America and the United States where it entered the repertory of popular instrumental ensembles performing social dance music, and also became associated with rural popular music. In Mexico the schottische (*chote*) gained popularity during the reign of Maximilian. Although the *schottische* derives its name from the German word for Scottish, its ultimate origins are contested; what is clear is that this quick, duple-meter dance form gave rise to a vibrant set of Latin American variants. While some scholars identify the *schottische* as rooted in nineteenth-century German and Bohemian round dances, others link it to the French *ecossaise*, a *contradanse* (country dance) dating back to the 1700s. All agree that by the mid-nineteenth century versions of the *schottische* for couple dancers entered the repertory of the international ballroom dance fashion radiating from Paris. Like other ballroom dances it was adopted around the world and acquired regional names. Reflecting this legacy, the *chote* enjoys continued popularity in mariachi repertory, in *música norteña,* as well as in the folk music of Hispanic instrumentalists in New Mexico and Southern California. Popular Mexican titles, such as "chote vaquero" (cowboy dance) and "chote zapatilla" (shoe dance), reflect the genre's regional and folk heritage. The *chote* can be identified by its "loping" rhythm in 4/4 time with the strong off-beat accents in the accompaniment on counts 2 and 4.

The second number in *Chin Chun Chan* is a waltz, the "Chorus of the Chanteuses" featuring French show girls staying at the hotel, a nod to Porfirio Díaz's continued fascination with all things French. The girls sing of the seductions of the waltz and how it, like wine and women, evokes paradise.

Song No. 3 is a two-step called "Coplas de las Polichinelas" (Verses of the Pulchinela). Sung by female street entertainers reminiscent of classic characters from *commedia dell 'arte*, the masked popular drama of sixteenth-century Italy, the lyrics recount a saucy story of Felipe, the bell ringer for the Church of San Juan, who feared climbing the bell tower alone and brought along the pretty Nicanora to quell his fears. Soon the couple were happily ringing more than one kind of bell. The rhyme scheme of the *coplas*, rhyming with chin, chun or chan, adds to the humor of this song.

The fourth number, the "Coplas del Charamusquero" (Verses of the Candy Vendor) features the rhythmic interplay of two against three that we explored in Chapter 4's review of the Mexican *son*, and the quality of improvised verse associated with regional *son*. The vendor's song mimics different conversations he and other retailers have with American tourists, who have plenty of money to spend but who resist communicating in Spanish. His tale incorporates various English phrases mangled by the vendors such as *Guan cen di* (Give me one cent), *veri güel* (very well), and *ol rait* (all right). Two of his male buddies from the street, Telesforo and Ponciano, chime in help him tell the story. For Mexican audiences these statements would also evoke slang curse words. (See Ezequiel Ojeda, 1986). This satiric presentation foreshadows the tone of the *revista* (musical revue) that will later dominate the popular stage in twentieth-century Mexico.[11]

The sentiment of No. 6, "El Teléfono sin Hilos" [7.1] has been discussed, but not its musical rhythm or form. The song of the Telefonistas is set as a lively but somewhat genteel *galop*, a European ballroom dance in duple meter that gained popularity in Paris in the 1820s and which influenced both the *can can* and the *polka*. As we shall see, this line of influence also shaped Mexican music arranged for piano solo and salon style performance, as well as dance music performed in cantinas by mariachis or by accordion-led *conjuntos* in northern Mexico. The polka rhythm undergirds countless Mexican songs, including *corridos* and *rancheras*.

The seventh number in *Chin Chun Chan*, is a "Baile de Pastel" or Cake Walk featuring the march-like rhythm of the African-American cakewalk dance. The ragtime number, titled "Bunch of Blackberries," a vaudeville hit composed by Abe Holzmann, was added to the original show in this place. Vaudeville, the theater style in vogue in the United States from the 1880s to 1930s, was mixed variety entertainment with shows that combined circus acts, musical performance, dramatic skits, and other entertainment. This musical inclusion underscores the references in the plot of *Chin Chun Chan* to the love–hate relationship with the United States in Mexico and the fascination of cosmopolitan Mexican audiences with American trends.

The eighth and final number in *Chin Chun Chan*, simply titled "Final" is a musical reprise of No. 3 song of the Polichinelas, but with new lyrics. To conclude the show, the cast presents a *despedida*, a farewell message common to many Mexican songs, in this case serving to close the entire show. The singers thank the audience for its kind attention and ask attendees to applaud if they liked the show, pleading with them not to hiss if they didn't (this surprising plea reflects of theater manners of the time).

SIGNIFICANCE OF *CHIN CHUN CHAN*

We've explored the zarzuela *Chin Chun Chan* in detail in this chapter to illustrate how this show, and theater in general, treated audiences to dramatic treatments of timely topics blended with ear-catching musical fashions. The persistent influence of the show confirms the success of this strategy. The enduring popularity of individual songs, in particular the "Danza (Romance) de *Chin Chun Chan*," points to how the zarzuela contributed to the national imaginary. An additional legacy exists in verbal conventions, such as the Mexican custom of cursing-without-cursing by saying the words: "Chin Chun Chan."[12] Less directly, but more significant, is the manner in which musical theater reinforced the popularity of rhythms and genres that spread throughout Mexico and flourished in new musical contexts. The repertory of many an instrumental *banda típica* includes songs that were first heard on the musical stage, and in many instances contemporary performers are unaware of this legacy. Finally, many of the conventions of staged musical theater like the zarzuela, and the edgier cabaret-style revue known as the *revista*, transferred directly to the musical films of Mexico's golden era of cinema in the 1940s–1950s.

THE NATIONAL CONSERVATORY AND FORMAL MUSICAL INSTITUTIONS

The Porfiriato was an era of building and development and many important musical institutions were established or bolstered during the years between 1876 and 1911, particularly in Mexico City. As the economy improved, a wave of new construction supported efforts to improve health and sanitation, and transformed urban centers with paved roads and new boulevards, new statues, and modern public buildings. As noted earlier, the building spree included new theaters, not just in Mexico City but also in each of the provincial capitals. Competing with the established theaters were the circus tents and coliseums. All of these venues provided work for skilled and trained musicians. The National Conservatory of Music (Conservatorio Nacional de la Música) was one of the many initiatives begun in previous administrations and brought to fruition by Porfirio Díaz (however, the current building for the institution was built in 1949, well after his administration). The roots of the school date from 1866, with the founding of the Conservatorio de Música de la Sociedad Filarmónica Mexicana (the Music Conservatory of the Mexican Philharmonic Society). That organization, inspired by French trends, added theatrical training to the artistic curriculum in 1869 and added "Declamation" to the name of the school. In 1873, just before Díaz assumed office, the Conservatory already had 43 professors, 763 male students, 260 female students, and two choirs with more than 300 singers in total. When the Sociedad Filarmónica Mexicana disbanded in 1876, President Díaz decreed the school under national supervision, naming it the Conservatorio Nacional de Música y Declamación. He wanted the institution and its graduates to equal any of their European counterparts.

Among the directors at the Conservatory during the Porfiriato was the French-born musician, journalist, and culture critic Alfredo Bablot, who served from 1881–1892. Not only did Bablot push forward curricular reforms but his presence confirmed the still powerful link to French culture and to Paris, recognized by Díaz, and many other turn-of-the-century intellectuals, as the cultural capital of the world. While director, Bablot established the Conservatory orchestra. He also accepted a young violinist and budding composer, Juventino Rosas (profiled below) as a Conservatory student. Another celebrated director of the Conservatory, much favored by the President, was the Durango-born Ricardo Castro Herrera, the composer and pianist introduced in the Chapter 6. Castro briefly assumed the post in 1906 after returning from three years of study in Europe (courtesy of a scholarship from President Díaz), only to die in the following year.

Developing orchestral music may have been one of Porfirio Díaz's goals and he sent promising Mexican composers to Europe to study and promote this idea, but Mexico did not distinguish itself in orchestral concert music apart from theater and opera during this era. Staffing professional orchestras required the interaction of formally trained musicians with popular and folkloric artists in order to muster sufficient forces. John Koegel (2005) reports that in 1880 the national conservatory maintained a symphonic orchestra that performed for special occasions. Musical life in Mexico City was supported by two other, smaller orchestras, probably with about 20 musicians each. One operated in the metropolitan Cathedral and the other in the *Coliseo*, both places where concerts were regularly offered. The repertory included the works of Mexican composers alongside compositions by revered European masters, particularly Handel, Haydn, Mozart, Beethoven, and Mendelssohn.

JUVENTINO ROSAS, A CROSSOVER ARTIST

We can gain some insight into the strain of establishing a professional musical career during the Porfiriato through the life of Juventino Rosas (1868–1894; full name, José Juventino Policarpo Rosas Cadenas—he may have been the inspiration for the character of Policarpo and the bell-ringer in *Chin Chun Chan*). In 1888, Rosas wrote a waltz that became an international sensation. His traversal of the divide between the cultivated conservatory and the popular stage, and his peripatetic relationships with elite patrons and fickle fans, relayed by his biographers Hugo de Grial (1965) and Helmut Brenner (2000) unite many of the topics examined in this chapter.

Born in Guanajuato, Juventino Rosas was a prodigy violinist who moved with his family to Mexico City so that he might study at the National Conservatory in 1875, beginning at the age of seven. After the death of his parents in 1885, he took up permanent residency in the capital. He signed on to perform at the Teatro Nacional as a violinist, playing in a duo with his friend Pepe Reina who played *bandolón* (a guitar-like instrument with 18 metal strings in 6 courses). The duo performed Rosa's composition "La Sonámbula" at a celebration of the Battle of Puebla attended by Porfirio Díaz and his cabinet, earning the young composer kudos from the President.

Despite the attention of President Díaz and patrons in elite circles, Rosas struggled to make a living and became a heavy drinker. He combined performing with street musicians along with playing in formal orchestras. An enterprising freelance musician, he also rang the bells at the Tepito Church in Mexico City, played for theatrical shows, and directed military bands. His patrons included the nation's elite and despite the impermanence of those encounters, they led, in chain-like fashion, to some of his greatest achievements. For a brief period Rosas directed the city orchestra that played for the Alberca Pane (a boarding house) and the Baños de Factor (public baths), both frequented by well-to-do patrons. This post landed him an invitation to perform in the orchestra at the casino Tivoli de Cartagena in Tacubaya (known as Mexico's Monte Carlo). While playing in the Tivoli orchestra, Rosas was invited by the wealthy Calixta Gutiérrez and her husband Vicente Alfaro to write a set of danceable songs for a saint's day festival that they planned to sponsor.

Supposedly while thinking of the music for this event Juventino Rosas went bathing in the Magdalena River with his friend Pepe Reina and the water's motion inspired the young composer to hum a few bars of a lovely melody. His friend Pepe rushed for paper and insisted that Rosas write down his ideas; later they became the waltz "Sobre las olas." He later dedicated the waltz to his benefactress Calixta Gutiérrez. After the premier of the composition at the Saint's Day Festival, Casa Wagner, the leading publishing company of the era bought it from Rosas for only 17 pesos. Fortunately, he eventually received from the company more than 100,000 pesos from the many sales of copies of the sheet music for "Sobre las olas," his most famous composition.

Rosas was not a good money manager and frequently drank to excess. His talent was often overlooked and he lived a bohemian life. Nonetheless, President Díaz commissioned him to compose a composition for the birthday of his wife, Carmen Romero Rubio de Díaz, resulting in the waltz named *Carmen*. Despite this commission, many of the president's foreign guests refused to believe that a Mexican composer was responsible for such beautiful music.

Like many musicians seeking their fortune in Mexico City, Rosas was unable to secure a steady appointment, so he continued to freelance as an orchestral player. In 1894 he signed on to play in the orchestra of a Cuban zarzuela company while they were in Mexico. He agreed to return to Cuba with the company for a series of tours, but while on the island he became gravely ill and the company had to leave him behind. Without a salary or home, he was left to the mercy of friends. A local physician whom he had met while playing with the zarzuela company came to his rescue, but just as Rosas thought he had recovered sufficiently to return to Mexico, he collapsed with hepatitis. He was only 26 years old when he died in Cuba that June of 1894.

In 1909 a group of famous musicians brought his remains back to Mexico for a parade of honor at the Conservatory and interment at the Rotunda of Illustrious Persons (then known as Rotunda de los hombres ilustres) in Mexico City. The arrival of the ship carrying Rosa's coffin to the port of Veracruz opens the 1950 film *Sobre las olas*, Ismael Rodríguez's cinematic dramatization of the composer's life, with Rosas played by Pedro Infante.

🎧
7.2

🎧
7.3

Listening to "Sobre las olas" (Over the Waves) by Juventino Rosas in two different versions performed by the Quinteto Típico [7.2] and the Banda Los Mochis de Porfirio Amarillas [7.3]. Sources: *Bicentenario 200 Años de Música en México; Bandas Sinaloenses Música Tambora*.[13]

The waltz "Sobre las olas" provides an example of the relationship between music created for high-status patrons and performers in elite venues with music heard in the contexts of the theater, circus, ballroom dancing, and other entertainments that brought large crowds of people together across social and economic class divisions. Rosas composed many waltzes, the most fashionable dance of the nineteenth century. Popular tunes were quickly published in sheet music formats that appealed to pianists, singers, and instrumentalists wanting to perform them in their homes. Known as "salon music" or "parlor music," this was music destined to be heard in the homes of modest residents, as well as in the elegant drawing rooms of wealthy patrons. Friends and acquaintances invited to these musical gatherings might be expected to participate by singing or playing an instrument like the guitar or violin, and in many instances, by dancing.

We can easily imagine dancing to the sounds of the Quinteto Típico heard in the Audio Example 7.2, and we can imagine Rosas himself playing with such a group in fancy settings. A rather different scenario comes to mind when we listen to the version of "Sobre las olas" for wind band [7.3] as recorded by the Banda Los Mochis de Porfirio Amarillas in the 1950s. Los Mochis is a northern coastal city in the state of Sinaloa and the name means "the land of the turtles." In Sinaloa the wind band developed a special tradition of its own, known as *tambora*, and we can hear the signature bass drum and energetic tuba performing a "walking" bass line

Figure 7.5A
Photo of Juventino
Rosas, 1894.

**Figure 7.5B
(see Plate 9)**
Cover of sheet music
for "Sobre las Olas."
Courtesy Collection of
Carlos Monsiváis.

of that style in their version of this perennially popular song. The performers play with a delightful slow *rubato*, a flexible treatment of melodic and rhythmic phrasing that stretches the beat for more expressive playing.

THE *ORQUESTA TÍPICA*

Changing Mexico's image abroad was something President Díaz felt was essential for improving the economic status of the nation. He also wished to quell lingering rebellion in the states along the U.S.–Mexico border, necessary not only for stabilizing his own rule, but also as a means of preventing U.S. troops from crossing into Mexico. Fostering international relations via travel promised to advance both goals. In 1884, after taking a four-year hiatus from the presidency, President Díaz traveled to the United States to represent Mexico at the New Orleans World's Fair and he took with him as his calling card a group of musicians performing on symphonic and regional instruments dubbing them the *Orquesta Típica de la Ciudad de*

México. The orchestra combined the repertory and style of dance bands popular in the United States with Mexican instrumental music customs.

Not only were recordings of the Orquesta Típica de la Ciudad de México among the first Mexican music to appear on sound recordings, on the labels Edison, Victor and Columbia, leading to the international promotion of Mexican music, but they also inspired a spate of recordings of other typical orchestras made in the United States. In the 1996 Arhoolie Records compiled a reissued collection of the earliest recordings of Mexican-American *orquestas típicas*, from the cities of San Francisco, Los Angeles, El Paso, San Antonio, Dallas, and New York. Groups like these spread ballroom dance styles like the *pasodoble*, *danza*, one-step, waltz, mazurka, *huapango*, polka, fox-trot, march, *chotis*, tango and *danzones*, rhythms that persist in the repertories of twenty-first century *bandas*, *conjuntos* (combos), and *mariachis*.

The orquestas típicas played an important role in the history of music in states along the United States–Mexico border. Even as the orchestras integrated popular and regional styles into their repertory, they maintained a genteel and high-brow status, particularly when contrasted with the conjunto music performed in rural homes and cantinas. Mexican-American studies scholar Manuel Peña explores this contrast in detail showing how the accordion-led combos known as *conjuntos* came to represent laborers and poor migrants, while the orquestas enjoyed the support and status of the wealthy and urban middle class (see Peña 1985, 1999, and more on these popular styles in Chapter 9).

Listening to "Monterrey Alegre" performed by the Orquesta Mexicana Calvillo from San Antonio, Texas, originally recorded in 1928.[14]

7.4

"Monterrey Alegre" offers an example of the orquesta típica sound and an instrumental song in the pasodoble rhythm. Note the combination of strings, plucked and bowed, with wind instruments. This kind of instrumentation is similar to that of the orquesta típica promoted during Porfirio Díaz's presidency. The Orquesta Típica, founded by Carlos Curti, was designed for travel and to represent modern Mexico for civic occasions domestic and foreign.

TRAVEL AND COSMOPOLITAN SONG

As the economy in Mexico blossomed during the Porfiriato, many Mexican musicians were able, and even encouraged by the administration, to travel to cities in Europe and the United States. New York City was one of the most popular residency destinations for Mexican musicians and intellectuals, as well as for their Latin American counterparts, thus fostering inter-American artistic exchange (Koegel 2005:536). Musicologist John Koegel notes that travel to the United States continued, and even increased, during the years of the Mexican Revolution, to be discussed presently, when composers and musicians sought refuge from the tumult and uncertainty of the era. To close this chapter, we will explore briefly the travels of composers, who once directed Porfirio Díaz's celebrated Orquesta Típica de la Ciudad de Mexico: Carlos Curti (1861–1926) and Miguel Lerdo de Tejada (1869–1941).

Inspired by theatrical music, Carlos Curti enlisted a group of students and teachers from the National Conservatory to establish the Orquesta Típica so that the ensemble might represent Mexico at the 1884/1885 New Orleans Cotton Exposition. The instrumentation reflected an eclectic mix of strings and winds that permitted numerous combinations. The musicians played the bowed strings of the symphony orchestra alongside guitars, mandolins, the harp and even the psaltery, an old-world dulcimer. Trumpets, trombones, and sousaphones were also included, as was the tango accordion known as the *bandoneón*. The musicians did not limit themselves to any single style of music or instrumental combination. In the years that followed, the orchestra toured the United States and Europe playing *danzas mexicanas*, marches, arrangements of popular songs, and transcriptions of operatic numbers. Besides formal concerts, the orchestra played for genteel private and civic events, as well as weddings, patron-saint day festivals, and community dances, and contemporary composers and their talents were showcased.

In addition to directing, Curti also played xylophone and mandolin, and composed theatrical music and popular song. His stylized waltz, "Predilicta," offers an example of his work.[15] Curti's zarzuela *La Cuarta Plana* (The Fourth Page, about a newspaperboy) written in 1886 was one of his most popular compositions, but today his music is overshadowed by the attention given to his contemporaries, Ricardo Castro and Manuel Ponce (introduced in Chapter 6).

Composer Miguel Lerdo de Tejada, best known for his song "Perjura," [7.4] was a subsequent director of the Orquesta Típica de la Ciudad de México. Under Lerdo de Tejada's direction, the orchestra played for numerous world fairs: the 1901 Panamerican Expo in Buffalo; the 1904 World's Fair in St. Louis, Missouri; and the 1934/1935 World's Fair in Chicago (Koegel 2006:563). He performed in the most celebrated venues, at Carnegie Hall in 1917 and with some of the era's most famous musicians, including the operatic tenor Enrico Caruso. In the years after the Porfiriato, Tejada began a circuit of vaudeville performances in New York City with his own orchestra founded in 1928.

🎧

7.5

Listening to "Perjura," composed by Miguel Lerdo de Tejado (1900), performed in 1906 by the baritone Manuel Romero Malpica. Source: *Bicentenario 200 Años de la Historia de la Música en México.*

The historic recording of "Perjura" (Perjury)[16] in 7.5 illustrates a skillful blend of popular and classical styles in both the composer's style and the performer's delivery that led to a new kind of cosmopolitan song tradition in Mexico. Operatic renditions like that of Manuel Romero Malpica and the song's later inclusion in a 1938 film of the same name, where it was sung by Jorge Negrete, contributed to its classic status.[17] "Perjura" features lyrics by Fernando Luna y Drusino subtly set to the seductive rhythm of the *danza* by Miguel Lerdo de Tejado.

"Perjura"	**"Perjury"**
No se me olvida cuando en tus brazos al darte un beso mi alma te dí; cuando a tu lado tu amor gozando, ¡ay! delirando, morir creí.	I can't forget when in your arms I gave you my soul as I kissed you when I enjoyed love at your side Ah, delirious! I thought I died.
Cuando mis labios en tu albo cuello con fiebre loca mi bien posé; y en los transportes de amor excelso no sé hasta dónde mi alma se fue.	When my lips are on your white neck I am set with a crazy fever and in the transport of superior love I know nothing of where my soul went.
¿Por qué no fueron aquellas horas como soñé? ¿Por qué ¡ay! huyeron y ya no pueden jamás volver? ¿Por qué no he muerto cuando eras mía y yo tu dios? ¿Cómo es que vivo si éramos uno y hoy somos dos?	Why didn't those hours go as I dreamed? Why did they flee, ah, never to return? Why didn't I die when you were mine and I your god? How can I live if we were one and now are two?
Hoy que te miro pasar radiante con otro amante como yo fui, siento que mi alma en un infierno de amor y celos está por ti.	Today when I watch you passing, radiant with another lover, as I once was I feel my soul burning with love and jealousy for you.
Quiero tu imagen verla borrada con tanto llanto que derramé; quiero olvidarte, que tu recuerdo vaya al abismo de lo que fue.	I want to see your image erased with all the weeping tears I spilled I want to forget you, and for your memory to go to the abyss of what used to be.
Pero no puedo dejar de amarte mi dulce bien. Que es imposible que yo te olvide si eres mi ser. Ya ni la muerte podrá arrancarte del corazón,	But I cannot bear to stop loving you my sweet being. It is impossible that I would forget you if you are my own self. Not even death will tear you from my heart.
Que somos uno aunque tú digas que somos dos.	For we are one, although you say we are two.

Figure 7.6
Lyrics for "Perjura" composed by Miguel Lerdo de Tejada. Used by permission of Edward B. Marks Music Company.

OPERA IN MEXICO

The most distinguished route for composers seeking recognition in the world of classical music was to compose opera, although this was by no means the most practical choice considering the cost and forces required for production. Many of the earliest operas by Mexican composers have not survived to the present and the few of those that have are rarely performed today. Despite the formidable expense and logistics, a taste for opera flourished in Mexico and influenced much more than formal concert music. The first Mexican master of the Italian operatic style was Melesio Morales (1838–1908), who composed eleven operas and whose 1865 opera *Ildegonda* received the most lasting attention. His slightly younger compatriot Ernesto Elorduy (1845–1913) wrote only one opera (although it is really a one-act zarzuela incorporating spoken verse), and while in some ways it embraced the modern perspective supported by Porfirio Díaz, its use of exotic settings and characters provides a frame for exploring the dynamics of alluring but threating international forces (Saavedra 2012).

Elorduy studied composition and piano performance for seven years in Europe with some of the most celebrated artists of the time, including Clara Schumann, Anton Rubenstein, and George Matthias (Miranda 2001:157). He served as ambassador to Barcelona and lived in Paris from 1884–1891, and upon returning to Mexico gained renown for his light, agreeable salon music. His operatic *Zulema* premiered in Mexico City's National Conservatory Theater in 1902 with orchestration by fellow composer Ricardo Castro, whose own opera about the Tarascan princess *Atzimba*, premiered in 1900.

🎧

7.6

Listening to "Duo de Muley y Zulema," from *Zulema*, by Ernesto Elorduy (1902). Live concert recording of Luciano Marazzo, tenor and Mackenzie Romriell, soprano, and Lindsey McHugh, piano. Source: University of Arizona, Center for Latin American Music, 2011.

Elorduy's opera does not overtly address Mexican national themes, nor classic literature, but instead evokes the faraway land and customs of the near East. Set in Turkey, the plot concerns an illicit love affair between Zulema, the favorite harem girl of the Pasha, with a handsome Arab slave. The opera surprised audiences of the time for its audacious subject matter and its departure from the comfortable style of the salon compositions for which Elorduy was best known. Some of his contemporaries compared the intensity and epic aspirations of Elorduy's musical style to the celebrated Italian operatic master Giuseppe Verdi (1813–1901). Like Verdi's operas, *Zulema* can be interpreted in terms of musical and political references. Musicologist Leonora Saavedra (2012) links *Zulema* to a nineteenth-century European fascination with foreign exoticism, explored in French opera, and cultivated as well in the romanticization of the gypsy and moorish roots of flamenco by Spanish romantic composers. She notes that in 1899

Duet from *Zulema*

Tenor (Muley):
Amor, amor divino
que en ardoroso anhelo
nos transportas unidos
a las bodas del cielo

Soprano (Zulema):
Amor de los amores
Que en prado florido

Tenor (Muley):
Amor divino

Soprano (Zulema):
Nos brindaste deleites
En dulcisimo nido

Tenor (Muley):
Amor que mi alma hieres
con tu celestes dardos

Soprano (Zulema):
Amor que me embalsamas
con fragrancia de nardos

Juntos:
Amor sobre mis ojos
Tu sueño eterno vierte
Y que presa en tus brazos
Me soprenda la muerte

Soprano (Zulema):
Muley dulce amor

Tenor (Muley):
Reclinado en tus brazos
Mis cadenas de esclavo caer
Siento en pedazos

Soprano (Zulema):
Reclinado en tus brazos
No soy la pobre sierva de Selim
sino tuya!

Tenor (Muley):
Amor, mi ser enerva
Y teniéndote mía
No me siento ya esclavo de Selim
No siento esclavo
Sino príncipe
de mi desierto flavo! [sic]

Soprano (Zulema):
A tu desierto iremos

Tenor (Muley):
Y si tus gracias quema mi sol [sic]

Soprano (Zulema):
De amor tu eres mi sol

Tenor (Muley):
Ah mi Zulema
Te amo, te amo
Te amo y te adoro

Tenor (Muley):
Love, divine love
that with your burning desire
you transport us together
to a wedding in the sky

Soprano (Zulema):
Love of all loves
That in the flowering meadow

Tenor (Muley):
Divine Love

Soprano (Zulema):
You offered us delights
In the sweetest of nests

Tenor (Muley):
Love that that wounds my soul
with your celestial darts

Soprano (Zulema):
Love that infuses me
with the fragrance of lillies

Together:
Love, over my eyes
Your eternal dream spills
And imprisoned in your arms,
let death surprise me

Soprano (Zulema):
Muley, sweet love

Tenor (Muley):
Reclining in your arms
My chains of slavery fall away
I feel them broken

Soprano (Zulema):
Reclining in your arms
I am not the poor servant of Selim
but yours!

Tenor (Muley):
Love, makes me weak
And having you
I no longer feel like Selim's slave
I don't feel like a slave
Rather a prince
of my own desert

Soprano (Zulema):
To your desert we will go

Tenor (Muley):
And if your thanks burns, my sun

Soprano (Zulema):
Of love, you are my sun

Tenor (Muley):
Ah my Zulema
I love you, I love you
I love you and I adore you

Figure 7.7
Lyrics to the "Duo de Muley y Zulema," from *Zulema*. Lyrics by Ruben M. Campos, music by Ernesto Elorduy. Source: Escuela Nacional de Música. Biblioteca, CENIDIM, INBA.

the librettist, Rubén M. Campos first published the script for *Zulema* in the *Revista Moderna Arte y Ciencia* (Journal of Modern Art and Science), a publication that from 1898–1911 supported writers who shunned the aristocratic airs of the current government. Saavedra's analysis suggests that Zulema offered a frame for exploring nationalism in the guise of exoticism. The sensuous love story of Oriental and European conflict, represented musically by Oriental (more flamenco-like than Turkish or Arab) and European melodic and harmonic qualities, might well be viewed as a cautionary tale for a Mexico caught between the culture and political spheres of closer competing powers: Europe and the United States.

Individual numbers from *Zulema* were published as piano–vocal sheet music for singers to perform in a variety of musical gatherings from private *salones* to *tertulias* (artistic gatherings for learned audiences, usually in public places). The performances might have sounded like that in Audio Example 7.6. Notice that while the music exploits the grand but lyric dramatic qualities of the *bel canto* opera style that so captured the hearts of Mexican audiences, the lyrics are in Spanish, not Italian.

CONCLUDING REFLECTIONS

Taken as a whole, the music promoted by Porfirio Díaz represented Mexico City more than it did the entire country. The orchestras aimed for a cultivated style, even when playing popular music. The zarzuelas, while popular with audiences through the nation during first decade of the twentieth century, typically favored the perspective of the *chilango* (a slang term for residents of Mexico City) on topics such as cosmopolitan life, social interaction, and immigration. Bias aside, the fashion in the central capital set the tone for theaters and concert-going audiences in major cities in other Mexican states.

In addition to the transformation of Mexican instrumental practices, the *Porfiriato* initiated a new trend for cosmopolitan song and many factors contributed to its development. New and more daring forms of musical theater contributed to its formation, among them the short comic zarzuela (*género chico*), and the musical review (*revista*). Theater was the source for the latest fashion, particularly before the emergence of radio and film, which as we shall see in Chapter 8 transformed popular music still further. Audiences adopted songs from the stage, bringing them to their homes, where they acquired new lives as salon music. Musicians often adapted the music that they first performed for elite audiences in salons, cafés, clubs, and casinos to better suit the general populace in fairs, circuses, and cantinas.

As we will see, cosmopolitan song, music theater, grand opera, and the emerging orchestral style all contributed to the development of new music in Mexico—classical and popular—including the modern mariachi style that would come to represent Mexico in film and in recordings.

CRITICAL THINKING AND DISCUSSION PROMPTS

1. How well can you discern popular dance rhythms? Without looking at the track list, listen to the selections on the CD *Orquestas Típicas: The First Recordings: 1926–1938* and try to pinpoint what dance rhythm is featured in each song. What clues help you distinguish one dance type from another? Are any of the tunes familiar to you?

2. Who were some of the composers most associated with the Porfiriato? Choose two and draw comparisons between them. What aspects of their work were affected by the political climate of the era? What aspects of their work survive today?

3. The theatrical stage continued to provide a framework for the development of Mexican music. How did theater influence both popular and classical music in Mexico?

4. The Porfiriato was not the first era in which Mexicans traveled abroad. What made this era of travel different and important for Mexican music?

5. In what ways did music in *Chin Chun Chan* reflect and reinforce the cosmopolitan ambitions of Porfirio Díaz? Was this relationship accidental or intentional?

6. How did the divisions between social classes during the Porfiriato affect musical practice at the time?

7. Do any of the social class divisions fostered by Porfirian politics persist in contemporary Mexican musical practice? Offer at least one example to support your answer.

8. Compare the grand opera style of the Duet from *Zulema* with one of the songs from *Chin Chun Chan*, or any of the other songs presented in this chapter. What differences do you notice in musical style and delivery in performance? Are there any similarities?

KEY TERMS, PEOPLE, AND PLACES

zarzuela	habanera
opera	orquesta típica
orquesta típica	Porfirio Díaz
canción Mexicana	Luis G. Jordá
salon	José Elizondo
tertulia	Carlos Curti
bel canto	Miguel Lerdo de Tejado
danza	Juventino Robles

Melesio Morales	"Monterrey Alegre"
Manuel Ponce	"Perjura"
Chin Chun Chan	"Sobre las olas"
Zulema	waltz

NOTES

1. This passage and all other English translations used in this chapter come from the translation of *Chin Chun Chan* prepared in 2007 by Janet Sturman and the theatrical team at the University of Arizona (Tucson) for a bilingual production presented in that year.
2. Project Gutenberg. www.gutenberg.org/etext/10228. Recording of Porfirio Díaz greeting Thomas Edison.
3. The educational DVD, *La cuarta raíz: Asian diversity in Mexico: Interviews with scholars regarding the Asian diaspora in Latin America with a focus on Mexico* (Los Angeles: Latino Museum of History, Art, and Culture, 2006) edited by Chon A. Noriega, et al., addresses the relatively unrecognized presence of Asians in Latin America.
4. Italian comic theater dating from the fifteenth century and by the seventeenth century featuring a familiar roster of stock characters and predictable slapstick humor. In Italian spelled *commedia dell'arte*.
5. Likely also familiar to audiences from the female character sharing that name in Shakespeare's *A Midsummer Night's Dream*, which maintains the image of Hippolyta as a strong woman willing to stand up for her views.
6. Known initially for his roles in silent films, Noriega earned an Ariel nomination for "Best Actor in a minor role" for his performance in the 1946 film, *Pepita Jiménez,* a cinematic depiction of the famous novel by Juan Valera, which was also set as an opera in 1905 by Spanish composer Issac Albéniz, and reset in 1964 as a zarzuela by Pablo Sorozábal.
7. Encyclopedic Discography of Victor Records. http://victor.library.ucsb.edu/index.php/matrix/detail/600000079/60-Z-Coplas_del_charamusquero
8. Audio example 7.1: Silvia Navarette and Fernando de la Mora, Obras de Luis G. Jordá, CD recording (Mexico City: Mosaic); Video example 7.3— University of Arizona Center for Latin American Studies, Chin Chun Chan, DVD (Tucson, AZ: 2009).
9. Outside of Cuba and the Caribbean this pattern is called the "cinquillo cubano" whereas the word "cinquillo" by itself refers to a quintuplet.
10. Although the *schottische* derives its name from the German word for Scottish, its ultimate origins are contested; what is clear is that this quick, duple-meter dance form gave rise to a vibrant set of Latin American variants. While some scholars identify the *schottische* as rooted in nineteenth-century German and Bohemian round dances, others link it to the French *ecossaise*, a *contradanse* (country dance) dating back to the 1700s. All agree that by the mid-nineteenth century versions of the *schottische* for couple dancers entered the repertory of the international ballroom dance fashion radiating from Paris. Like other ballroom dances it was adopted around the world and acquired regional names.
11. For Mexican audiences these statements would also evoke slang curse words. See Ezequiel Ojeda, "Hablando de Chin Chun Chan. Una entrevista

con Enrique Alonso." *Tramoya*, 1986. http://cdigital.uv.mx/bitstream/
123456789/3763/2/19868P94.pdf

12. Reminiscences communicated personally with the author.

13. Various Artists, CDs to accompany, Jesus Flores y Escalante and Pablo
Dueñas, *Bicentenario 200 Años de la Historia de la Música en México*, (Mexico
City: Sony Entertainment, 2010); Various Musicians, *Bandas Sinaloenses
"Musica Tambora"* Historic Mexican American Music, Vol. 11, CD 7048
(Arhoolie, 2001).

14. Mexican–American Border Music, Vol. 4—Various Artists, *Orquestas Típicas,
The First Recordings 1928–1938* (Arhoolie, #7017).

15. A historic recording of this song scored for two mandolins and guitar
appears on the website: http://cylinders.library.ucsb.edu/mp3s/1000/1327/
cusb-cyl1327d.mp3

16. While the title literally translates to "perjurer," it is sometimes translated
as "Liar."

17. In the film Negrete begins singing "Perjura" with the second verse. A clip
appears on YouTube at http://youtu.be/PhWJEvau9yo

FOR REFERENCE AND FURTHER STUDY

Brenner, Helmut. 2010. *Juventino Rosas: His Life, His Work, His Time*. Warren,
MI: Harmonie Park Press.

Brill, Mark. 2011. "Mexico." In *Music of Latin America and the Caribbean*. New
York: Prentice-Hall (Pearson).

Canton Ferrer, Christian. 2010. *Vida i obra de Luis G. Jordá (1869–1951). El
músic de les Masies de Roda que va tromfar a México*. Barcelona: Ajuntament
de les Masies de Roda.

Chanda, Nayan. 1999. "Early Warning." *Far Eastern Economic Review*
162(23):46–48.

Chao Romero, Roberto. 2010. *The Chinese in Mexico, 1882–1940*. Tucson, AZ:
University of Arizona Press.

Compton, Timothy G. 1994. "Mexico City Theatre, Summer 1993," *Latin
American Theater Review* 27:133–138.

Flores y Escalante, Jesús and Pablo Dueñas. 2010. *Bicentenario. 200 Años de la
historia de la música en México*. With 4 CDs and 100 recordings from
1905–2010. Mexico City: Sony Music Mexico.

García Hernández, Arturo. 2010. "Lejos del fasto, el Conservatorio se suma a las
efemérides patrias," *La Jornada* 14. www.jornada.unam.mx/2010/06/14/
cultura/a08n1cul (accessed January 12, 2015).

Garner, Richard L. 1988. "Long-Term Silver Mining Trends in Spanish America:
A Comparative Analysis of Peru and Mexico." *The American Historical
Review* 93(4):898–935.

Garrido, Juan S. 1981. *Historia de la Música Popular en México, 1876–1973*.
Mexico City: Editorial Extemporáneos.

Grial, Hugo de. 1965. *Músicos Mexicanos*. Mexico City: Editorial Diana.

Hardison Londré, Felicia and Watermeier, Daniel J. 2000. *The History of North
American Theater*. London and New York: Continuum International
Publishing Group.

Haney, Peter. 2003. "Bilingual Humor, Verbal Hygiene, and the Gendered
Contradictions of Cultural Citizenship in Early Mexican American
Comedy." *Journal of Linguistic Anthropology* 13(2):163–188.

Haney, Peter Clair. 2004. "Carpa y Teatro, Sol y Sombra. Show Business and Public
Culture in San Antonio's Mexican Colony, 1900–1940." PhD diss.,
University of Texas at Austin. www.lib.utexas.edu/etd/d/2004/haneypc042/
haneypc042.pdf (accessed January 12, 2015).

Hu-DeHart, Evelyn. 1984. *Yaqui Resistance and Survival*. Seattle, WA: University of Washington Press.

Hu-DeHart, Evelyn. 2006. "The Chinese in Mexico, A Brief Historical Sketch of their Rise and Fall." In Khun Eng Kuah-Pearce and Evelyn Hu-DeHart (Eds.). *Volunteer Organizations in the Chinese Diaspora*. Hong Kong: Hong Kong University Press, 141–158.

Koegel, John. 2005. "La Vida Musical en México del Siglo XIX." In *Discanto: ensayos de investigación musical, vol. 1*, 79–108. Veracruz, Mexico: Universidad Veracruzana.

Koegel, John. 2006. "Compositores Mexicanos y Cubanos en Nueva York, 1880–1920." *Historia Mexicana*, 56(2):533–602. http://codex.colmex.mx:8991/exlibris/aleph/a18_1/apache_media/252JL62J79DQ2BVLI7NY2B1RAD9XLI.pdf (accessed January 12, 2015).

Leal, Juan Felipe, Carlos Arturo Flores, and Eduardo Barraza, 2005. *Anales del ciné en México, 1895–1911, vol. 7, part 1*. 2nd ed. Mexico City: Voyeur, 66.

Mano a Mano. *Mexican Culture Without Borders*. www.manoamano.us/en/mexican-migration.html (accessed January 12, 2015).

Manuel, Peter. 2011. *Creolizing Contradance in the Caribbean*. Philadelphia, PA: Temple University Press.

Medina, Rafael and Elizondo, José. 1904. *Chin Chun Chan. Conflicto chino en un acto*. Mexico City: Medina y Comp. Impresores.

Meyer, Michael C., Sherman, William L., and Deeds, Susan. 2007. *The Course of Mexican History*. 8th ed. New York: Oxford University Press.

Miranda, Ricardo. 2001. "De Estambul a Tuxtepec: Zulema." In *Ecos, alientos y sonidos: ensayos sobre música mexicana*. Veracruz, Mexico: Universidad Veracruzana, 155–170.

Monterde García Icazbalceta, Francisco. 1970 (reprint of 1933 ed.) *Bibliografía del Teatro en Mexico*. North Stratford, NH: Ayer.

Morales, Alfonso, et al. 1984. *El país de las tandas: teatro de revista 1900–1940*. Mexico City: Secretaría de Educación Pública, Museo Nacional de Culturas Populares.

Moreno Rivas, Yolanda. 1979. *Historia de la música popular mexicana*. México City: Alianza Editorial Mexicana (Consejo Nacional para la Cultura y las Artes).

Noriega, Chon A., et al. (Eds.). 2006. *La cuarta raíz: Asian Diversity in Mexico: Interviews with Scholars regarding the Asian Diaspora in Latin America with a Focus on Mexico*. Los Angeles: Latino Museum of History, Art, and Culture. DVD.

Ojeda, Ezequiel. 1986. "Hablando de Chin Chun Chan. Una entrevista con Enrique Alonso." *Tramoya*. http://cdigital.uv.mx/bitstream/123456789/3763/2/19868P94.pdf (accessed January 12, 2015).

Peña, Manuel. 1985. *The Texas-Mexican Conjunto*. Austin, TX: University of Texas Press.

Peña, Manuel. 1999. *The Mexican American Orquesta*. Austin, TX: University of Texas Press.

Pérez-Fernández, Rolando Antonio. "De China a Cuba. Una Mirada a su Etnomusicología." *Revista Cultural de Nuestra América* 13(48):41–44. http://ojs.unam.mx/index.php/archipielago/article/view/19768 (accessed January 12, 2015).

Pomeranz, Ken and Bin Wong. 2009. *China and Europe, 1500–2000 and Beyond. What is Modern?* Columbia University: Asian Topics in World History. http://afe.easia.columbia.edu/chinawh/web/s5/s5_4b.html (accessed January 12, 2015).

Pujols, Ana Cecilia. n.d. *Panorama de la música en México*. www.elportalde-mexico.com/arte/musica/musica.htm (accessed January 12, 2015).

Reyes de la Maza, Luis. 1910. *Cien Años de Teatro en Mexico: 1810–1910*. Mexico: SEP.

Reyes de la Maza, Luis. 1984. *En el nombre de Dios hablo de teatro*. México: Universidad Nacional Autónoma de México.

Saavedra, Leonora. 2007. "Staging the Nation, Race, Religion and History in Mexican Opera." *Opera Quarterly* 23(1):1–21.

Saavedra, Leonora. 2012. "Spanish Moors and Turkish Captives in fin de siècle Mexico: Exoticism as Strategy." *Journal of Musicological Research* 31(4):231–261.

Shaffer, Lynda. 1986. "China, Technology and Change," *World History Bulletin* 4(1):1–6.

Suárez-Orozco, C., Suárez-Orozco, M. and Baolin Qin-Hillard, D. (Eds.). 2005. *The New Immigration: An Interdisciplinary Reader*. New York: Routledge.

Strachwitz, Chris. 1990. *Orquestas Típicas: The First Recordings: 1926–1938. Pioneer Mexican-American Dance Orchestras*. 1-CD with notes. (Arhoolie Folklyric 7017) El Cerrito: Arhoolie Productions.

Sturman, Janet. 2000. *Zarzuela: Spanish Operetta, American Stage*. Urbana, IL: University of Illinois Press.

Truett, Samuel. 2006. *Fugitive Landscapes: The Forgotten History of the U.S.–Mexico Borderlands*. New Haven, CT: Yale University Press.

DISCOGRAPHY

Album musical de Juventino Rosas. Guanajuato: Gobierno del Estado de Guanajuato, 1995.

Bicentenario 200 Años de Música en México. 4 CDs and 100 recordings from 1905–2010. Mexico City: Sony Music Mexico.

Silvia Navarette and Fernando de la Mora, *Obras de Luis G. Jordá*, CD recording Mexico City: Mosaic, 1998.

Various Musicians, *Bandas Sinaloenses "Musica Tambora"* Historic Mexican American Music, Vol. 11, Arhoolie, CD #7048, 2001.

Various Artists, *Orquestas Típicas, The First Recordings 1928–1938*, Arhoolie CD #7017, 1991.

VIDEOS AND FILMS

Chin Chun Chan, directed and produced by Janet Sturman. 2009. Tucson, AZ: University of Arizona School of Music, Center for Latin American Music www.youtube.com/watch?v=qpEdlCytFt8.

La cuarta raíz: Asian diversity in Mexico: Interviews with scholars regarding the Asian diaspora in Latin America with a focus on Mexico. Los Angeles: Latino Museum of History, Art, and Culture. Edited by Noriega, Chon A., et al., 2006. DVD.

Silver Connects the World. Annenberg Foundation. www.learner.org/courses/worldhistory/unit_video_15–1.html

Sobre las olas (1950) directed by Ismael Rodríguez. Burbank, CA: Warner Home Video. 2007. A feature film about the life of musician Juventino Rosas, with Pedro Infante as the title character.

WEBSITES

Cylinder Preservation and Digitization Project. University of California, Santa Barbara. http://cylinders.library.ucsb.edu (accessed November 24, 2014).

Discography of American Historical Recordings, s.v. "Victor matrix 60-Z. Coplas del charamusquero/José Torres Ovando; Señoritas Pérez." http://adp. library.ucsb.edu/index.php/matrix/detail/600000079/60-Z-Coplas_del_ charamusquero (accessed November 24, 2014).

Historia de la Orquesta Típica de la Ciudad de México. www.danielzarabozo. com/zarabozo8e.html (accessed November 24, 2014).

Music for the Nation: American Sheet Music, American Memory Project. Library of Congress. (Mexican music scores). www.memory.loc.gov (accessed November 24, 2014).

Project Gutenberg. Recording of Porfirio Díaz greeting Thomas Edison. www.gutenberg.org/etext/10228 (accessed November 24, 2014).

Secretaria de Cultura. "Orquesta Típica de la Cuidad de México." www.cultura. df.gob.mx/index.php/programas2/otcm (accessed November 24, 2014).

CHAPTER 8

Gifts of the Revolution

Not all Mexicans benefited from the economic development and foreign investment that Porfirio Díaz brought to Mexico during his 35 years in power. Many ordinary citizens and laborers, particularly textile workers, railroad workers and miners, experienced discrimination to the point of being treated like slaves by the foreigners who owned and managed these enterprises. When workers enacted strikes, the president dealt harshly with them as with those supporting other domestic protests and uprisings, further exacerbating discontent.

We can learn the story of the Revolution the way that many Mexicans did over a century ago, through the stories told in the narrative ballads called *corridos*. Those narratives, like the *corrido* itself, circulated well before the onset of the Revolution in 1810 but the revolutionary cause gave them new significance, helping to make the genre one of the most important forms of Mexican expression.

PRE-REVOLUTIONARY *CORRIDOS*

The story should begin with pre-revolutionary *corridos* that tell the tales of peasant bandits who fought against injustice. Although the original circumstances of the conflicts told in the song occurred before the Revolution, such songs were sung to fuel the fires of dissent and inspire men to join the cause of the revolutionary fighters.

One example is the tale of the Sinaloan miner Heraclio Bernal, who was accused of theft and thrown into jail in Mazatlán. In 1885 he signed a proclamation denouncing the legitimacy of the presidency of Porfirio Díaz and the administration in Sinaloa. Authorities responded to this bravado by arresting and executing him in 1888.

Listening to "El Corrido de Heraclio Bernal," author unknown, as sung by the Trío Nava, recorded in New York in 1921.[1]

8.1

Figure 8.1
Lyrics for the corrido
"Heraclio Bernal."
Source: *The Mexican
Revolution.* Arhoolie
Folklyric (7041–7044).

"El Corrido de Heraclio Bernal"

Año de mil ochocientos,
noventa y dos al contar,
compuse yo esta tragedia
que aquí les voy a cantar

Estado de Sinaloa,
gobierno de Mazatlán
donde daban diez mil pesos
por la vida de Bernal.

Dijo doña Bernadina:
"Ven, siéntate a descansar,
mientras traigo diez mil pesos
pa' poderte reemplazar."

Oigan amigos que fue
lo que sucedió:
Heraclio no tenía armas,
por eso no les peleó.

Desgraciado fue Crespín
cuando lo vino a entregar,
pidiendo los diez mil pesos
por la vida de Bernal.

Agarró los diez mil pesos,
los amarró en su mascada,
y le dijo al comandante:
"Prevéngase su Acordada."

"Prevéngase su Acordada
y escuadrón militar,
y vámonos a Durango
a traer a Heraclio Bernal."

Les dijo Heraclio Bernal:
"Yo no ando de robabueyes,
yo tengo plata acuñada
en ese Real de los Reyes."

Adiós muchachas bonitas,
transiten por donde quieran,
ya murió Heraclio Bernal,
el mero león de la sierra.

Adiós indios de las huertas
ya se dormirán a gusto,
ya no hay Heraclio Bernal,
ya no morirán del susto

Ya con ésta me despido
no me queda qué cantar,
éstas son las mañanitas
de don Heraclio Bernal.

"The Ballad of Heraclio Bernal"

In eighteen hundred
and ninety-two
I wrote this song
that I will now sing to you.

In the State of Sinaloa,
the government of Mazatlán
offered 10,000 pesos to bring in
Bernal, dead or alive.

Doña Bernardina told him:
"Come, rest a while,
I'll pay the pesos
and save your life."

Listen, friends,
I'll tell you what happened:
Heraclio didn't fight
because he was unarmed.

Crespin was the traitor
who gave him away,
he asked for the 10,000 pesos
in exchange for Bernal's life.

He took the 10,000 pesos
and wrapped them in his bandanna,
telling the commander:
"Prepare your men."

"Prepare your men
and the firing squad,
and let's go to Durango
to get Heraclio Bernal."

Heraclio Bernal said:
"I'm not a cattle rustler,
I've got minted silver
down in the Real de los Reyes" [a mine]

Goodbye pretty girls,
you may go wherever you please,
Heraclio Bernal, the mountain lion,
is now dead.

Goodbye Indians of the fields
who will be able to sleep well
since there's not Heraclio Bernal,
and he won't scare you to death.

With this I say goodbye
I have nothing else to sing,
these are the morning verses
of don Heraclio Bernal.

The heroic portrayal of men who ran afoul of the law while standing against injustice set the tone for revolutionary fervor and established a pattern for narrative content of the corrido. Set to simple, repetitive music, the point of these songs was the story and the creation of heroes to represent the cause of ordinary people. The predictable features of the verse and narrative form helped listeners remember the stories and singers to create them.

Trío Nava's performance of "Heraclio Bernal" uses only two chords in the guitar harmony. The instrumentalists play a simple role in the narrative "drama" by supporting the verse, and while their parts may occasionally serve as instrumental commentary, they never play over the voice. The singers sing in close, parallel harmony; their parts do not diverge from the shared task of presenting the story. Their rhythmic approach is however more complex than may be evident at first. The song unfolds in a 6/8 meter, predominantly in duple meter. However at the end of every other line of text, the accentuation shifts to a triple meter to close the phrase. This results in a four-measure pattern where the first, third, and fourth measures are in 6/8 (felt in two beats) and the second measure in 9/8 (felt in three beats) to align the lyrics with shifts in the harmony. The subtle shift from duple to triple meter changes the pace and adds emphasis to the closing word of each phrase.

MADERO'S DECISIVE UPRISING

Landowners in the countryside lived well. Some owned estates, known as *haciendas*, some with as many as a million acres of land. In contrast, the peasants who worked the land lived in poverty and were treated hardly better than slaves. A new generation of Mexican politicians, intellectuals, and activists, supported by workers and peasants rose up against the inequities permitted by Díaz and his administration. Francisco Madero, the son of a wealthy landowner himself, responded to these protests, leading the call for a more democratic government with his famed *Plan de San Luis Potosí* and running against Díaz for the presidency in 1910.

In 1910 Porfirio Díaz defeated Madero and was re-elected as president. To secure his position, Díaz had Madero jailed, but he escaped and called for an armed uprising against the president. Madero and his revolutionary forces succeeded in ousting Díaz, who after his resignation went into exile in France, where he later died. Madero was sworn in as the new president on November 6, 1911. He did not stay in power for long. Challenged by Victoriano Huerta, originally a supporter of Díaz, Madero was deposed and assassinated and Huerta assumed the presidency in 1913, although he would not stay for long either. By 1914 a reconstituted alliance of revolutionary forces forced Huerta from office and Venustiano Carranza, an early supporter of Madero and the leader of the rebel forces known as the Constitutional Army, became the 37th president of Mexico.

CORRIDOS OF THE REVOLUTION

The musical genre most typically associated with the Revolution is the corrido, Mexico's signature narrative ballad form rooted in the romance tradition of golden age Spain. The custom of singing tales flourished as oral tradition, both by convention and necessity. Singers tailored the narrative ballads to elicit specific sympathies not mass appeal. Furthermore, during the drawn-out years of the Revolution, Mexico's nascent recording industry ceased operation, only to resume in 1926, and the first significant body of corrido recordings made during the genre's own golden age from 1928–1937 were made on the U.S. side of the border (Strachwitz and Nicolopoulos 1994:9). Many of the audio examples used in this chapter were recorded during that period and the authors of most of the lyrics remain unknown today. It appears that the information conveyed took precedence over authorship within these popular circles of exchange.

8.2 Listening to the "Nuevo Corrido de Madero" as sung by Manuel Camacho y Regino Pérez, recorded in 1930. *The Mexican Revolution. Corridos about the Heroes and Events 1910–1920 and Beyond!*

Camacho and Pérez's recording of the "Nuevo Corrido de Madero" [8.2], made during the golden age of corrido recordings, features a more elaborate instrumental accompaniment than the simple "oom-pah-pah" heard in Audio Example 8.1. Note the driving walking bass-line performed by the *bajo sexto* player (see Fig. 8.5), and notice also that the same subtle shift from duple to triple accentuation that we heard in the previous example.

PANCHO VILLA IN SONG

A major leader during the Revolution was Doroteo Arango (1878–1923), better known by his pseudonym, Francisco "Pancho" Villa and through the legends and songs about him. General Villa fought in the initial uprising in 1911, winning a battle against Pascual Orozco in Ciudad Juárez. He fought for Madero in 1913 and won fame for his victory in Zacatecas where he opposed the federal forces of Carranza. Villa's famed North Division forces were defeated by future presidential challenger, Álvaro Obregón at the battle of Celaya in the state of Guanajuato in 1915. Villa attacked the garrison in the town of Columbus, New Mexico, in protest of the U.S. government's support of the President Carranza. In response, U.S. General Pershing pursued Villa, following him to Mexico where he eluded capture. In 1920 the Mexican government gave Pancho Villa and his men a ranch in return for laying down their arms, but they were soon assassinated in 1923, likely by order of Álvaro Obregón.

8.3 Listening to "Gral [General] Francisco Villa" as sung by Los Cuatezones in 1965. Source: *The Mexican Revolution.*

"Nuevo Corrido de Madero"

En mil novecientos diez,
en la ciudad de San Luis
expidió su plan Madero
pa' Porfirio combatir:
empezó por Ciudad Juárez
a recorrer el país.

¡Ah, qué Madero tan hombre,
le conozco sus acciones!
Derecho se fue a la cárcel
a echar fuera las prisiones:
Virgen Santa'e Guadalupe
lo llene de bendiciones.

Aquí me siento a cantar
estos versos familiares:
comenzaré con la muerte
de Madero y Pino Suárez,
que a México traicionaron
esas fuerzas federales.

La viuda le dice a Huerta
que no subiera al sillón,
que no después anduviera
con dolor de corazón,
porque allá viene Carranza
con nueva revolución.

Carranza le puso un parte,
que no perdía la esperanza
de tumbarlo de la silla
con su puñal y su lanza,
para que gritaran todos:
"Muchachos, ¡viva Carranza!"

Pancho Villa y Maytorena,
que en el norte se voltearon,
reconocieron las causas
que de un principio pelearon,
y se unieron al partido
que ellos mismos derrotaron.

"The New Ballad of Madero"

In nineteen hundred and ten,
in the city of San Luis Potosí
Madero set up his plan
to battle Porfirio Díaz:
he set out from Ciudad Juárez
on a nationwide campaign.

What a man Madero was!
I know his deeds,
he went straight to the jails
and set free the prisoners,
may the Saintly Virgin of Guadalupe
fill him with blessings.

Here I sit to sing
these familiar lyrics,
I'll begin with the deaths
of Madero and Pino Súarez
and how those federal forces
betrayed Mexico.

The widow (of Madero) told Huerta
not to assume the presidential seat,
because it would end up
breaking his heart,
and Carranza was coming right behind
with another revolution.

Carranza sent (Huerta) a message
saying he didn't lose hope
of toppling his government
by sword and knife,
so that everyone would shout:
"Viva Carranza!"

Pancho Villa and Maytorena,
who switched sides up North,
acknowledged those they had
originally fought against
and joined the forces
they had once defeated.

Figure 8.2
Lyrics for "Nuevo Corrido de Madero." Source: *Corridos & Tragedias de la Frontera. Mexican–American Border Music*, vols 6 & 7, 1994, pp. 9, Arhoolie Records, CD 7019/7020.

Figure 8.3
Portrait of Pancho
Villa. Source:
Biografías Selectas
(Mexico: Editorial
Argumentos, January
2, 1960).

As befitting a song about the commander of the Northern Division, and the *de facto* warlord of the state of Chihuahua, Los Cuatezones sing "Gral Francisco Villa" in true *norteño* (northern) style, with a *conjunto* (combo) of players using button accordion, bajo sexto, and guitar to accompany the singers. The reference to the 30–30 rifle in this song is taken up again in another corrido about Pancho Villa, "Carabina 30–30" [8.4].

Listening to "Carabina 30–30 [Treinta-Treinta]," performed by Los Lobos and recorded in 1993. Source: *Just Another Band from East L.A.*

8.4

The 1993 rendition of "Carabina Treinta-Treinta" by Los Lobos (The Wolves), a popular Chicano band from East Los Angeles in the United

"Gral Francisco Villa"

Francisco Villa nació
con el valor mexicano,
para ayudar a los pobres
contra el yugo del tirano

Villa salió del Parral
a defender su partido,
por eso los federales
lo trataban de bandido.

Villa con un compañero
hizo correr a cincuenta,
con su pistola en la mano
su rifle treinta-treinta.

¡Ay, qué cabeza de Villa
que ni un momento vacila!
Tomó el fortín más pesado
del cerrito de La Pila.

Los de Camargo dirán,
los que tuvieron presentes
cuantos pelones quedaron
antes de pasar el puente.

¡Ay, qué combate tan fuerte
el que Villa ha preparado!
La primera contraseña
era un paño colorado.

"éntrale Pascual Orozco,
tú decias que eras la fiebre,
que en el sitio de Reyames
tú corriste como liebre."

Gritaba el mocho Obregón:
"Aquí me hicieron salvaje,
ya me acabaron los yaquis
en este rancho de Guaje."

Pobres de los federales
que defendieron Torreón:
contra las fuerzas de Villa
era parar un ciclón.

"General Francisco Villa"

Francisco Villa was born
with Mexican courage,
to help the poor
against the rule of tyrants.

Villa, left Parral
to defend his cause
that's why the federal forces
called him a bandit.

Villa, with a friend,
routed out 50 men,
with his pistol in his hand
and his 30–30 rifle.

What a sharp mind Villa had,
he was never indecisive,
he captured the heaviest stronghold
at La Pila hill.

The people of Camargo will tell you,
the one who were there,
they'll tell you how many *baldies*
fell before crossing the bridge.

What a heavy combat
Villa has set up,
the first signal was
a red bandanna.

"Come on, Pascual Orozco,
didn't you say you were the toughest?
But at the battle of Reyames
you ran like a hare."

The one-armed Obregón shouted:
"I'll lose everything here!
The Yaqui Indians already wiped me out
at El Guaje ranch."

Poor federal soldiers
who defended Torreón,
fighting against Villa's forces
was like stopping a hurricane.

Figure 8.4
Lyrics for "General
Francisco Villa."
Source: *The Mexican
Revolution.* Arhoolie
Folklyric (7041–7044).

Figure 8.5
The bajo sexto, with 12 strings in 6 courses. Courtesy of Reyes Accordion &
Bajo Sexto Forum [reyesforo.com].

"Carabina 30–30"	"30–30 Carabine Rifle"
Carabinas 30–30 que los rebeldes portaban y decían los federales² que con ellas no mataban. [x2]	Carabines 30–30 that the rebels carried and the federal agents said that they didn't kill with them. [x2]
Con mi 30–30 me voy a marchar a engrosar las filas de la rebelión si mi sangre piden mi sangre les doy por los habitantes de nuestra nación.	With my 30–30 I am going to march to increase the ranks of the rebellion if they ask for my blood, my blood I give them for the inhabitants of our nation.
Gritaba Francisco Villa: ¿dónde te hayas Argumedo? ven párate aquí adelante tú que nunca tienes miedo. [x2]	Francisco Villa shouted: where are you Argumedo? you see trouble ahead and yet continue you who is never scared. [x2]
Con mi 30–30 me voy a marchar . . .	With my 30–30 I am going to march . . .
Ya nos vamos pa' Chihuahua, ya se va tu negro santo si me quebra alguna bala ve a llorarme al campo santo.	We're heading to Chihuahua, your black saint has already gone If I take a bullet, Go cry for me in the cemetery.
Con mi 30–30 me voy a marchar . . .	With my 30–30 I am going to march . . .

Figure 8.6
Lyrics for "Carabina 30–30." Attributed to Coronel José Isabel de los Santo Montalvo.
(Public Domain).

States illustrates the continued popularity of the corrido and its iconic images. This group of stellar musicians present an enriched combination of instruments, including the trap drum set and the baritone saxophone, along with electric guitar and bass. In earlier versions of this song the word "federales" appears as "maderistas" confirming the protagonists' alignment with Madero.

In this rendition, the lyrics offer fewer historic details regarding Pancho Villa's activities, and allow the historic revolutionary to speak for himself. Villa taunts his adversary Benjamin Argumedo. Known as the fearless "Lion of the Laguna," Argumedo supported Huerta's efforts to oust Madero, and challenged Villa for control of the northern states of Coahuila and Durango. The final verse expresses a common sentiment in corridos, the hope that the protagonist might be remembered after his inevitable death in battle.

WOMEN IN *CORRIDOS*

In the examples to this point, the women represented in the corridos have largely played supporting roles as mothers, wives, or represented the subject of the protagonist's affections.

Corridistas also sang about the roles that women played in combat as *soldaderas* (female soldiers) during the Revolution. The most celebrated soldaderas were reputedly named Adelita and Valentina, and songs exist about both. Technically classified as lyric songs rather than traditional corridos, both have been treated as corridos by performers and listeners alike. In 8.5, a historic rendition of "La Adelita," the iconic and much adored soldadera, is sung by the Trío González to a spirited polka rhythm. Historical records indicate that the real Adelita joined the revolutionary forces as a nurse, helping to form the Mexican Red Cross (Lavin 2011). The fighting role of Adelita is never mentioned in the song lyrics. Instead, Adelita appears to be the woman of a soldier's dreams, and alas his unrequited love.

> Listening to "La Adelita" as sung by the Trío González, recorded in 1919. Source: *Bicentenario 200 Años de Música en México.*

8.5

All performances of corridos are not the same. The famous recordings by Lydia Mendoza, known as the "Lark of the Border," show the popularity of the song "Adelita" with audiences who lived and worked along the Texas–Mexico border. Mendoza's recording illustrates her communicative vocal technique and her skillful guitar playing. The context, obviously a live performance where she was taking requests, reminds us of another traditional feature of corridos: to document and reinterpret conflict. In the context of the bracero movement of the 1940s, a program from 1942–1963 during which the United States formally imported temporary contract labor from Mexico, listeners may perceive parallels between the isolation and conflict of war with those experienced by migrant laborers who missed

Figure 8.7
Lyrics for "Adelita."
Traditional (Public
Domain).

"La Adelita"

Adelita se llama la ingrata,
la que era dueña de todo mi placer,
nunca pienses que llegue a olvidarla,
ni a cambiarla por otra mujer.

Si Adelita quisiera ser mi esposa,
y si Adelita ya fuera mi mujer,
le compraría un vestido de seda
y la llevaba a dormir al cuartel.

Si Adelita se fuese con otro
le seguiría la huella sin cesar,
en aeroplano y en buques de guerra,
y si se quiere hasta en tren militar.

Ya me llama el clarín de campaña
como valiente guerrero a pelear,
correrá por raudales la sangre
pero olvidarte jamás lo verás.

Y si acaso yo muero en campaña
y mi cadáver en la tierra va a quedar
Adelita por Dios te lo ruego
que con tus ojos te vayas a llorar.

Adelita por Dios te lo ruego
nunca vayas a hacerme traición.
Sabes bien que mi amor es ya tuyo
como lo es todo mi corazón.

"Adelita"

Adelita is the name of the ungrateful one,
the one who owned my love.
Don't ever think that I would forget her
or exchange her for another woman.

If Adelita wanted to be my wife,
if Adelita were to be my woman
I would buy her a silk dress
and take her to the barracks to sleep
with me.

If Adelita were to leave with another
I'd follow in her footsteps endlessly
on an airplane, on a warship, even on a
military train.

Now the bugle is calling me
a brave warrior to battle.
The blood will run in torrents
but I will never forget you.

If by chance I should die in battle
and my body be left on the land
Adelita, by God I beg you
to cry for me with those eyes of yours.

Adelita, by God I beg you
please never betray me.
You know my love is yours
as is all of my heart.

their loved ones as much as the protagonist feared losing the love of Adelita. In contemporary times corridos, new and old, continue to address the ongoing conflicts that shape life along the United States–Mexico border, a subject all its own.

8.6

Listening to "Adelita" as sung by Lydia Mendoza. Source: *La Alondra de la Frontera—Live!*

The music of Houston-born Lydia Mendoza (1916–2007) served as a symbol of Mexican and Mexican-American pride from her first recordings in 1928 until a stroke ended her career in 1986.[3] During and after the Civil Rights movement, she came to represent the community of Mexican origin in the United States. She sang only in Spanish and geared her performances for the working people of Mexican ancestry who lived and worked along

the United States–Mexico border. Her popularity with these audiences earned her the sobriquet "Lark of the Border." Without fanfare, she also came to represent the strong, confident, and capable Mexican woman, an image that continued to inspire her audiences, particularly as social policies changed to give women more rights. Given this background, it is not surprising that "Adelita" was one of her most requested songs.

While Mendoza made several of her first recordings in the late 1920s with her family as back-up musicians, she later recorded and performed solo, accompanying herself on the guitar. She developed a special playing style on the guitar where she would pluck the bass notes with her thumb and strum the harmony with her fingers. This technique allowed her to combine the bass and harmony parts traditionally played by two separate players.

THE TUMULTUOUS 1920S

While we have focused on corridos of the Revolution in this chapter, the genre is not the only important kind of music associated with that period of time, nor is the corrido associated only with revolutionary concerns. The tumult of the Revolution persisted throughout the 1920s and did not abate until the presidency of Lázaro Cárdenas in 1938. The post-revolutionary reforms begun during the presidency of Plutarco Elías Calles (1924–1932) and subsequent administrations will be discussed in Chapter 9 in connection with the rise of the film industry. Throughout the fractious era following the revolutionary war, music continued to be important to Mexicans. People used music to help them unify experience, entertain, relieve stress, share tales, and win the hearts and minds of listeners on all sides of issues.

Chapter 7 noted that during the first decades of the twentieth century many musicians left Mexico to seek their fortune elsewhere, particularly in the United States. Some, like Maria Grever, the great composer of popular songs for film and stage never returned, others like Manuel Ponce and Lucha Reyes, discussed in Chapter 9, did return, to great effect. The Mexican recording industry stalled in the 1920s and the earliest recordings of Mexican popular music were pressed in the United States during that decade. However, the Mexican entertainment industry gained strength in the 1930s and 1940s, becoming an international force as discussed in Chapter 9.

The migration of musicians from rural to urban areas within Mexico during the 1920s fostered the growth of the urban mariachi tradition, as previously noted. President Lázaro Cárdenas's sponsorship of the mariachi promoted the greater inclusion of select regional styles helping to make that ensemble the signature sound of Mexican popular music. Civic leaders linked the music played by these groups to other prominent symbols of nationality. It is during this era that musicians begin dressing in the distinctive *charro* suits of the well-to-do ranch owners, used first by musicians in the orquestas típicas, then gradually adopted by mariachis. It is during the 1920s and 1930s that the image of the China Poblana gained national prominence.[4] The pretty mestizo girl with her country dress, be-ribboned braids and silk shawl appeared everywhere dancing with her charro partner in hundreds of announcements, paintings, engravings, magazines, and of course, in the dress of staged folkloric dancers.

There is not time nor space to explore here other forms of music that also served the project of creating a new and more equitable nation. Wind bands, once the servants of the church and military, gained importance as patriotic symbols during this era. Also the ministries of culture and education, under the direction of composer Carlos Chávez, began a program of new concert composition and education to represent post-revolutionary ideals. The composition *Sones de Mariachis* [5.14] resulted from a request by Chávez for that program. We will have occasion to return to the movement of post-revolutionary composition in later chapters.

CONCLUDING REFLECTIONS

The decision to emphasize the corrido as the genre at the heart of this chapter was designed to illustrate the artistic, political, and social value of the genre during the period when it emerged as an exceptionally potent means of communication. Its role in the revolutionary times cemented its persisting role in Mexican and Mexican-American life to the present. Our brief exploration of the music of singer Lydia Mendoza introduced the value of the corrido to the Mexican migrant, a topic that Martha Chew explores in detail in her book *Corridos in Migrant Memory* (2006). Chew illustrates how the corrido has served individuals and communities in creating cultural memory, shaping social, and individual identity in the process. Programs such as the University of Arizona Poetry Center's annual corrido competition for high school students promote the corrido as a format for addressing topics of personal and current concern.[5] The Smithsonian Institution in the United States maintains a dynamic website introducing the corrido as a means of documenting and reflecting on the American experience, inviting visitors to try their hand at creating their own corrido.[6]

The examples explored in this chapter illustrate many of the predictable conventions of corrido format. These include patterns of poetic form, thematic concern, narrative customs, and descriptive convention, as well as customs of musical form. As we have seen the verses in a corrido build a story. Early in the song the narrator may introduce himself along with the protagonists in the story. The opening verses typically set the scene by providing specific dates, times, and names of places. To further frame the story, the singer often closes the song with a concluding message or a farewell, called the *despedida*. The poetry follows a conventional line-end rhyme scheme: ABCB, a popular format for the four-line quatrain. The narrative process in the corrido typically offers perspective on the subject, allowing listeners to understand the story from a particular angle. The music employs a predictable alternation between two or three main chords (I, V7, IV) and is typically in the upbeat rhythm of a waltz or a polka, no matter how sad the topic. For centuries such ballads have helped people make sense of experiences that involved love, loss, betrayal, prejudice, as well as demeaning and exploitative treatment. Today the corrido enjoys tremendous commercial popularity. Our single example of the corrido performed in the norteño style by the band Los Lobos offered an initial link to modern interpretations of the corrido.

We will have an opportunity to explore in more detail the contemporary corrido, including those that address drug trafficking, known as narcocorridos, in subsequent chapters in this book. Despite what may appear as a dramatic change in topic, the corrido in modern times continues to serve many of the same purposes that it did in revolutionary period by offering an entertaining perspective on current concerns and connecting them to timeless sentiments.

CRITICAL THINKING AND DISCUSSION PROMPTS

1. Examine each of the corridos presented in this chapter with the intent of answering the questions below.

   A. Identify recurring or defining:

      1. poetic conventions;

      2. narrative conventions;

      3. descriptive conventions;

      4. musical conventions.

   B. What is the lasting significance of the corridos presented in this chapter?

   C. What do you learn from the corridos that you might not learn from a history book?

D. Are elements of the stories told in corridos transferrable to other circumstances?

E. How does the music relate to the story?

F. Is the music transferrable?

G. Do the performers use different playing techniques or instrumentation?

2. Create your own corrido. Find a corrido that you like and use that melody as your frame. Write your own lyrics to that melody. Use your personal experience, or tell the story of someone or something you wish to commemorate. Partner with some classmates who can accompany you on guitar and sing your corrido for the class. Visit www.corrido.org for additional ideas.

3. Investigate the life and production of one of the bi-national composers mentioned in passing in this chapter, such as María Grever.

KEY TERMS, PEOPLE, AND PLACES

Heraclio Bernal	Los Lobos
Nuevo Corrido de Madero	Trío González
Gral Francisco Villa	button accordion
Carabina Treinta–Treinta	despedida
Adelita	cuatrain
Trío Nava	soldadera
Francisco L. Madero	China Poblana
Victoriano Huerta	Lydia Mendoza
Venustiano Carranza	corrido
Manuel Ávila Camacho	conjunto
Regino Pérez	bajo sexto
Pancho Villa	haciendas
Los Cuatezones	golden age of the corrido

NOTES

1. *The Mexican Revolution. Corridos about the Heroes and Events 1910–1920 and Beyond!* 4 CDs, Disc 1: 7. Arhoolie Folklyric (7041–7044). 1996.
2. In earlier versions of this song the word "federales" appears as "maderistas" confirming their alignment with Madero.
3. Details regarding the life and music of Lydia Mendoza can be found in the works by Yolanda Broyles-González (2001), and Chris Strachwitz and James Nicolopoulos (1993).
4. William Beezley notes that scholars have traced the model for the "China Poblana" to the popular Saint, Caterina de San Juan (1609–1684), a Hindu girl brought to Mexico by route of Manila and raised as a servant in Puebla (Beezley 2008:120, 177). She was dubbed "China Poblana" to indicate that she was of Oriental ancestry raised in Puebla. This image is only part of the story. During the colonial era when trade with China supplied New Spain with fine goods to satisfy the fashionable taste for things oriental, the term China was also applied to anything foreign. It was also applied to all people not of European ancestry, including Indians and mestizos. "China" eventually became the term for a non-creole woman. By the nineteenth century, the term "China," was regularly used to refer to a pretty woman of the Mexican countryside, and had nothing to do with Chinese ancestry. In the era of Independence the China Poblana became a national symbol of the typical and virtuous Mexican woman. Her artistic image, later copied in life, was standardized to reflect this national status. She wore white to symbolize independence, green to symbolize unity, and red to symbolize devotion and passion; the same colors as the flag of Mexico. See also Lucía Chen (Hsiao-Chuan Chen), "Desvistiendo un símbolo nacional: ¿es china la China Poblana?" In Lucía Chen and Alberto Saladino García (Eds.), *La Nueva NAO: De Formosa a América Latina*: Intercambios culturales, económicos y políticos entre vecinos distantes. (Taipei: University of Taiwan, 2008), pp. 255–272.
5. http://poetry.arizona.edu/k-12/corrido-poetry-center
6. Corridos Sin Fronteras. A New World Ballad Tradition. Smithsonian Institution Traveling Exhibition Service, at: www.corridos.org

FOR REFERENCE AND FURTHER STUDY

Beezley, William. 2008. *Mexican National Identity: Memory, Innuendo, and Popular Culture*. Tucson, AZ: University of Arizona Press.

Beezley, William H., English Martin, Cheryl, and French, William E.. 1994. *Rituals of Rule, Rituals of Resistance: Public Celebrations and Popular Culture in Mexico*. Latin American Silhouettes. Wilmington, DE: SR Books.

Broyles-González, Yolanda. 2001. *Lydia Mendoza's Life in Music: La historia de Lydia Mendoza—Norteño Tejano Legacies*. New York and London: Oxford University Press.

Castañada, Daniel. 1943. *El corrido mexicano, Su técnica literaria y musical*. México City: Editorial Surco.

Chen, Lucía (Hsiao-Chuan Chen), 2008. "Desvistiendo un símbolo nacional: ¿es china la China Poblana?" In Lucia Chen and Alberto Saladino García (Eds.), *La Nueva NAO: De Formosa a América Latina: Intercambios culturales, económicos y políticos entre vecinos distantes*. Taipei: University of Taiwan, 255–272.

Chew, Martha. 2006. *Corridos in Migrant Memory*. Albuquerque, NM: University of New Mexico Press.

Fernández Poncela, Anna M. [n.d.] *La soldadera y la coronela en los corridos de la revolución Mexicana.* http://bvirtual.ucol.mx/archivos/450_0102082307.pdf (accessed January 12, 2015).

Gómez Maganda, Alejandro. 1970. *Corridos y cantares de la revolución mexicana.* México: Instituto Mexicano de Cultura.

Lavin, Monica. 2011. *Las Rebeldes*, Mexico City: Editorial Grijalbo.

Meyer, Lorenzo. 1978. *History of the Mexican Revolution Period 1928–1934: The Beginnings of the Institutionalization and the Policy of the Maximato.* Mexico: Colmex.

Moreno Rivas, Yolanda. 2008. *Historia de la música popular mexicana.* Mexico City: Editorial Oceano.

Sánchez Vazquez, Maria Trinidad. 2010. *El uso de corrido como recurso para mantener el interés de los alumnos en la clase de historia.* Cuautlancingo, Puebla: SEP.

Strachwitz, Chris and Nicolopoulos, James. 1994. Notes for *Corridos & Tragedias de la Frontera. Mexican-American Border Music*, vols 6 & 7. Arhoolie, CD 7019/7020.

Velázquez, Marco and Vaughan, Mary Kay. 2002. "Mestizaje and Musical Nationalism in Mexico." In Mary Kay Vaughan (Ed.), *The Eagle and the Virgin: Nation and Cultural Revolution in Mexico, 1920–1940.* Durham, NC: Duke University Press, 95–118.

DISCOGRAPHY

Bicentenario 200 Años de Música en México. Four CD set. Mexico City: Sony Music (2010).

Corridos & Tragedias de la Frontera. Mexican-American Border Music, vols 6 & 7. Arhoolie, CD 7019/7020.

Jorge Gamboa. *El Incomparable de Sinaloa. Puros Corridos Pesados.* Hyphy Music/Discos Linda (2011).

Just Another Band from East L.A.: Los Lobos. A Collection. CD 282268, 1993 Slash Records (Warner Bros.).

Lydia Mendoza. *La Alondra de la Frontera—Live!* Arhoolie (2001).

The Mexican Revolution. Corridos about the Heroes and Events 1910–1920 and Beyond. Four CD set of historic recordings made between 1904 and 1974 in the USA and Mexico. Edited and annotated by Guillermo E. Hernández. Arhoolie Folklyric 7041–7044.

WEBSITES

Corridos Sin Fronteras. A New World Ballad Tradition. Smithsonian Institution. Traveling Exhibition Service, at: www.corridos.org (accessed November 24, 2014).

CHAPTER 9

Cinema, Radio, and the Celebrity Cantante

TRANSFORMATIVE IMAGINATION: PICTURE THIS

Imagine sitting in the living room of your family home in 1930 when radio was still young and television had not yet appeared. All ears are tuned to the radio XEW, the most powerful station of the decade. The signal is so strong that listeners in Cuba and Central America are hearing the same programs and you feel connected to the larger world. Station owner Emilio Azcárraga Vidaurreta has arranged for the celebrated Agustín Lara to host his own nightly show, "La Hora de Agustín Lara," broadcast live from a special studio. You can picture Lara, seated at his jet black grand piano, with a bottle of cognac at hand, holding forth for his radio audience. It feels as if each song is sung directly to you. Certainly that is what your mother, listening intently as she bustles about the house, believes. What a treat to hear "Solamente una vez," "Sabor a mí," "Amor de mis amores," "Alma corazón y vida," "Amorcito, corazón," "Piensa en mí," "Arráncame la vida," and "Mujer," delivered free to your home! It's as if each night the singer is a guest in your home sharing with you the premier of a new hit song.

TECHNOLOGICAL INTERPLAY AND THE COLLECTIVE IMAGINATION

Two years after Mexico's first radio station began in 1923, the Mexican government was broadcasting educational programs, *radionovelas* (radio soap operas), sporting events, and above all, music. The power of broadcast music changed the collective experience of the nation. The legendary Mexican essayist and critic of social and cultural issues, Carlos Monsiváis recalled scenes like the above and concluded that radio "created the Mexican housewife."[1] Certainly this new mode of access created a new option for bringing music into the home, connecting women whose work limited their mobility. Later, radio helped make music portable. We like

Figure 9.1
Agustín Lara at his piano.
Source: Sociedad de Autores y
Compositores de México.

to think of the twenty-first century as the age of technological marvel, but
the early decades of the twentieth century launched the interplay among
the technologies of sound and visual reproduction that made possible the
formation of modern entertainment industries. That interplay transformed
all music, but especially popular music, forever changing the meaning of
that term.

By the 1930s sound recording was no longer a novelty and its links
to other media provided mutual benefits. Radio, originally broadcast live,
began to incorporate recorded music. The culture industries competed but
also worked in tandem. As recordings featured more music and artists made
famous from film, radio followed suit.

Not only did radio help create stars, but musical formats changed to
conform to the new media. Recording companies favored a standard length
for a recorded song: the three-minute track. In response, composers of
Mexican song limited their creation to the three-minute frame. Lengthy
dance songs, like the widely popular bolero, were compressed. That format,
Monsiváis says, was ideal "for housewives"; we might say that music became
domesticated in the hands of the culture industries.

Other critics refer to the media's transformative processes in different
ways, but all agree that the interaction of film, radio, and recording resulted
in a national song repertory. Instead of domestication, historian Luis
Coronado Guel (2009) refers to the formation of national stereotypes. The

word stereotype carries a negative image in English, but Coronado Guel's concern lies with how the entertainment industry helped generate iconic representations of national values. No medium was more successful at this than film.

THE GOLDEN ERA OF MEXICAN FILM 1930–1960

The defining era of Mexican cinema that began in the 1930s and lasted until the mid-1950s exerted a profound influence on the conception and character of Mexican music and transformed popular traditions into stylized national entertainment and international exports. To discuss film without considering its connections to expanding modes of distribution such as radio, jukeboxes, and sound recording would obscure the full impact of the media. Together the new modes of delivery promoted the formation of nationalized music genres, promoted the mariachi, and propelled singers like Jorge Negrete, Pedro Infante, and Lucha Reyes to international stardom.

Initially the *ranchera* comedy, the most popular genre of Mexican film, took its cues from the *revistas*, *zarzuelas*, *comedias teatrales*, and opera of the previous decades. Film scripts employed stock characters and framed stories with musical moments in formats taken directly from the stage. This close relationship between the dramatic stage and song in Mexico has long been the case.[2] Recall that many popular songs during the colonial period traced their origins to theatrical works and those songs later resurfaced as regional and rural expressions. Film kept the cycle rolling as traditional songs found their way into film and newly created songs moved into the popular domain.

The *canción ranchera* and the bolero owe their signature status and popularity to the Mexican film industry. So effective was the imagery established in film, and so widespread was the distribution completed by the network of media linking film, radio, and sound recording, that these genres continue to stand for tradition and national identity.

The process of constructing a national music via film might be best understood as an array of parallel efforts to establish immediate connections—connections between regions, political positions, listeners, and with the media as a consumer good. We can better understand that process by examining music from select films, taking into account matters of design, presentation, distribution, and reception. Just as film-makers were exploring ways to capture audiences with new imaginings of popular and folkloric forms, singers and composers were fashioning their own images to define their careers in this era of new media opportunity. One such composer-singer was Agustín Lara (1897–1970). Films and radio helped make his songs classics throughout Latin America and the Spanish-speaking world.

Selections from two films made in the 1930s offer an introduction to the iconic individuals, formats, and styles that invited listeners and viewers to reflect on their own social experience and its fit with their own goals as well as the ideals of the Mexican nation. Our first two selections also address the popular topic of gender roles and proper action.

ICONIC PERFORMANCE AND THE REFLECTIVE GAZE

Listening to "Santa," composed and sung by Agustín Lara. Source: *The Originals—Agustín Lara Sings His Songs.*[3]

9.1

The film *Santa* (Saint) was the first sound film produced in Mexico. Released in 1931, it neatly illustrates the close ties between the styles of music popular from the theatrical *revistas*, the musical-theatrical revue that built upon the legacy of the zarzuela, examined in Chapter 7. The title song, composed by Agustín Lara is a romantic bolero and it affords us the opportunity to explore several topics including how the *compositor-cantante* (the singer-songwriter) helped establish archetypal images in film and song. Signature musical genres, in this case the bolero, arose in the process.

As early as 1908, the bolero arrived in Mexico from Cuba, likely arriving first in the Yucatan. By the 1920s Mexican musicians, among them the celebrated Guty Cárdenas (1905–1935), adopted the genre and transformed it into an exclusively Mexican genre (see Torres 2002). Mexican film helped transmit the bolero around the world, establishing it as a standard genre for romance, particularly in other Spanish-speaking nations. Similarly, the format of three singing instrumentalists, promulgated by groups such as Trío los Panchos and the Trío Calaveras, established a standard model for performance of this enduring genre. While Agustín Lara is renowned as the master of the Mexican bolero, many other composers followed his example, including María Grever, Tata Nacho, Gonzalo Curiel, all of whom also profited from an affiliation with the film industry.

The characteristic and engaging rhythm of the Mexican bolero results from the interaction of a long-short-short pattern in the bass against a syncopated treble pattern emphasizing the second half of each beat above it (Fig. 9.2).

Listen for this rhythmic interaction in "Santa" [9.1]. Note also how the song falls into sections and which lyrics are associated with each

Bolero rhythm				
maracas	>	>	>	>
treble	1 + 2	+ 3	+ 4	+
bass	>		>	>
count	1	2	3	4

Figure 9.2
Bolero rhythm. Figure prepared by author.

"Santa" [9.1]	"Santa" [Saint—A beautiful woman with a saintly character named Santa]
En la eterna noche de mi desconsuelo tú has sido la estrella que alumbró mi cielo.	In the eternal night of my discontent you have been the star that illuminated my heaven.
Y yo he adivinado tu rara hermosura y has iluminado toda mi negrura.	And I have guessed your rare beauty and you have illuminated all my darkness
Santa, santa mía mujer que brilla en mi existencia Santa, sé mi guía en el triste calvario del vivir.	Santa, my saint woman who shines on my existence Santa, be my guide on the sad march through life.
Aparta de mi senda todas las espinas calienta con tus besos mi desilusión.	You remove the thorns from the pathway warm with your kisses my disillusion.
Santa, sé mi guía alumbra con tu luz mi corazón.	Santa, be my guide illuminating with your light my heart

section. Lara was famous for contrasting two sections in his boleros, allowing him to use harmony and meter to further advance the appeal and sentiment of his songs. See if you can distinguish the sections while listening.

Santa is a film based on a 1903 novel by Federico Gamboa. The film adaptation of the book, created a generation later,[4] promotes Mexican faith and values over foreign ways and presents a cast of archetypal characters that appear again and again in Mexican cinema.

Feminist scholars point out a tendency in Mexican culture to view women as either saints, cast in the mold of the Holy Virgin, or sinners and temptresses, aligned with legendary traitors such as Malinche or la petenera, what Julia Tuñón calls "women of light and shadow" (Tuñón 1998). In the film, the female protagonist embodies both. Santa is an impoverished young woman whose beauty attracts the attention of many men. She submits to the seduction of a soldier who leaves her. As an abandoned, unmarried woman, she is scorned by her family and community and is forced to support herself by becoming a prostitute. In the brothel she falls in love with a foreign *matador* (bull-fighter) who does not appreciate her. At the same time a local man, a blind pianist, secretly loves her.

While the film presents its melodramatic characterization of protagonists, it also invites reflection and critique of life as currently lived in the nation. We can ask similar questions of the songs associated with this and other films: What kind of reflection does the song and its lyrics invite? Does the song have an independent appeal, apart from the film? Where might, or do, we hear it today?

RE-IMAGINING THE MEXICAN COWBOY IN *ALLÁ EN EL RANCHO GRANDE*

The hero of the ranchera film genre was the stereotypical Mexican cowboy, a character who personified the idealized noble nature of post-revolutionary Mexico. The singing cowboy merged the power and grace of the opera singer with the proletarian sensibilities and virility of the working man.

> Listening to "Allá en el rancho grande" by Emilio Donato Uranga with lyrics by Juan Díaz del Moral as sung by Tito Guízar. Source: Vintage Music.[5]

9.2

"Allá en el rancho grande" (1936) was the title song in the eponymous film, directed by Fernando de Fuentes that launched the career of the singer-actor Tito Guízar. The film was a box-office sensation that later became a classic of Mexican cinema. It also began a process that Donald Henriques (2011) describes as the "reimagining of mariachi."

Figure 9.4
Promotional Poster for *Alla en el Rancho Grande*. Source: Cineteca Nacional de México. Used with permission. Photographic image used courtesy of Diana International Films, S.A. de C.V., all rights reserved.

Films that glorified the ranching life, melodramas, or comedias rancheras were numerous. It is easy to argue, as does Moreno Rivas (2008) that the enthusiastic reception of these films was largely due to the music that drove the drama, not the other way around. Singers who trained for opera were cast in these musical films and the male opera star became essential to the ranchera comedy and transformed the delivery of Mexican popular song.

🎧
9.3

Listening to Jorge Negrete sing "Allá en el rancho grande," composed by Emilio D. Uranga with lyrics by Juan Díaz de Moral. Source: *Jorge Negrete— Sus 40 Grandes Canciones 1911–1953*.[6]

The singer-actor Tito Guízar (1908–1999) introduced "Allá en el rancho grande" in the film, but it was Jorge Negrete (1911–1953) who became the idealized representative of the handsome, heroic rancher [9.3]. It is interesting to compare recorded performances of "Allá en el rancho grande" by both of these trained singers. Guízar sings with an elegant power, while Negrete performs with seductive bravado. Musicologist Yolanda Moreno Rivas describes Negrete as "a cross between a fighting rooster and a peacock," a blend that helps explain his appeal (1979:81). The apotheosis of the *charro* singer (Fig. 9.6), Negrete later became an icon of mariachi and many modern performers have imitated his style.

Figure 9.5
Lyrics for "Allá en el rancho grande." Composer Emilio D. Uranga. Written by Silvano Ramos on behalf of Edward B. Marks Company. Used with permission.

"Allá en el rancho grande"	"Back at the Big Ranch"
Allá en el rancho grande,	Back at the big ranch
allá donde vivía,	where I once lived
había una rancherita,	there was a little ranch girl
que alegre me decía;	who made me happy saying
que alegre me decía:	who made me happy saying:
"Te voy a hacer tus calzones	"I'm going to make you trousers
Como los usa el ranchero	Like they use on the ranch
Te los comienzo de lana	I'll begin with wool
Te los acabo de cuero"	and finish them with leather"
Allá en el rancho grande . . .	Back at the big ranch . . .
El gusto de los rancheros	The taste of the ranchers
es tener el bueno caballo	is to have a good horse
para ensillarlo por la tarde	so they can ride it in the afternoon
y luego darle la vuelta al vallado	and later give it a turn 'round the fenced gully
Allá en el rancho grande . . .	Back at the big ranch . . .

Figure 9.6
Jorge Negrete in charro dress. Source: Conaculta.

The song "Allá en el rancho grande" has become a staple of contemporary mariachi repertory, an iconic example of the ranchera music genre, with its signature "oom-pah" accompaniment performed in a lively duple meter. The song follows a strophic verse–chorus format that beckons listeners to sing along. In the film, the ranchers gather around the handsome *charro cantante* singing the chorus and responding to his verses with *gritos*, cries of encouragement that resemble calls used to prod cattle during round-ups and drives. It may not surprise you to learn that the ranchera inspired American cowboy music (Lomax 1938; Lewis 1993). Songs such as "El Paso," sung by the Phoenix-born American singer Marty Robbins, are examples.[7] The swaggering cowboy represented American freedom and manliness on both sides of the Rio Grande. Some of the greatest American singers, including Bing Crosby, Nat King Cole, and Elvis Presley, sang versions of "Allá en el rancho grande."

The music and lyrics to "Allá en el rancho grande" were originally composed in the 1920s for a music theater work, but most Mexicans associate the song with the 1936 film and even more with mariachi, considering it a song of the people.[8]

INDIO FERNÁNDEZ'S SYNTHESIS OF ROMANCE AND POLITICS

We can see the impact of presidential policies in the music from the cinema of the golden era. The most successful films bore patriotic themes but that did not prevent them from embodying criticism of social policy or historical practice. Important post-revolutionary reforms began during the presidency of Plutarco Elías Calles (1924–1928). To bring together the disparate and still often belligerent forces of the Revolution, Calles founded the national political party PNR (Partido Nacional Revolucionario), eventually renamed the PRI (Partido Revolucionario Institucional—the Institutional Revolutionary Party), which retained power for the next 70 years, peaking during the golden era of cinema. The party promoted the revolutionary aim to integrate laborers, women, and indigenous people into a new and prosperous nation. Calles's reforms included land redistribution, advancement of public health initiatives, and enforcement of the anti-clerical segments of the constitution. The latter sparked a revolt of Catholic officials and devout parishioners, known as the Cristero War, and it took the negotiations of president Emilio Portes Gil to reach a truce. The subsequent president, Lázaro Cárdenas (1934–1940), nationalized the oil industry, reformed the unions, and raised the minimum wage. President Cárdenas gained respect for the attentions he devoted to the rural poor. His continued land reforms led to the demise of the traditional *hacienda*, the large farm owned by a single family for whom peasants worked as indentured servants, by reducing its reach and redistributing land to workers through the *ejido* system. Women began pushing for voting rights during this era, and although the effort was not realized during this period, some of the films from this era include strong female characters who challenge the male protagonists in the drama.

Culture and education were important tools for fostering political and social solidarity, as well as for critiquing the virtues and defects of the nation and its people. With social reforms underway and the turbulence of the revolutionary period behind them, film-makers could focus on inspiring patriotic solidarity while still drawing attention to conditions of society needing reform. Emilio "El Indio" Fernández (1904–1986), regarded by many as the greatest of the Mexican cinema directors of the golden era, exemplifies that double consciousness. His films were particularly popular for their portrayal of Mexico's landscape and daily life in the nation's contrasting regions and settings. We will thus look at music from two of Indio Fernández's most famous films, *Flor silvestre* with its examination of rural life, and *Salón México*, where the juxtaposition of sound and image invites reflection on urban life and the corresponding difficulties of merging cosmopolitan values and identities with traditional *Mexicanidad* (Mexicanness).

Both films appeared in the 1940s, a very productive period for Mexican film and mass media. Industry was growing and the economy along with it. Mexican actors, musicians, and film-makers had already developed ties with the Hollywood film industry in the United States, but whereas Hollywood's experiments with producing Spanish-language films in the 1930s were unsuccessful, Mexico quickly rose to prominence as a provider of film not just for domestic audiences but also for audiences throughout Latin America. World War II furthered this development of Mexican cinema. In 1939, German submarines bombed the Mexican oil tankers belonging to the petroleum company Pemex, prompting Mexico to align with the Allies in the war. During the war, most of the Allied nations, including the United States, focused on war films, leaving Mexico free to offer contrasting entertainment with international impact. Mexican films distributed Mexican music and culture around the world, gaining particular acceptance in Latin America and Europe.

INTEGRATING THE RURAL LIFE OF THE NATION IN *FLOR SILVESTRE*

In *Flor silvestre* (1943) director Emilio Fernández depicts rural life and invites compassion for those trapped by poverty and illiteracy. In the course of his story-telling, he essentially evaluates the Mexican Revolution and attempts to show how corruption, fanaticism, and authoritarianism threaten the realization of revolutionary goals. Three of the songs in the film support the narrative and carry its social criticism. Examining these songs thus allows us to explore conceptions of Mexican identity while also meeting some of the nation's legendary *cantantes*.

> Listening to "El Herradero" composed by Pedro Galindo as sung by Lucha Reyes. Source: *Nuestra Tradición.*[9]

9.4

The ranchera "El Herradero" is sung by one of Mexico's first women of song, Lucha Reyes (1906–1944), in a scene that reveals the co-existence of the social classes, despite the continuing inequities of daily life, at the celebration of the *herradero*, a cattle round-up much like a rodeo. This tradition, also known as the *charreada*, began in colonial times when Spanish law required hacienda owners to annually round up all cattle for purpose of branding and collecting taxes. During this time the laws then in place restricting Indians and mestizos from riding horses were temporarily suspended in order to complete the arduous work. Even with this provision, the workers on a single hacienda could not complete the task in time. *Hacendados* (estate owners) solved this problem by inviting *vaqueros* (cowboys) and farmhands from nearby haciendas to assist with the annual round-up. The round-up became a time for festivity as food, drink, and music were provided in exchange for the help. Horse-riding competitions became part of the entertainment hosted by the hacendados, providing the vaqueros a chance to display their bravery and win the hearts of young Mexican girls (Sands 1993; Nájera-Ramírez 1997). This tradition in its post-revolutionary continuation is depicted in the film *Allá en el rancho grande* as well as in the song "El Herradero."

The lyrics of "El Herradero" appear to celebrate the rodeo fiesta, but while praising cowboy skill, Chinas Poblanas,[10] and mariachis, the singer also offers a thinly veiled critique of the unjust treatment of women by the wealthy landowner and patriarchs of the haciendas. The strength of Lucha Reyes's delivery reinforces that message of pride and caution, helping explain her own celebrity.

Lucha Reyes began her singing career as a light soprano. After working in the United States and touring Europe, an illness resulted in a change to a deeper, rougher voice. When she returned to Mexico in 1928, she began

"El Herradero" [9.4]	"The Cattle Branding"
¡Ay! Qué linda qué rechula Es la fiesta de mi rancho Con sus chinas, mariachis y canciones Y esos charros que traen sombrero ancho	Oh, how beautiful, how nice Is the party at my ranch With its pretty women, mariachis and songs And those riders who wear a wide hat
Qué bonita Esa yegua alazana y pajarera Pa' enseñarles a echar una mangana Y montarla y quitarle lo matrera	How pretty that sorrel and alert mare To teach everyone to throw a lasso and to mount her and train her at her best
Qué bonita es la fiesta del bajío Y ay que linda sus hembras y sol Rinconcito que guarda el amor mío ¡ay! Mi vida tuyo es mi corazón	How pretty is the party of the bay region And oh, how pretty its women and its sun Little place where my heart is kept, ah! My dear, my heart is only yours.
Y ahora es cuando Valedores a darse un buen quemón Que esa yegua que viene del potrero Solo es buena pa'l diablo del patrón Las mujeres han de ser como todas las potrancas Que se engrían y se amansan con su dueño Y no pueden llevar jinete en ancas	And now is the moment You brave men dare to stand for a challenge 'Cause that mare who comes from the paddock Is only good for the brave boss The women have to be like all the good fillies, that are arrogant but tame only for their owners And no other rider can mount them
Qué bonita es la fiesta del bajío Y ay que linda sus hembras y sol Rinconcito que guarda el amor mío ¡ay! Mi vida tuyo es mi corazón.	How pretty is the party of the bay region And oh, how pretty its women and its sun Little place where my heart is kept, ah My dear, my heart is only yours.

Figure 9.7
Lyrics for "El Herradero." Written and composed by Pedro Galindo Galarza; English translation by Luis Coronado Guel.

Figure 9.8
Photo of Lucha Reyes.
Photo courtesy of
Olivia Yolanda
Sánchez Reyes, niece
of Lucha Reyes.

singing rancheras with mariachis, a move that shocked many Mexican listeners at a time when women did not perform with mariachis.

"El Herradero" remains a standard in the mariachi repertory and was recorded by numerous female stars including Lola Beltrán (1932–1996), and Chayito Valdéz (b. 1945). In 2011 yet another new interpretation was released by the quartet of Mexican-American women known as Sparx.[11]

> Listening to "Flor silvestre" composed by Los Cuates Castilla (Miguel Angel Díaz Miron, José Manuel Díaz Miron, and González de Castilla) performed by Trío Calaveras. Source: *Bicentenario 200 Años de Música en México.*
>
> 9.5

In keeping with his emphasis on regional customs, Emilio Fernández uses the revered trio of guitarist-singers known as Trío Calaveras to deliver two of the film's most important songs. The trio sings in the *campirano* (country style) popular in the northern and central states of Mexico. Their delivery is smooth, polished, and genteel, in contrast to the bold *bravo* style of Jorge Negrete, whom they often accompanied.[12] In Mexican Spanish, a *calavera* is a skull, but it also is slang for a debonair Casanova. The trio played with both of those images. Miguel Bermejo, Guillermo Bermejo and Raúl Prado formed the group that made their first film appearance in 1937 in the film *Las Tres Milpas*. Over time the members of the trio have shifted and none of the original members still live, but the Trío Calaveras still perform in the 2010s in a continuation of that legacy.

The song "Flor silvestre" is a beautiful huapango about the attractions of the wildflower, the peasant girl of the title. The song appears in a scene where the grandfather of the humble Esperanza (the "wildflower" referred to in the song title) talks with her new husband, who assures him that he respects his granddaughter despite the disparity in their social standing. While "Flor silvestre" was originally composed by a trio of performers from Veracruz known as Los Cuates Castilla, who helped popularize the Huastecan style of falsetto singing. In the film the song is performed by the Trío Calaveras who appear on-screen singing as they follow the family walking along the country path.

9.1

Listening to and viewing "El hijo desobediente" [9.1], composed by Miguel Bermejo, as sung by Trío Calaveras.[13] Source: YouTube.

In another scene in the film, we hear "El hijo desobediente" (The disobedient son). It is a corrido of the revolutionary period, and as such it invites comparison between the era depicted in the film and the values of revolutionary heroes who shared their fate and fortune with the poor.

Figure 9.9
Lyrics for "Flor Silvestre" by Cuates Castilla. Copyright © 1949 by Promotora Hispano Americana de Música, S.A. Administered by Peer International Corporation. Copyright Renewed. Used with permission. All rights Reserved.

"Flor silvestre" [9.5]	"Wildflower"
Flor silvestre y campesina Flor sencilla y natural No te creen una flor fina por vivir cerca del nopal	Wild flower and from the country Simple and natural flower They do not believe you are a fine flower because you live near the cactus
No eres una rosa, no eres un lirio, mucho menos flor de liz Tu perfume es mi delirio con él me haces feliz	You are not a rose, you are not an iris, not even a lily flower Your perfume is my delirium and with it you make me happy
Como tú mi flor silvestre ahí fue en mi tierra un amor Nunca este tuvo suerte pero mucho del dolor	Like you my wild flower, I had a love there in my place Which never was lucky but much pain instead
Flor silvestre, flor del campo que engalanas el zarzal Yo te brindo a tí mi canto Florecita angelical	Wild flower, you raise the level of the field with your presence I offer to you my song angelical flower
Mientras duermes en el suelo, tu eres protegida por el matorral, El carrillo y cornizuelo ellos forman tu vaya nupcial	While you sleep in the ground, you are protected by the scrub, the cheek and cornfield they form your nuptial pathway
Siempre tú has sido mi esperanza, linda flor espiritual Yo te he dado mi confianza Florecita del zarzal	Always you'll be my hope, pretty and spiritual flower I have given you my confidence Little flower from the thicket

"El hijo desobediente" [9.1]

Un domingo estando [h]errando
se encontraron dos mancebos
echando mano a sus fierros
como queriendo pelear

Cuando se estaban peleando
pues llego su padre de uno
"hijo de mi corazón
ya no pelees con ninguno"

Quítese de aquí mi padre
que estoy más bravo que un león
no vaya a sacar la espada
y le atraviese el corazón

"Hijo de mi corazón
por lo que acabas
de hablar antes
de que raya el sol
la vida le han de quitar"

Lo que le encargo a mi padre
que no me entierre en sagrado
que me entierre en tierra bruta
en donde me trille el ganado

Con una mano de fuera
y un papel sobre dorado
con un letrero que diga
José Luis fue desgraciado

El caballo colorado
que hace un año que nació
ahí se lo dejo a mi padre
Por la crianza que me dio

De tres caballos que tengo
ahí se los dejo a los pobres
para que si quiera digan
José Luis dios te perdone

Bajaron al toro prieto
que nunca lo habían bajado
pero ahora si ya bajo
revuelto con el ganado

Y con ésta me despido
con la estrella del oriente
esto le puede pasar
a un hijo desobediente

"The disobedient son"

One Sunday when they were branding
Two young men met each other
Suddenly they reached for their daggers
as if they wished to fight

When they were already fighting
the father of one of them arrived [saying]
"Son of my heart, please
don't fight with anyone now"

Father, get out of here
'Cause I am angry like a lion
If you don't go I'll take out my sword
and with it cross your heart

"Son of my heart
because of what
you just said,
before the sun shines
your life will be taken."

What I ask of my father is
to not bury me in sacred soil
Please bury me in the brutal earth
where the cattle trample me

With a hand outside the casket
and a golden paper on top
with a sign that says
Jose Luis was disgraced

The red horse
that was born just a year ago
I leave to my father
as payment for breeding me

All three horses that I have
I leave them to the poor
So at least they may say
Jose Luis, God pardons you

They took down a dark bull
who had never bowed before
but who now is already
turned under with the cattle

And with this I say goodbye to the story
with the star of the east
this same story might happen
to a disobedient son

Figure 9.10
Lyrics for "El hijo desobediente." Composed by Miguel Bermejo. Source: *Trío Calaveras-Estrellas de Fonógrafo*. Public Domain.

The scene [45:06–50:30] begins with a group of men lying in the dark, surrounded by empty liquor bottles, strumming guitars and singing themselves to sleep.

The haunting song "El hijo desobediente" was not created for the film *Flor silvestre*. Like the others from this film, it was a well-known traditional song. Indio Fernández recognized that to effectively create images and stereotypes that might represent the nation he needed to take material from the everyday life of ordinary people (Coronado Guel 2009). His attentions matched the political reforms of the era. The procedure was so effective that it also breathed new life into the music he chose. His films continue to live in the collective memory of the Mexican people, especially now that modern technology has made it possible for new generations to view them. Even more so, the songs have never faded from circulation and are still sung by contemporary performers in modern versions and settings, their legacy in film adding yet another layer to the meanings people attach to them.

Among the famous performers who have recorded "El hijo desobediente" was film star and singer Antonio Aguilar (1919–2007). He performed it live with numerous mariachis in concerts and rodeos around the world, particularly in Mexico and Colombia, where large cheering crowds sang the verses along with him. The legendary female singer Lucha Villa (b. 1936) performed it for the 1968 film *El corrido del hijo desobediente*, directed by Emilo Gómez Muriel, and the contemporary music star from Sinaloa, Jorge Gamboa (b. 1978) released a norteño version, accompanied by the typical accordion-led conjunto (band). The iconic themes of the song resonate with many listeners but must carry special meaning for Gamboa, a recovered drug addict whose music raised him from poverty.

COSMOPOLITAN INTEGRATIONS AND THE DANZÓN IN *SALÓN MÉXICO*

As a film celebrating night-life in Mexico City in the 1940s, *Salón México* (1948) represents a very different musical vision of the nation, emphasizing its urbanity and cosmopolitan nature. The signature music of this film is *rumba matancero* (rumba from Matazanas, Cuba) and danzón. Both genres, but particularly the danzón, were adopted and adapted by Mexicans as their own.

The film tells the story of Mercedes who works as bargirl in the famous dancing hall El Salón México so that she can finance the education of her sister Beatriz, who studies in an exclusive school. To earn prize money, Mercedes participates in a dance contest, dancing with the insolent pimp Paco. His refusal to share the prize money with her leads her to rob him. Paco's later attempts to blackmail Mercedes and compromise her sister's plans for marriage to a World War II war hero, prompt Mercedes to stab Paco, but before dying he shoots her. The melodramatic plot reveals dark and light qualities in the characters and the settings it depicts, and by extension, governmental institutions as well. Historian Luis Coronado Guel writes: "It is as if the dance between sin and virtue remains a part of the post-revolutionary nation and people continue to pin their hopes on the next generation."[14]

The night club Salón México was a real place. It opened on April 20, 1920 in a building once the home of a bakery called Los Gallos on the street Pensador Mexicano. People of all social classes came to dance from dusk to dawn in rooms with evocative names. The poor danced in the "*sebo*" (tallow) room, the middle class in the "*manteca*" (fat) room, and the elite in the "*mantequilla*" (butter) room, although it was permitted for dancers to move among the rooms (Buffington 2010). Overall however the urban setting and international popular dance repertory fostered integration among the social classes in Mexico. The vibrant atmosphere of the dance hall, inspired the famous composition *El Salón México* by American composer Aaron Copland, who visited it in 1932 in the company of the Mexican composer Carlos Chávez.

Of the songs heard in the film, three are danzones: "Almendra" by the Cuban composer Abelardo Valdés, "Nereidas" by the Mexican composer Amador Pérez Torres, and "Juárez did Not Have to Die," also known as "Danzón Juárez," by the Mexican Esteban Alfonso. "Almendra" is heard first and the film closes with "Danzón Juárez," underscoring Mexican adoption of the Cuban genre. It is worth noting that the film helped make "Almendra" the most internationally adored of all Cuban danzones. "Nereidas" and "Danzón Juárez," have become classic examples of the Mexican danzón and standard repertory for Mexican musical ensembles of all types, especially wind bands.

Listening and viewing "Las nereidas" (The Nereids) [9.2] by Amador Pérez Torres as performed by Acerina y su Danzonera.[15]

9.2

"Las nereidas" (The Nereids) were the sea nymphs, the daughters of Nereus, presumably an inspiration to the Oaxacan-born composer Amador Pérez Torres (1902–1976), who was one of the celebrated band leaders who led a dance band at Salón México. In the film *Salón México* the song is performed by the band Son Clave de Oro.[16] Our complete audio example features another danzón orchestra, that of Consejo Valiente Robles known as "Acerina" (1899–1987), whose group performed at El Salón México for more than 50 years. Initially a percussionist, Acerina was born in Santiago, Cuba where he developed a deep fascination with the rhythm of the danzón, the romantic dance derived from the creole Cuban *danza* created by Miguel Failde y Pérez. At the age of 14, after a family visit to Veracruz, Acerina moved to Mexico to perform with the dance orchestra of Tiburcio Hernández "Babuco," and from there he continued to perform in Mexico. Over the course of his career in his adopted country, he recorded more than 200 danzones (Díaz Ayala 1994; Orovio 1992).

The classic danzón structure is designed to optimize variety and familiarity in a prolonged format to retain the interest of dancers, by alternating a refrain (*estribillo*) with contrasting melodies. As you listen to the recording try to identify the return of the introductory theme, and note what features distinguish the contrasting B, C, and D sections. For example, can you hear a change of texture in the B section with the clarinets and woodwinds in the melody? The final section of a danzón is often a *montuno* (literally from the mountain), here a faster, brasher section with an improvised feel, set over a repeated and syncopated accompaniment pattern, designed to enliven and conclude the dance.

As with "Las nereidas," the "Danzón Juárez," written in homage to President Benito Juárez, is performed in the film as a purely instrumental version. The lyrics aren't heard. Viewers familiar with the song would have known the lyrics that express a lament on the president's assassination: Juárez, did not have to die, if he had not died, another rooster would sing to us, and the mother country would be saved. Listeners hearing this instrumental version might well recall the partisan patriotic verse and agree with the film's sentiment that work of nation building continues.

Listening to "Juárez," a danzón attributed to the composer Esteban Alfonso García (1888–1950) in an instrumental version performed by the Carlos Campos orchestra. Source: *Baila Como Las Estrellas Danzón.*[17]

9.6

Historian Robert Buffington (2010) points out that the dance salon brought men and women of different social classes together in a shared setting quite distinct from their segregated sites of work or relaxation, such as the marketplace or *cantina*. The dance hall, and the danzón itself, provided space for women to embody idealized romantic love in a polite, yet public context. Furthermore, it was working-class women who helped to liberate bourgeois women in the dance setting with their embrace of the controlled erotic dance that enacted idealized male–female relations.

FROM CLUB TO CONCERT HALL

Listening to "Danzón No. 2" by Arturo Márquez as performed by the OFUNAM—The Symphony Orchestra of Mexico's National University (UNAM).[18]

9.7

The romance of dance, radio, and film continues to promote idealized visions of historic and contemporary realities. The music of the danzón and its rich legacy, inspired contemporary Mexican composer Arturo Márquez (b. 1950), who wrote a set of *Danzones for Symphony Orchestra* in 1993. *Danzón No. 2*, premiered by OFUNAM—The Symphony Orchestra of the Mexico's National University (UNAM), is by far the favorite of the set. Its quick rise to popularity established the international reputation of the composer and the international appeal of the music.

In listening to the work you can hear the melodies of "Juárez" and other legendary danzones, set with modern energies that helps explain its attraction to modern performers and listeners. Márquez describes how he came to write the *Danzón No. 2* in 1993 while on a trip to Malinalco, in the south-west of the state of Mexico. He was traveling with the painter Andrés Fonseca and the dancer Irene Martínez, both experts in salon dances, who shared with him their special passion for the danzón. Together they listened to old recordings by Acerina and his Danzonera Orchestra, and from these experiences he learned the rhythms, form, and melodic characteristics of the danzón:

> I was fascinated and I started to understand that the apparent lightness of the *danzón* is only like a visiting card for a type of music full of sensuality and qualitative seriousness, a genre which old Mexican people continue to dance with a touch of nostalgia and a jubilant escape towards their own emotional world; we can fortunately still see this in the embrace between music and dance that occurs in the State of Veracruz and in the dance parlors of Mexico City. The *Danzón No. 2* is a tribute to the environment that nourishes the genre. It endeavors to get as close as possible to the dance, to its nostalgic melodies, to its wild rhythms, and although it violates its intimacy, its form and its harmonic language, it is a very personal way of paying my respects and expressing my emotions towards truly popular music. *Danzón No. 2* was written on a commission by the Department of Musical Activities at Mexico's National Autonomous University and is dedicated to my daughter Lily.[19]

Danzón No. 2 by Márquez is a favorite with modern conductors; it has become a signature work for the Venezuelan-born conductor Gustavo Dudamel, now conductor of the Los Angeles Philharmonic, and has been a showcase number for Alondra de la Parra, the talented Mexican-born conductor the Jalisco Philharmonic and founder of the Philharmonic Orchestra of the Américas, based in New York City.

CONCLUDING REFLECTIONS

The golden era of Mexican song and the bolero parallels, and in many ways resembles, the American jazz age. This is no accident since as discussed in the previous chapters, many Mexicans traveled to, lived, and worked in the United States, often going back and forth with regularity. This dynamic included those involved with film and media. Agustín Lara, is a case in point. Lara might be viewed as the George Gershwin of Mexico, and certainly his songs contribute to the canon of traditional song to which Mexicans might metaphorically refer as the *Cancionero mexicano* (The Mexican Songbook), in the same way that Gershwin's songs anchor the metaphorical American Popular Song Book. Other great composers, including Guty Cárdenas, Maria Grever, to name just two, also profited from the rise of film and mass media to create songs shared by a nation, and later the world, rather than an isolated single community or region.

We have also seen how a roster of celebrated singers profited from the golden era of Mexican film, as they contributed to its success. Any student of Mexican music should know something about Tito Guízar, Jorge Negrete, Pedro Infante, and Lucha Villa, and how their performances set new standards for vocal performance while promoting a collective vision of idealized Mexican identities.

The great Mexican films from the 1930s–1960s invited Mexicans to reflect on their own lives as they gazed at the screen. The stereotypes depicted in song and film have acquired mythic qualities. They stand as measures of past values and action, and serve as models of reflection for the present. As such they invite our critique for, like other iconic images, they limit as well as empower.

A single chapter permits only a limited introductory exploration of the ways that historic film-makers and artists responded to social and political policies. The aim of this chapter has been to direct attention to relationships between production, policy, and artistic expression, and to invite exploration of how the means of distribution shapes the meaning of music to people past and present. There are many ways to critique the music we have examined, as well as the social policies engaged in performance. You might ask which social and ethnic groups are not given voice in song or film, or what problems were overlooked or persist. Golden age efforts to celebrate traditional values offer limited solutions to the complexities of urban and modern life, yet music from this period continues to serve modern needs, entertaining us while evoking former contexts and serving new needs.

CRITICAL THINKING AND DISCUSSION PROMPTS

1. While critics often charge that the commercial entertainment industry negatively influences folkloric musical practice, it might also be argued that the entertainment industry helped contribute to the vitality of traditional culture in Mexico. How did film and radio both promote and transform the music of the Mexican people? Did the aims of producers, performers, and promoters differ from those of listeners and viewers in regard to the music; how? What do you see as positive or negative results of the entertainment industry on the trajectory of Mexican folk music?

2. The chapter states that Indio Fernández recognized that to effectively create images and stereotypes that might represent the nation he needed to take material from the everyday life of ordinary people. Give examples of how such stereotypes are intentionally constructed and propagated through music, and the potential outcomes of them.

3. Lucha Reyes, who performs "El Herradero," represents a challenge to both gender and socio-economic norms of her time. Elaborate on both the societal standards of the time and the significance of the performativity of her song.

4. How do the target audiences for *bolero*, *danzón*, and *ranchera* differ? What features of the genres indicate to you a difference in scope and purpose?

5. Drawing from the resources listed at the end of this chapter, investigate further the music of any of the composers mentioned in this unit. Include in your study a reflection on how, where, when, and why the music may be heard today.

KEY TERMS, PEOPLE, AND PLACES

canción mexicana	Tito Guízar
China Poblana	Lucha Reyes
bolero	Trío los Panchos
contradanza	Pedro Galindo
habanera	golden era of the bolero
danza	*Salón México*
danzón	Arturo Márquez
Las nereidas	Emilio "El Indio" Fernández
ranchera	Allá en el rancho grande
Amador Pérez Torres	Radio XEW
Agustín Lara	rumba mantancero
Pedro Infante	Los Cuates Castilla
Jorge Negrete	

NOTES

1. Carlos Monsiváis quoted in Xavier Gómez, Entrevista a Carlos Monsiváis: "No sólo lo fugitivo permanece y dura" (Interview with Carlos Monsiváis: It's not just the fugitive that remains and lasts.) www.babab.com/no17/Monsiváis.htm.
2. For extended examination of this critical relationship, see: Yolanda Moreno Rivas, *Historia de la Música Popular Mexicana* (Mexico City: Alianza Editorial Mexicana, 1979), 65–79.
3. Agustín Lara, *The Originals—Agustin Lara Sings His Songs* (YoYo USA—Discográfica, remastered 2000). A video with photos of Agustín Lara and clips from the film *Santa* appear on the YouTube video: http://youtu.be/2p-tYDmDkxs

4. There was an earlier film version of *Santa* in 1918, but of course it did not have sound.

5. Tito Guizar, *Tito Guizar* (Vintage Music, Remastered LP #86, 2010). Also footage from the original film can be found on YouTube: http://youtu.be/5hB2nb_75YQ

6. Jorge Negrete, *Sus 40 Grandes Canciones*, 1911–1953 (Rama Lama, 2002).

7. "El Paso" appears in Stanley Kramer's U.S. film *High Noon* (1953). José E. Limón (1999) has analyzed the song as evidence of affirmative moves on the part of Americans towards Mexicans and Mexican-Americans during this decade. He examines *High Noon* noting its positive portrayal of Mexican women but concludes that despite this sympathetic tone, the plot ultimately confirms the deep social discrimination faced by Mexican-Americans in the American Southwest, part of what he calls "Greater Mexico."

8. The Mexican Society of Authors and Composers (SACM) registered a copyright for "Allá en el rancho grande" in 1920. See information in the SACM biography for Juan Díaz de Moral, at: www.sacm.org.mx/archivos/biografias.asp?txtSocio=02507

9. Lucha Reyes, *Nuestra Tradición*, (Compilation CD, Sony BMG, 2007). See also http://youtu.be/dzmyDz7HllI

10. See definition in Chapter 8.

11. Sparx. *Con mariachi*, vol. 3. Striking Music, 2011. The group began performing when still children in the 1980s.

12. "Triologia—Flor Silvestre—Trío Calaveras." YouTube video, 2:28. Posted April 27, 2011. http://youtu.be/sMQEETPYjrQ The Trío Calaveras and their music are profiled in a weblog on the bolero: http://elblogdelbolero.wordpress.com/2008/03/06/trio-calaveras-malaguena/

13. "El hijo desobediente, Pelicula *Flor silvestre*, Trío Calaveras." YouTube video 3:05. Uploaded February 8, 2011. www.youtube.com/watch?v=LQ7TEG4_tmg

14. Luis E. Coronado Guel, "Mexican Music in Film: Depiction, Stereotype or National Reality?," paper delivered at the Joint Meetings of the Rocky Mountain Chapter of the American Musicological Society, the Society for Music Theory and the Southwest Chapter of the Society for Ethnomusicology, Boulder, CO, April, 2009.

15. A clip showing these instrumentalists appears as "Acerina y su Danzonera," YouTube video 1:46. http://youtu.be/1kkW_gwj8rs. See also "El Blog del Bolero," posted September 18, 2008. http://elblogdelbolero.wordpress.com/2008/09/18/acerina-y-su-danzonera-salon-mexico/

16. "Nereidas—(Extracto de la pelicula *Salón México*)" YouTube video, 3:04. Posted June 9, 2011. http://youtu.be/0NidMgS5iiI

17. Various Artists. *Baila Como Las Estrellas Danzón*. Balboa—Musart, 2005.

18. Arturo Márquez. OFUNAM—Orquesta Filarmónica de la UNAM, Ronald Zollman, Director. *Música Sinfónica Mexicana*. Difusión Cultural UNAM (Voz Viva de México) MN30 (1995).

19. "peermusic classical—Danzón No. 2, Arturo Márquez" www.peermusicclassical.com/catalog/catalog_detail.cfm?catalog_id=1017

FOR REFERENCE AND FURTHER STUDY

Beezley, William. 2008. *Mexican National Identity: Memory, Innuendo, and Popular Culture*. Tucson, AZ: University of Arizona Press.

Buffington, Robert. 2010. "'La Dancing' Mexicana: Danzón and the Transform-ation of Intimacy in Post-Revolutionary Mexico City." *Journal of Latin American Studies* 14(1):87–108.

Coronado Guel, Luis E. 2009. "Mexican Music in Film: Depiction, Stereotype or National Reality?," paper delivered at the Joint Meetings of the Rocky Mountain Chapter of the American Musicological Society, the Society for Music Theory and the Southwest Chapter of the Society for Ethno-musicology, Boulder, CO, April, 2009.

Díaz Ayala, Cristóbal. 1994. *Discografía de la música cubana*. San Juan, Puerto Rico: Editorial Fundación Musical.

Gómez, Xavier. [n.d.] Entrevista a Carlos Monsiváis: "No sólo lo fugitivo permanece y dura." [Not only the fugitive remains and lasts]. Interview with Carlos Monsiváis. www.babab.com/no17/Monsiváis.htm (accessed December 11, 2011)

Halbwachs, Maurice. 1980. "Historical Memory and Collective Memory." In *On Collective Memory*. New York: Harper and Row, 50–187.

Henriques, Donald. 2011. "Mariachi Imaginings. Encounters with Technology, Aesthetics, and Identity." In *Transnational Encounters. Music and Performance at the U.S.–Mexico Border*. New York: Oxford University Press, 85–110.

Lewis, George H. 1993. "Mexican Influences on Country Songs and Styles." In George Lewis (Ed.), *All that Glitters. Country Music in America*. Bowling Green, OH: Bowling Green State University Press, 94–101.

Limón, José E. 1999. *American Encounters, Greater Mexico, the United States and the Erotics of Culture*. New York: Beacon Press.

Lomax, Alan. 1938. *Cowboy Songs and Other Frontier Ballads*. 3rd ed. New York: The Macmillan Co.

Madrid, Alejandro and Robin Moore. *Danzón: Circum-Caribbean Dialogues in Music and Dance*. London and New York: Oxford University Press, 2013.

Mistron, Deborah E. 1991. "The Institutional Revolution: Images of the Mexican Revolution in the Cinema." PhD diss., Indiana University.

Mora, Carl J. 1989. *Mexican Cinema: Reflections of a Society*. Rev. ed. Berkeley, CA: University of California Press.

Moreno Rivas, Yolanda. 2008. *Historia de la música popular mexicana*. Mexico City: Editorial Oceano.

Nájera-Ramírez, Olga, director. 1997. *La Charreada: Rodeo a la Mexicana*, a Documentary Film. San José: KTEH Public Television.

Orovio, Helio. 1992. *Diccionario de la Música Cubana*. Havana: Editorial Letras Cubanas.

Rodríguez, Dionisio. Agustín Lara: El Schubert Jarocho. www.babab.com/no27/lara.php (accessed January 12, 2015).

Sands, Kathleen Mullen. 1993. *Charrería Mexicana: An Equestrian Folk Tradition*. Tucson, AZ: The University of Arizona Press.

Slobin, Mark. 2008. *Global Soundtracks: Worlds of Film Music*. Music/culture. Middletown, CT: Wesleyan University Press.

Torres, George. 2002. "The Bolero Romantico. From Cuban Dance to International Popular Song." In Walter Aaron Clark (Ed.), *From Tejano to Tango: Essays on Latin American Popular Music*. New York: Routledge, 151–171.

Tuñón, Julia. 1998. *Mujeres de luz y sombra en el cine mexicano: La construcción de una imagen, 1939–1952*. Mexico City: Colegio de México and el Instituto Mexicano de Cinematografía (IMCINE).

DISCOGRAPHY

Agustín Lara, *The Originals—Agustin Lara Sings His Songs*. YoYo USA—Discográfica, remastered 2000.

Arturo Márquez. OFUNAM–Orquesta Filarmónica de la UNAM, Ronald Zollman, Director. *Música Sinfonica Mexicana*. Difusión Cultural UNAM (Voz Viva de México) MN30 (1995).

Bicentenario 200 Años de Música en México. 4 CDs and 100 recordings from 1905–2010. Mexico City: Sony Music Mexico (2010).

Carlos Campos. *Baila Como Las Estrellas Danzon*. Musart—Balboa (2005).

Jorge Negrete. *Sus 40 Grandes Canciones, 1911–1953*. Rama Lama, (2002).

Lucha Reyes. *Nuestra Tradición*, Compilation CD, Sony BMG (2007).

Sparx. *Con mariachi, vol. 3*. Striking Music (2011).

Various Artists. *Baila Como Las Estrellas Danzón*. Balboa—Musart (2005).

CHAPTER 10

New Song and Rock Mexicano

INTRODUCTION: THE LULL AND THE STORM

The 1960s were a watershed decade for the Americas and the world touched by American culture. Mexico was no exception. Historian Michael Meyer speaks of the period from 1958–1976 as "the lull and the storm," a designation that holds for music of this period as well (Meyer 2007:573). Music served the lull and fueled the storm. Two related, yet distinct, lines of popular music developed during this period: 1) Mexican rock 'n' roll known as *rocanrol* and subsequent branches of Mexican rock music; and 2) *canto nuevo* (also known as *nueva canción* and *nueva trova*), a new counter-cultural song movement that spread throughout the Americas. Both emerged as urban practices and both attracted students and young audiences, but there were important differences. The New Song movement spoke to an intellectual and literary community and embraced a political perspective that questioned the impact of capitalism and excoriated the lingering effects of colonialism. While New Song was fueled by a strong mistrust of commercial economics, the growth of rock music blossomed with financing from the international music industry, even when artists chose to challenge social norms. In both styles, musicians and listeners found distinctively Mexican ways to engage the spectrum of international fashion and activity.

THE LATIN AMERICAN NEW SONG MOVEMENT IN MEXICO

The New Song movement in Mexico drew inspiration from many sources, musical, artistic, literary, and political. Activities in Cuba, Chile, the United States, and Central America were particularly influential. The Cuban Revolution that began in 1953 installed Fidel Castro in 1959 as the leader of a new Communist government. Corresponding to this movement, a generation of singer-songwriters in Cuba created songs highlighting the plight of the poor and working classes, and urging action towards improving their lot. While committed to modern sensibilities, these artists also drew inspiration from older traditions of Cuban *trova* (poetic song) composed and performed by a previous generation of singing guitarists such as Sindo Garay, Rosendo Ruiz, and Alberto Villalón. The new generation also called themselves *trovadores* (poet-singers) and dubbed their music *nueva trova* (new lyric song), new because of its audience and political content. Most prominent among these newcomers were Silvio Rodríguez and Pablo Milanés. Mexican musicians and social activists, many who felt that the ideals of their own country's revolution had not been realized, found common cause with the direct style of the New Song movement and with the communist and socialist ideals expressed by many of these poet-composer-performers

Another fount of inspiration for Mexican singers came from the nueva canción movement in Chile, a practice rooted in the revalorization of regional folk song that began in the 1950s in that country. Two important female singers, Violeta Parra and Mercedes Sosa, each in their own manner, fostered new research into regional song and established performance venues and formats promoting urban performance of folk song (Fairley 1984).

Two Mexican musicians who may be viewed as counterparts to Parra and Sosa are Judith Reyes (1924–1988) and Chava Flores (1920–1978), both recognized for establishing antecedents to the New Song movement in Mexico (Barrales Pacheco 1994). Judith Reyes was born in Tamaulipas and established herself as a successful stage and cabaret performer in Mexico City in the 1940s. After 1953 she began working as a journalist and became interested in the plight of the *braceros*, the manual laborers who were imported to the USA between 1942 and 1962, writing songs and articles about her experiences with that labor movement and the abusive conditions she observed. She later wrote a series of corridos documenting the repression of student protests in 1968, collected in a volume titled *Cronología del movimiento estudiantil 1968*.[1] Her song "Coplas de las Medallas" (Couplets on the Medals) criticizes the actions of the Mexican government during and following the 1968 Olympics (Barrales Pacheco 1994:261). Her sense that the corrido continued to serve the Mexican people as a means of poetic music expression is shared by many of the later *cantadores nuevos*.

Another musician whose work inspired the New Song movement in Mexico was Chava Flores (born Salvador Flores Rivera, 1920–1978). He composed more than 200 songs chronicling daily life in Mexico City, marked by witty and satiric reflections and with down-to-earth titles like "Voy en el Metro" (I'm riding the Metro). Chava Flores self-identified as an urban folklorist and not as a performer. More than 82 musicians recorded his songs, including Pedro Infante, Jorge Negrete, and Amparo Ochoa. Although he attracted the attention of the recording and film industry, he never received sufficient compensation to make a real living solely from his compositions, but his focus on ordinary life and urban concerns found resonance in the New Song movement (Barrales Pacheco 1994:271). Chava

Flores did earn considerable renown for his appearances on television, particularly in *El Chavo del 8*, one of the most famous music and comedy shows in Mexican television history (Flores 1988).

In Latin America the New Song movement gained political potency in the 1970s when folk-inspired singers like Victor Jara and the ensembles Quilapayún and Inti-Illimani dedicated their music to the support of the socialist programs of Chilean president Salvador Allende. After Allende was unseated in 1973, his supporters were persecuted. The tragic story of Victor Jara's murder for his outspoken songs and their powerful influence, horrified a generation of musicians and fans. Fellow musicians, many of whom had to seek refuge outside of Chile, carried the banner with broader social messages and inspiring modern protest singers throughout America and Europe.

The movement in Mexico, as elsewhere in the Hispanic world, was led by students and intellectuals and these youthful performers developed first-hand connections with other performers in the New Song movement in Latin America. After an influential international *Encuentro de la canción de protesta* (Encounter for Protest Song) in the summer of 1967 in Cuba, there were annual festivals and gatherings in Europe and Latin America where New Song performers shared their music with each other and expressed solidarity with each other's causes (Fairley 1984:107). The video example of Gabino Palomares performing with Amparo Ochoa [10.1] was filmed at such an encounter in Managua, Nicaragua, in 1984.

Musicians also performed with each other across national boundaries in gathering places called *peñas* (cultural cafés). Javier Barrales Pacheco (1994) documents the importance of these sites for the development of the New Song movement in Mexico. The Café Negro in Mexico City, founded in 1962 by the Mexican singer-songwriter Salvador Ojedo Logio (b. 1936), was one of the most important of the peñas in that city. Here the musicians who co-founded the group Los Folkloristas (introduced briefly in Chapter 2) met, socialized, and rehearsed together. Sessions on Saturday evenings at the Café Negro included local and international performers, and visitors included some of the most prominent proponents of nueva canción, such as Victor Jara, Mercedes Sosa, Violeta Parra, and Silvio Rodríguez.

Political violence in Central and South America bought a wave of migration from those regions into Mexico as people sought refuge from violence and political persecution in the 1970s. Overlapping the involvement of the United States with the Vietnam War, the era of protest and civil rights activism in the United States spawned a generation of musicians who positioned themselves against cultures of patriarchy, wealth, and oligarchy.

The most celebrated of the Mexican singers who responded to these motivations in the tradition of nueva canción are Amparo Ochoa (1946–1994), and Gabino Palomares (b. 1950). Their lives, profiled in detail by Javier Barrales Pacheco (1994), reveal the complex lines of influence that characterized the movement. Amparo Ochoa grew up in the village of Costa Rica near Mazatlán, Sonora. She grew up listening to Cuban singers Pérez Prado, Beny Moré and Tin-Tan (a comedian and singer who sang Pérez Prado's songs in movies) and as a young woman hosted a radio show called *Amanecer Ranchero* (Ranch Daybreak). She studied public health and became a rural teacher before moving to Mexico City to study music. During her student years she developed connections with the guerilla theater movement and sang in cabarets with Óscar Chávez. In the 1970s she started performing alongside regulars in the Mexico City peñas, including the Café Negro. At the height of the New Song movement in the 1970s she represented Mexico at major festivals around the world, and recorded a series of television shows dedicated to the corrido (with Jorge Saldaña, one of the original Folkloristas). She did not compose her own material, but she dedicated her life and her lovely, haunting voice to performing songs of patrimony and social concern. In addition to "La Maldición de Malinche," [audio example 10.1] one of her most requested songs was the Francisco Madrigal corrido "Jacinto Cenobio" about the plight of the rural farmer dependent upon foreign imports now that he can no longer sustain himself with produce from his own harvests.

Gabino Palomares was born in 1950, in Guanajuato to parents of Otomí heritage. This great spokesperson for the dignity of ethnic identity grew up singing in *rondallas* and *estudiantinas*, school serenading groups. Palomares's early experience with the recording industry illustrates how the New Song movement in Mexico was overshadowed by activity in other Latin American countries. In 1972 the Philips recording company offered Palomares a contract to record his original songs, but wanted him to identify himself as Argentinian, under the premise that it would be easier to market his recordings. He refused, and it would not be until 1977 that he had a chance to record again (Barrales Pacheco 1994:372).

Apart from solo singers, ensembles of performers also took up the banner of New Song, and Mexico's foremost example is the ensemble Los Folkloristas, founded in 1966. This ensemble became known for their family-like identity and their community approach to performance.[2] Their efforts to resurrect lost indigenous traditions share some of the inspiration of folk music investigators like Violeta Parra and Mercedes Sosa and to some degree built on Mexico's own tradition of folk music study initiated by scholars like Vicente Mendoza, Blas Galindo, and Manuel Ponce. For those engaged in the New Song movement, the aim of folk music research was not to incorporate the oral tradition into cultivated formats, in the manner of classical composers, but rather to continue tradition, by creating new songs that embodied the direct expression and narrative power of folk songs, but which spoke to urban audiences. The new songsters sought respect for the races who were suppressed in the process of colonization and who remained outside the circles of power in contemporary society.

10.1

10.1

Listening to "La Maldición de Malinche" performed by Amparo Ochoa with Los Folkloristas and viewing a live performance of the same song by Gabino Palomares and Amparo Ochoa, live in Managua in 1983 [video example 10.1]. Sources: *El Cancionero Popular*,[3] and YouTube.[4]

"La Maldición de Malinche"

Del mar los vieron llegar
mis hermanos emplumados,
eran los hombres barbados
de la profecía esperada.

Se oyó la voz del monarca
de que el Dios había llegado
y les abrimos la puerta
por temor a lo ignorado.

Iban montados en bestias
como Demonios del mal,
iban con fuego en las manos
y cubiertos de metal.

Sólo el valor de unos cuantos
les opuso resistencia
y al mirar correr la sangre
se llenaron de vergüenza.

Por que los Dioses ni comen,
ni gozan con lo robado
y cuando nos dimos cuenta
ya todo estaba acabado.

Y en ese error entregamos
la grandeza del pasado,
y en ese error nos quedamos
trescientos años de esclavos.

Se nos quedó el maleficio
de brindar al extranjero
nuestra fé, nuestra cultura,
nuestro pan, nuestro dinero.

Y les seguimos cambiando
oro por cuentas de vidrio
y damos nuestra riqueza
por sus espejos con brillo.

Hoy en pleno siglo XX
nos siguen llegando rubios
y les abrimos la casa
y los llamamos amigos.

Pero si llega cansado
un indio de andar la sierra,
lo humillamos y lo vemos
como extraño por su tierra.

Tú, hipócrita que te muestras
humilde ante el extranjero
pero te vuelves soberbio
con tus hermanos del pueblo.

Oh, Maldición de Malinche,
enfermedad del presente
¿Cuándo dejarás mi tierra
cuando harás libre a mi gente?

"Malinche's Curse"

From the sea they saw them arrive
my feathered brothers
they were the bearded men
of the awaited prophecy.

They heard the voice of the monarch
saying that the god had arrived
and we opened the door to them
out of fear of the unknown.

They came mounted on beasts
like demons of evil
they carried fire in their hands
and were covered with metal.

Only the courage of a few
put up any resistance to them
and when they saw the running blood
they were filled with shame.

Because gods don't eat,
nor do they enjoy what they've stolen
and by the time we realized
everything was over.

In that mistake we gave up the greatness
of the past
and in that mistake
we remained as slaves for 300 years.

The curse remained with us
of offering the stranger
our faith, our culture,
our bread, our money.

Today we continue exchanging
gold for glass beads
and we give up our wealth
for shiny mirrors.

Today, in the middle of the twentieth
century blond people keep coming to us
and we open our homes to them
and we call them friends.

But if there arrives an Indian,
tired of walking the mountains
we humiliate him and we see him
as a stranger in his own country.

You, hypocrite, you who appear humble
before the stranger
but become arrogant
with your peasant brothers.

Oh, Malinche's curse,
sickness of the present,
When will you leave my land?
When will you make my people free?

Figure 10.1
Lyrics for "La Maldición de Malinche." Courtesy of Gabino Palomares.[5]

The lyrics of the song "La Maldición de Malinche" represent a distinctive Mexican approach to New Song with a focus on the lingering and insidious damage to the native psyche resulting from the colonial culture. Malinche, Cortés's native-born interpreter, is excoriated for her role in facilitating the domination of the Spaniards. Even more abhorrent is the practice of *malinchismo*, the derogatory term for preferring things foreign as better and more valuable (Barrales Pacheco 1994:38).

In an essay on this topic Marcelo Colussi (2007) identifies a companion attitude to malinchismo, charging Europeans with often assuming that Latin America remains hopelessly primitive. He writes:

> In general Latin America is not associated with science and technology, art, and philosophy; but yes, it is associated with backwards society, with primitiveness, and with societies fixated by years of Spanish colonial domination, profoundly Catholic and filled with prejudice.[6]

In his song, Gabino Palomares asks listeners to reject such views and to value the indigenous people, honor the peasant laborers, and resist the tendency to submit to European values of merit that exclude native peoples from having genuine power and influence. In comparing the two performances, we may note that presentation of the verse and the sincere quality of the vocal delivery is more prominent than the signature acoustic guitar accompaniment in the duo rendition [video example 10.1], while in the musical rendition with Los Folkloristas [audio example 10.1] the inclusion of Andean flutes (newly popular with non-Andean listeners at the time) and later, mariachi instruments establish a link between Mexican and Latin American concerns.

Los Folkloristas made their own recordings on their own label, Discos Pueblo, and sold them via non-traditional avenues in supermarket chains. Over time they gained mainstream recognition and their success brought charges of commercialism. Los Folkloristas have been criticized for their recording policies, charged with appropriating and profiting from other people's songs. We might ask if it is fair to charge them with commercializing folk culture (see Seeger 1991).

Before we move on to examine the tradition of rock music and the conditions that influenced its development in Mexico, it should be noted that not all New Song artists focused on folkloric music. Freshly composed songs, like those of Gabino Palomares, Federico Arana, Guillermo Briseño, Óscar Chávez, Eugenia León, and Tania Libertad, were vitally important.[7] Furthermore, the popularity of canto nuevo did not end in the 1960s, 1970s, or 1980s; the movement persists to the present day, aided by new recording releases, and by a new generation of poetic bards and performers.

THE SOCIAL ENVIRONMENT DURING THE EARLY ROCK ERA

Like nueva canción, rock mexicano took root in urban settings. As with rock in the United States, and the UK, Mexican rock first emerged as commercial entertainment in the late 1950s, blossoming in the 1960s. The 1960s was the first decade in Mexican history where the urban population of the country outnumbered the rural population. President López Mateos bought the film industry and electrical utilities back from U.S. control and his profit-sharing plan increased the earning power of wage laborers, boosting the growth of a middle class. Alongside national progress in public health, improved sanitation, the reduction of infectious diseases, and the virtual eradication of malaria, the public debated issues of birth and population control. The government launched new efforts to improve education and combat illiteracy and established an independent foreign policy in regard to Cuba and the Soviet Union.

Television and improved communications connected Mexicans to events around the world. Student protests of the U.S. military engagement in Vietnam created a supportive environment for protests of local politics. When Mexico City hosted the Olympic Games in October of 1968 the government prepared a parallel cultural Olympics to enrich the gathering. Protestors, led by public high schools and public university students, denouncing lack of autonomy and democracy, also objected to the expense for these events, arguing that resources would be better spent to alleviate poverty. Dissension reached a tragic climax in the Plaza de las Tres Culturas, located in Tlatelolco a few blocks from the National Palace in Mexico City, when the paramilitary *granaderos*, police, and Mexican soldiers opened fire with tear gas and automatic rifles on the more than 5,000 protesters.[8] Official accounts list the deaths at 48 but those present assert a much higher number of fatalities ranging closer to 300 including those who disappeared when they were taken by the police and army to their facilities. The massacre at Tlateloco on October 2, 1968 marks the end of the early rock era, let's look at its beginning.

Rocanrol in the 1950s

In the 1950s the media of film and television spread the new rock 'n' roll music, targeting young fans at home and abroad. The first Mexicans to access this music were middle- and upper-class residents of Mexico City and other urban centers who traveled and studied in the United States. Mexicans watched a domesticated portrayal of rock on the television show *American Bandstand*, that began its 37 years of promoting Top 40 hits in 1952. American movies also brought rock 'n' roll to Mexico. Veteran Mexican rocker Fito de la Parra (2008) remembers the impact of the 1955 American film *The Blackboard Jungle* on him and other young Mexicans of the era in the film.[9] The film portrayed rock 'n' roll as music of frivolity and rebellion. Mexican directors responded with their own movies, among them the 1956 film *La locura del Rock'n Roll* (The madness of Rock'n Roll).

Mexican fans of *rocanrol* were largely cosmopolitan and upwardly mobile youth and the formats for its consumption were nurtured by both Mexico's own entertainment industries and those abroad. In 1961 the Mexican recording company Orfeón launched the television show *Premier*

Figure 10.2
Lobby card for the film
*La locura del Rock'n
Roll.* Provided by La
Cineteca Nacional.
Used with permission.

Orfeón, later known as *Orfeón A Go-Go* which presented the most popular rock and roll artists each Friday.[10] In these early years entire families listened to the hip new style of rocanrol music and CBS records responded by releasing Spanish-language versions or covers of English-language hit songs. These covers were known as *refritos* (refried), or when the translations were direct: *fusiles* (literally guns, but here meaning "covers"). Apart from youth interest, another reason why Mexican musicians released covers in Spanish of English rock 'n' roll songs was in response to the law imposed by the Dirección general de radio, televisión y cinematografía (RTC) limiting the number of broadcast songs in foreign languages. Covers thus became an important marketing strategy for recording labels in response to the growing local and international popularity of rock. "El Relojito" [video example 10.2] sung by Gloria Ríos is an example of a refrito of "Rock around the Clock," the first rock 'n' roll hit recorded by Bill Haley and his Comets in 1955. In *Refried Elvis* (1999), an important study of Mexican rock music and counterculture, Eric Zolov maintains that such versions by Mexican performers like Gloria Ríos (1922–2002) domesticated rock music for widespread Mexican consumption. Introducing rock music to Mexican listeners in their native language not only made commercial sense, but it also supported a Mexican law that limited the number of songs in foreign language broadcast over Mexican airwaves.

10.2

Listening to "La Mecedora" (Rocker Girl) performed by Gloria Ríos, 1956. Source: *30 Mexican Rock N' Roll Classics.*[11]

10.2

Viewing "El Relojito" (Rock around the Clock) performed by Gloria Ríos, composed by Mario Patrón. Source: YouTube.[12]

One of the earliest stars of Mexican rock music on television and recording was the lovely Gloria Ríos, known as La Reina del Rocanrol (The Queen of Rock 'n' Roll). Born in San Antonio, Texas she moved to Mexico City when she was 15 years old.[13] Both "La Mecedora" (Rocker Girl) performed by Gloria Ríos, [audio example 10.2] and "El Relojito." [video example 10.2] come from the 1956 film *La locural del Rock'n' Roll*. As you listen to these examples, notice how jazz-like the music sounds, particularly in "El Relojito." The division between jazz and the early rock of American rhythm and blues was rather fine in the 1950s and the band supporting Ms. Ríos in the film is led by pianist Mario Patrón, a jazz musician who became her second husband and with whom she toured Europe. Music for this film was directed by Juan García Esquivel,[14] another jazz great, who appears in the film in the role of Juan. Esquivel gained fame as the founder of the jazz style dubbed "space pop." The video clip confirms the resemblance between early rock and jazz dance bands and reminds us that jazz, especially Latin jazz, was another style of music embraced by Mexican musicians. The simple lyrics of "La Mecedora": "I want to rock, I want to roll" illustrate the playful attitude that dominated this early style of dance music.

As rock music quickly became a style dominated by male performers, Ríos's legacy faded from public memory. While television screens and record covers in the 1950s appeared to project conformity and intergenerational acceptance, in everyday life rocanrol created a space for young people to exert new control over their lives by developing a separate youth culture.

CHANGING PRACTICES

Eric Zolov observes that as a rock culture developed it began transforming Mexican traditional culture and the customs of shared activities linking families and communities through intergenerational participation. Families felt the loss when young people favored gathering at *tardeadas* (afternoon gatherings for rock fans) at the *cafes a gogo* instead of participating in seasonal music events, such as *fiestas patronales* or the annual *posadas* (a Christmas tradition of song and pageantry recalling Joseph and Mary's search for lodging and the birth of the infant Jesus).

Despite the emerging youth culture, at first rock in Mexico enjoyed support across generations. Many economically comfortable urban families accepted the early rocanrol sound, integrating it into multi-generational family gatherings. For example, in the film *Rock 'n' Roll Made in Mexico*, singer and guitarist, Armando Molino (of the band La Maquina del Sonido) describes how he attended the Avándaro Festival (discussed below) with his father.

Around the world, rock music was intimately tied to the English language and another early stage of the native rock scene in Mexico was marked by Mexican artists singing in English. The names of Mexican bands Los Blues Jeans, Los Sparks, Los Hooligans, Los Teen Tops, Los Loud Jets, are a few examples of groups that integrated and transformed this Anglo-bias into formats that spoke to Mexican audiences. Two examples by Javier Bátiz, one of most important of early Mexican rock figures, allow us to compare the rock in English movement with the competing creation in Spanish.

10.3

Listening to Javier Bátiz [10.3] "Hard Life" and [10.4] "Si Estuvieras Aqui" (If You Were Here). Sources: Batiz and Hair, Vam Records and 16 Grandes Éxitos, Discos Denver.[15]

10.4

Javier Bátiz was born in 1944 in the city of Tijuana, a city greatly influenced by its proximity to the United States, and still a center of innovation in popular music. In 1957 Bátiz formed his first rock group, the TJs, and developed a sound influenced more by American downhome blues than by the cheerful pop of the bandstand groups. You can hear the twelve-bar blues harmonic structure, the blues poetic frame, the gritty vocal timbre, and the guitar-centric character of blues-rock in Audio Example 10.3, "Hard Life." Bátiz's influence on Mexican rock was enormous and long-lived. He is credited with teaching guitar to Carlos Santana, Alex Lora, Abraham Laboriel, and Guillermo Briseño. Despite his preference for R&B inflected music, Bátiz also released rock music with Spanish lyrics and rhythms. In the late 1960s he sang for audiences that included fans of all ages and occupations, including police and government officials at the Mexico City bar Terraza Casino. His fame in Mexico City led to his prominent role in the development of La Onda Chicana (the Chicano Wave) and the Avándaro Festival.

LA ONDA CHICANA

By the mid-1960s, Mexico boasted a homegrown counter-cultural movement linked simultaneously to the counterculture abroad and to a musically diverse and vibrant scene locally. Called "La Onda Chicana," (the Chicano Wave) this rock counter-culture peaked in the fall of 1971, at the Avándaro music festival, when over 200,000 youth from across the social spectrum gathered at the racetrack near Avándaro Lake to experience two days of music, freedom, and *desmadre* (wild abandon or outrageous behavior—the subversion of social boundaries of propriety). Organizers of the event never expected it to draw as many participants as it did. Originally the musical entertainment was to support a car racing event, but young rock fans flocked to the site, turning Avándaro into Mexico's Woodstock. While participants report that the gathering was initially peaceful and rather orderly, an ill-timed burst of profanity from the stage prompted the broadcasters to cut power and caused the scattering of attendees.[16] Major newspapers reported on the event as if it was an orgy of sex, drugs, and rock, denouncing participants and the music as a threat to civil order (Zolov 1999:205). The response to Avándaro ended any previous support of rock by the government, and local recording and broadcast media. In response,

Figure 10.3
(see Plate 11)
Alex Lora, lead singer
of the legendary
Mexican band El Tri,
poses for a photo on
Sunset Blvd., in Los
Angeles. (AP
Photo/Nick Ut, file).
Used with permission.

rockers moved underground, attending clandestine concerts in makeshift spaces they called *hoyos funquis* (funky holes). Because of the illicit nature of these concerts, these spaces developed connections with illegal drug dealing, reinforcing pejorative views of independent rock. When the ever-vigilant police found these spots, they were quick to shut them down or blackmail the organizers (de la Peza Casares 2007:208).

Listening to "Abuso de Autoridad" performed by El Tri. Source: *Three Souls in My Mind—Grandes Éxitos, originally released in 1974 on the Album Chavo de Onda.*[17]

10.5

El Tri was founded in 1968 by bass guitarist and composer Alex Lora, along with Ernesto de Leon on lead guitar, and Carlos Hauptvogel on drums as the band Three Souls in My Mind. Known to fans as El TRI the nickname became official in 1971, and the fact that it's shared with Mexico's national soccer team—Tri from the football team stands for Tricolor, in reference to the flag and representing the Mexican Federation of Associated Football—only underscores the band's current claim to represent authentic Mexican rock (de la Peza Casares 2007:207). Like the Rolling Stones, El Tri continues to perform today,[18] and like so many Mexican rock bands, the musicians of El Tri have experimented with a range of styles over their long career. The personnel has also changed from the early years to the present, however, Alex Lora remains as the leader of the group. Prior to the band's performance at Avándaro, they performed many songs in English, but at that event they began performing in Spanish and in 1973 recorded an album of original songs entirely in Spanish that soundly criticized social and political policies of the times.

In "Abuso de Autoridad" Alex Lora names the culprits he feels are abusing authority in Mexico, including the police and the president, as he also celebrates the alternative circles that allow him to share this exposé. Note the direct reference in the lyrics to president Gustavo Díaz Ordaz Bolaños who served in office from 1964–1970. He oversaw the suppression of student protesters in Tlateloco in 1968 and is considered to be one of the most repressive presidents of the twentieth century, directly implicated in the 1968 massacre. The reference situates this song in the context of the government's broader repressions of youth resistance and expression

Figure 10.4
Lyrics to "Abuso de Autoridad." Composed by Alejandro Serna Lora (Alex Lora). Copyright: Producciones Lora S.A. De C.V.

"Abuso de Autoridad"	"Abuse of Authority"
Vivir en Mexico es lo peor	Living in Mexico is the worst
Nuestro gobierno esta muy mal	Our government is very bad
Y nadie puede protestar	And nobody can protest
Porque lo llevan a encerrar	Because they'll be locked up
Ya nadie quiere ni salir	And no one wants to go out
Ni decir la verdad	Nor tell the truth
Ya nadie quiere tener	And no one wants to have
Más líos con la autoridad	More trouble with the authority
Muchos azules, en la ciudad	Many "blues" (cops) in the city
A toda hora queriendo agandallar	Abusing all the time
No, ya no los quiero ver más	No, I don't want to see them any more
Y las tocadas de rock	And rock gigs
Ya nos las quieren quitar	They want to take them away from us
Ya solo va a poder tocar	The only one who will be able to play is
El hijo de Díaz Ordaz[19]	The son of [President] Díaz Ordaz

during that decade. The musicians on this hard rocking recording are: Alex Lora on bass and lead vocals, Sergio Mancerra on guitar, and Carlos "Charlie" Hauptvogel on drums.[20]

THE MOVE UNDERGROUND

As noted earlier, home-made rock moved underground and developed teeth during the 1970s. During that decade Mexico suffered a period of economic recession and political repression to prevent any '68 comeback that profoundly affected the middle class who initially supported rock. The grittier rock that developed in response attracted new fans in the poorest neighborhoods of Mexico City. Rather like the underground spaces that nurtured early disco and rap in the United States, the *hoyos funquis* (funky holes) where underground rockers and fans gathered were temporary meeting places in abandoned buildings and parking lots in the poorest, toughest neighborhoods. The temporary nature of the gatherings kept young rockers on the move as they tried to make it difficult for authorities to monitor or harass participants (Zolov 1999:251).

NEW OPPORTUNITIES IN THE 1980S

By the 1980s rock Mexicano had regained a mainstream status and the decade saw the formation of a range of groups with broad international appeal and stature. In 1985 the rock group Maldita Vecindad y los Hijos del Quinto Patio (The Damned Slum and the Sons of the Fifth Patio) formed. They pioneered new Mexican approaches to *rock en español*, along with the equally important groups Caifanes, Café Tacuba, and Maná (both of the latter remain active), enjoying new support and promotion from the international recording industry. Until their break-up in August 2011, Maldita Vecindad (as they were known for short) explored a blend of styles including ska, heavy metal, and traditional Mexican music, and band members dressed in *Pachuco* garb of baggy pants, long coat, and pork-pie hat.[21] In this same era, bands from Argentina (Soda Stereo, Miguel Mateos and ZAZ, Fito Paéz, Enanitos Verdes, GIT, Los Fabulosos Cadillacs), Colombia (Aterciopelados, and later Shakira and Juanes) and Spain (Nacha Pop, La Unión, Héroes del Silencio) began selling to larger audiences and labels like BMG, RCA, and Sony International began promoting cross Latin marketing of *rock en tu idioma* (rock in your language, meaning Spanish).

> Listening to "Kumbala" as sung by Maldita Vecindad. Source: *El Circo* (1991).

10.6

The music of "Kumbala" may remind some listeners of the soundtrack for a 007 movie. It certainly reflects Maldita Vecindad's attraction to Cuban and tropical dance music. The strongly accented *clave* rhythm (sounded

Figure 10.5
Maldita Vecindad.
The artists engaged in
a legal battle regarding
the rights to their
name after their
breakup. Sep. 11,
2011. Photo by
Archivo Agencia
EL UNIVERSAL.
(Copyright GDA/El
Universal/México via
AP Images). Used with
permission.

on wooden percussion sticks known as *claves*), heard in the first half of the song, gives way to an aggressive 4/4 rock back-beat, only to return at close the song. The music captures the alluring sensuality of the tropical dance club mentioned in the lyrics. Opening the selection is a muted trumpet, suggesting a stage band more than a rock band. The inclusion of instruments beyond the traditional amplified guitars and drums of the classic rock band is a hallmark of Maldita Vecindad's blended style.

The lyrics evoke the atmosphere of the Dance Bar Kumbala, with its neon red light signal, the passion of the night, the nearby sea, and dancing couples falling in love. Absent are bold political messages; instead this song emphasizes sensuality and evokes the qualities of magical realism popularized in literature of the era and particularly in Gabriel García Márquez's novel *Cien Años de Soledad* (One Hundred Years of Solitude). Not all of Maldita Vecindad's songs adopt this smooth sound and pictorial approach; some draw upon ska, punk, and edgier hip hop aesthetics. "Kumbala" illustrates only one response by this band to the opportunities that opened in the 1980s. It appears on the CD *El Circo*, an album released in 1991 that has been called the "*Sgt. Pepper* of Latin music" for its similar mix of styles in a compiled set of songs that might accompany a staged revue of skits presented in a cabaret or circus tent, reflected in the cover art for the CD. The album's metaphorical big tent included songs with political messages, such as the song "Un gran circo" (A big circus) and "Un poco de sangre" (A little blood) denouncing social inequality.

THE 1990S TO THE PRESENT

Since the 1990s rock Mexicano has continued to be linked to the international entertainment industry and new performers continue to arrive on the scene, others continually evolve to retain both Mexican and international fans. One of the most successful artists in this latter category is Saúl Hernández and Jaguares.

> Listening to "Las ratas no tienen alas" (The Rats Don't Have Wings) by Jaguares. Source: *El Equilibrio de los Jaguares.*

10.7

The alternative rock band Jaguares (Jaguars) was founded in 1996 by Saúl Hernández, the lead singer who co-founded Caifanes in 1987. Reportedly, Hernández had a dream that prompted him to leave Caifanes and form the new group, after he had a dream of singing in a jaguar's mouth—a powerful blend of mystic and pre-Cortesian imagery. His new direction reinforced his solidarity with indigenous Mexicans and their quest for recognition and civil rights. Hernández expressed support for the Zapatista Movement—EZLN—in various declarations to the media and in his concerts. The lyrics in "Las ratas no tienen alas" (Fig. 10.6) exhort ordinary people to persevere against the "rats," the police who persecute or disparage them. They don't have wings, they can't reach the heights that you can, the song implies. To an interviewer, Hernández explains:

> This is a reference to the system, to the people or whomever you wish. Remember that in the 1970s when you had long hair and walked on the street people whistled at you or grabbed you? That abuse of rights is very sad, it moves from a personal problem to a country's problem. The song "The Rats Don't Have Wings" speaks to this. [Abusers] can beat you, rob you, stab you in the back, they can stay, they can betray you, but they are never going to be able to fly.[22]

The cryptic quality of lyrics is supported by the band's musical performance, with the laid-back delivery of Saúl's singing, and the bursts of instrumental sound that punctuate the trance-like character of the song. Saúl has cultivated and acquired a reputation for being a shaman, a spiritual leader, typically of indigenous ancestry, who has the ability to create links between the natural and supernatural worlds.

BI-NATIONALISM AND BEYOND IN THE TWENTY-FIRST CENTURY

This chapter began by introducing Gloria Ríos as one of the first Mexican women to align herself with rock, albeit it temporarily, and it will close with Julieta Venegas, another multi-talented woman. Like Ríos, Venegas

Figure 10.6
Lyrics for "Las ratas no tienen alas." (Alfonso Hernández Estrada) Copyright 1996 by El Gorila con Alas y El Cocodrilo Emplumado and Peermusic Ltd. Peermusic administers on behalf of itself and El Gorila con Alas y El Cocodrilo Emplumado. Used by permission. All rights reserved.

"Las ratas no tienen alas"

Voy cambiándome de piel
sintiendo la metamorfosis
Voy rastreando el camaleón
siguiendo su cinismo interno

Voy contigo a dominar las leyes
que no son la forma de nuestra razón
Y verás que al despertar
tus pies no pisarán
la mugre que dejó Luzbel
con su traición.

Laberintos incansables
recorren la ruta
de mi insomnio
Y de mi historia.

Acuérdate que las ratas
no tienen alas
Acuérdate que las ratas
no tienen alas
Acuérdate que las ratas
no tienen alas
Acuérdate que las ratas.

Si alguna vez me viste
arrastrándome entre cuerpos
Fue por la nauseabunda
mezcla de dolor y odio
Si alguna vez me viste
desnudo fue para no ocultarme
tus visiones
Nunca ocultarme menos de ti.

Laberintos incansables
recorren la ruta
de mi insomnio
Y de mi historia.

Acuérdate que las ratas . . .
Recuerda

"The Rats Don't Have Wings"

I am changing my skin
feeling the metamorphosis
I am tracking the chameleon
Following its internal cynicism

I go with you to dominate the law
that don't form our reasoning
And you will see that when you awake
your feet will not step upon
the dirt left by Lucifer
with his betrayal.

Restless labyrinths
Go across the route
of my insomnia
and of my history

Remember that the rats
don't have wings
Remember that the rats
don't have wings
Remember that the rats
don't have wings
Remember that the rats

If you ever saw me
dragging myself among the bodies
It was because of the nauseating
Mix of pain and hate
If you ever saw me naked
it was so as not to hide myself
from your visions
I'd never hide myself, less from you

Restless labyrinths
Go across the route
of my insomnia
and of my history

Resolve that the rats . . .
Remember

also was born in the United States but was raised in Mexico. A bi-national status is shared by Mexicans in all fields, although not all have the financial means to leverage the experience as successfully as Venegas. With her residences in Mexico, Europe, and the United States, Venegas enjoys close affiliation with multiple cultures. Her experience calls to mind the position of social scientist Roger Rouse (1991), who was one of the first scholars to maintain that modern Mexican identity is shaped by the necessity of integrating geographically disparate connections.

Born in 1970 in Los Angeles, singer Julieta Venegas was raised in Tijuana, Mexico. Her early rock performances were with the Tijuana-based ska band Tijuana No!, but Venegas soon established herself as a singer in an eclectic blend of pop and rock styles building a fan base in Mexico, the United States, and around the world, winning multiple Grammy and MTV awards over the course of her career. Her song "Me voy" (I'm Going) [10.8] infuses the pop ballad with the distinctive harmonic rhythm of the ranchera strummed on the guitar, supported by the rock drum kit, while her voice alternates melodic passages with the accordion player.

Listening to "Me voy," sung by Julieta Venegas. Source: *Limon y Sal*, Ariola.[23]

10.8

The ultimate break-up song, "Me voy" offers a commonly felt female perspective on failed love, likely contributing to its extraordinary popular success. Each verse begins with an explanation, closing with the strong refrain, a statement of farewell: "Because you didn't know how to understand my heart and what it had in it; because you didn't have the courage to see who I am . . . Because you don't listen to what is so close to you . . . What a shame, but goodbye. I say goodbye to you and I'm going." The song, like the woman who delivers it, presents the world with a strong, confident stance. With its no-tears *despedida* (farewell), "Me voy" serves as a fitting close to our brief set of examples of rock, pop, and New Song in Mexico.

CONCLUDING REFLECTIONS

This chapter introduced two important and often antagonistic lines of urban musical expression that emerged in the middle of the twentieth century and which continue to influence greatly Mexican music today. In addition to their urban setting the two lines of practice, nueva canción and rock, share other important characteristic. Perhaps none is more important than the formation of social spaces for building communities of support and inspiration. While the peñas were crucial to the trajectory of the New Song movement in Mexico, so also were the cafés a go-go and hoyos funquis to their respective stages of rock music. The face-to-face contact of these gathering spaces served as a counterbalance to the acquisitive power of the commercial entertainment industry.

The opposing views that separated New Song from rock 'n' roll centered on attitudes regarding capitalism, either resisting or embracing it. Proponents of New Song considered it a response to the rockers and their compromised ideals of commercialism (Barrales Pacheco 1994:258). The high regard for folklore that motivated and inspired the trovadores set them apart from the rockers, but folkloric music was not the only repertory that shaped these musicians. Many of them, including Amparo Ochoa, Salvador Ojeda, and José "Pepe" Ávila, grew up listening to, and in some cases performing, jazz and Cuban-Mexican music. Just as the dance bands that played the mambos and boleros of Pérez Prado adopted rocanrol as a new rhythm to please audiences, the vocal traditions associated with these popular styles informed the contemporary technique of some of the trovadores.

As rock matured, the themes addressed by its practitioners overlapped with those of New Song. A number of Mexican groups such as Javier Bátiz, Los Dug Dugs, Love Army, Los Sinners, and Three Souls in My Mind, aligned themselves with the protest movement. It should be noted that New Song composers and performers did not limit themselves to political themes alone; songs of love and romance are also part of the repertory. Barrales Pacheco offers Óscar Chávez's romantic ballad of anguished love "Por ti" as an example, noting that "no cause or movement among the people can triumph unless its leaders show that they are human too" (Barrales Pacheco 1994:341). Socially conscious rockers fought their own battles with the authorities and commercial interests as the trajectory of rock after 1968 and the Avándaro festival illustrates. In 1991 Gabino Palomares reflected upon the historic confrontations between rockers and the new folk movement regarding capitulation to capitalist values; he stated "we made some mistakes in assuming that rock and its electric guitars were instruments of imperialism," wistfully concluding that in the end "Televisa of Mexico won" (Barrales Pacheco 1994:385–386).

On August 17, 2009 Alex Lora received the Medal for Artistic Merit (Medalla al Mérito artístico) from the Legislative Assembly of Mexico City, an official recognition of rock 'n' roll music and of someone that started his career as an underground performer in a repressive era.

Neither New Song, nor rock, may be reduced to a uniform body of practice. Diversity in goals, formats, and style characterize both. Few trovadores, then or now, play folkloric music exclusively; much of their repertory is modern and contemporary in character and theme. Similarly, even the small sample of examples in this chapter indicate that Mexican rock performers have embraced a full range of rock styles from rhythm and blues, to metal, and hip hop, as well as Latin dance rhythms such as salsa, bachata, or cumbia.

CRITICAL THINKING AND DISCUSSION PROMPTS

1. Describe the two approaches to early rock. How did Mexican *rocanrol* compare to Mexican rock 'n' roll in the 1960s?

2. How did the youth culture that developed around rock 'n' roll challenge traditional culture in Mexico?

3. Why did the federal government attempt to control media representation of rock?

4. What events changed this sunny public image of rock and led to a more directly engaged Mexican rock music?

5. What parallels and contrasts can you draw between the rock music scene in Mexico today and developments prior to 1980? To answer this question more thoroughly, consult one or more of the references listed for this chapter.

6. Rock 'n' roll in the 1950s was closely aligned with jazz and this chapter mentions the prominence of Mexican jazz band leaders and composers Mario Patrón (1935–1981) and Juan García Esquivel (1918–2002). Esquivel composed the bulk of his music before 1970, but he gained new attention in the 1990s, not without some controversy. Investigate the life of Esquivel or Patrón and their musical legacies. Apart from place of birth, what makes their music Mexican? Would it be better to define either, and their music, as international or universal? Why or why not?

7. A team that blends country and rock styles is the popular bi-national duo Jesse y Joy, whose song "¡Corre!" earned No. 1 status on pop charts in the United States and Mexico and won "Best Song" in 2012. Originally released on the CD *Con Quién se Queda el Perro?* (Who Gets the Dog?), the duo released a bachata version in collaboration with the Dominican band La Republica in 2013 (see Pacini-Hernandez, 1995, for some background on bachata). Born in Mexico City, Jesse and Joy Huerta, also spent time with their American mother and her family in Wisconsin while growing up.[24] Their experience calls attention again to the role of bi-national exchange and status in Mexican pop music. Conduct some research about the lives of Jesse and Joy and their work. How has their bi-national experiences influenced the way they create and perform their music? Do you think that their bi-national status has influenced the way that audiences have responded to their music? How does their experience compare to artists discussed in this chapter?

8. Identify at least one additional Mexican rock or pop artist and compare his or her work to one of the artists introduced in this chapter.

9. A new generation of *canto nuevo* artists continue to perform in Mexico today. Locate a song by one of the performers whom Fernando Delgadillo identifies as a contemporary performer of *trova nueva* and compare it to "La Maldición de Malinche." Does the artist you selected speak to international or distinctly Mexican issues? How does the sung delivery and music contribute to the poetic expression? Delgadillo offers the following list of recent Mexican proponents of New Song: Alejandro Filio, Alejandro Santiago, Alberto Escobar, Alfredo Saras, Alfredo Soto Mayor, Angel Galván, Carlos Varela, Cesar Lazcano, Daniel Del Rincón, Daniel Venegas, Edel Juárez, Edgar Oceransky, Eduardo Ulloa, Efrain Inclán, Enrique

Quezada, Félix García, Fernando Delgadillo, Genaro González, Gerardo Peña, Gibran Hernández, Gonzalo Ceja, Gustavo Lastra, Hernaldo Zuñiga, Jaime Ades, Juan Carlos Bidault, Laura Abitia, Mexicanto(+), Oscar Fuentes, Rodrigo Solís, and Sergio Merino.

10. Watch the film *Hecho en Mexico*, a film that explores how contemporary Mexican musicians are using music to address the issue of division—between social classes, nations, and musical styles, as well as the borders separating individual versus collective experience. How do the artists and the music shown in that film compare to those introduced in this chapter?

KEY TERMS, PEOPLE, AND PLACES

nueva canción	*tardeadas*
nueva trova	festivals a go-go
canto nuevo	*posadas*
rocanrol	Javier Bátiz
trovador (trovadores)	La Onda Chicana
Violeta Parra	Avándaro
Mercedes Sosa	*hoyos funquis*
Victor Jara	Alex Lora
Silvio Rodríguez	El Tri
Fidel Castro	Maldita Vecindad
Gabino Palomares	Pachucho
Amparo Ochoa	Quilapayún
Los Folkloristas	Inti-Illimani
Malinche's curse	*rock en tu idioma*
Tlatelolco	Saúl Hernández
La locura del Rock'n Roll	Jaguares
fusiles	Caifanes
refritos	shaman
Orfeon A Go-Go	bi-nationalism
Gloria Ríos	Julieta Venegas
Juan García Esquivel	Jesse y Joy

NOTES

1. Judith Reyes, "Los Rebeldes," from the album *Mexico Oprimido*. YouTube Video, 3:18, posted November 4, 2011. www.youtube.com/watch?v=4r8Z 1aA8mlQ

2. Performers on the group's first recordings, *Los Folkloristas: Repertorio 1966–1968*, vols 1–4 were: Salvador Ojeda, Milla and Rosa Elena Domínguez, Jorge Saldaña, Emiliano and Sara Rosa Ávila, Héctor Sánchez, Jas Reuter, Efrain Trillo, Rubén and María Elena Ortiz, José Ávila, Gerardo Támez, and Rene Villanueva. Ojeda would leave the group in 1968 and Ávila and Villanueva assumed new leadership roles.

3. Amparo Ochoa with Los Folkloristas, *Cancionero Popular*, Mexico City: Discos Pueblo (1975) DP 1006.

4. Amparo Ochoa and Gabino Palomares. "Maldición de Malinche," Antropofobia Records, posted December 18, 2006. www.youtube.com/watch?v=eyUwolkWINk

5. "Tlaxcala. The Translator's Network for Linguistic Diversity." www.tlaxcala.es/detail_artistes.asp?lg=en&reference=183 (accessed September 20, 2014). The English translation included in this text reflects minor edits by Janet Sturman.

6. "En général l'Amérique Latine n'est pas associée à la science, à la technologie, à l'art et à la philosophie; mais oui on l'associe à une société arriérée, primitive, à des sociétés figées aux siècles de la colonie espagnole, profondément catholique, pleines de préjugés."

7. The work of these artists and more is examined by Javier Barrales Pacheco in his PhD dissertation, "History, identity, and the new song movement in Mexico City: A study in urban ethnomusicology," available from the University of California, Los Angeles (1994). It is the only really thorough study of New Song in Mexico and is the source for much of the information reported in this chapter.

8. The three cultures that come together at this site include the Aztec, as represented by the archaeological ruins, the Spanish, as represented by a church called the Templo de Santiago, built in the 1600s, and modern Mexico, as represented by a set of office complexes that now belong to the National Autonomous University of Mexico (UNAM) and privately owned apartments. Given the tragedies associated with the site, it seems ironic that only a year before the student massacre in 1968, leaders of Latin America and Caribbean nations signed on this very site a treaty prohibiting the proliferation of nuclear weapons in their countries, known today as the Treaty of Tlateloco.

9. *Rock 'n' Roll Made in Mexico: From Evolution to Revolution*. DVD, film in English with Spanish subtitles. Los Angeles: Heart Drum/Happy Trailers (Canned Heat Productions), 2008. www.cannedheatmusic.com

10. "Vuelve Primavera: El Rock de los 60 en México." Posted August 4, 2009. http://estroncio90.typepad.com/blog/2009/08/introducción-y-algo-de-historia.html

11. *Master Classics Records, 2010.*

12. "Gloria Ríos. El Relojito (Rock around the Clock), Mexico 1956," excerpt from the film *La locura del Rock'n'Roll*. YouTube Video, 2:45, posted by maph49, August 29, 2006. www.youtube.com/watch?v=GILybBOmMrc

13. "Gloria Ríos. La reina ignorada del rock and roll mexicano." www.maph49.galeon.com/avandaro/gloriarios.html (accessed September 20, 2014).

14. IMDb. *La locura del rock and roll*. www.imdb.com/title/tt0272705/ (accessed September 20, 2014).

15. Reissued on *Batiz and Hair*, Vam Records, 2014; and *16 Grandes éxitos*. Discos Denver, 2014.
16. Armando Molino in the film *Rock 'n' Roll Made in Mexico*.
17. El Tri. *Los Numero Uno. Exitos 1968–2003* [Original Recording Remastered] Sony. Also on: *Three Souls in My Mind—15 Grandes éxitos*, 2010.
18. TRI stands for Three Souls in My Mind, but due to a dispute between Alex Lora and Carlos Hauptvogel about the ownership of the name. Lora decided to settle the dispute by using TRI instead and adding "de México" and Hauptvogel kept the rights to the name Three Souls in My Mind. The name became official in 1985, after Lora lost the dispute.
19. President Gustavo Díaz Ordaz Bolaños served in office from 1964–1970. He oversaw the suppression of student protesters in Tlateloco in 1968.
20. "Una Breve Historia y Algunas Photos del TRI." www.angelfire.com/co/LaDiablarock/historiatri.html (accessed September 20, 2014).
21. The term "Pachucho" emerged to describe Mexican-American youth in the 1930s and 1940s who dressed in flashy suits with baggy pants known as "zoot suits," and pork-pie hats. They cultivated a gang persona and conversed in their own hip jargon.
22. Mi Sitio Web. La Entrevista. Saúl Hernández. (Interview with Saúl Hernández). www.geocities.ws/misitioweb/entrevistas.htm (accessed September 20, 2014).
23. Originally released on the album *Limón y Sal* (Mondomix, 2006).
24. "Bachata Nueva 2012. Corre corazón. Jesse y Joy Ft. la republika." Posted June 13, 2012. www.youtube.com/watch?v=Z3uwOsMFe8c

FOR REFERENCE AND FURTHER STUDY

Barrales Pacheco, Javier. 1994. "History, Identity, and the New Song Movement in Mexico City: A Study in Urban Ethnomusicology." PhD diss., University of California, Los Angeles.

Colussi, Marcelo. 2007. L'interminable complexe d'infériorité de l'Amérique Latine. [The interminable inferiority complex of Latin America]. *El Correo (Paris)*, October 27. http://dev.elcorreo.eu.org/?L-interminable-complexe-d&lang=fr (accessed January 12, 2015)

de la Peza Casares, María del Carmen. 2007. "El Tri: Memory, Imagination and Politics?" *Intercultural Communication Studies* 16:206–213.

Fairley, Jan. 1984. "La Nueva Canción Latinoaméricana." *Bulletin of Latin American Research* 3(2):107–115.

Flores Rivera, Salvador. 1988. *Relatos de mi barrio: Autobiografía de Salvador Flores Rivera (Chava Flores)*. Mexico CIty: EDAMEX.

Garofalo, Rebee. 2004. *Rockin' Las Américas: The Global Politics of Rock in Latin/o America*. Pittsburgh, PA: University of Pittsburgh Press.

Gavagnin, Stefano. 1986. "Sobre la 'orquesta' en la Nueva Canción" [On the orchestra style in the Nueva Canción]. *Literatura chilena: Creación y crítica* 10(1):5–7.

González, Juan Pablo. 1991. "Hegemony and Counter-Hegemony of Musician Latin-Americans: The Chilean Pop." *Popular Music and Society* 15(2):63–78.

Martínez, R. 1992. *The Other Side: Fault Lines, Guerrilla Saints, and the True Heart of Rock N' Roll*. New York: W.W. Norton.

Meyer, Michael C., et al. 2007. *The Course of Mexican History*. 8th ed. New York: Oxford University Press.

Moreno, Albrecht. 1986. "Violeta Parra and la nueva cancion Chilena." *Studies in Latin American Popular Culture* 5:108–126.

Pacini Hernandez, Deborah. 1995. *Bachata: A Social History of a Dominican Popular Music*. Philadelphia, PA: Temple University Press.

Palacios Franco, Julia. 2004. *Memoria y Rock. La historia oral como otra forma de grabación*. Proceedings of the Fifth Congress of the Latin American Branch of the International Association of the Study of Popular Music. www.iaspmal.net/wp-content/uploads/2011/12/JuliaPalaciosFranco.pdf (accessed January 12, 2015).

Palacios Franco, Julia. 2004. "Yo no soy un rebelde sin causa . . . O de cómo el rock & roll llegó a México." In *Historias de los Jóvenes en México. Su presencia en el siglo XX*, edited by José Antonio Pérez Islas, et al.. Mexico City: Secretaría de Educación Pública; Instituto Mexicano de la Juventud: Archivo general de la Nación, México, 341–348.

Palacios Franco, Julia and Estrada, Tere. 2004. "A Contracorriente: A History of Women Rockers in México." In Rebee Garofalo (Ed.), *Rockin' Las Américas. The Global Politics of Rock in Latin America*. Pittsburgh, PA: University of Pittsburgh Press, 142–159.

Reyes, David and Waldman, Tom. 2009. *Land of a Thousand Dances: Chicano Rock 'n' Roll from Southern California*. Albuquerque, NM: University of New Mexico Press.

Rouse, Roger. 1991. "Mexican Migration and the Social Space of Post-modernism." *Diaspora: A Journal of Transnational Studies* 1(1):8–23.

SACM. *Sociedad de Autores y Compositores Mexicanos*. [Society of Mexican Authors and Composers]. www.sacm.org.mx/archivos/biografia.asp (accessed January 12, 2015).

Seeger, Anthony. 1991. "Singing Other People's Songs." *Cultural Survival Quarterly* 15(3):36–39.

Taffet, Jeffrey F. 1997. "'My guitar is not for the rich': The New Chilean Song movement and the politics of culture." *The Journal of American Culture* 20(2):91–103.

Zolov, Eric. 1999. *Refried Elvis: The Rise of the Mexican Counterculture*. Berkeley, CA: University of California Press.

DISCOGRAPHY

Amparo Ochoa with Los Folkloristas, *Cancionero Popular*, Mexico City: Discos Pueblo (1975) DP 1006

El Tri. *Los Numero Uno. Exitos 1968–2003* [Original Recording Remastered] Sony.

Julieta Venegas. *Limón y Sal*. Mondomix, 2006.

Los Folkloristas. *Nuevo Canto*. Mexico City: Discos Pueblo (1976) DP1016.

Maldita Vecindad y Los Hijos del Quinta Patio. *El Circo* (1991)

Rock 'n' Roll Made in Mexico: From Evolution to Revolution, CD collection. Canned Heat Productions, 2008.

FILMS AND VIDEOS

Hecho en Mexico. Director. Duncan Bridgeman. Performers. Alejandro Fernández and Los Tucanes de Tijuana. Lionsgate, DVD (2012).

Rock 'n' Roll Made in Mexico: From Evolution to Revolution. Directed by Lance Miccio, produced by Fito de la Parra. Canned Heat Productions. DVD (2008). [www.cannedheatmusic.com/merchandise.html]

Rojo Amanecer. Hector Bonilla, Maria Rojo. Mexcinema Video Corp. (1983).

CHAPTER 11

Competing Popular Styles

THE WEDDING PLAYLIST AS POP CATALOG

Few events bring together a wider array of popular dance music styles than a wedding and these stylistic differences provide a useful starting point for exploring unities and polarities in popular Mexican music. The DJs who mix and spin the songs for a Mexican wedding, whether for the entire event or between sets of a live band, must provide music that satisfies the full spectrum of ages present. Despite a general shared culture, there are different views regarding what music represents the couple, and most importantly, what songs will reliably bring the guests together on the dance floor. We don't have to travel to Mexico to see those differences in action. Writing from the perspective of Mexicans living in California, journalist Gustavo Arellano reminds his readers that "Mexicans in the United States come from different parts of Mexico." Southern Californian weddings are "chockablock with banda sinaloense, Chalino Sánchez wannabes, rancheras, Sierreño, sonidero, and conjunto norteño (and the mashing of them all), the Texas airwaves play a different style . . .grupero, tribal, and northern Mexico-style cumbias rule."[1]

In 2012, Arellano, stacked his list of the "ten most overplayed songs at Mexican weddings" against a list published by his friend, Houston journalist Marco Torres, to see how they compared.[2] As predicted, there was some overlap, but there were notable differences. In Houston, Mexican wedding guests shake their booties to more cumbias than rancheras, and Torres's list includes cumbias by 3BallMTY, Aniceto Molino, and Fito de Olivares; while in California tambora, bachata, and almost anything by Banda El Recodo tops the list. Both reporters' playlist included a line dance: Los Indomables, "La víbora del mar" and music originating outside of Mexico: King Africa's "Humahuaqueño Carnavalito," a Peruvian huayno for the California crowd; and the Honduran *punta* "Sopa de caracol," by Banda Blanca in Houston. On one other point both agreed: the signal that the party's over is when all one's drunken relatives are prompted to sing along with the mariachi star Vicente Fernández belting out "El Rey."

Arellano and Torres focus on Mexican weddings in the United States, but similar lists could be prepared for different cities in Mexico. Cultural historian María Concepción Márquez Sandoval notes that geographic region isn't the only factor shaping the music at a wedding; the socio-economic class status of the couple and the hosting families determines music choices as well.[3] After all, Mexico remains a highly stratified society.

An upper-class couple will likely hire at least two live bands and sometimes three to play for the reception and it is common for those bands to perform songs in Spanish and English. The wealthier the couple, the more English-language music performed. As for American weddings, the love songs chosen have lasted for decades, such as "I Will Always Love You" (Whitney Houston), and "Unchained melody" (Righteous Brothers). The reason to have two bands is to have non-stop music. A string quartet may play classical music to open the reception and sometimes will play while meals are served. A live band with electric instruments will entertain guests with more festive music for dancing. And if a mariachi is hired to perform earlier in the ceremony, it may play at the reception as well; as in the Mexican-American weddings, mariachi is often the final music heard to close the reception.

A middle-class couple will typically hire only one live band that alternates music with a disc jockey who plays recorded music, the *sonido* (sound). Advertised as *Luz y Sonido* (light and sound), DJs usually provide both music and stage lights to light up the dance floor (*pista de baile*). In the past decade, *sonidos* have become more popular than live musicians as they have a vast repertoire on cue for different moments during the reception, such as the welcome, serving meals, dance time (always after the meals), and farewell. Sonidos tend to be cheaper than a live band, although if the equipment is more lavish they can be as expensive or even cost more than a live band. To compete, live bands (*grupos musicales*, or *grupos de variedad*) now offer both services; they perform live and play recorded music during their breaks.

Lower-class weddings may also combine live bands and DJs. For these weddings the best man or men pay the expenses for the music and are known as *padrinos de música*. Whether there is a live band or a DJ the preference will be for performing and dancing to a mix of songs in Spanish, most commonly Banda music (Banda El Recodo, Banda Machos, Jenni Rivera), norteña (Los Tigres del Norte, Ramón Ayala), quebradita, cumbia, reggaeton, and salsa.

Geographic location also matters. Almost any wedding from the Yucatan Peninsula, no matter what social class, will certainly include danzón (see Chapters 1, 6), as that music is particularly important in the area. In Chiapas, a marimba orchestra will supplant the mariachi. Weddings in central Mexico often have the most diverse repertoire, with parties including música tropical (salsa, merengue, cumbia, and other Caribbean dance rhythms) and música norteña (combo bands playing corridos and other dance rhythms). While in the northern regions of the country, norteño and banda music rule. In Nuevo León, huapangos (particularly the northern commercial style with accordion, as played by Los Hechizeros) bring guests to the dance floor.

Weddings in Mexico City stand apart because residents there come from all parts of the country, each with their own customs. For those born in Mexico City (*chilangos* or *defeños*), especially among the working class, cumbia reigns supreme. Performed by DJs known as *sonideros*, this cumbia, like Mexico City, is a mix blending guaracha, vallenato, salsa, and even South American inspired cumbia (Cumbia Andina Mexicana) from bands like "Los Askis" and "Los Llayras."

The many types of popular music from recent decades that come together at weddings form the heart of this chapter and we will explore examples of several of the styles included in those wedding playlists. We'll review the roots of the competing styles, follow some trends, and consider shifting patterns of dominance to better understand when and why different pop music matters to listeners within Mexico and beyond.

TWO PILLARS OF NORTHERN DOMINANCE

Any story of contemporary Mexican popular music must address the development of two major iconic styles: 1) the *conjunto* or combo style of the northern Mexican states that share a border with the United States, also known as *música norteña*; and 2) the dance music popularized by wind bands from the state of Sinaloa known as *banda sinaloense*, or simply *banda*. These styles form the pillars around which a full range of new popular music has developed.

Our story must also acknowledge the manner in which modern popular music from the northern territories resulted in a new locus for Mexican popular identity. So influential are these styles, that Mexican literature and cultural studies scholar Juan Carlos Ramírez-Pimienta (2010) maintains that northern Mexican music has replaced the mariachi in representing modern Mexicans to the world. Even if we do not accept wholeheartedly such a bold claim, we must acknowledge that the northern territories, once considered by central Mexicans as the backward provinces, are recognized today for creating music that speaks to a contemporary Mexican identity. This new identity is no longer tied to cultural production managed by the central Mexican states. Furthermore, the identities promoted by the popular musical styles of the north are truly transnational, for while musicians and fans maintain affiliations with specific places, they regularly transcend any single geographic locale as they engage in ongoing exchanges across international and stylistic borders.

THE CONJUNTO STYLE FROM EARLY TO MODERN PRACTICE

The northern style of music called *conjunto*, *norteño*, *tejano*, and Tex-Mex, depending on subtle differences of perspective and practice, developed from regular musical and cultural exchange across the Texas–Mexico border. The history and contemporary significance of that exchange and its accompanying tensions have been widely studied by leading scholars including Américo Paredes (1970), Manuel Peña (1985), Guadalupe San Miguel (2002), José Limón (2011), and Cathy Ragland (2012). An engaging early treatment can be found in two films by Les Blank: *Chulas Fronteras* (Beautiful Borders, 1976) and *Mero Corazón* (Real Heart). Together they offer an excellent introduction to the roots of the northern style of popular music and its Texas–Mexican proponents. In Blank's classic films we meet local superstars Don Santiago Jiménez, Flaco Jiménez, Narciso Martínez, Rumel Fuentes, Lydia Mendoza, Los Alegres de Terán, Los Pingüinos del Norte, and Ramiro Cavazos. Footage was filmed in the Rio Grande Valley, in Texas, at the Del Valle Record pressing plant, and in several cantinas and an onion warehouse (*bodega de cebolla*) in San Benito and McAllen, Texas. Viewers meet the legendary Narciso Martínez (who was born in Reynosa, Tamaulipas but grew up in the Rio Grande Valley) working at his day job at the Gladys Porter Zoo in Brownsville, TX. The message is clear: norteño music may be big business today, but the original conjunto stars came from humble backgrounds.

The roots of the conjunto style of music date from the 1860s when German, Polish, and Czech immigrants imported the accordion to northern Mexico and what is now southern Texas. The practice of pairing the accordion with the bajo sexto guitar and a side snare drum eventually led to a standard instrumentation for performing songs and dance music for working-class laborers. Mexican musicians adapted the popular salon dances of Europe: the Polish polka and mazurka, the Czech *redowa* (a leaping waltz-like dance), and the already popular Viennese waltz, giving them a Mexican flavor. Local dances like the huapango from Tamaulipas joined the repertory.

Beginning in the 1920s norteño musicians began to make gramophone recordings and the circulation of recorded performances both enriched and helped standardize the genres associated with conjunto. We find an example in how musicians merged the tango, the Argentine dance that gained international popularity in the 1930s, with Mexican regional song forms, resulting in popular hybrid forms like the tango-waltz and the tango-ranchera [see 11.4]. After 1960 a similar embrace occurred with the *cumbia*, originally a dance from Colombia, as it became a favorite rhythm in norteño conjunto music.

EARLY NORTEÑO MASTERS

Listening to "Flor Marchita" as performed by Narciso Martínez, originally recorded in 1937.[4]

11.1

The early northern conjunto style is represented on our listening list by the music of the legendary accordion master Narciso Martínez (1911–1992), known as "El Huracán del Valle" (the Hurricane of the Valley). He was greatly admired by his contemporaries and imitated by other regional musicians to this day, including Native American *waila* musicians from the borderlands, discussed later in this chapter.

Martínez developed a new technique for playing the button accordion. Unlike German musicians, he dropped the left-hand bass chords and focused on elaborating the right-hand melody lines. He let his bandmate, the masterful bajo sexto player Santiago Almeida, handle the bass lines. Martínez's lighter, brighter sound set a new standard for Tex-Mex accordion players, while Almeida's approach to the bass guitar line became the model for future players of bajo sexto.[5]

"Flor Marchita" (Withered Flower) is also the title of a Mexican film released in 1969. The song is a *chotis* which shares a duple meter with the polka but differs in that the chotis features a lilting dotted-rhythm in the melody and a heavy accent on beat two of each measure. The musical form of the tune unfolds as a string of alternating and repeating melodic phrases: AABBAABBAABBAA, alternating repetition with contrast in a predictable manner well suited for dancing.

We've encountered the chotis in our previous discussion of how the salon and ballroom dance styles of Europe were popularized in Paris and later absorbed into international repertories in the late nineteenth and early twentieth centuries. Theater music also included the chotis rhythm, further spreading it and other dance rhythms. Mexican popular musicians adopted the rhythm for social dances, as did the Tohono O'odham, discussed below.

THE TEXAS–MEXICAN CONJUNTO

Defined by its signature accordion-driven sound, Texas–Mexican conjunto (the name for the ensemble and the style), also called tejano music or Tex-Mex, resulted from the talents of other musicians performing along the border, among them the family of Santiago Jiménez. Born in San Antonio, Texas, musician Santiago Jiménez, Sr. (1913–1984) learned accordion from his father, Patricio Jiménez, and began playing professionally when he was only eight years old. In the 1930s, Santiago began recording and playing live for the radio on the two-row button accordion, the iconic instrument of conjunto. After living and working for years in Dallas, Texas, he returned to San Antonio at the age of 64 where he performed and recorded with his sons Leonardo "Flaco" (the skinny one) and Santiago, Jr., for the remaining seven years of his life.

Leonardo "Flaco" Jiménez (b. 1939) developed a style distinct from his father, becoming a virtuoso legend in his own right and leading his generation's approach to the Texas–Mexican conjunto style by connecting it with other popular musical styles from the 1950s to the present. He began performing at an early age, playing in his father's band Los Corporates when he was only seven years old. As an adult, Flaco Jiménez moved to New York City where he collaborated and made recordings with a wide range of artists including Stephen Stills, John Hiatt, Dwight Yoakam, Linda Ronstadt, Emmy Lou Harris, Ry Cooder, and Bob Dylan. The exposure made him known to audiences worldwide. He was inducted as an NEA National Heritage Fellow in 2012, and has won five Grammy awards: three for his solo work and two for collaborative performances of rock, country, and Mexican styles, including one for his work with the Texas Tornados, the band that he and fellow musicians Freddy Fender, Doug Sahm, and Augie Meyers formed in 1990. Flaco Jiménez's renown as a master accordionist led the Hohner accordion company to create an accordion named after him. Audio Examples 11.3 and 11.4 offer two contrasting examples of his playing.

> Listening to "Marina" as performed by Leonardo "Flaco" Jiménez with Los Lobos. Source: *Flaco Jiménez: Partners* (1992).

11.2

Flaco Jiménez's accordion playing in the song "Marina" illustrates his virtuosic technique. He introduces the tune with an ornamented passage, and inserts decorative interludes between each verse. These passages are known among players as *adornos* (adornments) and each player creates his own distinguishing adorno style. Notice that no matter how many flourishes Jiménez adds, he never loses the fundamental dance beat. "Marina" is a song that Jiménez has been singing in South Texas for many years, but for this recording he sings it with the band Los Lobos and includes English-language lyrics alongside the original Spanish verses.

> Listening to the "West Texas Waltz" performed by Flaco Jiménez and Emmy Lou Harris. Source: *Flaco Jiménez: Partners* (1992).

11.3

The merger of Tex-Mex and Southwest country music can be heard in the recording of the "West Texas Waltz" performed by Flaco Jiménez and Emmy Lou Harris. It illustrates the often unrecognized affinities between Tex-Mex music and country music in the United States. Flaco Jiménez's abilities to perform with musicians in many styles helped secure his fame and bring wider attention to Tex-Mex music.

LYDIA MENDOZA'S BREAKING OF GENDER RESTRICTIONS

Virtually all the performers of early música norteña and Tex-Mex were men, and most still are. Outside of the home environment, the primary venues for performance prior to 1950 were bars and cantinas, places respectable women did not generally frequent. Lydia Mendoza (1916–2007), introduced in Chapter 8, represents an important exception to the exclusion of women performers in working-class border communities. Even more significant were Mendoza's commercial recordings which spread her fame throughout the south-west and into Mexico.

The "Lark of the Border," or "La Alondra de la Frontera," as Lydia Mendoza was called, was more than an accomplished singer; she also developed a method of playing the solo guitar that allowed her to integrate an articulated bass line into the harmony part, thereby condensing the parts usually played by a trio of male instrumentalists. This solo female singer regularly performed the parts of three men. Details of Mendoza's life make for fascinating reading and scholars have only recently come to appreciate how her music and life represented the transnational experience of the Mexican migrants who became her greatest fans (Broyles-González 2001; Strachwitz and Nicolopoulos 1993).

11.4

Listening to "Mal Hombre" sung by Lydia Mendoza in 1934. Source: *Mal Hombre and Other Original Hits from the 1930s.*

"Mal Hombre" (Evil Man) was Mendoza's first recorded song in 1934 and its success helped launch her touring career. Set to the rhythm of a tango, an international sensation of the time, this *canción* became her most requested number.

Over her long career, Lydia Mendoza acquired a vast repertoire of songs in many popular styles, but she never turned her back on the working-class Mexican people to whom she catered and with whom she most identified. The ranchera song "Pajarito prisionero" illustrates her sensitivity towards Mexican migrants and the difficulties they faced.

11.5

Listening to "Pajarito prisionero" sung by Lydia Mendoza, recorded live in Santa Barbara, California in 1982.

The early performances of La Alondra took place in humble settings such as tent shows and fairs across the American Southwest and in various cities of Mexico. Mendoza always took requests from her audience and we can hear that kind of interaction in the live recording of "Pajarito herido" [11.5] made by her biographer Yolanda Broyles-González at a 1982 concert in Santa Barbara. The recording appears on the CD *Lydia Mendoza, La Alondra de la Frontera* erroneously subtitled "live from New York," and the song is labeled "Pajarito prisionero" (Imprisoned Little Bird) rather than "Pajarito herido" (Wounded Little Bird). Either way, Mendoza's song conveys a sense of entrapment and feelings of conflict regarding love lost that makes for an interesting comparison to heartache caused by the cage of gold told in "Jaula de oro" as sung by Los Tigres del Norte [11.8]. Do you suppose that migrants found themselves relating metaphorically to the little bird caged by a love gone wrong?

WAILA: AN INDIGENOUS RESPONSE TO EXPANDING INFLUENCES

Both Tex-Mex and norteño musical styles influenced rural popular music along the Arizona–Mexican border, including the social dance music of

"Mal Hombre"

Era yo chiquilla todavía
cuando tu casualmente me encontraste
y merced a tus artes de mundano
de mi honra el perfume te llevaste.

Luego hiciste conmigo lo que todos
los que son como tu, con las mujeres,
por lo tanto no te extrañe que yo, ahora,
en la cara te diga lo que eres.

(Estribillo):
Mal hombre . . .
tan ruin es tu alma que no tiene
nombre,
eres un canalla . . . eres un malvado . . .
eres un mal hombre.

A mi triste destino abandonada
entablé fiera lucha con la vida
ella, recia y cruel me torturaba
yo agotada al fin . . .caí vencida.

Tu supiste a tiempo, mi derrota,
mi espantoso calvario conociste,
te dijeron algunos . . . ve a salvarla . . .
y probando quien eras . . . te reíste . . .

Poco tiempo despúes en el arroyo
entre sombras mi vida se perdía.
Una noche con otra tu pasaste
y al mirarme oí que te decía . . .

Quien es esa mujer . . . tu la conoces . . .
y tu voz contestaba . . . na cualquiera . . .
y al oír de tus labios tal ultraje
me mostraba . . . fingiendo que tu no
eras . . .

"Bad Man"

I was still just a little girl
when you casually met me
and at the mercy of your mundane tricks
you took away the scent of my virtue.

Later, you did with me what all
who are like you do with women
and so it should not seem strange that now
I tell you to your face what you are.

(Chorus)
Bad man . . .
Such a ruin is your soul that it has no
name,
you are despicable . . . you are an
evildoer . . .
you are a bad man.

Abandoned to my sad destiny
a fierce struggle with life faced
strong and cruel, it tortured me
and, I exhausted in the end . . . fell
vanquished.

You knew at the time, my defeat,
my frightful Calvary you knew,
Some told you . . . you saw it could be
saved . . .
and showing who you are . . . you
laughed . . .

Some time later in the gully
among the shadows my life was lost.
One night you passed by with another
woman
and while watching me I heard her say
to you . . .

Who is that woman . . . you know her . . .
and your voice answered . . . a fallen
woman . . .
and to hear from your lips such an insult
showed me . . . pretending what you are
not . . .

Figure 11.1
Lyrics for "Mal Hombre" by Lydia Mendoza. San Antonio Music Publishers, Inc., BMI. Used with permission.[6]

Figure 11.2
Lyrics for "Parjarito herido" by Lydia Mendoza. San Antonio Music Publishers, Inc., BMI. Used with permission.[7]

"Pajarito herido"	**"Wounded Little Bird"**
Un lindo pajarito, cierta noche herido refugiarse en mi ventana y yo le recogí compadecida brindándole el calor que le faltaba	One night, a lovely wounded little bird took refuge in my window, and I, feeling compassion, took him into the warmth of my home
Le puse en un jaula primorosa cuidábale con mimo noche e día y siempre que sus trinos escuchaba cantaba así, con gran melancolía	I placed him in a beautiful cage and looked after him night and day, and every time I heard the warble of his song, singing like that, with great sadness,
Pajarito, pajarito que en tu jaula vives prisionero yo también por un amor igual que tu cautiva muero (se repite)	Little bird, little bird prisoner within your cage I am languishing too As a prisoner of love (repeat)
De un hombre zalamero y engañoso sentíame a poco tiempo enamorada al ver que mi galán era tan falso rompí con su querer, desengañada	From a man full of flattery and deceit and I quickly fell in love with when I found out my lover was so untrue disillusioned, I broke up our affair
Hoy día que ha pasado tanto tiempo recuerdo que le quiero todavía y siempre que recuerdo al pajarito suspiro así, con gran melancolía	Even today after such a long time has passed, I realize that I still love him and whenever I think of that little bird I sigh with great sadness
Pajarito etc.	Little bird etc.

the Tohono O'odham Indians (also known as Papago), who live in southern Arizona and northern Sonora, Mexico. This dance music called *waila* developed along parallel lines as música norteña beginning in the 1880s and O'odham musicians still perform it the twenty-first century.

11.6 "First Stop Waila," performed by the band Southern Scratch. Source: *Dancing in the Dust* (2000).[8]

Waila bands perform the same array of dance rhythms as norteño performers, including the chotis (chote), mazurka, waltz, cumbia, and polka. The polka stands as the signature rhythm of the waila tradition, and thus players call it "waila" rather than polka. The polka is characterized by a quick duple meter, but the tradition manner in which O'odham dance waila is with smooth gliding steps, not with the bouncing steps associated with polkas danced in central and eastern European style. Our example, "First Stop Waila" [11.6] is performed by the band Southern Scratch. The band takes its name from "chicken scratch" an early term for waila music. Note the prominence of the saxophone and accordion in the band.

The saxophones and accordions take the role of singers. It is rare to hear any human voices in old-school waila performance. O'odham musicians, particularly those living on the U.S. side of the border, more readily adopted Mexican musical practices than the Spanish language.[9] The practice is slowly changing today as young musicians adopt and favor the new international rhythms of Latin music (Sturman 2012). The cumbia now dominates waila events geared for youthful audiences and young performers are creating lyrics for some of their songs and occasionally sing during shows and dance sessions.

While it may seem as if waila music is simply música norteña by a different name, several important distinctions allow musicians to project a nuanced identity highlighting the relationship of place and indigenous ethnicity. In addition to favoring a purely instrumental performance, O'odham musicians also tend to play their instruments differently than norteño musicians; waila is typically less ornate and showy.[10]

LOS TIGRES DEL NORTE

As this book is being written in 2014, Los Tigres del Norte (The Tigers of the North) are entering their sixth decade of performance, continuing to represent contemporary música norteña. They sing polkas, waltzes, ballads, and especially the cumbia, the most popular dance rhythm since 1970. The group's founder and lead guitarist is Jorge Hernández,[11] who formed the band with his brothers and cousins after moving to San Diego. The men grew up in the little town of Rosa Morada in the state of Sinaloa and when they began playing music they moved to larger cities along the Pacific Coast, including Mexicali where they lived and worked while in their teens. They played their first concert in Soledad, California in a prison. After releasing in 1974 "Contrabando y traición," the song that came to define the narcocorrido genre, the group earned fame on both sides of the United States–Mexico border, launching a sensational career that continues to the present. In 2000, rather like the bandit heroes in some of their songs who direct their riches towards the good of the people, the band created the Los Tigres del Norte Foundation at UCLA which supports an archive and library of border music. Our two audio examples featuring Los Tigres del Norte [11.8, 11.9] illustrate how Los Tigres updated traditional instrumental and structural formats to address controversial modern concerns.

THE NARCOCORRIDO

> Listening to "Contrabando y traición" performed by Los Tigres del Norte. Source: *Contrabando y Traición* (Fonovisa, 1984).

11.7

The music of "Contrabando y traición" has all the qualities of the classic norteño conjunto: twangy guitars marking the harmonic rhythm, discreetly supported by bass and snare drum, with accordion passage work serving as a kind of Greek chorus providing "commentary" to the sung verse. Notice that the accordion entrances are predictable, always between lines 5 and 6 of each verse, and again in the interlude between verses. In the final verse, we hear the sounds of gunshots included in the recording sound mix.

The original name of the song "Contrabando y traición," was "La Camelia" written by Ángel González in 1972. It was not the first, nor the last, narcocorrido written but it has become legendary. It established models for future corridos, including some composed in response to it, such as "Ya encontraron a Camelia" (They've Found Camelia), and "El hijo de Camelia" (The Son of Camelia) (see Herrera Sobek 2006:132). The 1977 Mexican movie *Contrabando y traición*, directed by Arturo Martínez enacts and elaborates the story told in the song, which also served as inspiration for the video-chamber opera *únicamente la verdad* (2008) by Mexican composer Gabriela Ortiz.[12]

🎧

11.8

Listening to "A mis enemigos" as sung by Valentín Elizalde.

Another famous early singer of narcocorridos was Chalino Sánchez (1960–1992), who first rose to prominence via the underground circulation of his cassette recordings and when a concert attendee opened fire on him while singing on-stage in 1992. The event led to his unsolved murder in Culiacán later that year. He has been the subject of several films, including the documentary *Al Otro Lado* (2006), that explores the violence surrounding this genre,[13] and his corrido "El crimen de Culiacán" appears in the soundtrack of the 2010 Mexican film *El Infierno*.

Mark Edberg argues that the narcocorrido persona as "badass" has become a marketing tool in its own right, overriding any actual circumstance or connection to crime (Edberg 2011:67). However, there can be no denying that some singers send threatening or coded messages from one cartel to another in their songs. An example is the late Valentín Elizalde "El gallo de oro" (The Golden Rooster) (1979–2006). Reputedly, after singing the taunting "A mis enemigos" (To My Enemies) [11.8] during a concert in Reynosa, Tamualipas, he was gunned down by members of the Zeta Cartel. While he was alive, he never had a Billboard hit, but after his death, his songs gained immense popularity on YouTube and a posthumous album, *Vencedor* (Winner), rose to the top of the charts in 2009. The lyrics of "A mis enemigos" include references to Elizalde's place of birth, Navajoa in the state of Sinaloa, as well as the town of Guasave, where he lived and performed with his father and brothers.

The song opens with a boastful shout out in street slang: *Y esto va pa' toda la bola de envidiosos ay'jo [ay, hijo]!*—"This goes out to all the envious ones!" followed by a question: "how did the burned ones die?" The next verse compares barking dogs to jealous gossips: "The dogs continue barking (*siguen ladrando los perros*), a sign that I am moving forward." The follow verse is more menacing: "They don't play around with me, why would they risk their life, I have a super kick gun (*traigo una súper patada*), and

"Contrabando y traición"

Salieron de San Isidro,
procedentes de Tijuana
traían las llantas del carro
repletas de hierba mala
eran Emilio Varela,
y Camelia, la Texana.

Pasaron por San Clemente
los paró la emigración
les pidió sus documentos
les dijó: "¿De donde son?"
ella era de San Antonio,
una hembra de corazón.

Una hembra así quiere a un hombre
por el puede dar la vida
pero hay que tener cuidado
si esa hembra se encuentra herida,
la traición y el contrabando
son cosas incompartidas

A Los Angeles llegaron
a Hollywood se pasaron
en un callejón oscuro
las cuatro llantas cambiaron
ahí entregaron la hierba,
y ahí también les pagaron.

Emilio dice a Camelia
"Hoy te das por despedida,
con la parte que te toca,
tu puedes rehacer tu vida
yo me voy para San Francisco
con la dueña de mi vida."

Sonaron siete balazos,
Camelia a Emilio mataba
los policia solo halló
una pistola tirada
del dinero y de Camelia
Nunca más se supo nada.

"Contraband and Betrayal"

They left San Isidro,
heading for Tijuana
carrying car tires
filled with marijuana
They were Emilio Varela,
and Camelia, the Texas woman

While passing by San Clemente
they were stopped by immigration
they asked for their documents
they asked "Where are you from?"
She was from San Antonio,
a woman of strong heart.

If a woman loves a man
she will give her life for him
but one must be careful
if that woman is wounded
betrayal and contraband
are incompatible things

They arrived in Los Angeles
and moved on to Hollywood
In a dark alley
and changed the four tires
there they delivered the weed
and there they were paid.

Emilo says to Camelia
"Today I say goodbye to you,
with the part you made
you can remake your life
I am going to San Francisco
with the love of my life."

Seven bullets sounded
Camelia killed Emilio
the police found only
a gun left behind
about the money and of Camelia
Nothing more was ever known.

Figure 11.3
Lyrics for "Contrabando y traición" as sung by Los Tigres del Norte. Originally "La Camelia" by Ángel González in 1972. Copyright EMMAC (Mexican Music Publishers Association AC).

have them in sight." Elizalde taunts his adversaries: "Don't talk behind my back . . . go on risk it," and then exhorts his band mate and composer of the song Francisco Lira Murillo: *Y échele compa Lira*—"Go for it, my pal Lira," praising his hometown roots. The closing verses of the song, as with older corrido poetic models, offers an elegy to place and an homage of devotion to his hometown: *Navojoa como te quiero, Guasave tierra querida.* A self-referential turn finishes the song with a final boast: "Keep crying snakes, I will take you out on the road, for those who truly care for me, here you have a friend. I just sang this song to all my enemies."

Among the contradictory aspects of the narcocorridos is the bouncy dance music that we might describe as "celebratory" in atmosphere (Edberg 2011:78). As the music industry and singers exploit the drug smuggler as (anti-)hero, they ultimately connect fans with a universal human fascination with the social bandit, and particularly to rebels willing to take on power. Just as all rap fans are not gangsters, many young listeners who listen to narcocorridos are not proponents of drug gangs. Nonetheless, violence associated with drug trafficking in Mexico has escalated since 2006, when the election of President Felipe Calderón (2006–2012) continued the shift of power away from the long-ruling PRI party initiated by Vicente Fox, the first president of the Partido Acción Nacional–PAN.[14] Calderón, like President Fox before him, and President Enrique Peña Nieto, who took office in 2012, lobbied for federal and state regulations prohibiting the public broadcast of narcocorridos. The restrictions are highly controversial eliciting praise from some and charges of harm to freedom of speech and artistic expression from others (see Grey and Johnson 2013; Madrid 2011).

Fans may find avenues for social connection via modern corridos and listeners may relate to the songs' protagonists who challenge a legal system that often fails poor people, country laborers, migrants, or themselves. Plenty of fans also seem to find fun and fantasy in the clashes of power depicted in narcocorridos, akin to the cathartic and entertaining adventures of power enjoyed in comic books and movies. As Edberg (2011) reminds us, narcocorridos, join a vast repertory of songs styles around the world that celebrate acts of rebellion.

MIGRATION AND CROSS-BORDER EXCHANGE

The push and pull factors of migration across the United States–Mexico border have varied, shifting from the bracero movement (1942–1964), to the waves of migration in response to NAFTA after 1993. Narcotics traffickers took advantage of the newly opened borders for trade, and in 1994 the importation of drugs across the United States–Mexico border increased by 24 percent.[15] The violence of the drug trade affected migration as well. The tightening of U.S. border security in 2001, initially in response to the 9/11 attacks by al-Qaeda, and later with the construction of the physical barrier along the United States–Mexico border called for in the "secure fence act" of 2006, led to additional dangers and trials faced by migrants seeking work and residency.

Roger Rouse (1991) has argued that Mexican migrants live in multiple places simultaneously, essentially living in an extended border zone, often because they cannot live securely in one place or the other. When scholars discuss musical transnationalism—and all the examples in this chapter in one way or another can be defined as such—they explore, as we have, how musical sound and performance reflect the give-and-take of cross-border exchange. Their studies of listener reception confirm the difficulties of tying music to any single place. Recognizing the transnational character of music reveals how people use music to help construct comfortable spaces between geographic localities and social communities. The song lyrics of "Jaula de oro," performed by Los Tigres del Norte directly address the psychic pain many people experience while living in such in-between spaces, as does their song "Mis dos patrias" (My Two Homelands). The discussion of tecnobanda and associated dance practices that follows explores more joyful responses to cross-border identity.

Listening to "Jaula de oro" performed by Los Tigres del Norte and Juanes, recorded live at the Hollywood Palladium in Los Angeles, February 28, 2011.[16]

11.9

The Colombian pop star Juanes (born Juan Esteban Aristizábal Vásquez in 1972) joined Los Tigres for the 2011 performance of the song "Jaula de oro." The sentiments expressed in the lyrics reflect the views of immigrants who have come from Mexico to the United States, feelings shared by many who may not be able to return to their homeland. The collaboration of Juanes with Los Tigres del Norte illustrates the popularity of the conjunto style across the Americas, as well as how popular music from northern Mexico and the U.S. borderlands has come to broadly represent Mexican identity. Claims that modern cultural identity is shifting from the central to northern states of Mexico, as noted by Ramírez-Pimienta and others, is further reinforced by a range of new popular music styles, to be discussed presently.

FROM REGIONAL BANDA TO TRANSNATIONAL *TECNOBANDA*

As noted at the opening of this chapter, the two pillar styles of popular Mexican music since 1960 cohere around either the northern conjunto sound, or the dance band tradition that developed in Sinaloa, known simply as banda. In this section we will examine the transformation of the regional popular wind band into an international commercial pop medium signaling transnational Mexican identity. The transition involved a change of instrumentation, performance practice, and new attitudes shared by musicians and their fans.

The banda in the Pacific Coastal state of Sinaloa, often called the *tambora*, after the name for its bass drum, differed from the military and

"Jaula de oro"

Aquí estoy establecido,
en los Estados Unidos,
diez años pasaron ya,
en que crucé de mojado,
papeles no he arreglado,
sigo siendo un ilegal.

Tengo mi esposa y mis hijos,
que me los traje muy chicos,
y se han olvidado ya,
de mi México querido,
del que yo nunca me olvido,
y no puedo regresar.
De qué me sirve el dinero,
si estoy como prisionero,
dentro de esta gran nación,
cuando me recuerdo hasta lloro,
aunque la jaula sea de oro,
no deja de ser prisión.

"Escúchame hijo,
¿Te gustaría que regresáramos
a vivir México?"
"Whatcha talkin about Dad?,
I don't wanna go back to Mexico,
no way Dad"
Mis hijos no hablan conmigo,
otro idioma han aprendido,
y olvidado el español,
piensan como americanos,
niegan que son Mexicanos,
aunque tengan mi color.

De mi trabajo a mi casa,
no sé lo que me pasa,
que aunque soy hombre de hogar,
casi no salgo a la calle,
pues tengo miedo que me hallen,
y me pueden deportar.
De que me sirve el dinero,
si estoy como prisionero,
dentro de esta gran nación,
cuando me recuerdo hasta lloro,
aunque la jaula sea de oro,
no deja de ser prisión.

"Cage of Gold"

Here I am established
in the United States
ten years have already passed
since I crossed as a wetback,
I have not yet arranged my papers,
I continue being an illegal

I have my wife and my children
that I brought so young,
and they have already forgotten
my beloved Mexico
that I will never forget, and
to which I cannot return.
What is money worth,
If I am like a prisoner,
trapped in this great nation,
I even cry when I remember this,
although the cage is made of gold,
it is still a prison.

"Listen to me son,
Would you like for us to return
and live in Mexico?"
"whatcha talkin about Dad?,
I don't wanna go back to Mexico,
no way Dad"
My children don't talk with me,
they've learned another language,
and have forgotten Spanish,
They think like Americans,
denying they are Mexicans,
although they have my color.

From my work to my house,
I don't know what happens to me,
for although I am the man of the house,
I hardly even go out to the street,
because I fear I will be found,
and they could deport me.
What is money worth,
If I am like a prisoner,
trapped in this great nation,
I even cry when I remember this,
although the cage is made of gold,
it is still a prison.

civic wind bands that flourished in the 1800s. Unlike the more formal wind bands with trained musicians who played pre-composed music, the civilian popular bandas were comprised primarily of amateur musicians who played popular music by ear.

The Sinaloan banda gained prominence with the emergence of the Banda Sinaloense El Recodo, led by Don Cruz Lizárraga (1918–1985), a self-taught clarinet player who nonetheless professionalized banda in a manner not unlike what Gaspar Vargas did for mariachi. El Recodo (The Bend) is a small village near the beach resort and port town of Mazatlán, Sinaloa. El Recodo resident Cruz Lizárraga played with his first band in 1938. He recounted that he was promised a set of cymbals from the municipal president if he played well when hired for a civic function. He did not expect much, but he played so well that the official gave him a full complement of eight instruments to begin his own band.[17] He founded Banda El Recodo in 1951 with two clarinets, two trumpets, two trombones, along with bass and snare drum. The group played a mixture of styles including popular Mexican favorites, Latin dance tunes, swing jazz, and classical music. Recodo made its first recording in 1958, making it the first banda from the region to be recorded. Having released more than 178 recordings since, Recodo continues to perform and record six decades later, still under the direction of Lizárraga family members. The current Banda El Recodo has increased instrumentation as it has grown in stature, and now includes four clarinets, three trumpets, three trombones, a tambora (bass drum with cymbal), a *tarola* or snare drum, a tuba (Sousaphone), three lead singers, and three harmony singers. Since 1980, El Recodo has integrated more tropical dance rhythms into its repertory including more salsa and cumbia.

Listening to "El Caballo Bayo" (The Bay Horse)[18] by Banda El Recodo de Cruz Lizárraga.[19]

11.10

"El Caballo Bayo" illustrates Banda El Recodo's instrumental approach to a popular ranchera song first made famous by Antonio Aguilar (1919–2007) and later popularized by Vicente Fernández (b. 1940). The lyrics, not heard here, depict a man ostensibly singing to his horse: "My faithful dappled horse no longer returns to its stable, it no longer responds to my caresses. Damn the lucky dog who took it from me." It's not hard to read between the lines.

Like the other dance music, the form follows a traditional alternation between the full ensemble with a contrasting section that highlights one or two instruments. Here the A section begins with a loud, full, and almost chaotic presentation of a lively melody in 6/8 time played by the full band, followed by a B section with a waltz-like triple meter and the tuba supplying oom-pah support in the bass, where the trombones carry the melody. After the return of the A section with the full band, the B section returns with the clarinets and saxophones taking the melody and the tuba again

Figure 11.5
(see Plate 12)
Mexican performers
Banda El Recodo sing
during the Billboard
Latin Music Awards at
the Bank United Center
in Miami Thursday
April 28, 2011. (AP
Photo/Carlo Allegri)

supplying oom-pah support in the bass. The song closes with a final return of the A section and the full band.

🎧

11.11

Listening to "Te quiero a morir" written by Alfonso 'Poncho' Lizárraga, performed by Banda El Recodo from the album *La Mejor de Todas* (The Best of All) (2011).[20]

Earning number one hit status in Mexican regional popular music in 2011 and also in Latin pop and rock, "Te quiero a morir" [11.11] also enjoyed popularity on radio stations in the south-western United States, such as Tucson's "La Caliente," FM 102.1. It illustrates Banda El Recodo's incorporation of vocals and recognition of the popular ballad ranchera style.

This is party music; people listen to it forget their troubles and to dance. The lyrics convey an expression of romantic love. Saying "Te quiero a morir" is a way of saying that you love someone to death, akin to saying "I love you to the moon and back." The essential quality of banda remains its danceability, and the responses of fans in that context, particularly young fans connected to the worlds of MTV and a wide range of popular styles, have propelled the reinvention of *banda* music for young contemporary listeners in ways that compete and supplement rock and other forms of popular music. Banda expert Helena Simonett notes that the appeal of the music extends into the United States: "Participation in banda events allowed both Mexican immigrants and Mexican Americans to reclaim and renovate their own tradition while enjoying the commercial seduction and standards of MTV and its related industry" (Simonett 2001:29).

Although this chapter has examined banda and conjunto as separate lines of music-making, contemporary performers often move comfortably between the genres, particularly because bandas and conjuntos often play the same rhythms and songs. The wildly popular singer, accordionist, actress, and television producer Jenni Rivera (born Dolores Janney Rivera, 1969–2012) provides one example. Known as "La Diva de la Banda" she sang with bandas, conjuntos, and full orchestras, as well as mariachis.

BALADA AND THE GRUPERA MOVEMENT

With roots in the 1960s, a musical movement that came to be called *la onda grupera* took off in the 1970s as commercial approaches to the modern romantic pop ballad, known as *balada*, reflected the growing acceptance of the cumbia as the ultimate Latin dance rhythm. Drawing equal inspiration from the dance orchestras that catered to upper and aspiring classes, and the emergence of electronic musical options, dance orchestras began to shrink. In the hands of a single skilled player of keyboard synthesizer, it became possible to reproduce an entire string or brass section with the touch of a key. Grupera was as much a practical format for playing urban pop music as it was a distinct style.

Chapter 10 includes a quip by Gabino Palomares in which he notes the power of Televisa to control the musical tastes of Mexican audiences. Alejandro Madrid (2012) explains how rise of the balada pop ballad song format has been intimately tied to a network of distribution cultivated by this media empire. Televisa emerged in 1972 from the merger of Mexico's two largest television companies, TIM (Televisión Independiente de México) and Telesistema Mexicano and soon came to control radio stations, recording companies, and cable broadcasts. Another media conglomerate, OTI (Organización de Televisoras Iberoamericanas) linked all countries with Hispanic and Portuguese audiences, with the exception of Cuba. The television variety show *Siempre en domingo* (Always on Sunday), hosted by Raúl Velasco, introduced Mexican and Latin American audiences to new pop performers from 1970–1998. Originally catering to middle-class tastes, it slowly grew more progressive over time. Mexican and international pop ballads were also performed by scrappy local bands, calling themselves *grupos*. Madrid (2012) maintains that these groups served as working-class alternatives to the polished artists supported by the entertainment industry. To simulate the impact of a bigger orchestra, the groups of four to six musicians used synthesizers and electric instruments to create their signature, easy-listening *grupera* sound mix.

The onda grupera trend continued through the 1980s and 1990s, interacting with parallel trends in Mexican rock, as well as international and regional popular styles. The emphasis on electronics and synthesized sound helped generate new styles of *tecno* music, including *tecnobanda* and corresponding dance fads such as quebradita and pasito duranguense.

Early onda grupera artists were Los Bukis, Grupo Brindis, Los Temerarios, Liberación, and Los Fugitivos (Olvera 2008:21). In 1993, Fonovisa, a division of the world's largest Spanish-language media company, began publishing the magazine *Furia Musical* (Musical Fury) to promote grupera nationally and internationally. With publication bases located in both Mexico City and Miami—sites renowned for their cosmopolitan aesthetics and commercial media geared towards attracting a broadly-defined, international Latino audience—the magazine reinforced the economic power of this new avenue of musical exchange across national boundaries.

COMMERCIALIZING THE *BALADA*

11.12   11.1

Listening to and viewing "El triste" by José José [11.12] Source: *Serie Platino, 20 Exitos* (BMG 1997) and [11.1]. Source: YouTube.

The song "El triste,"[21] sung by José José (b. 1948), exemplifies the polished *balada* song style popular in the 1970s. The video of his award-winning performance at the Festival OTI, the International Festival of Latin Song,[22] shows the finesse and formality of his passionate singing, the impressive instrumental arrangement supporting the song, and the emotion expressed by the audience. At that event superstars such as Angélica María, Marco Antonio Muñiz, and Alberto Vázquez roared in response to his perform- ance and as a validation of his quality. Since that remarkable debut, José José has enjoyed a long career, performing on stage and in film and on television—earning international stardom and multiple awards. Health problems and alcohol led to a serious deterioration of his voice in the 1990s and his work since then has focused on collaborations and retrospectives and acting. The influence of the style he pioneered persists and can be heard in the music of many popular artists, including the grupero singer Marco Antonio Solís, who began his career as a founding member of one of the most popular groups, Los Bukis.

11.2

Listening to and viewing "Yo te necesito" by Los Bukis.[23] Source: YouTube.

Los Bukis (The Kids, in Purépecha), originally from Michoacán, are the most celebrated representatives of the grupera style from the 1970s. The performance is notably a collaborative effort, all the musicians in the group are featured as players or singers. There is no star with anonymous back- up. Prominent in the sound mix is the electric organ and the percussion, and in this example, the tambourine played by José Solís is particularly captivating.

The consolidation and exchange of contemporary Mexican popular music styles across national divides was furthered by the 1993 signing of the NAFTA treaty which linked Mexico, the United States, and Canada in the North American Free Trade Agreement. NAFTA lifted tariffs on products crossing those national boundaries, increasing commercial exchange and investment. The precise effect of NAFTA on the culture industry is difficult to pinpoint, but the impact was both direct and indirect. Free trade strengthened the power of the recording, film, and broadcast entertainment industry. As the major recording labels consolidated in the 1990s, Miami became the most important center of the Latin American music industry. The industry established three big categories for Latin music: 1) Latin rock and pop, 2) Afro-Caribbean, and 3) Mexican regional. These same categories shaped radio broadcast and television programming and helped companies promote concerts and recordings across geographic and stylistic boundaries. Listeners and performers were not necessarily confined by these categories; they continued to recognize many distinct styles and genres within each of these broad categories.

NAFTA policies adversely affected the economic viability of traditional agriculture and indigenous livelihoods, increasing internal migration in Mexico from rural to urban areas and the United States as laborers sought work. Migrants living in Los Angeles, Houston, Chicago, and other cities in the United States, developed musical tastes and practices that in turn promoted new fashions in Mexico, creating a circuit of exchange.

CUMBIA, QUEBRADITA, **AND YOUTH DANCE CLUBS**

As bandas incorporated the electric guitars and keyboards of the grupos, and the saxophones of the jazz and tropical dance bands, they also cultivated new blends of Afro-Caribbean *música tropical* with a further merger of Mexican regional styles, norteño, tejano, and banda. The quebradita, basically a very fast cumbia, is an excellent example. The word means "little break," a reference to the way that way a man will bend and swing his partner while dancing.

> Listening to "De dónde es la quebradita" as performed by Banda Arkangel R-15. Source: *10 de Colección* (Sony, 2008).

11.13

We can explore the origins of this style as musicologist Sydney Hutchinson (1997) does, using Banda Arkangel R-15's quebradita song "De dónde es la quebradita" ("From where does quebradita come?"). Hutchinson notes that some musicians trace the roots of quebradita to the rise of tropical music in Mexico City during the 1950s. Others root it in norteño practices, claiming that the first example was "El Ranchero Chido," known as the song "with the little skip" recorded in 1978 by the group Los Huracanes del Norte (Hutchinson 1997:32). Still others trace the style to banda from Guadalajara, as does Helena Simonett (2001: 29). Precise origins remain uncertain, but what is clear is that the genre pulls from a mix of influences and by 1993 several influential bands, including Banda Machos and Banda Maguey from Jalisco, Banda Vallarta Show from Nayarit, and Banda Arkangel R-15 were all playing quebradita for dances in Southern California and the American Southwest. In the song "De dónde es la quebradita" [11.13] the singers in the Banda Arkangel R-15 offer their own answer to the question of the style's origins by citing a long list of Mexican states, adding California, concluding that quebradita belongs to all Mexicans, no matter where they currently reside.

Figure 11.6
Quebradita Dancers at a *quinceañera* in Indianapolis, Illinois. Photo by Ted Sommerville. Used with permission.

As you listen to "De dónde es la quebradita" [11.13], try to hear the reference to state names in the lyrics. Note also how the brass parts respond to the vocal statements, operating in manner similar to the accordion in música norteña.

The acrobatic couple dance associated with quebradita is what really spread the practice and has kept the style alive to the present. The best way to comprehend this is to watch a video of young dancers. Once the practice of urban high school youth who wanted to exhibit their skills and celebrate their Mexican identity, quebradita has now become formalized in dance schools and folkloric dance events in Mexico City, and is even taught as a mode of exercise in gyms and community centers. The video clip 11.3 illustrates the fringed garments and cowboy-inspired dress, as well as the acrobatics, and the musical collage of ballad, merengue, polka, and cumbia music associated with stylized competitive quebradita dancing.

11.3

Viewing the video of *Quebradita Sexi Salto Mortal*. Source: YouTube.[24]

PASITO DURANGUENSE

The curious paradox of deterritorialization and geographical affiliation made possible by transnational musical forms is neatly illustrated by the rise of *música duranguense* (music from Durango), another type of tecno-banda dance music that emerged in Chicago, Illinois *circa* 2003. Our review of this style draws upon research of the style published by Sydney Hutchinson (2007). Duranguense is popular with working-class Mexican youth who wear gang style street clothes, or clean-cut youth who wear stylized cowboy garments, and who perform acrobatic couple dances known as *pasito duranguense* (the little-step from Durango) at parties or clubs. Duranguense resembles quebradita and borrowed some of its choreography and sounds. It spread quickly from Chicago to other places in the United States and in Mexico and returned via recordings by Mexican bands, many with members born in the United States.

The electronic character of the audio mix is one of the distinguishing characteristics of duranguense which favors a preference for artificial, circus-style party sounds with a mix resembling an amusement park calliope (steam organ) more than an acoustic band. Other electronic elements include the electronic tuba of tecnobanda, and the *melodica* (a musical keyboard played by blowing through a mouthpiece; see Fig. 11.7).

> Listening to "El Sube y Baja" (The Rise and Fall) performed by Grupo Montéz de Durango. Source: *El Sube y Baja* (Disa, 2002).

11.14

"El Sube y Baja" (The Rise and Fall), a pasito duranguense by the Grupo Montéz de Durango is a remake of the norteño polka by Paulino Vargas, originally recorded by Los Broncos de Reynosa, transformed to a fast-tempo merengue (Hutchinson 2007:167).[25] It illustrates the merger of tropical dance music with elements of banda that is typical of the duranguense style. The sound mix displays a preference for the artificial timbre of various electronic instruments. The bouncy duple rhythm provides a catchy frame for the saucy lyrics. The singing opens with the suggestive statement: "I want to be glass from which you drink, and kiss your sugared mouth." Statements in subsequent verses are bolder and increasingly salacious, stating a desire to be "the mascara on your lashes," or "a fine pearl necklace by your breast." Those verses contrast with the refrain: *Que sube y que baja, que llega hasta Aztlán*—"That rising and that lowering (or the up and down), that reaches Aztlán." Mixing sex with pride in historic patrimony with

Figure 11.7
A Hohner melodica.
Wikimedia.

references to the mythic homeland of the ancient Aztecas, the refrain closes with questions: "Where are the dead going? Who knows where they will go?" Like a corrido, the singers break the narrative frame by pointing to themselves in the moment. They exhort Montéz, and jokingly exclaim "ay, what's up?"

In addition to merengues, other dance rhythms favored by duranguese groups are cumbias and rancheras, often as remakes of traditional songs and norteño hits. Some duranguese songs are northern Mexican versions of American songs, for example, the band K-Paz, one of the most representative and popular of this genre, released a version of the Hank Williams song "Jambalaya" (Hutchinson 2007:175).

Surprisingly, given the preponderance of symbols used by dancers, musicians, and fans—like the image of the scorpion, associated with the state of Durango where these arthropods are common—duranguense music originally had little to do with the Mexican state of Durango. It was invented by Mexican and Mexican-American youth living in Chicago, Illinois. For example, several of the members of Grupo Montéz de Durango

Figure 11.8
Tribal Dance Crew in pointy boots. Martín Hernández Rodríguez (right), Saúl Nicolás Coronado (center), and Gabriel Rodríguez Flores (left) are a dance crew from Buenavista. Photo by Edith Valle for VICE Media LLC (April 2011).

grew up in the Chicago suburb of Aurora, although some had family in Durango. Lead singer Alfredo Ramirez attributes the success of the band to its roots in regional popular styles, explaining to Sydney Hutchinson, in a mix of English and Spanish: "we are from the *rancho, el pueblo* and we have our feet planted firmly *en la tierra*" (2007:171). Current performers of duranguense in bands like K-Paz de la Sierra, Patrulla 81, Los Alacranes, hail from many Mexican states, as do their fans, and thus the style, while ostensibly identified with Durango, is not really rooted in any single place.

Like quebradita in the American Southwest, pasito duranguense is also practiced by high school youth who formed clubs where dancing Mexican style is cultivated with pride, free from social stigma. Sydney Hutchinson (2011) describes these dance spaces as "kinotopias," a riff on the concept of "audiotopia" used by Josh Kun (1997) to describe an idealized social environment defined by sound. The ability of musicians and fans to fashion the community they value through music and dance, bridging geographic and historic space, may be the most significant feature of duranguense and similar twenty-first-century musical practices.

TECHNO CUMBIA AKA *MÚSICA "TRIBAL"*

Another kind of party music, known as *música tribal*, eschews live instrumentalists and the acrobatic couple dancing associated with quebradita and pasito duranguese. *Tribal*, the digital, electro-fusion style of popular music that closes this chapter is also closely tied to the northern part of Mexico. Tribal DJs concoct their own cocktails of electronic and live sounds blended with tropical dance beats. The name exemplifies another kind of invented affiliation, for although the beat tracks are inspired by global rhythms, particularly African and Latin American tribal music, there is very little direct connection to Mexican indigenous musical practice or culture. The heroes of this music are the DJs or *sonideros* who create the mixes and the dancers who dress in exaggerated cowboy shoes. Audio Example 11.13, "Inténtalo" by 3BallMTY moved from the Mexican regional pop charts to international hit lists in 2012. Two singers from Sinaloa, the lovely América Sierra and the tecnobanda singer "El Bebeto" (Carlos García Alberto Villanueva) from Sinaloa join forces on this number.

> Listening to "Inténtalo" (Try It) featuring América Sierra and El Bebeto, with the DJ crew 3BallMTY. Source: *Inténtalo* (Fonovisa, 2011).[26]

11.15

The tribal movement emerged around the year 2000 in Mexico City dance clubs, where DJs favored a sound mix of vaguely defined Aztec-inspired sounds mixed with música tropical, particularly Colombian cumbia and Cuban *guaracha*. In Monterrey, Tribal is also known as *tribal guaracha*. The members of 3BallMTY (shorthand for Tribal Monterrey) are DJs Erick Rincón, Alberto Presenta "DJOtto," and Sergio Zavala "Sheeqobeat." The group is credited with bringing international attention to the underground

Tribal style, when they were invited to perform at the Worldtronics Festival in Germany in 2010 and when they signed with Universal Records in 2011. Rincón is featured in the video short *Mexican Pointy Boots* that documents the style of dress worn by young men at "tribal" dances.[27]

11.4

Viewing *Mexican Pointy Boots* [11.4][28]

The Tribal dance performed by young men who dance wearing cowboy boots with extended and extremely long, pointy toes has spread across Mexico (see Fig. 11.8), as far south as Oaxaca. Many of the dancers craft this boot extension themselves, covering plastic hose with leather, paint, screws, and other hardwear and sequins, and the most skilled craftsmen sell their *botas vaqueras exóticas* (exotic cowboy boots) called exotic for their design as well as for their leather from exotic animals such as the ostrich, snake, and crocodile (Jardin 2011). The boots are a status symbol for those who can afford them. Young men form crews and compete in contests to determine the best dance crew while young women watch from the sidelines, creating spaces defined by gender, as most of these contests are male only.

CONCLUDING REFLECTIONS

Several themes connect the examples in this chapter. First is the new prominence of the music from the northern states of Mexico. The influence of the two dominant instrumental formats, the conjunto norteño and the banda persists, albeit with many variants, linking the twentieth and twenty-first centuries. Both formats absorbed influences from the grupera movement that arose in the 1970s, which emphasized the romantic balada and launched the trend for using increasingly sophisticated electronic and digital instruments. The recording and entertainment industry grew more sophisticated and powerful, it promoted consolidation by promoting regional forms as international fare.

Almost as quickly as the music industry helped promote new pride in the northern region, regional affiliation grew more complex. Migration and transnational exchange led people to identity simultaneously with more than one place. The *ida y vuelta* (going and coming; departure and return) of people, imports, and industry between Mexico and the United States transformed musical practice at an unprecedented rate. As a result it has become increasing difficult to link musical styles and practices to a single site or source. While we might argue that it was never possible to identify pure musical styles or link traditions to a single site of origin, our examination of regional popular music forms in this chapter illustrates the challenge of fixing place and ownership for Mexican popular music in the twentieth and twenty-first century. Like migration, technology, and media—particularly the international music and entertainment industry— changed forever the rate of exchange between Mexico and the United States.

We can lament the deterritorialization of Mexican popular music, but that process has its benefits as well. Once music is decontextualized, a range of new options opens for creators, fans, and consumers. In his book *Ethnicity, Identity and Music*, Martin Stokes wrote: "music can be used as a means of transcending the limitations of our own place in the world, of constructing trajectories rather than boundaries across space" (Stokes 1994:4). For those who love popular music, of any kind, this statement surely rings true. Who has not felt an indefinable bond with an unseen but strongly felt community when listening to a favorite song? That bond, whether we immediately recognize it or not, is more than personal. Stokes reminds us that music provides more than an avenue by which people find shared interests; it also provides a way to transform social space. This chapter has offered many examples of how musicians, listeners, and dancers have used music to transform social space. The building of communities around music, however temporary, is one of the most important themes of this chapter. From Josh Kun's "audiotopias" to Sydney Hutchinson's "kinetopias," music and dance provide a means for people to cross artistic, social, geographic, and personal boundaries, while constructing new, and sometimes idealized, personal identities, and community affiliations.

We may conclude that the blurring of boundaries so characteristic of competing forms of Mexican popular music may help people make sense of a paradox of modern life—the increasing irrelevance of place, despite its continued importance.

CRITICAL THINKING AND DISCUSSION PROMPTS

1. Mark Edberg (2011) argues that narcocorridos join a vast repertory of songs styles around the world that celebrate anti-heroes and rebellion. Find an example from that world of examples and compare it to a narcocorrido of your choice.

2. Do you agree with movements in some states of Mexico to censor narcocorridos? Investigate the situation before offering your response. How do those efforts compare to the censorship experienced by performers in other styles, such as nueva canción?

3. Gender emerged as an important marker in several of the examples included in this chapter. Choose one example and discuss in more detail how that music contributes to the performance of gendered identity.

4. Roger Rouse has argued that Mexican migrants live in multiple places simultaneously, essentially living in an extended border zone. How does contemporary popular music help musicians and their listeners address that border experience?

5. Attend a live performance or an event featuring one of the musical styles featured in this chapter. Observe the performance so that you may describe it in detail. What was the setting like? How was the space laid out? How was it decorated? How many musicians were in the group and what instruments did they play? Who was in the audience?

How did they dance or otherwise react to the music and/or interact with the musicians? How did you personally react to the music? Note as best you can the kinds of songs played and the sequence in which they occurred. If possible, when the musicians are on break, ask them for some details about themselves—who they are, where they're from, how long they've been playing, etc. Relate your observation experience to material covered in class.

6. Listen to a local Spanish-language radio station that broadcasts Latin pop and regional popular music. Make a list of what you hear during 15 full minutes of broadcast. Many radio stations have parallel websites that you can visit to review playlists by the time of day. This will help you acquire titles and artist names for what you hear. How does what you hear on the radio compare to the examples discussed in this chapter?

7. If you have a chance to attend a Mexican or Mexican-American wedding, reflect on the music you hear at the event. In what ways does it reflect the styles and issues discussed in this chapter?

KEY TERMS, PEOPLE, AND PLACES

música norteña	José José
norteño	Los Bukis
conjunto	Marco Antonio Solís
El Huracán del Valle	Grupo Montéz de Durango
Los Lobos	Banda Arkangel R-15
Lydia Mendoza	tecnocumbia
corridos	tecnobanda
bajo sexto	música "tribal"
accordion (acordeón)	deterritorialization
Los Tigres del Norte	pasito duranguense
Banda El Recodo	cumbia
Santiago Jiménez	quebradita
Chalino Sánchez	banda sinaloense
balada	waila
grupera	bi-national
la onda grupera	narcocorrido

transnational	Sydney Hutchinson
NAFTA	kinetopia
melodica	*ida y vuelta*
Josh Kun	3BallMTY
audiotopia	

NOTES

1. Gustavo Arellano. "The Ten Most Overplayed Songs at a Mexican Wedding," California Edition, OC Weekly Blogs. Web. November 28, 2012. http://blogs.ocweekly.com/heardmentality/2012/11/la_vibora_de_la_mar.php
2. Marco Torres. "The Ten Most Overplayed Songs at Mexican Weddings, Texas edition," Houston Press Blogs. Web. November 29, 2012. http://blogs.houstonpress.com/rocks/2012/11/mexican_wedding_songs.php
3. Personal communication with the author, October 8, 2014.
4. *Norteño and Tejano Accordion Pioneers, 1929–1939*. Arhoolie Folklyric, Compact Disc Recording 7016 (1995).
5. An informative video compilation of Nacisco Martínez performing can be found on YouTube at: www.youtube.com/watch?v=vWYRtRfjbZY#at=19
6. The Mudcat Cafe. Lyrics and Knowledge. Web. October 2014. <http://mudcat.org/thread.cfm?threadid=107285>
7. Ibid.
8. Various Artists. *Dancing in the Dust: The Waila Festival Live!* CD. Crow Hang, Santa Rosa Band, San Xavier Fiddle Band, Jam Band 'D,' Papago, Desert Suns, with comments by Angelo Joaquin, Jr. Debra Narcho, Ofelia Zepeda, Ben Jose, Jim Griffith, and Ron Joaquin. Blue Bhikku Records 88014. (2000), USA.
9. The Tohono O'odham (Desert People) are a bi-national nation within nations. Their native and protected territory extends onto land on either side of the border established in 1854 with the Gadsden purchase between the U.S. state of Arizona and the Mexican state of Sonora.
10. Janet Sturman, "Movement Analysis as a Tool for Understanding Identity: Retentions, Borrowings, and Transformations in Native American Waila." *The World of Music* 39/3 (1997): 51–70.
11. See the informative interview of Hernández by Josh Kun, "Jorge Hernandez, Los Tigres del Norte," *Bomb* (New Art Publications, Winter 2007), 98: 54–59.
12. The opera premiered August 8–9, 2008 in a production offered by the Contemporary Vocal Ensemble of Indiana University under the direction of Carmen Hellena Téllez and Marianne Kielian-Gilbert at the Buskirk-Chumley Theater in Bloomington, Indiana.
13. *Al Otro Lado*. A documentary film by Natalia Almada (SubCine 2006). *Contrabando y traición (Camelia la Texana)*, directed by Arturo Martínez (San Luis Potosí, Mexico: Hermanos Benítez Producciones, 1977). *Chalino Sánchez—Vida de Peligros* (Mexico City: Image Entertainment studio, 2004).
14. An informative BBC report on the shifting influence of various drug cartels and deaths from drug violence, "Who's Behind Mexico's Drug-related

Violence?" February 10, 2014, at: www.bbc.co.uk/news/world-latin-america-10681249

15. Ryan Grim, "NAFTA and the Drug Cartels," *Huffington Post*, July 1, 2009, at: www.huffingtonpost.com/ryan-grim/nafta-and-the-drug-cartel_b_223705.html

16. *MTV Unplugged: Los Tigres del Norte and Friends*. Fonovisa, 2011.

17. Banda Recodo de Cruz Lizárraga—Don Cruz Lizárraga, at: www.bandaelrecodo.galeon.com/familia1038384.html (accessed October 2014).

18. When used to describe a horse, the word bayo, like the English term "Bay," refers to the color of the horse's hair. Bayo is a light yellowish tone, like a cream color.

19. *Que siga la tambora*, Banda Sinaloense "El Recodo" de Cruz Lizárraga (1997).

20. Banda El Recodo, *La Mejor de Todas*, Fonovisa (2011).

21. José José—"El Triste" (En Vivo). YouTube video clip uploaded June 29, 2010. www.youtube.com/watch?v=MKhuZGk5qZ8

22. This festival gave rise to the OTI song festival, sponsored by the Organización de Televisión Iberoaméricana) that ran from 1972–2000. See Madrid 2012:73.

23. "Yo te necesito." Los Bukis. Video uploaded to YouTube, January 27, 2009. www.youtube.com/watch?v=xqDcF7sXrxA

24. *Quebradita Sexi Salto Mortal*. Video clip uploaded to YouTube March 13, 2009. www.youtube.com/watch?v=u8FtpFNMwpg

25. Paulino Vargas's recording is itself a remake of the song "Sube y Baja" by Felipe Valdéz Leal y Ramón Ortéga Contreras, associated with the golden era of Mexican cinema, and sung by actor Eulalio González (El piporro) in the film *El terror de la frontera* (1963). Vargas, also known as the "father of the narcocorrido," transformed such popular songs into narratives of the rural northern states and border regions.

26. A video of this song appears in the web article by Federica Longo, "America Sierra: Billboard's Latin Music Breakout Star," April 15, 2013. www.voxxi.com/america-sierra-billboard-breakout-star/

27. Informador.mx. "Populariza 3BallMTY el gusto por la música tribal." Web. February 14, 2012. www.informador.com.mx/entretenimiento/2012/357316/6/populariza-3ballmty-el-gusto-por-la-musica-tribal.htm

28. *Mexican Pointy Boots*. Vice presents video posted on YouTube April 7, 2012. www.vice.com/en_uk/video/watch/behind-the-seams/mexican-pointy-boots

FOR REFERENCE AND FURTHER STUDY

Broyles-González, Yolanda. 2001. *Lydia Mendoza's Life in Music: La historia de Lydia Mendoza—Norteño Tejano Legacies*. New York: Oxford University Press.

Carrizosa, Toño. 1997. *La onda grupera: historia del movimiento grupero*. Mexico: Edamex.

Edberg, Mark. 2011. "Narcocorridos: Narratives of a Cultural Persona and Power on the Border." In Alejandro Madrid (Ed.), *Transnational Encounters: Music and Performance at the U.S.–Mexico Border*. New York: Oxford University Press, 67–84.

Grey, Jonathan and Johnson, Derek (Eds.). 2013. *A Companion to Media Authorship*. Malden, MA: John Wiley and Sons.

Herrera-Sobek, María. 2006. *Chicano Folklore*. Westport, CT: Greenwood Publishing.

Hutchinson, Sydney. 1997. *From Quebradita to Duranguense Dance in Mexican American Youth Culture*. Tucson, AZ: University of Arizona Press.

Hutchinson, Sydney. 2007. *From Quebradita to Duranguense Dance in Mexican American Youth Culture*. Tucson, AZ: University of Arizona Press.

Hutchinson, Sydney. 2011. "Breaking Borders, *Quebrando Fronteras*: Dancing in the Borderscape." In Alejandro L. Madrid (Ed.), *Transnational Encounters: Music and Performance at the U.S.–Mexico Border*. New York: Oxford University Press, 41–66.

Jardin, Xeni. 2011. "Mexican Music Tribal, Point Boots, Los Parranderos and 3Ball MTY," *Boing Boing Blop*, September 12. http://boingboing.net/2011/09/12/mexico-musica-tribal-pointy-boots-los-parranderos-and-3ballmty.html (accessed January 12, 2015).

Kun, Josh. 1997. "Against Easy Listening: Transnational Soundings and Audiotopic Listenings," In José Esteban Muñoz and Celeste Fraser Delgado (Eds.), *Every-night Life: Culture and Dance in Latin/o America*. Durham, NC: Duke University Press, 288–309.

Kun, Josh. 2007. "Jorge Hernández, Los Tigres del Norte," *Bomb* 98:54–59.

Lewis, George H. 1991. "Ghosts, Ragged but Beautiful, Influences of Mexican Music on American Country-Western and Rock N' Roll," *Popular Music and Society* 15(4):85–103.

Limón, José. 2011. "This is Our *Música*, Guy! Tejanos, and Ethno-Regional Musical Nationalism." In Alejandro L. Madrid (Ed.), *Transnational Encounters: Music and Performance at the U.S.–Mexico Border*. New York: Oxford University Press, 111–128.

Madrid, Alejandro. 2008. *Nortec Rifa! Electronic Dance Music from Tijuana to the World*. New York: University of Chicago Press.

Madrid, Alejandro. 2011. *Transnational Encounters: Music and Performance at the U.S.–Mexico Border*. New York: Oxford University Press.

Madrid, Alejandro. 2012. *Music in Mexico*. New York: Oxford University Press.

Olvera G., José Juan. 2008. "Las Dimensiones del Sonido. Música, frontera e identidad en el noreste." *Trayectorias* 10(26):20–30.

Paredes, Américo. 1970. *With his Pistol in his Hand*. Austin, TX: University of Texas Press.

Peña, Manuel. 1985. *The Texas-Mexican Conjunto: History of a Working-Class Music*. Austin, TX: University of Texas.

Ragland, Cathy. 2004. *Música Norteña. Mexican Migrants Creating a Nation between Nations*. Philadelphia, PA: Temple University Press.

Ragland, Cathy. 2012. "Tejano and Proud: The Accordion Traditions of South Texas and the Border Region." In Helena Simonett (Ed.), *The Accordion in the Americas: Klezmer, Polka, Tango, Zydeco, and More*. Urbana, Chicago and Springfield, IL: University of Illinois Press, 87–111.

Ramírez-Pimienta, Juan Carlos. 2010. "Chicago lindo y querido si muero lejos de ti: el pasito duranguense, la onda grupera y las nuevas geografías de la identidad popular mexicana." *Mexican Studies / Estudios Mexicanos* 26(1):31–45.

Reid, Jan and Shawn, Sahm. 2010. *Texas Toronado. The Times and Music of Doug Sahm*. Austin, TX: University of Texas Press.

Rouse, Roger. 1991. "Mexican Migration and the Social Space of Post-modernism." *Diaspora: The Journal of Transnational Studies* 1(1):8–23.

San Miguel, Guadalupe. 2002. *Tejano Proud. Tex-Mex Music in the Twentieth Century*. Laredo, TX: Texas A&M International University.

Simonett, Helena. 2001. *Banda: Mexican Musical Life across Borders*. Middletown, CT: Wesleyan University Press.

Sturman, Janet. 2012. "Preserving Territory: The Changing Language of the Accordion in Tohono O'odham Waila Music." In Helena Simonett (Ed.), *The Accordion in the Americas: Klezmer, Polka, Tango, Zydeco, and More*. Urbana, Chicago and Springfield, IL: University of Illinois Press, 112–135.

Stokes, Martin (Ed.). 1994. *Ethnicity, Identity and Music: The Musical Construction of Place*. New York: Berg Publishers.
Strachwitz, Chris and Nicolopoulos, James. 1993. *Lydia Mendoza: A Family Autobiography*. Houston, TX: Arte Público Press.

DISCOGRAPHY

3BallMTY Inténtalo, Fonovisa, 2011.
Banda Arkangel R-15. *10 de Coleccíon*. Sony, 2008.
Banda El Recodo. *Que siga la tambora Banda Sinolense "El Recodo,"* 1997.
Banda El Recodo, *La Mejor de Todas*, Fonovisa, 2011.
Flaco Jiménez, *Partners*. Reprise Records, WEA International, 1992.
Grupo Montéz de Durango. *El Sube y Baja*. Disa, 2002.
José José. *Serie Platino, 20 Exitos*. BMG, 1997.
Los Bukis. *Yo te Necesito*. Fonovis, 1982.
Los Tigres del Norte. *Contrabando y Traición*, Fonovisa, 1984/1994.
Los Tigres del Norte. *MTV Unplugged: Los Tigres del Norte and Friends*. Fonovisa, 2011.
Lydia Mendoza. *Mal Hombre and Other Original Hits from the 1930s*. Arhoolie Records, 1993.
Lydia Mendoza. *La Alondra de la Frontera—LIVE!* Arhoolie Records, CD release of 1982 recording (2001).
Valentín Elizalde. *Vencedor*, Universal, 2006.
Various Artists. *Dancing in the Dust: The Waila Festival Live!* CD. Blue Bhikku Records 88014, 2000.
Various Artists. *Norteño and Tejano Accordion Pioneers, 1929–1939*. Arhoolie Folklyric, Compact Disc Recording 7016, 1995.

FILMS AND VIDEOS

Chalino Sánchez—Vida de Peligros. Mexico: Image Entertainment Studio, 2004.
Contrabando y Traición (Camelia la Texana), dir. by Arturo Marínez. San Luis Potosí, Mexico: Hermanos Benítez, Producciones, 1977.
El Infierno, directed by Luis Estrada. Bandidos Films, 2010.
El Valiente: Chalino Sánchez/Al Otro Lado. A documentary film by Natalia Almada. SubCine, 2006.

CHAPTER 12

Classical Contemporary Music: New Frames For New Audiences

THE NATIONAL INSTITUTE OF FINE ARTS: NEXUS AND RADIATING INFLUENCE

For many hoping to see the finest of classical music in Mexico, a visit to the Palacio de las Bellas Artes (the Palace of Fine Arts) is a must; it is the nation's center of arts; the nexus of the best and most distinctive performers from within the nation or visiting. Patrons may also seek out programs sponsored by the Instituto Nacional de Bellas Artes, (the National Institute for Fine Arts, known as INBA), also located in Mexico City. Although the Palacio de las Bellas Artes was planned by Porfirio Díaz and intended to commemorate the centennial of Independence in 1910, construction ceased with the Revolution and the building was not completed and opened until 1934.

Bellas Artes unites pre- and post-revolutionary aesthetics, and the art deco interior houses artwork by some of Mexico's most renowned artists, Rufino Tamayo, Diego Rivera, David Alfaro Siqueiros, and José Clemente Orozco. Murals and paintings by Rivera, Siqueiros, and Orozco address themes of social realism, the plight of laborers and the poor, and progress towards civic improvement and social justice. The fresco by Diego Rivera in Figure 12.2 is titled "Man at the Cross Roads"; "Man, the Controller of the Universe" appears on one of the walls. It captures the optimistic spirit of progress that characterized the social reformers of the 1930s, including musicians and composers. Depicted in the mural is the contrast between capitalism and socialism, and the reconciliation of this tension by forward-thinking leaders. The figures of Leon Trotsky and Vladimir Lenin as leaders of the Russian Revolution are depicted. Sympathy for proletariat reforms guided both Mexican and Russian revolutionaries, but Mexican socialism and Russian communism diverged significantly in the ensuing years, influenced in part by relations with the United States (see Spenser 1999).

The social themes depicted on the walls of the entrance way contrast with the gilded interior, and with the romantic depiction of the Mexican

Figure 12.1
The Palacio de las Bellas Artes. Photo by Carlos Ramírez. Used with permission.

valley on the glass curtain fashioned by Louis Comfort Tiffany that graces the stage and provides a stunning backdrop for many performances. The differences in the art displayed in the venue reflect the commissions awarded to artists with contrasting portfolios. Some, like Rivera and Orozco, were politically active and expressed their social and historical commitment in their work, but others like Tamayo and Comfort responded to the commission with non-overtly political art. The presences of such vastly different artistic expression by some of the most renowned artists of the era establishes the unique status of Bellas Artes among the public state-sponsored spaces of the twentieth century.

The home of the Orquesta Sinfónica Nacional, Mexico's national symphony, El Palacio de las Bellas Artes, is also a center for other important music and dance presentations, including the weekly performances of Amalia Hernández's Ballet Folklórico. The Palace of Fine Arts operates under the umbrella of Mexico's national arts institute, known as INBA-CONACULTA (National Institute of Fine Arts—National Council for Arts and Culture).[1] We might compare INBA to the NEA (National Endowment for the Arts), the largest annual national funder of the arts in the United States of America, but Mexico's national arts agency is more influential and directive in nature and invests nearly twice the amount on annual arts funding.[2] Today, in addition to onsite visits to Bellas Artes, patrons can visit its website which serves as a portal to the range of activities

Diego Rivera. (1886-1957)
El Hombre en el Cruce de Caminos
"El hombre controlador del universo"
1934. Fresco sobre bastidor metálico móvil
4.80 m x 11. 45 m

Instituto Nacional de Bellas Artes

(A CONACULTA
Consejo Nacional para la Cultura y las Artes

u·t·⊙ur

Figure 12.2
(see Plate 13)
Fresco by Diego Rivera,
"El hombre en el cruce
de caminos." Copyright
MPBA—Museo del
Palacio de Bellas Artes.
Photo by Tomás
Casademunt. ARS
Artists Rights Society.
Used with permission.

presented under the auspices of Mexico's national arts center.[3] Like the
mix of art, architecture, and perspectives embodied in the Palace of Fine
Arts, the calendar of the National Institute of Fine Arts reflects a blend of
new and old, experimental and traditional, elite and popular. The calendar
includes many free performances of music, dance, film, and theater in
addition to those with an admission charge. Above all, the site confirms
the vibrant classical music scene in Mexico. As we have seen in previous
chapters, even before the Revolution, the Mexican government supported
classical music as essential, not only for the development of a specialized
circle of performers and composers, but also for the enrichment of the
entire nation. The five composers presented in this chapter represent
different approaches to art music composition and you are invited to

Figure 12.3
(see Plate 14)
The glass curtain and
concert hall interior of
the Palacio de las
Bellas Artes. Photo by
Brenda Blanco Perea.

compare them and see which speaks most powerfully to you. Each of our featured composers offers a contrasting position in regard to Mexico's government-sponsored arts agenda and to their own right to shape international trends. In so doing, each confirms the radiating force of the arts from Mexico's capital.

SILVESTRE REVUELTAS AND THE POST-REVOLUTIONARY ARTS BRIGADES

The music of composer, violinist, and conductor Silvestre Revueltas (1899–1940) is enjoying renewed attention in the twenty-first century. Musicologist Aurelio Tello describes Revueltas as "the complement and counterpart of Carlos Chávez in the creation of a new musical reality" (2010:290). Like many composers before him, Revueltas moved from the provinces to Mexico City, leaving his hometown of Santiago Papasquiaro, Durango in 1913. He studied violin at the Conservatorio Nacional and played in the National Symphony. In 1917 he moved to the United States where he lived and completed additional studies in Austin, Texas and Chicago, Illinois. Upon his return to Mexico in 1924, he collaborated with Carlos Chávez on concerts of new music. Revueltas taught violin at the Conservatorio Nacional and later served as director. Today, a bronze bust of Silvestre Revueltas stands in the lobby outside the Conservatorio's main concert hall.

Revueltas developed his own perspective on nationalistic concert music, as Aurelio Tello (2010) explains. Whereas Manuel Ponce initiated a line of musical nationalism by establishing a curriculum for the study of the nation's folklore and turned to mestizo song as a resource for classical compositions, and Carlos Chávez turned to indigenous music for inspiration, Revueltas added individualistic interpretations of urban popular music and contemporary life. Some of Revueltas's most important compositions are: *Magueys, Esquinas, Feria, Tocata* (for percussion), *8 x Radio, Janitzio, Sensemaya, Planos,* as well as music for films, *Redes, La Noche de los Mayos, El Indio* and *Ferrocarriles de Baja California.* The work we will examine, *El renacuajo paseador,* was conceived as music for puppet theater in 1933 and later redesigned as a ballet in 1936. It was performed to great acclaim in a concert version in the Palacios de las Bellas Artes on the very night that Revueltas died of pneumonia in 1940.

🎧

12.1

Listening to *El renacuajo paseador* by Silvestre Revueltas as performed by the London Sinfonietta, directed by David Atherton. Source: *Revueltas Centennial Anthology, 1899–1999. 15 Masterpieces.* RCA (1999)

Revueltas created *El renacuajo paseador* (The Traveling Tadpole) as music for the puppet theater groups, who worked with the educational outreach groups of the 1930s. In order to implement the reforms mandated by the revolutionary constitution, the ministry of education initiated literacy

Figure 12.4
Photo of composer
Silvestre Revueltas
(1930). Wikimedia.

brigades to travel from Mexico City to the provinces. The arts were integral to the project and one of the tools used to reach children was puppet theater. The Fine Arts Puppet Theater, *El Teatro Guiñol de Bellas Artes*,[4] was founded in 1932 and sponsored by the Fine Arts Department of Mexico's Ministry of Public Education (known by its acronym SEP).[5] Carlos Chávez, then director of the Ministry of Fine Arts, oversaw the content of the dramas. In addition to promoting literacy, the puppet shows addressed anti-alcoholism, political engagement, aesthetic appreciation, class-consciousness, and social equity. We see similar goals extolled in campaigns for social welfare in many Latin American countries of the era. The Teatro Guiñol project advanced the goals of public education first launched during the administration of President Álvaro Obregón from 1920–1924, one of several initiatives aimed towards realizing the ideals of the Revolution and carrying them to the masses. By 1933 the Teatro Guiñol, and its SEP-sponsored affiliate touring companies were presenting as many as four shows a day, traveling to more than 87 schools around the nation, carrying among their props a phonographic record player.

Music was important to the puppet plays: each started with a musical prelude, others were even built around folkloric or popular musical selections, such as "La bamba," "El jarabe tapatío," and "La bicicleta" (Abarrán 2010). The composer Silvestre Revueltas, then serving as director of the National Conservatory, composed what may be the most celebrated original piece for Mexican puppet theater: *El renacuajo paseador*.[6] Both the story and Revueltas's music remain popular today. Visitors to the website for the National Institute of Fine Arts will see that children's theater and particularly puppet theater remains an important program option, not just in the nation's capital but in many of the states of Mexico such as Guanajuato and Michoacán. Puppet theater remains an important government-sponsored medium for inculcating civic, moral, and artistic values at the federal and state levels.

The story of *El renacuajo paseador* is based on the poem by Colombian author Álvaro Pombo (*c*.1880), that warns children to listen to their parents. A young frog (*renacuajo* or tadpole) who loves to drink and dance, disobeys his mother and sneaks out to party with his friend "rat." The party is disrupted by prowling cats who eat the rat, and later by a hungry duck, who gobbles the little frog. Revueltas remembers hearing this tale as a child, and crafted his musical score for the puppet show called *Rin Rin renacuajo*. His composition includes references to ranchera melodies and the prominent trombone represents the tipsy little frog, and by extension Revueltas himself, who was rather too fond of drink (Paraskavaidas 2011:6).

A careful listener will also notice accentuated rhythms, intense dynamic contrasts, and dissonant bitonal harmonies. *El renacuajo paseador* may remind some listeners of the Russian composer Igor Stravinsky, whose music was a great inspiration to composers around the world in the early twentieth century. Stravinsky's ballet *The Rite of Spring*, used bursts of melody and repeated rhythmic motives to evoke primitive energies in a sophisticated manner. Like Stravinsky, Revueltas and his contemporaries explored contemporary approaches that challenged the dominance of German compositional influence on classical music. His efforts contributed to a distinctive repertory of modern Mexican concert music.

EXTENDING NATIONALIST SENTIMENT: MONCAYO'S *HUAPANGO*

Music scholar José Antonio Alcaraz (1998:33) marks the beginning of the nationalist movement of composition in Mexico with the establishment of the Orquesta Sinfónica Nacional in 1928 and the end of nationalism with the death of composer José Pablo Moncayo (1912–1958). Moncayo was born in Guadalajara, Jalisco and began his professional studies in composition with Carlos Chávez at the Conservatorio Nacional in Mexico City. There Moncayo bonded with a distinguished group of fellow composers: Blas Galindo, Daniel Ayala, and Salvador Contreras, later called the "group of four" in recognition of their contributions to the ongoing movement of Mexican nationalist music. Chávez encouraged his students to travel to provinces around the country collecting regional music to inspire their compositions. For his symphonic fantasy *Huapango*, Moncayo made field recordings in the state of Veracruz and tried to convey the quality

Figure 12.5
Photo of José Pablo Moncayo. Photos provided by CENIDIM/INBA. Biblioteca de las Artes, CENART (México).

of the music he heard in his composition. *Huapango* includes the famous sones jarochos "Siquisirí," "El Balajú," and "El Gavilán," but it is more than a set of arrangements; it is a concert work in its own right. In many ways *Huapango* can be compared with *Sones de Mariachi* composed by Moncayo's classmate Blas Galindo, discussed in Chapter 5. The Orquesta Sinfónica Mexicana (OSM) premiered *Huapango* at the Palacio de las Bellas Artes in 1940, and in the following year the OSM performed it in New York City.

> Listening to *Huapango* (1940) by José Pablo Moncayo as performed by the Orquesta Sinfónica Nacional.[7]

12.2

Huapango is Moncayo's most famous composition and it has become as popular in contemporary Mexico as the national anthem. So popular is this composition that it overshadows the remainder of Moncayo's compositions, which include pieces for piano, chamber music groups, chorus, opera, and ballet, in addition to a rich body of symphonic works. Aurelio Tello summarizes the appeal of "El Huapango de Moncayo," as it is popularly known.

> It has been arranged for every imaginable instrumental format, from piano solo to mariachi, there is no group that doesn't wish to legitimize their Mexicanness by making their own version of this emblematic piece . . . the statistics are overwhelming, any Mexican (from Tijuana to Cancún, from Reynosa to Oaxaca, from Guerrero to Veracruz, from Monterrey to Chiapas) identifies lovingly with *Huapango* and this score says to that Mexican that it must belong to him.
>
> (Tello 2010:498)

POST-NATIONAL EXPRESSION: MANUEL ENRÍQUEZ

After 1950, the next generation of classical musicians turned away from incorporating overtly nationalist elements in their music, such as references to huapangos, sones, and pre-Hispanic instruments, and turned instead to experimenting with a range of non-representational techniques and international trends. Manuel Enríquez (1926–1994) emerged as a leader in this group. He was born in Ocotlán, Jalisco, to a musical family and began studying violin with his father. After continuing his studies at the Academy of music in Guadalajara and at the Conservatorio de las Rosas in Morelia, he moved to New York City to study at the Juilliard School of Music. He studied with two of the world's most famous master pedagogues of string performance, taking violin lessons with Ivan Galamian and chamber music with William Primrose, while studying composition with Peter Mennin, who introduced him to the expressionist approach. He later studied composition with Stefan Wolpe, a disciple of Anton Webern, who in addition to sharing his views on experimental composition, also engaged him in debates regarding politics and the humanities.

After receiving a Guggenheim Fellowship in 1971, Enríquez experimented with electronic composition at the Columbia-Princeton Electronic Music Center, a pioneering site for this work. His interest in electronic music continued and he attended conferences and workshops at the celebrated center for electronic composition in Darmstadt Germany between 1975 and 1977. Enríquez lived in Paris and was commissioned by the Mexican government to promote Mexican music in Europe. Along with the string quartet he founded, he gave recitals in major music centers of Vienna, Paris, Bonn, Warsaw, and Bourges, and lectured on new music in Mexico. He began teaching at the Conservatorio Nacional in Mexico City in 1964 and from 1979 to his death in 1994 he directed the International

Figure 12.6
Photo of Manuel Enríquez in his studio in 1981. Courtesy of Susana A. Enríquez, PhD, photographer and wife of the composer.

Festival of Music in Morelia, and the International Forum of New Music, the most distinguished and enduring contemporary music forum in Mexico, now named for him. The Foro de Música Nueva Manuel Enríquez takes place annually, sponsored by INBA with concerts at the Palacio de las Bellas Artes; the year 2014 marked its 36th season of operation.[8] Manuel Enríquez was the most important proponent of avant-garde music in Mexico during his lifetime and he left a lasting legacy, not only in his own compositions but in his critical writings and his support of other musicians in Mexico.[9]

> Listening to *Ritual* (1973) by Manuel Enríquez as performed by La Orquesta Filarmónica de la UNAM (the Philharmonic Orchestra of the National Autonomous University of Mexico).

12.3

Ritual illustrates some of Enríquez's experimental techniques and the philosophical and psychological motivations behind them. The composer explains:

> The majority of acts that govern our life constitute preconceived things that a man must complete like a ritual, that made me think of a work that illustrated something of my personal experiences through situations and successes. Thus, this piece has passages of mysticism as well as festive sections of simple celebration.
>
> (Alcaraz 2001:116)

Enríquez does not attempt to capture the sounds of an actual festival, but rather the sensation of feeling festive during a celebration. This focus on sensation over physicality is a characteristic of expressionist music of this period. He describes his attempts to convey the feeling of freedom in another section of *Ritual*, in which he leaves some of the performance up to chance, a technique famously explored by the twentiethth-century American composer John Cage. Musicians use the term "aleatoric" to describe the use of chance operations to compose or perform music. Enríquez describes his aleatoric procedures in the transition sections of *Ritual* which may strike the listener as uncertain despite their structured chance operations:

> It is in those sections of "free technique" that the instrumentalists have been instructed to play with a certain freedom. There is an overall plan, the random sections have already predetermined suggestions. The director is the only person who can actually transform the structure of the piece, since at any moment he can construct "at random" his own form, using the different sonic modules that he has at his disposition.
>
> (Alcaraz 2001:117)

Ritual is both highly organized and random, so listeners may find themselves working hard to make sense of the composition. Such techniques were fashionable in international composition circles from the mid- to late twentieth century. With compositions like *Ritual*, Enríquez positions himself, and Mexican music, as participating in that culture. He seeks an international as well as a Mexican audience.

THE MODERN COMPOSER AS PHILOSOPHER: MARIO LAVISTA

Like Carlos Chávez, Mario Lavista (b. 1943) has been a great teacher of musicians and composers, lecturing at the Conservatorio Nacional and from 1998 has been member of the Colegio Nacional, an institution that since 1943 recognizes its members as the most distinguished intellectuals and scientists in the country. One of Lavista's students, Alejandro Rossi, writes that he always asked his students "how can a sound be musical?" (1998:104). Lavista explored extending standard playing techniques for orchestral instruments to produce new sounds, working with flutist Marielena Arizpe, bassist Bertram Turetzsky, and oboist Leonora Saavedra, as well as the string quartet Cuarteto Latinoamericano,[10] among others. A master of words as well as tones, Mario Lavista builds support for new composition with his essays, poems, and collaborations with journalists and authors in the world of literature and theater. His literary acumen led him to compose a set of songs with texts by Nobel prize-winning author and diplomat Octavio Paz and an opera based on a story by the celebrated novelist Carlos Fuentes. Lavista founded and edited the journal *Pauta*, whose contents include scholarly essays and poems concerning musical topics. His compositions include songs, symphonies, electronic music, chamber pieces, works for solo instruments, and opera.

Lavista studied with the best musicians in Mexico and abroad. Another student of Carlos Chávez, he also studied in Mexico with the renowned

Figure 12.7
Photo of Mario Lavista. Fundación SGAE.

conductor and composer Eduardo de Mata. In Europe he studied with Nadia Boulanger, György Ligeti, and with Karlheinz Stockhausen, arguably the most famous of the founders of electronic composition. Drawing upon all these experiences, Lavista creates thoughtful compositions that link music in Mexico to the world's history and greatest literature.

> Listening to *Clepsidra* (1991) by Mario Lavista as performed by the Orquesta Filarmónica de la UNAM.[11]

12.4

Clepsidra (Clepsydra) is the name for a water clock used in ancient Egypt. The mechanism was used by several ancient civilizations and beginning in the Middle Ages as well during the Renaissance became an important symbol in Western art representing the time left for a human before meeting death. In his notes on the composition Lavista explains that he composed *Clepsidra* in 1991 for the San Antonio Symphony in the United States to perform on the 300th anniversary of the discovery of the San Antonio River. Lavista explained to musicologist Juan Arturo Brennan that he likes to think of music like a river, and both as images of the rhythm of time.

> The river tells us of the history of the water, while music tells us the history of sound. Both are, in some manner, clepsidras, water clocks for observing and mediating time, for transforming disorder into order, continuity into discontinuity, and noise and sound into feeling. The composition is inhabited by memories of my own music.
>
> (Brennan 2012)

For a performance of this work on his 60th birthday, Lavista shared virtually the same thoughts with another colleague, adding his view that the time of composers, is measured in works not in years. "Sixty years is not a line that distinguishes the past from the present but a point along the ascent to perfecting one's art. The artist's defense against time is the defense of culture and art" (García Hernández 2003).

In *Clepsidra* Mario Lavista quotes music that he created in his previous compositions including his opera *Aura* (Dawn), *Reflejos de la noche* (Reflections of the Night; for string orchestra), and *Ficciones* (Fictions). We all find ourselves reflecting on time and memory and *Clepsidra* provides a privileged frame for the composer's reflections, along with our own, as listeners.

DRAMATIC ALLIANCES: MARCELA RODRÍGUEZ

On January 8, 2013 the Palacio de Las Bellas Artes presented in its Manuel Ponce Hall the opera-film *La Bola Negra*, written by the author Mario Bellatín with music by the composer Marcela Rodríguez. This opera-film follows the experiences of a Japanese entomologist working in Africa and the dangerous lives of youth growing up in that Ciudad Juárez.[12] The prominent female composer, Marcela Rodríguez, born in Mexico City in 1951, is one of a small number of women composers who have been recognized for leaving their mark on Mexican music, and hers is the final profile in this chapter.[13] Listeners in Mexico recognize a strong feminist perspective in the music of Rodríguez, whose works often reference strong and brave women, like Sor Juana Inés in her dramatic composition *Funesta*, explored below.

Marcela Rodríguez studied with the great Cuban composer Leo Brouwer, and also with the great Mexican pedagogues of music and research Antonieta Lozano and Julio Estrada. Rodríguez composes works for solo instruments and voice, orchestra, chamber ensembles, as well as opera, theater, and film. Renowned as one of Mexico's most influential living composers, she points to Silvestre Revueltas as a composer who investigated sound, and one of her inspirations.[14] Since 1979 she has favored works with a theatrical element, a perspective evident in *Funesta*, the work we will examine in this chapter.

12.5

12.6

Listening to Aria No. 4 "De primer sueño" [12.5] and Aria No. 6 "Funesta" [12.6] from the song cycle *Funesta* (1995) by Marcela Rodríguez. Source: *Marcela Rodríguez. Funesta/Adultera enemiga/La fábula de las regiones (Trigo)*, Urtext Digital Classics.[15]

Figure 12.8
Photo of Marcela Rodríguez. Photo by Rogelio Cuéllar, courtesy of Marcela Rodríguez.

Funesta is a set of six songs for soprano, string quartet, string bass, and percussion, set to texts by Sor Juana Inés de la Cruz, the genius nun who lived from 1648–1695, who also composed poems, plays, and music. Sor Juana wrote a celebrated defense of the right of women to an education that continues to inspire modern readers and artists.[16] The texts for the fourth and sixth songs in *Funesta* are taken from Sor Juana's poem "Primer sueño." The other songs quote verses from Sor Juana's sonnets and romances (see Bergmann, 2009). "De primer sueño" is the title that Marcela Rodríguez gave to the fourth song in her cycle and is also the title of the theater piece in which her sister, the actress Juana Rodríguez, played the solo role of Sor Juana. The music of *Funesta* served as the score for the drama which takes us into the nun's dream, her tormented soul, and her vision of finally transcending repression.[17]

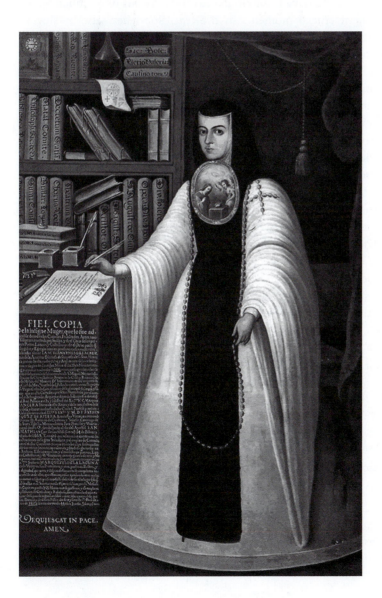

Figure 12.9
Portrait of Sor Juana Inés de la Cruz. Painting by Juan de Miranda in 1680. Wikimedia.

In the fourth song, as in the other movements of the cycle, Rodríguez has the soprano soloist sing in a deliberate manner, setting each syllable of text as a moment it its own right. The instrumental texture highlights the separation between the mournful bass lines played on the violoncello and anxious motives played in the highest registers of the violin. These techniques recall instrumental practices used by Baroque composers of the seventeenth century, when Sor Juana lived, and when so many of the customs that characterize Mexican music and culture were established.

Single pitches are struck on a steel drum, punctuating the silence, and perhaps reminding the listener of tolling church bells. The tones have an insistent quality, like dripping water or a metaphoric sounding of the passage of time. Although Rodríguez favors modern harmonic elements, the tonality hovers between Aeolian and Dorian modes, the old church modes that would have been familiar in the religious order inhabited by Sor Juana. At crucial moments in the text, Rodríguez sets the singer's melody to recall religious chant, giving words like "grave" a more melodic and *melismatic* setting, with multiple notes per syllable, that contrasts with the single pitch per syllable approach elsewhere in the song. Using scratchy sounds made by drawing the bow close to the bridge, the cello and bass players enrich the dark texture in later sections of the song, contrasting with the warm and sensuous quality of the voice.

As you listen to the fourth song of *Funesta*, consider how the music makes you feel. You might ask: Who are the birds of darkness in Sor Juana's poem? Does Rodríguez's music enhance that image and make the birds relevant to contemporary listeners?

In the sixth and closing aria of the cycle, Rodríguez expands upon the techniques heard earlier to create the most dramatic of all the songs in the cycle. The extreme dynamic contrasts lead us to share in Sor Juana's anguish. While the music focuses our attention upon a specific world, the techniques connect to a broad universe of experience. The foreboding bass motives share the interval of the ancient requiem chant the *Dies Irae* (Day of Wrath),[18] used also by John Williams in his film score to *Jaws*. The motive

---

Excerpt from Aria No. 4. "Primer sueño" (First Dream)

y en la quietud contenta de imperio silencioso,	And in the soundless purview of its silent realm,
sumisas sólo voces consentía de las nocturnas aves,	it brooked none but the muted voices of the birds of darkness,
tan obscuras, tan graves,	[sounds] so deep and dim
que aun el silencio no se interrumpía.	as not to break the silence.

Figure 12.10 Excerpt of lyrics from Aria No. 4. "Primer sueño" (First Dream), music composed by Marcela Rodríguez, poetry by Sor Juana Inés de la Cruz. (*Obras Completas de Sor Juana Inés de la Cruz*, edited by Alberto G. Salcedo and Alfonso Méndez Plancarte. Mexico City: Fondo de Cultura Economica, 1951, vol. 1, p. 335. English Translation: Alan Trueblood, *A Sor Juana Anthology*. Cambridge: Harvard University Press, 1988, p. 117.)

Aria No. 6 "Funesta" (Foreboding)

Piramidal, funesta,	Pyramidal, lugubrious,
de la tierra nacida sombra	a shadow born of earth,
yo, la peor de todas.	I, the worst of all.

Figure 12.11 Lyrics from Aria No. 6 "Funesta," music composed by Marcela Rodríguez, poetry by Sor Juana Inés de la Cruz. (*Obras Completas de Sor Juana Inés de la Cruz*, edited by Alberto G. Salcedo and Alfonso Méndez Plancarte. Mexico City: Fondo de Cultura Economica, 1951, vol. 1, p. 335. English Translation: Alan Trueblood, *A Sor Juana Anthology.* Cambridge: Harvard University Press, 1988, p. 117.)

in Rodríguez's setting also seems to be a compact reference to the final sections of the Symphony No. 8 of Gustav Mahler. The soprano's sensuous melody paradoxically also recalls religious chant and her vocal delivery is interrupted by long pauses and eerie instrumental interludes.

There have been multiple performances of *Funesta* in combination with the drama *Primer sueño* since its premier in 1995 at the Centro Cultural Universitario in Mexico City—the latest was in 2009. The drama is distinctly modern performance art, but it also draws upon memories of the ancient *autos sacramentales*, the religious plays that supported conversion of Mexico's indigenous people, and which in turn inspired them to create new dramas to support their changing life.

Alone, as a concert piece, the song cycle *Funesta* is powerful, but the coincidence of the composition and its theatrical staging is even more powerful, prompting new ways of thinking about music, theater, and the legacy of Sor Juana one of the most important cultural references in Mexican history, and today an icon of feminism. Marcela Rodríguez and her collaborators invite us explore the profound significance of these three perspectives.[19]

CONCLUDING REFLECTIONS

This chapter offered a brief survey of music created by five of the most famous composers associated with classical art music in Mexico from the twentieth and twenty-first centuries. It bears noting that all of them have favored symphonic compositions, the medium that garners supreme status as the measure of a modern nation's prominence in the world of inter-national concert music. The status of the symphony orchestra is tied to the health and status of music education and each depends upon the other.

The composers in this chapter also explored a wider sound palette, turning to electronically generated sounds, expanded instrumental tech-niques, and instruments from other world music traditions. The composers here belong to an intellectual circle that includes leading musicians, artists, writers, actors, directors, and film-makers around the world. We can see the continued interest of composers in creating for film, stage, and visual media that have long nurtured musical life in Mexico. Revueltas's 1936 scores for the movies *Redes* and *¡Vamonos con Pancho Villa!*, for example, stand as two of the earliest and finest examples of serious, original music composed for film. Even when composition is not directly tied to a dramatic frame, as with Marcela Rodríguez's *Funesta* or Silvestre Revueltas's *El renacuajo paseador*, the strong imagery, psychic sentiment, and sonic textures evoked in the compositions by Manuel Enríquez and Mario Lavista bring to mind film scores to many listeners.

Legacy emerges as an important personal and cultural issue. Each of the composers profiled in this chapter emphasizes their debt to the masters who guided them. The influence of Carlos Chávez looms large and all five composers profiled here either studied or worked with Chávez in some way. As testimony to his enormous influence, Mexico's national music research center, known as CENIDIM, bears the name of this important maestro: Centro Nacional de Investigación de Música Carlos Chávez.

The trajectory of classical music in Mexico has shifted. Modern composers favor abstract reflection over concrete reference and turn their gaze ever outward towards the world (although we have seen plenty of historical precedent for this focus). While Pablo Moncayo directly integrates traditional national music into a symphonic frame, Manuel Enríquez and Mario Lavista favor more abstract and experimental approaches to a wide range of sound resources. Contemporary living composers may not share a common musical language, but most share an interest in experimenting with new compositional techniques and ideas, seeking pathways of expression that will interest citizens of the world as well audiences in Mexico.

Mario Lavista directly invites his listeners to ponder the passage of time through music. The ways that each of the composers featured in this chapter explores the passage of time, a universal concern, provides a satisfying conclusion to our survey. On a very basic level, whether they state so or not, *all* composers are concerned with the passage of time, especially the quality of time during their compositions and experienced by listeners. Each of the Mexican composers explored in this chapter approaches time differently. By offering listeners ways of connecting the present to the past, while pointing to the future, each composer speaks to concerns that have always engaged Mexicans, and the entire world as well.

CRITICAL THINKING AND DISCUSSION PROMPTS

1. The title of this chapter, Classical Contemporary Music: New Frames for New Audiences, suggests that the audiences for contemporary classical music in Mexico have changed over time. Who constitutes these new audiences? Ground your answer by reflecting on the audience for one of the compositions introduced in this chapter or by exploring the Bellas Artes website and identifying the audience(s) it aims to reach.

2. How is Mexican identity represented in the compositions presented in this chapter? Is that a concern that should always define a Mexican composer or Mexican music? Explain your answer.

3. Compare one of the compositions in this chapter to one or more selections introduced in a previous chapter. Offer your analysis of the character of the music itself, the motivations for composition, the experience the music invites or makes possible (for players, listeners, promoters, communities, as relevant), how people have responded to the music, and who or what the music serves.

4. Choose one of the compositions in this chapter. Examine in detail how the composer treats the passage of time and connects the present to the past. Identify a moment or strategy that you find particularly powerful or appealing.

KEY TERMS, PEOPLE, AND PLACES

Palacio de las Bellas Artes	dynamic contrast
INBA-CONACULTA	nationalism
Silvestre Revueltas	SEP
Pablo Moncayo	autos sacramentales
Manuel Enríquez	steel drum
Mario Lavista	Teatro Guiñol
Marcela Rodríguez	*El renacuajo paseador*
Sor Juana Inés de la Cruz	*Ritual*
Carlos Chávez	*Huapango*
aleatoric	*Clepsidra*
symphonic orchestra (importance)	*Funesta*
chance operations	

NOTES

1. www.bellasartes.gob.mx/index.php/engli.html
2. The budget of the INBA is approximately twice the size of the NEA, the largest annual national funder of the arts in the United States, according to the annual reports posted on their respective websites. In the financial year of 2010, the NEA invested nearly $139 million through more than 2,700 grants across the country. The expenditure of INBA for 2011 was $277,520,000.

3. Instituto Nacional de Bella Artes. Website, at: www.bellasartes.gob.mx (accessed October 4, 2014).

4. While *titeres* is the generic word for puppets (marionettes), teatro guiñol typically features hand puppets. Guiñol (also, Guignol) was the name of a nineteenth-century Italian puppeteer who popularized children's puppet theater throughout Europe, at a time when puppet theater was largely for adult audiences. Guiñol has a long association with Punch and Judy style drama where one character typically beats another, an aspect exploited in many Mexican puppet plays as well. For more on children's puppet plays in Mexico, see Albarrán (2010).

5. SEP is an abbreviation for "Secretaría de Educación Pública."

6. A recording of Revuelta's music for *El renacuajo paseador* can be heard on Open Source Audio at Community Audio—Internet Archive (March 10, 2001), at: www.archive.org/details/ElRenacuajoPaseadorDeSilvestreRevueltas

7. *Huapango.* Orquesta Sinfónica Nacional de Mexico. Mexico City: Musart-Balboa, 1991.

8. INBA—Bellas Artes, Música. Website 2014, at: www.forodemusicanueva. bellasartes.gob.mx

9. Pytheas Center for Contemporary Music. Biographies of Manuel Enríquez by Aurelio Tello and Armando Torres Chibrás. Website created 2008, at: www.pytheasmusic.org/enriquez.html

10. Peermusic Classic. Mario Lavista. Biography, at: www.peermusicclassical. com/composer/composerdetail.cfm?detail=lavista (accessed October 4, 2014).

11. Orquesta Filarmónica de la UNAM, Ronald Zollman, Director. Difusiona Cultural UNAM (Voz Viva de México) MN30 (1995).

12. Estrenan Bola Negra, ee Mario Bellatin, con Música de Marcela Rodríguez, (El INBA Informa, January 9, 2013). www.bellasartes.gob.mx/prog_art/ minxmin/mostrar_completa.php?id=3130

13. For more on women composers, musicians, and scholars in Mexico, see: González and Saavedra (1982) and Vilar-Payá (2010).

14. "Los jóvenes compositores sólo miran hacia europa: Marcela Rodríguez," *La Jornada,* February 27, 2005, at: www.jornada.unam.mx/2005/02/27/ index.php?section=cultura&article=a02n1cul

15. Classics Online. Rodríguez, M. *Funesta,* (2014 Naxos Digital Services). www.classicsonline.com/catalogue/product.aspx?pid=785177. A full performance of *Funesta* appears on YouTube, at: www.youtube.com/watch? v=IRwDv1uzHV4 (posted April 3, 2013).

16. Mario Lavista wrote music for a film about Sor Juana.

17. Staged dramatization performed by the composer's sister available at: http://hemi.nyu.edu/journal/4.2/eng/en51_pf_cabranes_grant.html

18. This chant from the Mass for the Dead has been used by many different composers throughout the ages.

19. This topic has been explored in depth by Luisa Villar Payá from the University of the Americas in Puebla, Mexico.

FOR REFERENCE AND FURTHER STUDY

Albarrán, Elena Jackson. 2010. "Comino vence al Diablo and other Terrifying Episodes: Teatro Guiñol's Itinerant Puppet Theater in Mexico, 1923–1940." *The Americas: A Quarterly Review of Inter-American Cultural History* 67(3):355–374.

Alcaraz, José Antonio. 1975. *La obra de José Pablo Moncayo.* Cuadernos de música, nueva serie 2. México: UNAM/Difusión Cultural, Departamento de Música.

Alcaraz, José Antonio. 1998. *En la más honda música de selva* [In the Deepest Music of Jungle]. Mexico City: Consejo Nacional para la Cultura y las Artes.

Alcaraz, José Antonio. 2001. *Manuel Enríquez: Canciones para un compañero de viaje*. Mexico City: INBA-CENIDIM.

Alvarez Coral, Juan. 1972. *Compositores Mexicanos*. Mexico City: Edamex

Azar Manzur, Carlos. 2001. "Funesta de Marcela Rodríguez." *Letras Libres*. www.letraslibres.com/revista/letrillas/funesta-de-marcela-rodriguez (accessed January 12, 2015).

Bergmann, Emilie. 2009. "Sor Juana's 'Silencio Sonoro': Musical Responses to her Poetry." *Cuadernos de Música, Artes Visuales y Artes Escénicas* [Journal of Musical, Visual and Performing Arts] 4(1–2):177–206. http://cuadernosmusic ayartes.javeriana.edu.co/images/stories/revistas/RevistaV4N1y2/CUADERNO S_volumen_4_11%20BERGMANN.pdf (accessed January 12, 2015)

Brennan, Juan Arturo. 2012. Programa 2. Segunda Temporada. Mario Lavista (1943) Clepsidra. Músic UNAM. www.musica.unam.mx/index.php?option =com_content&view=article&id=2179:programa-2&catid=79:segunda-temporada-2012&Itemid=150 (accessed January 12, 2015).

Cárdenas, Sergio. 2010. "Ritual de Manuel Enríquez." *Onomatopeya de lo Indecible Blog*, May 12. http://onomatopeyadeloindecible.blogspot.com/2010/05/ritual-de-manuel-enriquez.html (accessed January 12, 2015).

Cortéz, Luis Jaime. 2000. *Favor de no disparar sobre el pianista. Una vida de Silvestre Revueltas. Teoría y Práctica del Arte*. Mexico City: Conaculta.

Cortéz, Luis Jaime (Ed.). 1990. *Mario Lavista: Textos en torno a la música*. 2nd ed. Mexico City: CENIDIM.

García Hernández, Arturo. 2003. "Festejaron a Mario Lavista por tanta vida hecha música." *La Jornada*, July 22. www.jornada.unam.mx/2003/07/22/ 02an1cul.php?origen=cultura.php&fly=2 (accessed January 12, 2015).

González, María Angeles and Saavedra, Leonora. 1982. *Música Mexicana Contemporanea*. Mexico City: Fondo de Cultura Económica-SEP.

Grant, Leo Cabranes. 2008. "A Failed Mass: Jesusa Rodríguez and her 'Striptease de Sor Juana'." *e-mférica*. http://hemi.nyu.edu/journal/4.2/eng/en51_pf_cabranes_grant.html (accessed January 12, 2015).

Lago, Roberto. 1987. *Teatro guignol mexicano* [Mexican Puppet Theater]. 3rd ed. Mexico City: Federación Editorial Mexicana.

Lavista, Mario. "El Lenguaje del músico." *Istor* 34:89–100. www.istor.cide. edu/archivos/num_34/textos_recobrados.pdf (accessed January 12, 2015).

Murray Prisant, Guillermo and Iglesias Cabrera, Sonia. 1995. *Piel de papel, manos de palo: historia de los títeres en México*. [Paper Skin, Stick Hands: The History of Puppets in Mexico]. Mexico City: Espasa Calpe.

Paraskavaidas, Graciela. 2011. Homenage a Revueltas, *Magma*. www.gp-magma. net/pdf/txt_e/Revueltas%202011.pdf (accessed January 12, 2015).

Ramírez Sánchez, Rogelio. 2013. *Origen motívico-estructural de Clepsidra, obra para gran orquesta de Mario Lavista*. www.scribd.com/doc/131310274/Clepsidra-Mario-Lavista (accessed November 24, 2014).

Rossi, Alejandro. 1998. "Contestación al Discurso de Ingreso del Maestro Mario Lavista como Miembro del Colegio Nacional." *Istor* 34:101–107. www. istor.cide.edu/archivos/num_34/textos_recobrados.pdf (accessed January 12, 2015).

Spenser, Daniela. 1999. *The Impossible Triangle. Mexico, Soviet Russia, and the United States in the 1920s*. Durham, NC: Duke University Press.

Tello, Aurelio. 2010."La Creación de Música en el siglo XX." In *La música en México: Panorama del Siglo XX*, edited by Aurelio Tello. Mexico City: FCE/ Conaculta, 486–555.

Tello, Aurelio (Ed.). 2010. *La música en México: Panorama del siglo XX*. Mexico City: FCE/Conaculta.

Vilar-Payá, María Luisa. 2010. "La Mujer Méxicana como creadora e investigadora de la música del concierto del siglo XX y principios del XXI." In *La música en México, Panorama del siglo XX*, edited by Aurelio Tello. Mexico City: FCE/Conaculta, 569–588.

DISCOGRAPHY

Marcela Rodríguez. Funesta/Adultera Enemiga/La Fabula de las Regiones (Trigo), Urtext Digital Classics (2000).

Orquesta Filarmónica de la UNAM, Ronald Zollman, dir. *Música Sinfónica Mexicana*, Revueltas, S.; Ibarra, F.; Ortíz, G.; Enríquez, M.; AMG-Rovi, (1994).

Orquesta Sinfónica Nacional de Mexico. *Huapango*. Mexico City: Musart-Balboa (1991).

Various Artists. *Revueltas Centennial Anthology, 1899–1999, 15 Masterpieces*. RCA (1999).

FILMS AND VIDEOS

La Bola negra—el musical de Ciudad Juárez, directed by Eduardo Márquez. Mexico City: Marisa Leon, 2012.

CHAPTER 13

A Despedida *and* Closing Reflections

INTEGRATION, INFLUENCE, AND CONFLUENCE

The organizing thesis of this book is that an ongoing process of selective integration accounts for the distinctive character of Mexican music and its value to Mexicans and the larger world. The material in the previous chapters was presented to illustrate some of the forces that account for those processes of selection. Understanding the reasons why musicians make music in a particular way not only helps us understand Mexican music itself but also helps us to understand the social customs and trends that have shaped culture, past and present, within Mexico and beyond.

Over the course of the semester we have examined a broad collection of musical examples that illustrate the diversity of music in Mexico and changing attitudes towards that diversity. Examples have ranged from indigenous expressions such as the Yaqui deer dance songs to classical concert music by living composers like Marcela Rodríguez. The reasons that the deer dance persisted while other Yaqui rituals faded may be credited to the parallels missionaries were able to draw between narratives regarding Christ and the redemptive power of the death of the deer. The Mexican government originally regarded the fierce Yaqui as threats to the formation of a unified Mexican nation, but today, the state of Sonora has officially chosen the deer dancer and the accompanying music as iconic representations of state identity. We observed a different choice of historic identities when Marcela Rodríguez used both modern and ancient European musical techniques to explore the poetry of the nun Sor Juana Inés de la Cruz. Considered a rebel because her academic activities, Sor Juana once posed a threat to the Catholic Church, but she is now revered as symbol of female strength. Despite choosing different threads of influence for their musical tapestries, Rodríguez and the Yaqui both engage history, religion, and rebellion as fundamental to contemporary Mexican identity.

We have explored only some of the factors that have influenced the choices musicians made when creating or performing music in the service of establishing ritual order, confirming community cohesion, inciting rebellion, reconciling conflict, or projecting personal, group, or national identity. As a reader, you are now in a position to reflect more on these dynamics and how they have changed depending on time and place.

One conclusion suggested by our exploration is that there is no single type of Mexican music that truly represents all Mexicans. From the decades immediately following the Revolution to the present, mariachi has been developed to consciously represent the breadth of the Mexican experience and population, but in practice the tradition celebrates an ongoing reimagining of mestizo traditions. Mexico's residents of African or Chinese ancestry are not overtly represented in mariachi repertory, nor in most other styles. Classical composers have embraced minority musics, but in general their music maintains a dialogue with their European and American counterparts. Circumstances have forced indigenous communities to adopt European and mestizo practices like banda and waila and develop them as their own. Film, radio, audio recording, and television helped Mexicans share music among themselves and with others around the world, and while popular music linked audiences across social and geographic divides, it also reinforced pride in competing regional customs.

This text opened with a quote from *Harvest of Empire*, a book that explores how the United States' role in Latin America has influenced immigration to the United States from Mexico and other Latin American countries. First Spain, and later the United States, profited by being present in Mexico. Spain and the United States have also profited from the presence of Mexicans in their nations. In the realm of music, we have seen how mariachi, música norteña, and other popular styles have influenced American music from classical concert music to country music, and have led to the formation of new styles like tejano, duranguense, and Western swing exchanged freely across the borders. Spain's trajectory of New Song and rock en español would have developed very differently without Mexican influence, and much of that influence arrived virtually, via film, recordings, and radio. And these examples don't address other international exchanges, such as the popularity of mariachi in many Latin American countries, including Costa Rica and Colombia, or música norteña in Nicaragua. Like the butterflies that pollinate the fields and ensure a bountiful harvest, music flies above and across the physical boundaries separating nations.

BEAUTIFUL LITTLE SKY—"CIELITO LINDO"

Musical examples have formed the core focus in this text, hence it is fitting that we close with one final example, providing one more chance to explore contrasting perceptions of value and meaning. While not all of the music we have examined is for singing, there can be little question that the lyric tradition forms the heart of Mexican music. One of the most attractive characteristics of Mexican music life is how common it is for people to know so well a body of beloved traditional songs that they are ready to sing them spontaneously at gatherings of family and friends, parties, and other celebratory occasions. In these settings singing is not reserved for superstars and recordings do not replace the experience of joining fellow friends and family in song. The emphasis is on participation, not presentation, a distinction anthropologist Thomas Turino (2008) makes in his book *Music in Social Life*.

We began our study with an invitation to sing to the song "Sandunga"; and now we close with the invitation to sing another song loved by Mexicans of all ages: "Cielito lindo." In the United States, this song acquired a demeaning association with the commercial marketing of Frito-Lay corn chips and a simplistic view of Mexican identity for many Americans. Yet, this song has a more complex reputation among Mexican musicians and is often chosen by students of Mexican ancestry when asked to name ten examples of Mexican music that they view as essential to know. In the quote below, one young woman explains her choice and introduces veteran and new performances.

> I chose "Cielito lindo" because it is one of the few rancheras that I recognize immediately. Written in 1882 by Quirino Mendoza Cortés, it has been performed by many well-known artists; one example is Vicente Fernández. I chose Marta Gómez's version of the song instead of [a rendition by] Vicente Fernández or any of the others because I thought it was interesting to hear a woman sing the song instead of a man. This particular version is taken from the soundtrack of the [2011] film *From Prada to Nada*. I thought it was interesting that over 100 years after the song was written, it is still being used in a contemporary film. This shows that these lyrics and melody have a lasting effect on people.

The title "El cielito lindo" literally means "beautiful little sky" but is more accurately understood as an endearment equivalent to "sweet little one" or "darling." The song is known throughout Mexico. "It is everywhere where Mexico is present . . . all around the world" another student wrote. She added:

> This was the favorite song of my *abuelo* [grandfather] and he would always sing it under his breath. I distinctly remember him telling my brother that if he wanted to win a girl's heart all he would have to do is sing this song to her.

Using the music and lyrics in Figures 13.1–13.2, sing "Cielito lindo." Perhaps a classmate who plays guitar can accompany you. Observe the syncopations that link this song to the 6/8 meter of traditional sones. Observe also how the lyrics for the opening verse of "Cielito lindo," the oldest of the set, have a narrative tone quite different from the romantic supplications that characterize the subsequent verses. The reference to unnamed smugglers of contraband recalls a theme popularized in corridos, prompting some people to consider "Cielito lindo" to be one of the first

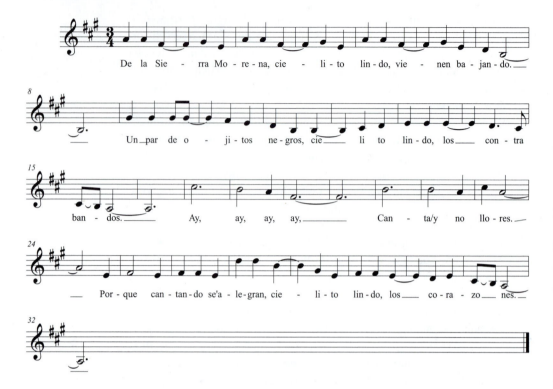

Figure 13.1
Score for "Cielito lindo" by Quirino Fidel Mendoza Cortés. Copyright 1948 by Promotora Hispano Americana de Música, S.A. Administered by Peer International Corporation. Copyright Renewed. Used by permission. All Rights Reserved.

narcocorridos. Yet, that initial theme is quickly abandoned. The romantic quality of the remaining lyrics surely accounts for the popularity of this song with mariachis hired to play at sentimental occasions, such as Mother's Day and birthdays. It is frequently sung in *serenatas* (serenades), typically when a man wishes to proffer his love for a young woman, starting courtship, or ask her to marry him. For this purpose a suitor may hire mariachis or a trio to perform after nightfall, usually after midnight, in the street facing the home of his sweetheart, to awaken her with songs of love. This tradition, popularized in Mexican films of the 1930s–1950s, was adopted across Latin America. As confirmation of such influence, the author remembers noticing the vast number of mariachis that advertised their services in Bogota, Colombia in the 1990s. When she posed the question "Why are mariachis so popular in Colombia?" she was told they were regularly hired by suitors for serenades. In that country in particular, contemporary mariachi singers Vicente Fernández and his famous son Alejandro Fernández have performed to sold-out stadiums and concert venues, and their recordings peaked the charts on Colombian radio.

13.1

Listening to "Cielito lindo" as sung by Marta Gómez.

Marta Gómez, the singer on Audio Example 13.1 is a cosmopolitan singer with international ties linking her to the great singer-songwriters of Latin America. Born in Colombia, Gómez earned a degree at Berklee College of Music in Boston. She makes her home in the United States but travels

"Cielito lindo"	"Pretty Little Sky"
[1] De la Sierra Morena, cielito lindo, vienen bajando Un par de ojitos negros, cielito lindo, de contrabando	[1] From the bronze mountains, lovely sky (darling), coming down are a pair of dark eyes, darling, with contraband.
[Estribillo] Ay ay ay ay, canta y no llores Porque cantando se alegran, cielito lindo, los corazones	[Refrain] Ay ay ay ay, sing and do not cry because by singing, pretty little heaven, hearts cheer up.
[2] Ese lunar que tienes, cielito lindo, junto a la boca No se los des a nadie, cielito lindo, que a mi me toca	[2] That mole that you have, darling, beside your mouth Don't give it to anyone, darling, because it is for me.
[Estribillo]	[Refrain]
[3] De tu casa a la mía, cielito lindo, no hay más que un paso Ahora que estamos solos, cielito lindo dame un brazo	[3] From your house to mine, darling, there is no more than one step Now that we are alone, darling, Give me a hug
[Estribillo]	[Refrain]
[4] Una flecha en el aire, cielito lindo lanzó cupido Y como fue jugando, cielito lindo yo fui el herido	[4] An arrow in the air, darling Cupid shot And as he was shooting (playing), darling, I was wounded
[Estribillo]	[Refrain]

Figure 13.2
Lyrics for "Cielito lindo" by Quirino Fidel Mendoza Cortés. Copyright 1948 by Promotora Hispano Americana de Música, S.A. Administered by Peer International Corporation. Copyright Renewed. Used by permission. All Rights Reserved.

widely, concertizing around the world, including performances in Mexico. Her polished skills and sophistication have not diminished her respect for the humble beauty of folkloric expression. The union of the contrasting worlds of traditional and modern cultures is a theme in the film *From Prada to Nada*, where Marta Gómez is heard on the soundtrack. The film plot, a loose adaptation of Jane Austen's *Sense and Sensibility* of 1811, concerns two spoiled girls who learn to truly appreciate their Latin ancestry only after their father's death forces them to move from Beverly Hills to live with their Mexican-born aunt in East Los Angeles. As a comedic melodrama, *Prada to Nada* attempts to explore stereotypes of Mexican and American identity, while relying on its own broadly drawn caricatures. Within the film, the song "Cielito lindo" stands as symbol of complex identity, representing at different points in the film, old-country Mexican traditions, nostalgic love, family ties, and modern love. Consider your own associations with "Cielito lindo." Are you able to hear it with fresh ears when you reflect on it as a ranchera waltz with a rich and ongoing history?

DEPARTURES

This text closes with the hope that each reader develops his or her own affinity with Mexican music. It is hoped that readers now know a representative collection of Mexican music by song title, composer, performer, and sound. This foundation should serve as a base for continuing to explore the sounds, sentiments, and social value of Mexican music in its many varieties. Like music anywhere, Mexican music gains value through the way people respond to it. Cultivating the ability to listen in an informed manner, to hear musical sounds as they connect to individual and collective voices, to recognize what is included along with what is omitted, is a skill that will not only enhance the pleasure you have in listening to music, but will also transfer to other areas of life. What better activity than sensitive listening to prepare oneself to see beyond stereotypes and to engage with people in meaningful ways? As our study has shown, Mexican musicians have been delivering this message for centuries.

CLOSING QUESTIONS

There are many questions that we might ask to reflect upon and summarize points raised in this book. A valuable exercise that will allow you to draw upon examples explored across our units is to relate that material to big questions regarding the role of music in society. Like the contents of this course, the questions are not exhaustive, but hopefully they will prompt you to draw connections among styles and examples and to think of more questions, for having questions drives knowledge.

CRITICAL THINKING AND DISCUSSION PROMPTS

1. Does music have any power to change society? Explain your answer drawing upon at least one example from class.

2. Can any single style of Mexican music represent all Mexicans? Why or why not? Again, use examples from class to support your answer.

3. Why is the concept of identity so important to a study of music? Explain your answer drawing upon at least one example from class.

4. What can we learn from the choices people make when creating music? Explain your answer by drawing upon at least one example from class.

5. What can we learn from the choices people make when responding to music? Explain your answer by drawing upon at least one example from class.

6. To what degree does place matter to contemporary Mexican music makers? Use at least one example from class to explain your answer.

7. To what degree does place matter to contemporary listeners (including dancers, or fans) of Mexican music? Explain your answer by drawing upon at least one example from class.

8. How do composers and performers draw upon historical references to communicate contemporary messages via their music?

9. Despite their differences, what is shared by contemporary popular styles of Mexican music (post-1950 to the present)? Name specific examples from our course of study to support your answers.

10. In what realms of musical activity, past and present, has the theater provided a critical frame? Name specific examples from our course of study to support your answers.

11. In what ways have Mexican musicians exploited options for sending hidden, or coded messages via their music?

12. What distinguishes Mexican music from other kinds of music?

13. Were the issues facing composers or performers in the past completely different from those today? Choose a contemporary composer or performer and compare him/her to one of the individuals introduced in this text.

FOR REFERENCE AND FURTHER STUDY

Gonzalez, Juan. 2000. *Harvest of Empire: A History of Latinos in America*. New York: Penguin Books.

Turino, Thomas. 2008. *Music as Social Life: The Politics of Participation*. Chicago, IL: University of Chicago Press.

DISCOGRAPHY

From Prada to Nada (Original Motion Picture Soundtrack). Nacional Records, iTunes Digital Release, 2011. [Includes the track of "Cielito lindo" sung by Marta Gómez]

Audio Examples and Credits

AUDIO EXAMPLES

Video Examples
and Credits

VIDEO EXAMPLES (Credits and Links for accessing files appear on the website).

Index